THE NAVARRE BIBLE

EXODUS

Volumes in This Series

THE NAVARRE BIBLE

Exodus

The Book of Exodus
in the Revised Standard Version and New Vulgate
with a commentary by members of the
Faculty of Theology of the University of Navarre

FOUR COURTS PRESS • DUBLIN
SCEPTER PUBLISHERS • NEW YORK

Typeset for
FOUR COURTS PRESS
7 Malpas Street, Dublin 8, Ireland.
www.fourcourtspress.ie

Distributed in North America by
SCEPTER PUBLISHERS, INC.
P.O. Box 211, New York, NY 10018–0004
www.scepterpublishers.org

Nihil obstat: Martin Hogan, LSS, PhD, *censor deputatus*.
Imprimi potest: Desmond, Archbishop of Dublin, 17 February 1999

A catalogue record for this title is available from the British Library.

The content of this paperback book is also published as part of the *Pentateuch* in
The Navarre Bible: The Pentateuch (4th printing, 2008).

ISBN 978-1-84682-207-0

Library of Congress Cataloging-in-Publication Data for: The Navarre Bible: The Pentateuch

Bible. O.T. English. Revised Standard. 1999.
    The Navarre Bible. – North American ed.
        p.   cm
    "The Books of Genesis, Exodus, Leviticus, Numbers, Deuteronomy in the Revised Standard
        Version and New Vulgate with a commentary by members of the Faculty of Theology of the
        University of Navarre."
    Includes bibliographical references.
    Contents: [1] The Pentateuch.
    ISBN 1-889334-21-9 (hardback: alk. paper)
I. Title.
    BS891.A1 1999.P75   99-23033
    221.7'7—dc21   CIP

The title "Navarre Bible" is © Four Courts Press 2003.

ACKNOWLEDGMENTS
Quotations from Vatican II documents are based on
the translation in *Vatican Council II:*
The Conciliar and Post Conciliar Documents,
ed. A. Flannery, OP (Dublin, 1981).
Quotations from the following editions published by
the Catholic University Press of America are used with permission:
Origen, *Homilies on Genesis and Exodus*, trs. R. Heine;
St Augustine, *De civitate Dei*, trs. G. Walsh and G. Monaghan;
St John Chrysostom, *Homilies on Genesis*, ed. Robert Hill.

The English translation of the *Catechism of the Catholic Church* is copyright for Ireland
© 1994 Veritas Publishers and Libreria Editrice Vaticana. All rights reserved.

Printed and bound in Great Britain by MPG Books, Bodmin, Cornwall.

Contents

Preface and Preliminary Notes

The text of this book has already been published, and is in print, as part of the hardback *The Navarre Bible: The Pentateuch* (2004).

The Commentary

The distinguishing feature of the *Navarre Bible* is its commentary on the biblical text. Compiled by members of the Theology faculty of the University of Navarre, Pamplona, Spain, this commentary draws on writings of the Fathers, texts of the Magisterium of the Church, and works of spiritual writers, including St Josemaría Escrivá, the founder of Opus Dei; it was he who in the late 1960s entrusted the faculty at Navarre with the project of making a translation of the Bible and adding to it a commentary of the type found here.

The commentary, which is not particularly technical, is designed to explain the biblical text and to identify its main points, the message God wants to get across through the sacred writers. It also deals with doctrinal and practical matters connected with the text.

The first volume of the *Navarre Bible* (the English edition) came out in 1985—first, twelve volumes covering the New Testament; then seven volumes covering the Old Testament. Many reprints and revised editions have appeared over the past twenty years. All the various volumes are currently in print.

The Revised Standard Version

The English translation of the Bible used in the *Navarre Bible* is the Revised Standard Version (RSV) which is, as its preface states, "an authorized revision of the American Standard Version, published in 1901, which was a revision of the King James Version [the "Authorized Version"], published in 1611".

The RSV of the entire Bible was published in 1952; its Catholic edition (RSVCE) appeared in 1966. Whereas the Spanish editors of what is called in English the "Navarrre Bible" made a new translation of the Bible, for the English edition the RSV has proved to be a very appropriate choice of translation. The publishers of the *Navarre Bible* wish to thank the Division of Christian Education of the National Council of the Churches of Christ in the USA for permission to use that text.

The Latin Text

This volume also carries the official Latin version of the New Testament in the *editio typica altera* of the New Vulgate (Vatican City, 1986).

PRELIMINARY NOTES

The headings within the biblical text have been provided by the editors (they are not taken from the RSVCE). A full list of these headings, giving an overview of the Book of Exodus, can be found at the back of the volume. *Some headings carry an asterisk*; this means there is an asterisked note below, more general than usual and one which examines the structure or content of an entire passage.

An asterisk *inside the biblical text* signals an RSVCE 'Explanatory Note' at the end of the volume.

References in the margin of the biblical text or its headings point to parallel passages or other passages which deal with the same theme. References given in *italics* show the place in the New Testament which most directly touches on the subject. With the exception of the New Testament and Psalms, the marginal references are to the New Vulgate, that is, they are not normally adjusted (where applicable) to the RSVCE.

Abbreviations

1. BOOKS OF HOLY SCRIPTURE

Acts	Acts of the Apostles	1 Kings	1 Kings
Amos	Amon	2 Kings	2 Kings
Bar	Baruch	Lam	Lamentations
1 Chron	1 Chronicles	Lev	Leviticus
2 Chron	2 Chronicles	Lk	Luke
Col	Colossians	1 Mac	1 Maccabees
1 Cor	1 Corinthians	2 Mac	2 Maccabees
2 Cor	2 Corinthians	Mal	Malachi
Dan	Daniel	Mic	Micah
Deut	Deuteronomy	Mk	Mark
Eccles	Ecclesiastes (Qohelet)	Mt	Matthew
Esther	Esther	Nah	Nahum
Eph	Ephesians	Neh	Nehemiah
Ex	Exodus	Num	Number
Ezek	Ezekiel	Obad	Obadiah
Ezra	Ezra	1 Pet	1 Peter
Gal	Galatians	2 Pet	2 Peter
Gen	Genesis	Phil	Philippians
Hab	Habakkuk	Philem	Philemon
Hag	Haggai	Ps	Psalms
Heb	Hebrews	Prov	Proverbs
Hos	Hosea	Rev	Revelations (Apocalypse)
Is	Isaiah	Rom	Romans
Jas	James	Ruth	Ruth
Jer	Jeremiah	1 Sam	1 Samuel
Jn	John	2 Sam	2 Samuel
1 Jn	1 John	Sir	Sirach (Ecclesiasticus)
2 Jn	2 John	Song	Song of Solomon
3 Jn	3 John	I Thess	1 Thessalonians
Job	Job	2 Thess	2 Thessalonians
Joel	Joel	1 Tim	1 Timothy
Jon	Jonah	2 Tim	2 Timothy
Josh	Joshua	Tit	Titus
Jud	Judith	Wis	Wisdom
Jude	Jude	Zech	Zechariah
Judg	Judges	Zeph	Zephaniah

Abbreviations

2. RSV ABBREVIATIONS

In the notes indicated by superior *letters* in the RSV biblical text, the following abbreviations are used:

Cn   a correction made where the text has suffered in transmission and the versions provide no satisfactory restoration but the RSV Committee agrees with the judgment of competent scholars as to the most probable reconstruction of the original text

Heb   the Hebrew of the consonantal Masoretic Text of the Old Testament.

Gk   Septuagint, Greek Version of the Old Testament

Lat   Latin Version of Tobit, Judith, and 2 Maccabees

Ms   manuscript

Mss   Manuscripts

MT   the Hebrew of the pointed Masoretic Text of the Old Testament

Sam   Samaritan Hebrew text of Old Testament

Syr   Syriac Version of the Old Testament

Tg   Targum

Vg   Vulgate, Latin Version of Old Testament

N.B. See the explanation given in footnote **f** on p. 53 regarding the significance of the rendering of LORD in capital latters in the RSV text.

3. OTHER ABBREVIATIONS

AAS	*Acta Apostolicae Sedis*	f	and following (*pl.* ff)
ad loc.	*ad locum*, commentary on this passage	ibid.	*ibidem*, in the same place
		in loc.	*in locum,* commentary on this passage
Apost.	Apostolic		
can.	canon	loc.	*locum*, place or passage
chap.	chapter	par.	parallel passages
cf.	*confer*, compare	Past.	Pastoral
Const.	Constitution	*pl.*	plural
Decl.	Declaration	RSV	Revised Standard Version
Dz-Sch	Denzinger-Schönmetzer, *Enchiridion Biblicum* (4th edition, Naples-Rome, 1961)	RSVCE	Revised Standard Version, Catholic Edition
		SCDF	Sacred Congregation for the Doctrine of the Faith
Enc.	Encyclical	sess.	session
Exhort.	Exhortation	v.	verse (*pl.* vv.)

The Old Testament in the
Context of the Bible

1. HOLY SCRIPTURE IN THE MYSTERY OF
CHRIST AND HIS CHURCH

1. Analogy with the Word made flesh

Jesus Christ is the key to understanding the nature and message of the sacred books of the Bible. Through these books God has deigned to speak to us in a human language, in the same way as the Eternal Word of the Father condescended to take up our human nature and become one of us.[1] In Holy Scripture God speaks to us through the human authors of the various books (the hagiographers), using their words. The books of the Old Testament, containing the word of God that prepared the way for the coming of the Redeemer, were a first step towards the incarnation of the Eternal Word of the Father. The books of the New Testament bear witness to the zenith of God's revelation—Jesus Christ—and record his words and doings. Jesus Christ is, then, the goal towards which the entire Bible tends; he is its heart, the source of its life; he is its deepest meaning.

Because they are inspired by the Holy Spirit, the books of both Testaments are means whereby God (Father, Son and Holy Spirit) and man communicate. It was God's saving plan that those books should proclaim the new life that flows from the crucified and risen Jesus as from a spring, and that is spread abroad through the preaching of the Gospel and through the sacraments of the Church. The Holy Scriptures are not, then, the basis of Christianity, as if Christianity were a "religion of the book". Christianity is "the religion of the 'Word' of God, a word which is 'not a written and mute word, but the Word which is incarnate and living';"[2] it is the life which flows from the Son of God made man into the hearts of his followers. So, for us to understand the true scope of the Holy Scriptures, "Christ, the eternal Word of the living God, must, through the Holy Spirit, 'open [our] minds to understand them' (cf. Lk 24:45)".[3]

Like the mystery of Jesus Christ the words of the Bible have a divine dimension and yet at the same time are truly human; what is termed the "law

---

1. Cf. Vatican II, *Dei Verbum*, 13. **2.** *Catechism of the Catholic Church*, 108. **3.** Ibid.

of the Incarnation" applies to them: "To compose the sacred books, God chose certain men who, all the while he employed them in this task, made full use of their powers and faculties so that, though he acted in them and by them, it was as true authors that they consigned to writing whatever he wanted written, and no more."[4] Therefore, in order to understand the meaning of the sacred books one needs to call into play all available resources (linguistic, historical, literary, etc.), given the fact that these books were written in times and cultures different from our own. However, scholarship of this sort is inadequate on its own; we need to have the guidance of the Holy Spirit and for this, in turn, John Paul II pointed out, "one must first be guided by the Holy Spirit and it is necessary to pray for that, to pray much, to ask in prayer for the interior light of the Spirit and docilely accept that light, to ask for the love that alone enables one to understand the language of God, who is 'love' (1 Jn 4:8, 16)."[5]

2. God speaking to his Church

Being docile to the Holy Spirit implies being faithful to the Church, the community of salvation founded by Christ; the texts of Holy Scripture have been entrusted to the Church "in order to nourish faith and guide the life of charity [. . .]. Being faithful to the Church, in fact, means resolutely finding one's place in the mainstream of the great Tradition that, under the guidance of the Magisterium, assured of the Holy Spirit's assistance, has recognized the canonical writings as the word addressed by God to his people and has never ceased meditating on them and discovering their inexhaustible riches."[6] So, the Scriptures entrusted to the Church are a treasure that belongs to all believers: "Sacred Tradition and Sacred Scripture make up a single sacred deposit of the Word of God, which is entrusted to the Church. By adhering to it the entire holy people, united to its pastors, remains always faithful to the teaching of the apostles."[7]

Because of its essential link to the Church, Holy Scripture is part and parcel of the hierarchical and charismatic dimension of the Church. The Magisterium has a God-given charge authentically to interpret the word of God, whether oral or written, on behalf of Jesus; and when it propounds the teaching of Revelation it is interpreting and "actualizing" Scripture, that is, applying it to the cultural and historical circumstances in which the faithful find themselves. As successors of the apostles, bishops are the first witnesses to and guarantors of the living tradition in which the Scriptures are interpreted from age to age. And priests, as co-workers of bishops, have a special charism to interpret Scripture when, conveying not their own personal ideas but the Word of God, they apply the eternal truth of the Gospel to the concrete

---

4. Vatican II, *Dei Verbum*, 11.   5. Cf. John Paul II, 'Address on the Interpretation of the Bible in the Church', *L'Osservatore Romano*, weekly edition in English, 28 April 1993, published in an edition of Pontifical Biblical Commission, *The Interpretation of the Bible in the Church* (1994).   6. Ibid. 7. Vatican II, *Dei Verbum*, 10; cf. 21.

circumstances of life.[8] The Spirit has also been given to individual Christians to enable them to burn with the love of God when, in a group or on their own, they prayerfully study the Scriptures.

However, there are two areas in the life of the Church where Holy Scripture is most directly interpreted and presented to us—the liturgy, and the *lectio divina* or spiritual reading of the biblical texts.

The Second Vatican Council teaches that, in the liturgy of the Church and especially the celebration of the Eucharist, all the baptized come to experience the presence of Christ in his word, "since it is he himself who speaks when the holy scriptures are read in the Church".[9] By the very fact of listening to the word, the people of God contribute to the supernatural meaning of faith. In principle, it is in the celebration of the Eucharist that the sacred texts are most vividly brought alive, for it is in the Mass that the Word of God is proclaimed among the community of believers gathered around Christ "to give glory to God and to effect the work of salvation which Holy Scripture proclaims".[10]

Lectio divina, or the spiritual reading of Scripture done in a group or on one's own, is another way to go deeper into its meaning and apply it to one's life, and thereby obtain a growing love for the Word of God, the source of interior life and apostolic fruitfulness.[11] This reading is never private, because the believer always reads and interprets in the context of the Church's faith—and this reading in turn enhances that faith's treasury.[12] That is why the Second Vatican Council called for the faithful to be given every facility to access the Scriptures.[13]

2. THE OLD TESTAMENT AND ITS INTERPRETATION

1. Books of the Old Testament

The Old Testament is an indispensable part of Holy Scripture. Its books are divinely inspired and "retain a permanent value, for the Old Covenant has never been revoked. In fact, the economy of the Old Testament was deliberately so oriented that it should prepare for and declare in prophecy the coming of Christ, redeemer of all men."[14]

The canon of the Old Testament comprises 46 texts (45, if Jeremiah and Lamentations are counted together), which in Catholic editions are grouped into three blocks:

(1) *Historical books*: the five that make up the Pentateuch (Genesis, Exodus, Leviticus, Numbers, Deuteronomy), plus Joshua, Judges, Ruth, 1 and 2

---

8. Cf. Vatican II, *Presbyterorum ordinis*, 4. **9.** Vatican II, *Sacrosanctum Concilium*, 7. **10.** Ibid., 6.
11. Cf. Vatican II, *Dei Verbum*, 21. **12.** Cf. Pontifical Biblical Commission, *The Interpretation of the Bible in the Church*. **13.** Cf. Vatican II, *Dei Verbum*, 22 and 25. **14.** *Catechism of the Catholic Church*, 121-122, quoting *Dei Verbum*, 14–15.

Samuel, 1 and 2 Kings, 1 and 2 Chronicles, Ezra, Nehemiah, Tobit, Judith, Esther and 1 and 2 Maccabees.

(2) *Didactical, poetical or wisdom books*: Job, Psalms, Proverbs, Qoheleth (Ecclesiastes), Song of Songs, Wisdom and Sirach (Ecclesiasticus).

(3) *Prophetical books*: Isaiah, Jeremiah, Lamentations, Baruch, Ezekiel, Daniel, Hosea, Joel, Amos, Obadiah, Jonah, Micah, Nahum, Habakkuk, Zephaniah, Haggai, Zechariah, Malachi.

Being the word of God, the books of the Old Testament are timeless, they have an enduring value; yet they do reflect the times and circumstances in which they were written. Therefore, "'even though they contain matters imperfect and provisional,' the books of the Old Testament bear witness to the whole divine pedagogy of God's saving love: these writings 'are a storehouse of sublime teaching on God and of sound wisdom on human life, as well as a wonderful treasury of prayers; in them, too, the mystery of our salvation is present in a hidden way' (*Dei Verbum*, 15)."[15]

2. Interpreting the Old Testament

The Church reads the Old Testament books for the testimony they bear to the history of salvation. But because that history found its fulfilment in Christ and is illuminated by Christ, the Church interprets these books in the light of the paschal event—the death and resurrection of the Lord; this light exposes a radically new meaning and a definitive one.[16] This new insight into the meaning of the ancient Scriptures is an integral part of the Christian faith. This means that reading the Old Testament in the light of the death and resurrection of Jesus does not change the original meaning of the texts—but it does enable us to go deeper and to reach its fullest meaning by the light of Christ's definitive revelation; so, not only does the Old Testament continue to be valid, but we are enabled to understand it better. Any attempt to set aside the Old Testament or to change its substance would deprive the New Testament of its roots in history.[17]

Two basic principles need to be borne in mind in order to interpret the books of the Old Testament properly:

(a) *Any biblical text has to be read first in the context and in the light of Scripture as a whole.*
"Attention must be devoted to the content and unity of the whole of Scripture, if we are to derive their true meaning from the sacred texts . . .".[18] At times the Bible, particularly the Old Testament, can look like an agglomerate of books rather than a single coherent work; however, all the biblical texts have, under

---

15. Ibid., 122. **16.** Cf. Vatican II, *Dei Verbum*, 4. **17.** Cf. *Catechism of the Catholic Church*, 123. **18.** Vatican II, *Dei Verbum*, 12.

God's inspiration, come into being from within the community of believers, and they have been passed on as something that is all of a piece. Each of these books, therefore, needs to be read and interpreted as part of the entire Bible, if we are to see the way that divine Revelation develops and the various ways it is communicated to man. But it is also the case that "the texts of the Bible are the expression of religious traditions which existed before them. The mode of their connexion with these traditions is different in each case, with the creativity of the authors shown in various degrees. In the course of time, multiple traditions have flowed together little by little to form one great common tradition. The Bible is a privileged expression of this process: it has itself contributed to the process and continues to have controlling influence upon it."[19]

These connexions between texts and traditions or between one text and another do occur within the Old Testament, but they really come into their own in the New Testament, containing as it does many explicit and interpreted quotations from the Old. This fact shows that the New Testament writers recognized that the Old Testament was divinely inspired and that the revelation it contained reached its fulfilment in the life, teaching and, particularly, the death and resurrection of Jesus. When they went to the Old Testament texts to obtain light on the salvific meaning of Jesus' words and deeds, they necessarily had to rely on the methods of interpretation and the skills available in their own time. It would have been anachronistic for them to use the methods of modern scholarship. By contrast, when we read the Old Testament we should indeed interpret it with the aid of what modern science has to tell us about the world and with the help also of modern scholarship and of what we now know about the methods of interpretations available to the ancient writers. But no matter how much light these new resources provide, the fact remains that the Old Testament and the New Testament are closely linked;[20] indeed, St Augustine's words are much easier to understand now than when they were first written: *Novum in Vetere latet et in Novo Vetus patet* (The New is hidden in the Old, and the Old is made manifest in the New).[21]

(b) *The Bible should be interpreted in the context of Church Tradition.*
Biblical tradition extends into the living Tradition of the Church. God entrusted the Bible not to any one individual, but to the Church.[22] It is only through the Church that we come to have the canon of Holy Scripture, that is, to know which books are inspired, which books form part of the Bible. "Guided by the Holy Spirit and in the light of the living tradition which it has received, the Church has discerned the writings which should be regarded as Sacred Scripture [. . .]. The discernment of a 'canon' of Sacred Scripture was the result of a long process."[23]

---

19. Pontifical Biblical Commission, *The Interpretation of the Bible in the Church.* 20. Cf. Vatican II, *Dei Verbum*, 16. 21. St Augustine, *Questiones in Heptateuchum*, 2, 73 (PL 34, 623). 22. Cf. Vatican II, *Dei Verbum*, 11. 23. Pontifical Biblical Commission, *The Interpretation of the Bible in the Church*, B. 1.

The Church identified which books are inspired (both the Old and the New Testaments), and by discerning the canon of Scripture she discerned her own identity: the Scriptures are, from then on, a mirror in which the Church is constantly enabled to see herself and to check, century after century, how she should be responding to the Gospel.[24] The Church is aware that it was the Holy Spirit himself who moved the hagiographers to write the sacred books—and it is he who guided her to recognize which books were inspired and who always helps her to correctly and authentically interpret them. Any interpretation of of Holy Scripture which wants to respect the nature of those books must, therefore, be done *in sinu Ecclesiae*, in the bosom of the Church.

There is, then, a close connexion between Tradition, Scripture and Magisterium. Tradition has been set down in writing in certain books, and these books have been recognized as sacred, as part of Scripture, by that same living Tradition which interprets them as being the genuine Word of God. Thus, the third element, interpretation, is part and parcel of Scripture itself, because Scripture is shaped by a series of actions taken by the Church which is, by virtue of its constitution, a community of tradition.

In the course of this great Tradition, the Fathers provided an exegesis which drew out of Scripture guidelines for the doctrinal tradition of the Church; their work has made a rich theological contribution to the instruction and spiritual nourishment of the faithful. The Fathers' reading and interpretation of Scripture are a treasury, from which the Church is forever drawing— this, despite the fact that the methods the Fathers used to explore the meaning of the texts were those of the times and cultures in which they lived, and in many instances have lost their scholarly validity.[25] Ever since the epoch of the Fathers, preaching and study have produced an enormous amount of commentary, providing further insights into the meaning of Scripture.

Be that as it may, the interpretation of Scripture should never be approached as a research exercise dependent on the researcher's technical skills. It is, rather, an encounter with the Word of God in the living Tradition of the Church, an encounter with an immense multitude of men and women who have rooted their lives in the Church and made their services available to her.

---

24. Cf. Vatican II, *Dei Verbum*, 18. **25.** Cf. ibid., 23.

Introduction to the Pentateuch

The "Pentateuch" is the name given to the first five books of the Bible—Genesis, Exodus, Leviticus, Numbers and Deuteronomy. Taken together, the sacred texts form something like a work in five parts. The name "Pentateuch", coming from the Greek *Pentateuchos*, means "a book composed of five rolls" and from the start of the Christian era it was applied to the case or container in which the rolls of these five books were stored. Jews, and often Christians too, call the Pentateuch the "Law", in Hebrew *ha-Toráh*.

1. STRUCTURE AND CONTENT

The general content of the Pentateuch can be seen from the titles given to the books that make it up. *Genesis* deals with the origin of the world, mankind and the people of Israel; *Exodus*, the Israelites' escape from Egypt; *Leviticus*, the levitical laws on holiness and worship; *Numbers*, censuses and lists of those who came out of Egypt and wandered about the desert; *Deuteronomy*, the second Law, laid down by Moses before the entry into the promised land.

However, when we look more closely at the content of the Pentateuch we see it as something quite complex. On the one hand, there is a line of narrative running from Adam to Moses; and on the other a series of laws and regulations which really have to do with various different circumstances experienced by the people of Israel. We have in the Pentateuch a mesh of narrative accounts and laws: there is no book like it. The events it narrates, from the creation of the world to the end of the people of Israel's pilgrimage in the desert, provide the setting for the laws; and the laws, in their turn, originate in, derive from, the events described. If we look at the Pentateuch as a whole, it is easy to see that God reveals himself by means of events and words which are intrinsically connected with one another, in such a way that the works performed by God bear out the doctrine signified by the words, and the words, for their part, throw light on the works.[1]

The division into five books does not exactly keep step with the historical narrative; in fact the narrative is interrupted at various points to take in blocks of laws. Here is an outline of the narrative:

---

1. Vatican II, *Dei Verbum*, 2.

Exodus

1	Gen 1–11	The Creation and the history of humankind up to Abraham. Prehistory.
2	Gen 12–50	The history of the patriarchs: Abraham, Isaac, Jacob and his sons.
3	Ex 1–18	Sojourn in Egypt; deliverance from slavery and escape into Sinai.
4	Ex 19–40	The Covenant made in Sinai. A huge collection of laws: the Ten Commandments, the Code of the Covenant and ritual regulations.
5	Lev 1–27	Laws about sacrifices, priests, ritual purity and holiness.
6	Num 1–10	Preparations for leaving Sinai; some laws.
7	Num 11–36	Stages in the journey from Sinai to Moab, with a long intermediate stop at Kadesh; further laws about sacrifices and priests.
8	Deut 1–30	Three wide-ranging discourses given by Moses in Moab recalling the stages of the Israelites' pilgrimage in the desert and reminding them of the commandments.
9	Deut 31–34	Moses' last instructions. His death (in Moab).

The history narrated in the Pentateuch is clearly a selective one. The book of Genesis, in its early stages, covers humankind as a whole—creation, the drama of the first sin, the human race spreading across the earth, and the growth of evil which earns the punishment of the flood. With Noah, however, mankind gets a new start; but the text focuses on the descendants of Shem (one of Noah's sons), whose line continues right down to Abraham, the man to whom God promises the land of Canaan and countless offspring. The biblical narrative then follows the sons of Abraham, first Isaac's line and then that of Jacob, ignoring that of Ishmael and later that of Esau (these receive only a mention). It then concentrates on the twelve sons of Jacob, from whom will come the twelve tribes that go to make up the people of Israel; the most mention is given to Judah and Joseph. The book of Exodus focuses on Moses and Aaron, descendants of Levi. However, from this stage onwards the main protagonist is the people of Israel. So, by this process of selection the narrative moves from humankind as a whole to direct its attention to just one nation, God's chosen people.

2. COMPOSITION

The laws by which Israel was governed were known as the "Law of Moses" (cf. Deut 31:9; Josh 8:31–35; 23:6; 25:25). Thus, in Exodus 34:27–28 we are told that God commanded Moses to write the words of the Covenant on tablets of stone; and in the book of Nehemiah we hear that on the return from the Babylonian exile the book of the "law of Moses which the Lord had given to Israel" was read out in public (cf. Neh 8:1–8). Much later on, shortly before the time of Jesus Christ, these passages were taken to mean that Moses himself was the author of the Pentateuch. Statements to this effect (which are also to be found in the New Testament: cf. Mt 8:4; Mk 7:10; Luke 24:24; Jn 1:45; 5:46; Acts 3:22; Rom 10:5, 19; 1 Cor 9:9; 2 Cor 3:15) show the great authority these five books had as the word of God written down by the great prophet Moses and given to the people of Israel. From this time onwards, in both Jewish and Christian tradition, we find constant references to Moses' being the author of the Pentateuch.

From very early times, however, biblical scholars were aware that the Pentateuch as we now know it comes from the time of the return from exile in Babylon (6th–5th centuries).[2] But in more recent times, beginning in the eighteenth century, the sources of the Pentateuch have been the subject of careful scholarly research. What that research shows is that the final redaction used materials from many different periods, some of them very old indeed—materials which were rearranged and rewritten by the inspired writers; this edited text consists of the five sacred books as they reached the Jewish people—and later the Church. In them is revealed a core teaching which was particularly meaningful to the Jews after their experience of exile—that Israel is God's chosen people, who have received the gift of the Law, and they must keep that Law if they are to remain as a people and dwell in the promised land. God used certain men, at different times, to compose the sacred books "so that, though he acted in them and by them, it was as true authors that they consigned to writing whatever he wanted written, and no more."[3]

We have no reliable information as to what form this material took prior to its being incorporated in the Pentateuch or what the history of that material was; but there is good reason to suppose that ancient traditions about the patriarchs, Moses and the wilderness years, and the conquest of the promised land, were all collected and expanded in various ways at peak periods of religious and cultural activity among the Jewish people.

During the period of the monarchy stress was laid on religious traditions such as the Covenant with God in the wilderness, obedience to what that

---

2. St Jerome explained that the account of Moses' death (cf. Deut 34), and some other remarks, such as when it says "to this day" (Gen 26:33; 35:20), are attributable to Ezra when he copied out the Law of Moses (cf. *De perpetua virginitate B. Mariae*, 7; PL 23, 190). **3.** Vatican II, *Dei Verbum*, 11.

Covenant laid down, and the transcendence of God. In their preaching, prophets like Amos and Hosea went deeper into the religous meaning that these traditions had for the people. It may well be that when the Northern kingdom fell to the Assyrians (9th century), many Israelites fled south and brought with them their own interpreted traditions containing that theological content. This Northern tradition is called the "Elohistic" tradition (E), because in its accounts God is referred to by the name of "Elohim".

The seventh century BC, under Kings Hezekiah and Josiah, saw profound religious changes which helped towards a new understanding of the past and brought about a literary revival; this in turn, during and after the Exile, led to the writing of a history of Israel from the conquest of the promised land onwards (the books of Joshua, Judges, Samuel and Kings). This account is usually described as the "Deuteronomic" account (D), because it included Deuteronomy, or part of it, as an introduction to the history narrated in those books. It expounds the Law of Moses in a series of great discourses and it stresses the gratuitous nature of God's choice of Israel, and the need to faithfully obey his commandment. It also makes the case for centralizing religious worship in one shrine only—the temple of Jerusalem.

The literary activity of the Deuteronomic reform may well have extended beyond the writing of the history of the period from Joshua to Kings. It probably helped form certain traditional accounts (written and oral) into narrative cycles—the story of the origin of the world and of man, the patriarchs, Israel in Egypt, the Exodus, the years in the desert before entering the land of Canaan. This laid the foundations for the composition of an elaborate prologue to Deuteronomy and to the history of the subsequent years, a prologue which would weave into a harmonious whole ancient tradition about the history of salvation, from the origin of the world to the early days of Israel's settlement in the land of Canaan. In those narrative cycles God is sometimes referred to as "Yahweh"; that is why the tradition from which these passages derive is called the "Yahwistic" tradition (for which the abbreviation J is used, from the German *Jahwist*).

The Exile in Bablyon (6th century BC) led to a period of deep religious soul-searching. The priests among the exiles had to try to keep the people's faith alive and to protect them from the influences of Babylonian religion which was full of pagan myths and ritual practices. To do this they kept reminding the people of the traditions of their ancestors, pointing out that the entire history of mankind and particularly that of the people of Israel involved a series of covenants made by God with men. The literary activity of these priestly groups in Babylon (which was kept up after the return from exile) is to be seen in elaborate collections of laws about worship, priestly purity, and the purity of the people. In modern scholarship all this literary activity is described as belonging to the Priestly tradition (P, from *Priester*, the German for "priest"), a tradition which has left a profound impression on our text of the Pentateuch.

Recent scholarship has tried (though no consensus has yet emerged) to identify which parts of the content of the Pentateuch date from which of these historical periods. It seems fairly clear that the teaching contained in these five books did not develop all of a sudden at the time of their final redaction or in the period immediately before that; rather, the basic elements—God's choice of the people of Israel, the Covenant, the Law, the form of worship—were part of the earliest traditions of the people.

3. THE FIVE BOOKS FORM A UNITY

All the various traditions which must have existed prior to the final redaction, even though they each have their own literary and doctrinal characteristics, were brought together by divine inspiration to form the great masterpiece we call the "Pentateuch" and become the "Law of Moses". If we look at the opening words of each of the five books (the title, as it were, given them by their authors), we will see the line of continuity running through them.

Genesis provides the reply (uttered by belief in the Lord) to the question: When and how did the people of Israel come into being? But obviously attention had to be paid to the existence of other nations more numerous than Israel—and the whole matter of the origin of the world and of humankind had to be addressed. To answer these questions, the writers availed themselves of traditions that spoke about the beginnings—the creation of the world and of man, the origin of the various peoples, particularly the origin of Israel, that is, Abraham, who had come from Mestopotamia (cf. Josh 24:2; Is 51:2), and Jacob the Aramean nomad who travelled down into Egypt (cf. Deut 26:5). All this is dealt with in the same book, Genesis, whose content justifies the words with which the Hebrew text begins—*Bereshit* ("In the beginning": Gen 1:1). This opens the way to describing the first stage in the history of the people, the stage when they were chosen by God as his own.

The book of Genesis ends with the Israelites living in Egypt. However, that was only the beginning of their history: it continued when they left that country. At this stage in the story Moses is the central figure: the narrative concentrates on him and on those who, along with him, were rescued from Egypt and who made a solemn undertaking to obey the will of God who had made them his chosen people among whom he was going to pitch his tent. It was very important to identify who precisely were those people who formed the core of the reinvigorated people of God; therefore, this stage in the story of the chosen people (covered by the book of Exodus) begins with the words "These are the names of the sons of Israel who came to Egypt with Jacob" (Ex 1:1). The book of Exodus covers all the traditions about the departure from Egypt, the Covenant and the Lord's coming to dwell in the midst of his people.

If God is dwelling among his people, then they have to live in holiness. However, the history of the people was a succession of infidelities followed by punishment and pardon. Would they ever manage to obtain forgiveness once-and-for-all, and live in holiness from then on? How could they come to know the will of God? The answer to these questions is to be found in the Law and in worship. There were all kinds of regulations about details of divine in worship (the product of priestly circles) and the third book (Leviticus) in this work made up of five rolls, the Pentateuch, was the natural place to spell out all these regulations. God himself tells his people, through Moses, how they are to serve him at all times. So, the book which gathers up all these laws begins with the words "The Lord called Moses, and spoke to him from the tent of meeting" (Lev 1:1), that is to say, he called the people to serve him and he gave them rules about how they should go about this.

The narrative was still incomplete, because in the previous book Israel was left at the foot of Sinai, whereas God had promised to give it the land of Canaan. So we are told about how the people set out marching across the desert again, in perfect formation, and we are told of all the trials they under-went. Some found it too much for them and they gave up. This explains why the Israelites spent forty years in the desert: that sinful generation needed to be purified and the new generation had to prove it was worthy to cross the Jordan and take possession of the land God had promised Abraham. This part of the work, the book of Numbers, is based on a mix of ancient accounts of the strife between Israel and the surrounding peoples. Its purpose is clearly to show the tension that exists between punishment and salvation. Punishment extends even to Moses and Aaron, who will not enter the promised land; salvation is detected in the name of the new hero, Joshua, meaning "Yahweh saves". Life in the desert has shaped the personality of this people which has been given the Word of God; so the book which covers all this material about the pilgrim-age in Sinai opens with the words "The Lord spoke to Moses in the wilderness of Sinai" (Num 1:1).

When they reached the plains of Moab, before entering the promised land, the time was right for the great discourses given by Moses, in which the history of Israel is clearly interpreted as salvation history: Israel has been chosen by God, not because it is a big nation or is exceptional in some way: it is chosen by God's great love; love is what lies behind God's choice. These Mosaic discourses become the fifth roll, Deuteronomy, and the content of the book is heralded by its opening lines: "These are the words that Moses spoke to all Israel" (Deut 1:1)—words which show the meaning and purpose of Israel's long history, namely, the fact that it is an expression of the paternal love of God and of his people's filial response to that love.

From the religious point of view, all the material assembled in the Pentateuch constitutes teaching to which the people of Israel must subscribe. It has now all become part of the "Law" of the Lord. This combination of vari-

ous traditions has an enriching effect: they complement one another and in no sense conflict. Now that they are integrated in a single whole (the "Law"), they show how God acts towards his people and the response he expects.

4. MESSAGE

The message contained in the Pentateuch is basically a religious one: it shows God at work in human history and his creation of the people of Israel,[4] and it spells out the kind of response the people must make to God. It identifies, therefore, the basis of Israel's faith and religion: we see Israel acknowledging and proclaiming how God intervened in its past history (cf. Deut 26:5–10; Josh 24:2–13), doing things which are otherwise inexplicable. At the same time it tells us that God makes his will known through people who speak on his behalf. Hence the importance of the words placed on Moses' lips. So, events, and the words that interpret them, that show what God's will is, are intrinsically linked. Both things—events and words—come from God and form part of the history of salvation.

The history of God's revelation as narrated in the Pentateuch is also a history of man's knowledge of the true God. By means of significant historical events and words uttered by God's spokesmen, Israel came to know the one and only God, transcendent and almighty (cf. Ex 34:1–6). This is the image of God portrayed by the first five books of the Bible.

The Pentateuch teaches that God has acted in human history by choosing a particular nation to be the means by which all nations will attain salvation. This election or choice, which is unmerited and entirely the product of God's love, is the key to understanding the story that unfolds not only in the Pentateuch but right through the Bible. The Pentateuch really begins with the singling out of one man, Abraham, and it develops to the point where that election extends to the entire people of Israel through the mediation of another chosen man, Moses.

Each election is accompanied by a *promise*. The Pentateuch is also the book of the promises. God promises Abraham and the patriarchs the land of Canaan and many descendants; he renews this promise to the people of Israel, whom he has rescued from Egypt; and he promises liberation and victory over evil to all of Adam's line (cf. Gen 3:15).

Election and promise are ratified by the *Covenant*. The Covenant between God and his people (mediated by Moses) constitutes the centre of the Pentateuch. But this Covenant is really the climax of a series of covenants which begins with Noah and then continues with Abraham and the other patriarchs down to Moses' time. Israel is quite right to see itself as the people of the Covenant.

---

4. For a summary of the stages of Revelation, cf. *Catechism of the Catholic Church*, 54–63.

The Covenant brings with it the *Law*, which is a series of injunctions or regulations the people must obey in order to maintain their pact with God. So, the Law has a deep meaning: if one accepts it, that means one is gratefully accepting God's will; keeping the Law means that one really and truly wants to obtain the promised gift. As we have seen, Jewish tradition calls the Pentateuch the "Law"; this means not just law in the sense of regulation but law as "God's saving intervention" as reported in these books.

5. THE PENTATEUCH IN THE LIGHT OF THE NEW TESTAMENT

When read in the light of the Christian faith, the Pentateuch does not lose any of its sublime religious meaning: rather, we perceive that meaning better than before, because we are able to see it in the context of divine biblical revelation as a whole. We recognize the Pentateuch to be, as it were, a stage in a process, the first stage in salvation history, a history which is on-going and which attains its climax in Jesus Christ and in the Church, the new people of God.

The God whom himself in Jesus Christ reveals is the same God as made himself known to Moses and the patriarchs, the one and only God, transcendent and merciful, who is active in human history. The New Testament teaches that this action of God went further than we could have dreamed: God became man in order to save man (cf. Jn 1:14). And in this central event of history, God revealed himself to be Father, Son and Holy Spirit, a Trinity of Persons in one God.

The aim of God's choice of Israel (to be a means whereby all nations will be blessed) is fulfilled in the New Testament by its showing us that the Saviour has come from within the people of Israel. Christ represents Israel, for he is the Chosen One of God who is to bring salvation to all mankind; with him and through him the number of the elect has no limit to it (cf. Gen 3:15).

In the Pentateuch election is linked to promise; in the New Testament we are shown that the promises have been fulfilled through Christ. He is the affirmation of the promises (cf. Rev 7:12), promises which, over the course of Old Testament salvation history, go beyond the boundary of one nation and point to a Kingdom of God. This is the Kingdom Christ will establish; and God has made an irrevocable promise that it will come about and that it will endure.

The covenants that ratified the original election and the promises reach their climax in the new and definitive Covenant sealed with the blood of Christ. But that Covenant cannot be understood without reference to the earlier covenants, which had special features of their own but were nevertheless a preparation for the definitive Covenant. The New Covenant exists because there previously existed an Old Covenant. And together with the New

Covenant a New Law is revealed which, based likewise on the Old (cf. Mt 7:12), is now presented as the Law of Christ, written on man's heart by the Holy Spirit.

In all these ways, the Law, that is, the Pentateuch as a whole, was and continues to be, as St Paul teaches, the tutor that leads us to Christ (cf. Gal 3:24–25). The *Catechism of the Catholic Church* explains that "the Law remains the first stage on the way to the Kingdom. It prepares and disposes the chosen people and each Christian for conversion and faith in the Saviour God. It provides a teaching which endures for ever, like the Word of God. The Old Law is a *preparation for the Gospel*: 'The Law is a pedagogy and a prophecy of things to come (St Irenaeus, *Adv. Haer.* 4, 15, 1).' It prophesies and presages the work of liberation from sin which will be fulfilled in Christ: it provides the New Testament with images, 'types', and symbols for expressing the life according to the Spirit. Finally, the Law is completed by the teaching of the sapiential books and the prophets which set its course toward the New Covenant and the Kingdom of heaven."[5]

6. INTERPRETATION

The Pentateuch gives an account of a key stage in salvation history—the origins of the people of Israel and its establishment as the people of God founded on the Covenant and the Law. In the events it describes and also in the laws it presents, the Pentateuch allows us to glimpse God's plans for the salvation of mankind. It therefore seeks to be, and is, a predominantly historical work; and at the same time it seeks to offer, and does offer, a code of human behaviour. As we have seen, it recounts the history of the Israelites' ancestors from the viewpoint of a faith that is based on later revelation (that of the events of Sinai and the teachings of the prophets). It deals with Mosaic law from the perspective of the Israelites' experiences over the course of centuries, from the very start down to the time of the Exile in Babylon. The kind of history found in the Pentateuch is of a very special kind: it is a history in which the most important element is not that it allows the reader to check whether events took place in this way or in some other way: what matters is that he can identify the teaching that the book is trying to get across. As far as the laws are concerned, the essential thing quite often is not the regulations being made for a particular situation in the life of the chosen people but the spirit behind the laws and the degree of universal validity they have. As the Second Vatican Council put it, the important thing is to ascertain "the meaning which the sacred writers really had in mind, that meaning which God had thought well to manifest through the medium of their words".[6] It is this meaning—usually termed the

---

5. Nos. 1963f. 6. *Dei Verbum*, 12.

"historical" or "literal" meaning—that we try in the first instance to bring out in our commentary on the text.

In addition to an "historical" interpretation, the books of the Pentateuch, like any other writings (or more so), are also open to a theological or spiritual interpretation. The early chapters of Genesis particularly lend themselves to this type of interpretation. In addition to the meaning they may have had at the time when they were written, they are open to being better understood and to taking on greater relevance when viewed from other cultural and religious standpoints (that is why, for example, our commentary on Genesis 1–3 includes teachings given by Pope John Paul II apropos of them). Moreover, when concrete individuals make an appearance in the Pentateuch narratives, it is possible also to interpret them symbolically in the sense that we can see in them models for how we ought to behave and the kind of attitude we should have towards God, and lessons about spiritual values. There is a tendency towards this kind of interpretation towards the end of the Old Testament (cf. Sir 44) and it extends into the New (cf. Heb 11); it was particularly to the fore in the Patristic period. In accounts about concrete individuals or events, this style of interpretation is able to uncover a spiritual meaning (compatible with the historical meaning) which helps us to read the texts of the Pentateuch as a catechesis of Christian life. Our commentary includes some interpretations of this sort.

Finally, reading the Pentateuch in the light of Christ's revelation, one comes to see that it is not just a stage in salvation history but also a direct announcement of the final outcome of that history, that is, Christ and the Church. We can see certain persons and things in these books as standing for Christ and his Church. In these instances we find a latent presence of Christ and his Church. This typological interpretation of the Pentateuch occurs in the New Testament (as when St Paul sees Hagar as standing for the Old Covenant and Sarah for the New: cf. Gal 4:21), but it is particularly a feature of the Fathers. Its main value is that it helps to show how Christ is present right throughout the Bible. In the commentaries that follow, the reader will find some of this typological interpretation which discloses "the inexhaustible content of the Old Testament [. . . and] indicates the dynamic movement towards the fulfilment of the divine plan when 'God [will] be everything to everyone' (1 Cor 15:28)."[7]

---

7. *Catechism of the Catholic Church*, 129f.

Introduction to the Book of Exodus

"Exodus" is the title the Greek translators gave to the second book of the Pentateuch, a title later adopted by the Latin version and by translations into modern languages. The Jews, who usually call the books of the Bible by their opening words, call this book *"We'elleh shemot"* ("These are the names") or simply *"Shemot"* ("The Names"). "Exodus" mean "leaving", "going out"; it applies particularly to the content of the first fifteen chapters of the book which tell how the Israelites managed to get out of Egypt; however, the word is perfectly suitable for the whole book, because it tells about how the Israelites escaped from slavery and gained their freedom, ceasing to be subject to Egypt and accepting the Covenant established on Sinai.

1. STRUCTURE AND CONTENT

The book of Exodus is made up of a number of interlinked accounts and lists of regulations which record most of the history of the children of Israel—from the time the incipient tribes settled in Egypt (thus it dovetails with the end of Genesis: cf. Ex 1:1–22) to their extended sojourn at the foot of Mount Sinai (which is where the book of Numbers finds them). The accounts cover the most important events in the history of Israel—its slavery in Egypt, the birth of Moses its leader, the signs God worked to release them from repression, the institution of the Passover, the making of the Covenant, the first apostasy and the establishment of religious worship. The laws assembled in the book of Exodus constitute the main corpus of law in the Pentateuch, and they cover the religious, moral and social life of Israel.

The book is usually divided into two main parts in line with the two key events it covers:

PART ONE: THE DEPARTURE FROM EGYPT (1:1—18:27) This is the epic account of the Exodus; it begins with the children of Israel in Egypt and follows them until they reach the foot of Mount Sinai (chaps. 1–18).

(1) The narrative begins with a short summary of the life of the tribes in Egypt—how they prospered (1:1–7) and their first setbacks (1:8–22).

(2) The following chapters contain an account of the calling of Moses, which goes from his infancy in the court of Egypt to his first interview with

the pharaoh on behalf of his people. It begins with his birth and rescue from the Nile by the pharaoh's daughter, and his upbringing at court (2:1–10). After killing an Egyptian and trying to make peace between two of his countrymen, Moses flees to Midian (2:11–25); there God reveals himself to him in the burning bush and tells him his name (3:1–22). In charging Moses with a mission to save his people, God gives him the power to work wonders (4:1–9) and designates Aaron as his spokesman (4:10–17). On his way back from Midian to Egypt, Moses and his son undergo circumcision, and Aaron and Moses meet in the desert (4:18–31). After this, the first interview with the pharaoh takes place; the pharaoh rejects Moses' request to let the people go into the desert for a religious feast: in fact, instead of his letting them off work for the occasion, he makes their work even heavier (5:1–18). Moses then pleads with God to come to the people's aid (5:19—16:1). The text then returns to the subject of the calling of Moses, and his mission (6:2–13). After giving details of the genealogy of Aaron and Moses we come to a new account of the interview with the pharaoh, in which the plagues are announced (6:14—7:7).

(3) The next five chapters deal with the plagues. In the course of the narrative, the theological meaning of each plague is underlined: thus, the magicians appear only in the account of the first three plagues (the waters of the Nile turning red, the frogs, and the gnats: 7:14—8:15); the next three (the flies, the cattle epidemic and the plague of ulcers prepare the way for the great storm which is recounted as a theophany of God in the face of which the pharaoh acknowledges God's sovereignty for the first time (9:13–35); and with the last three (the locusts, the darkness, and the death of the first-born) the pharaoh gradually comes round until eventually (after the death of the first-born) he gives in (10:1—11:10).

(4) In connexion with the last plague the rules for the Passover are spelled out. These rules deal with its institution (12:1–14), the celebration of the days of the unleavened bread (12:15–20), and various other instructions (12:21–28). We are then told about the death of the first-born (12:29–32) and the preparations for leaving Egypt (12:33–42), as well as new regulations about the Passover, the unleavened bread and the first born (12:43—13:16).

(5) The departure from Egypt is described with all due formality. It is all depicted as something planned by the Lord (13:17—14:4). Even though the Egyptians are in hot pursuit, the people of Israel manage to cross the Red Sea with the aid of divine marvels (15:1–21). The triumphal Hymn or Canticle of Miriam celebrates the wondrous deeds of the Lord (15:1–21).

(6) This part of Exodus reaches its climax with an account of the stages prior to their reaching the wilderness of Sinai—the episode of the bitter waters of Marah (15:22–27), the prodigy of the manna and the quails (16:1–36), the water from the rock (17:1–7), and the first battle and victory over the Amalekites (17:8–15). It ends with Jethro's visit to Moses and appointment of the judges (18:1–27).

PART TWO. THE PEOPLE OF ISRAEL IN THE SINAI (19:1—40:38) This deals with the main events that take place at Sinai—the making of the Covenant, the promulgation of the laws and precepts, and the building of the sanctuary:

(7) The theophany of the Lord is recounted in a solemn fashion which stresses its drama, and sets the scene for the Covenant and the promulgation of the Ten Commandments (19:1—20:21).

(8) The Code of the Covenant is then recorded as being part of the corpus of laws that God gives to Moses. The first section covers ordinances about worship (20:22–26), slaves, and penalties for injuries (21:1—22:16). These are followed by other regulations about social morality, trials, and treatment of enemies (22:17—23:9). Finally, it deals with sabbatical years, the sabbath and other cultic matters (23:10–19). It ends with a number of warnings and promises (23:20–33).

(9) The account of the theophany at Sinai concludes with the Ritual of the Covenant, which includes the rite of ratification (24:1–11) and Moses going up the sacred mountain again and staying there forty days and forty nights (24:12–18).

(10) There follows a section about rules to do with the Sanctuary. The first of these cover its construction and sacred objects (25:1—27:21); the section then goes on to deal with ministers and their roles in worship (28:1—31:18).

(11) Then comes an account of the most serious instance of apostasy to take place in the desert. This aberration consisted in the people adoring a golden calf, and it brought down the wrath of God (32:1–10). Moses intercedes for the people, but he fails to deflect God's punishment. The calf is destroyed (32:11–24), and the guilty die at the hands of the Levites (32:25–29). Moses again intercedes with the Lord, who, as a punishment for the sin, decides that only his angel and not He himself will accompany the people on their journey (32:30–35). After this episode the order is given to break camp and the Tent of Meeting is described (33:1–11). Finally, after Moses intercedes with God once more, He agrees to accompany the people personally (33:12–17). The section ends with the account of Moses' vision of the glory of the Lord (33:18–23).

(12) After the apostasy, everything had to be done all over again, as can be seen from the account of the renewing of the Covenant. This consisted of the handing over of the new tables of the Law (34:1–9), the so-called Ritual of the Covenant (34:10–28) and the appearance of Moses before the people, his face shining (34:29–35).

(13) The book ends with an account about how the rules for the construction of the sanctuary were followed in exact detail (35:1—36:38), as also those about the sacred objects (37:1—38:31) and the ministers (39:1–43). Once the construction and furnishing are completed, the sanctuary is consecrated (40:1–15); Moses does things exactly as the Lord directed him (40:16–33). By

way of epilogue, there is a short recapitulation about the protective function of the cloud that covered the tent of meeting: it is a sign that God is with his people and it is he who is leading them on their pilgrimage through the desert.

2. HISTORICAL BACKGROUND

The history recounted in Exodus should not be regarded as an exact, detailed chronicle. It is more a history of salvation which tells how the Lord made the "sons of Jacob" into the "people of God", that is, a people who have become part of the salvific mystery: he has chosen them to be the first fruits of salvation; he has established a Covenant of love with them and in his providence takes special care of them. The sacred writer has expounded this supernatural truth dressing events in a language of worship, theology and epic poetry. It is not always easy therefore to work out what the exact chain of events is.

What is certainly true (as even a non-religious historian will acknowledge) is that this book is telling us about key stages in the history of the people of Israel—(1) that the descendants of the patriarchs suffered ignominious oppression during the time they spent in the Nile delta; (2) that they managed to escape from there in very remarkable circumstances; (3) that during their lengthy stay in the desert region they developed a "national self-consciousness" with the help of Yahweh ("the Lord"), whom they acknowledged as the one true God; and (4) in the course of this remarkable adventure one figure stood out, that of Moses, who gave them cohesion and leadership and who was their great teacher.

(a) *Dating the Exodus*
The Israelites most probably left Egypt in the thirteenth century BC, the time when the main buildings of ancient Egypt were being constructed. In recent times historians and archeologists have added greatly to our knowledge of that culture; they tell us that there were thirty-one dynasties of pharaohs, divided over three empires: the Old Empire (2800–2300 BC) which was at its zenith in the third and fourth dynasties; the Middle Empire (2300–1500 BC) whose high point was in the eleventh to seventeenth dynasties; and the New Empire (1500–1000 BC). It was in this last period that Egypt reached the zenith of its power and prestige. Pharaohs Seti I (1291–1279) and Rameses II (1279–1212) came to the throne at a time of peace and stability and were responsible for important religious and cultural initiatives, the most outstanding of which included monumental buildings; in the construction of these, resident foreigners were used, Semites in particular.

One needs to remember that in the eighteenth–sixteenth centuries BC the Hyksos, who were probably Canaanites and Ammorites from the general region of Syria and Palestine, invaded Egypt and then dominated it for over

one hundred years. The Egyptians maintained a resistance against them until around 1500 BC, when they managed to expel or suppress them. It may have been during these centuries that the descendants of the patriarchs arrived from Canaan and settled down in Egypt in very favourable circumstances.

From this date on (1550 BC) the enslavement of the Israelites probably began. The statement in Exodus 1:8 (to the effect that "There arose a new king over Egypt, who did not know Joseph") may be a reference to the early years of the New Empire.

The book of Exodus, which makes no reference to dates, likewise gives no names of pharaohs. The only reference which may give a guide is in 1 Kings 6:1, which speaks about four hundred and eighty years as being the length of time between when the people of Israel came out of Egypt and the building of Solomon's temple. Since Solomon's reign began in 960 BC, this means the Exodus would have taken place around 1440 BC. However, the figure given in 1 Kings rather looks as though it is saying that there were twelve generations (each of forty years) in the span; in other words, there is nothing exact about it.

However, in Exodus 1:11 there is mention of the store-cities, in the building of which Israelites were involved; this seems to be a firmer piece of information and it leads one to suppose that it was in the thirteenth century that the people of Israel left Egypt. The kind of building programme promoted by Seti I and Rameses II had no parallels in previous centuries.

On the other hand, if one accepts that the Exodus began early in the thirteenth century, the conquest of Palestine must be set some forty years later, that is, in the second half of the same century, the date archeologists give for the destruction of many cities of Canaan, such as Lachish, and Jazer.

(b) *The figure of Moses*

The structure of Israelite religion and the socio-political organization of the people stem from and hinge on Moses. There was once a time (when rationalism and positivism were very much in vogue) when a question-mark was put against whether there was ever any such person as Moses. The accepted opinion nowadays is that there is sufficient archeological and historical evidence for saying that he did exist. The source of our knowledge of this distinguished personality is the book of Exodus. That book, written from the standpoint of faith, portrays him as a leader and guide, a prophet and teacher, and the prototype of Israel, since his own life was marked by the same ups and downs as the people had to cope with.

As a leader and guide, Moses—always at the Lord's bidding and under his protection—manages to overcome, firstly, opposition from the Israelites themselves, and then the stubbornness of the pharaoh, and later still the forces of nature. As regards his leadership, the best example is his struggle to keep up the people's spirits and to counter their lack of faith. This begins when Moses is still living in the court of the pharaoh (cf. 2:14), it springs up again when he

puts the Exodus project to the people (5:21), and it crops up again when they start complaining in the wilderness (cf. 15:22–24; 17:1–17). Gradually Moses manages to get them to follow him and to accept the Covenant of the Lord willingly and to take on board the requirements it lays down (on a number of occasions they make a promise to this effect: "All the words which the Lord has spoken we will do": 24:3, 7; 19:8; 25:9).

Future generations will acknowledge Moses as prophet and teacher (cf. Deut 18:18; Hos 12:14), because the Law reached them through him. The sacred writers place on Moses' lips all the rules and regulations to do with the moral, religious and social life of the people. In the book of Exodus three codes or groups of important laws are included. These codes may have been redacted before the book was composed; from very early on, the various traditions attributed them to Moses. They are the moral Decalogue or ten commandments (20:1–17), the Code of the Covenant (20:22—23:33) and the Ritual Code (34:14–26). The books of Numbers and Leviticus attribute to Moses the laws that they contain; and Deuteronomy takes the form of a long discourse spoken by Moses.

But, first and foremost Moses is regarded and projected as a model for his people, its paradigm. His life is an image of the life of Israel: his remarkable birth, "drawn out of the water" (2:10), prefigures the birth of the people in the waters of the Red Sea; his pleasant childhood in the pharaoh's court (2:10) is like the easy years the sons of Israel spent in Egypt (1:6); his flight, which brought him to live as a stranger in Midian (2:11–22) is also an image of the persecution of the people. Consequently, Moses' faith in God's design (4:1–17) will be the basis of the faith of the entire people.

In this sort of way the sacred writer points up how closely Moses is linked to his people. He is not just an intermediary: he is their representative before God. From this angle, too, he is a figure of Jesus Christ who, having taken on human nature, opened the way of salvation to all mankind through the waters of Baptism.

3. COMPOSITION

The basic facts recounted in the book of Exodus were retained in the folk-memory of the people and celebrated on the great feast-days; they were sung about in hymns and generally passed on as being an essential element of their faith. By recalling, as they did, the history of the origins of the nation, those who eventually settled down in Israel (around the 13th century BC) gave religious meaning to the institutions, laws and customs that they practised, gradually linking them to the original events of the Exodus and the desert years. This process, which took place by a special providence of God, is all consolidated in Exodus. To explain how it (and the rest of the Pentateuch) came to be written, exegetes over the past hundred years talk about there being a number of known sources or traditions. As regards this book, there seems to be more evi-

dence of the presence of the "Yahwistic" and "Priestly" traditions.[1] But we should also bear in mind that "codes" of law probably existed from much earlier on and were passed on quite independently of the traditions just mentioned.

Even though the book draws on a diversity of sources, there is a marked unity about it: there are repetitions (as we shall point out), but the narrative thread is maintained throughout. Undoubtedly the last editor was skilled at collecting old traditions and blending them skilfully into a harmonious whole, which, without betraying the facts, focuses on the key theological truths—the saving intervention by God, the election of the people of Israel, the doctrinal and moral implications of the Covenant, and the purpose and meaning of worship.

4. MESSAGE

The whole book is designed to exalt the greatness of God who has done so many wondrous deeds, and to stress the special nature of the people of Israel, the beneficiary of so many blessings. The choice of Israel, the Covenant and worship are the three things which constitute the structure of the people's faith and religious life.

(a) *The choice of Israel*
The greatest salvific act in the history of Israel, and the necessary point of reference for explaining God's other salvific interventions, is the deliverance of Israel from bondage in Egypt. Through this act, God—entirely on his own initiative—made the descendants of Jacob into a free people. In the light of this great event future generations will come to see that their existence as a people was the outcome of a very special divine intervention, comparable to the act of creation. This is why, in the Old Testament, creation is depicted as an act of election-salvation (cf. Is 45:12–13) and why, in turn, every salvific act can be described as a creational act: God chose to produce out of chaos such things as are created; from among these, he chose man; from among men, he chose the people of Israel.

The narrative of the salvific events God brought about in Exodus is interwoven with an account of the people's acts of infidelity: first, there is their failure to believe what Moses says; then there is the murmuring against Moses and Aaron in the wilderness; later on, the worshipping of the golden calf, etc. These sins provoke the Lord's anger so much that he is on the point of wiping the entire people out. However, time and again he forgives them and confines himself to punishing them—with punishments which are also salvific actions because they show that it is sin that leads the people back into a situation of slavery and subjection. Election-salvation is the way the living and true God behaves towards his people, and it prepares the way for complete revelation, when all mankind is called in Christ to form part of the New People of God.

---

1. Cf. "Introduction to the Pentateuch", pp 19–21, above.

(b) *The Covenant*
The choosing of Israel from among the nations was equivalent to establishing it
as the people of God by means of the Covenant. Already in chapter 6 it is spelled
out that their liberation from slavery and oppression has this as its aim: "I will
take you for my people, and I will be your God" (6:7). In the rite of the
Covenant as described in chapters 19–24 (and in its renewal in chapter 34) we
find phrases like "keeping the covenant" (19:5), "the blood of the covenant"
(24:7), "the words of the covenant" (34:28), etc. The Covenant does not just
mean the imposition of certain rules by God, which would mean a unilateral
requirement to obey certain laws coming from outside, designed to regulate the
religious and moral life of the people. Nor is it just the commitment the Israelites
made to God to put certain basic laws into practice. It is first and foremost a
bilateral pact whereby God, who is the one who takes the initiative, proposes to
the people that they and he commit themselves to carry out certain obligations;
for his part, God will protect Israel in a special way (it will be his people); and
Israel, for its part, will acknowledge him as its God, the one God, and will obey
all his commandments. The Covenant, therefore, is an event which regulates the
religious, moral and social life of the members of the people, but it affects, above
all, their innermost heart and it is what makes them the people of God, because
it shows the special relationship the Lord has with them.

The term "covenant", in Hebrew *berit*, seems to mean "between-two", that
is, a mutual agreement between two persons. It is likely that the way the establishment of the Covenant at Sinai is described is inspired not so much by private pacts such as those described in the book of Genesis between Jacob and
Laban (cf. Gen 31:41) or between Abraham and his neighbours (Gen 14:13),
as by the vassalage pacts which sealed the peace between peoples. The
(extant) wording of some pacts from the second millennium BC has many sim-
ilarities with the wording recorded in Exodus and in other books of the Bible.
However, it is worth pointing out that the Covenant of Sinai is different in this
respect: the Sinai Covenant includes the moral Decalogue (20:1–17), the Code
of the Covenant (20:22—23:19) and the Ritual of the Code (34:17–26), that
is, it regulates all aspects of the people's life, and its essence is that, by that
Covenant, God made Israel "a kingdom of priests and a holy nation" (19:6). It
is not just a peace pact or a vassalage agreement that is being sealed, but a pact
which makes it a people of the utmost dignity.

The Covenant will be constantly renewed in Israel's liturgy, and the
prophets are always reminding the people about it; when they break it, God
himself will restore it (cf. Jer 31:31–35). In the fullness of time, Jesus Christ
will seal with his blood the new and eternal Covenant (cf. Heb 8:6–13).

(c) *Worship*
Religious organization and religious worship had immense importance in
Israel. The main body of prescriptions about worship is to be found in the

book of Exodus. Like the rest of the laws, these were regarded as having Moses as their author, even though many of them seem to reflect the splendour of the liturgy in the temple of Jerusalem during the period of the monarchy. These laws fall into three main groups—Passover, the festivals or feasts, and the sanctuary and its institutions.

The *Passover*, which is mentioned in the Ritual Code (cf. 34:25) and in the Code of the Covenant (cf. 23:13–19 and 34:17–26) is fully described in chapter 12 where the institution, ritual and meaning of this sacrifice are attributed to Moses. The immolation of the lamb and family participation in the feast are indicative of the simplicity of a sacrifice typical of nomadic peoples; but for generation after generation it constituted a vivid memorial of the liberation from Egypt. As time went by ceremonies grew up, giving the people a deep appreciation of the Passover, and these also are recorded in the Exodus account; they made the Passover the most typical of all Israel's sacrifices.

The *feasts* and the other rules to do with worship (cf. 23:13–19 and 34:17–26) are described in fairly simple language—which is indicative of their antiquity. Although some of these rites and even some of the feasts existed in Canaan before the Israelites came back from Egypt, only in Israel did they acquire their specific religious character. They all acknowledge the Lord as the only God and they recall and re-enact the wondrous events of the Exodus.

The *sanctuary*, its institutions and its ministers are regulated by prescriptions recorded in chapters 25–31. Here again elements from the desert period are mixed up with other much later ones—some even from after the Babylonian exile (6th century BC). But all are treated as ordinances from the Lord or from Moses, to show their obligatory and sacred character.

These brief remarks, which will be expanded upon in the notes, help to show how elaborate the religious life of Israel was; and they are also the things that the book of Exodus gives pride of place to, over and above exactness in dating or topography.

5. EXODUS IN THE OLD AND THE NEW TESTAMENT

The salvific events recounted in the book of Exodus constitute the foundation of Israelite history and religion; they are things which the people will keep alive in their memory. Phrases like "God brought Israel out of Egypt" or "God brought Israel out of Egypt with his powerful hand and his outstretched arm" occur more than seventy-five times in the Old Testament.

When the Bible wants to draw a contrast between the blessings of God and the sins of the people, it always evokes the Exodus and the desert as a sign of God's special love: "I brought you up out of the land of Egypt, and led you forty years in the wilderness [. . .]. But you commanded the prophets, saying, 'You shall not prophesy' " (Amos 2:10–12; cf. Amos 3:1–2). The biblical texts

also reflect the fact that God's choice of Israel is enduring: "When Israel was a child, I loved him, and out of Egypt I called my son" (cf. Hos 11:1). The memory of the Exodus stirs them to repentance: "O my people, what have I done to you? In what have I wearied you? Answer me! For I brought you up from the land of Egypt, and redeemed you from the house of bondage" (Mic 6:3–4; cf. Jer 2:5–6). The Exodus is, therefore, the point of departure for praising the greatness and powerful love of the Lord: "He smote the first-born of Egypt. [. . .] and brought Israel out from among them, for his steadfast love endures for ever" (Ps 136:10–11; cf. Ps 78; 105; 106; 114; Wis 16–19; etc.).

When it comes to describing the dire consequences of the Assyrian invasion (721 BC) and the deportation to Babylon (587 BC), bondage in Egypt is the benchmark: "They shall return to the land of Egypt, and Assyria shall be their king because they have refused to return to me" (Hos 11:5). But the Exodus is above all, the ground of their hope, for God, who did such wonders in bringing them out of Egypt, is ready to do them again in order to bring about a new and more enduring deliverance. Therefore, the return from exile in Babylon will be described as a glorious new exodus: "Thus says the Lord, who makes a way in the sea, [. . .] 'Remember not the former things. [. . .] Behold, I am doing a new thing. [. . .] I will make a way in the wilderness and rivers in the desert. [. . .] The people whom I formed for myself (will) declare my praises" (Is 43:16–21; cf. 48:24; 52:10–12; etc.). Since the Exodus is seen as being like creation, the return from the Babylonian captivity, described as a new exodus, is also equated to a new creation (cf. Is 44:24–28; 45:12–13; 51:9–11).

The New Testament, too, contains many references to the Exodus. In St Matthew's Gospel Jesus is portrayed as a new Moses: to him are applied the words of Hosea: "Out of Egypt have I called my son" (Mt 2:15). Christ will spend forty days in the wilderness (cf. Mt 4:2), which is evocative of the forty years the people spent in the desert and the forty days Moses spent on Mount Sinai (cf. Ex 24:18). The beatitudes are enunciated on the Mount (cf. Mt 5:1) in the same sort of way as the Law of Moses was promulgated on Sinai; and the transfiguration will take place on a mountain (cf. Mt 17:1–8).

St Paul, for his part, will recall many of the wonders of the Exodus, seeing them as a figure of things in the new economy of salvation: the manna is a figure of the Eucharist, and the rock from which Moses caused water to spring is a figure of Christ (cf. 1 Cor 11:1–5). The Covenant of Sinai prefigured the Covenant established by Christ in his blood (cf. 1 Cor 11:24–25); the sanctuary and the form of worship used in the wilderness are a pale shadow of what obtains in heaven (cf. Heb 8:5). Many other events will later be evoked as figures of the new economy, in line with the words of St Paul who has this to say about Exodus events: "Now these things happened to them as a warning, but they were written down for our instruction, upon whom the end of the ages has come" (1 Cor 10:11).

EXODUS

PART ONE

The Departure from Egypt

1. THE SONS OF ISRAEL IN EGYPT

The prosperity of the sons of Israel in Egypt

Gen 46:1–27
Acts 7:14–17

1 ¹These are the names of the sons of Israel who came to Egypt with Jacob, each with his household: ²Reuben, Simeon, Levi, and Judah, ³Issachar, Zebulun, and Benjamin, ⁴Dan and Naphtali, Gad and Asher. ⁵All the offspring of Jacob were seventy persons; Joseph was already in Egypt. ⁶Then Joseph died, and all his brothers, and all that generation. ⁷But the descendants of Israel were fruitful and increased greatly; they multiplied and grew exceedingly strong; so that the land was filled with them.

Gen 46:27
Deut 10:22
Acts 7:15
Gen 1:27
Ps 105:24
Acts 13:17

1:1–7. The book of Genesis (cf. Gen 46:8–27) already provided a list of the descendants of Jacob who went down into Egypt; these are now mentioned in a summary form here. Thus, in his opening verses the sacred writer makes it clear that the events of the Exodus are a continuation of those recounted in Genesis, and that the members of the people of Israel which is going to be established are in direct line of descent from the patriarchs. The number of seventy (cf. Gen 46:27) conveys the idea of completeness: that is, all Jacob's descendants moved to Egypt. But it is also a small number, showing that only God could turn them into the sizeable people of Israel.

"They increased greatly; they multiplied and grew exceedingly strong"

(v. 7)—language identical to that used in the first account of creation, recalling the divine blessing which guaranteed that the first human couple would be fruitful (cf. Gen 1:27), as would those who are now the first links in the people of Israel.

*1:8–14. The situation of the children of Israel is dramatically portrayed: the more they are oppressed, the stronger they become (v. 12). The frequent contrasts in the account and the fact that no names are supplied give the impression that God himself (even though he is yet not named) is on the Israelites' side and is against the pharaoh and his people. From the very beginning, over and above the comings and goings of men, God is at work; a religious event is taking shape.

For the first time the Bible here

---

¹Haec sunt nomina filiorum Israel, qui ingressi sunt Aegyptum cum Iacob; singuli cum domibus suis introierunt: ²Ruben, Simeon, Levi, Iuda, ³Issachar, Zabulon et Beniamin, ⁴Dan et Nephthali, Gad et Aser. ⁵Erant igitur omnes animae eorum, qui egressi sunt de femore Iacob, septuaginta; Ioseph autem in Aegypto erat. ⁶Quo mortuo et universis fratribus eius omnique cognatione illa, ⁷filii Israel creverunt et pullulantes multiplicati sunt ac roborati nimis impleverunt terram. ⁸Surrexit interea rex novus super

Jud 5:11 **The sons of Israel are oppressed***

Acts 7:18–19 [8]Now there arose a new king over Egypt, who did not know Joseph. [9]And he said to his people, "Behold, the people of Israel are too many and too mighty for us. [10]Come, let us deal shrewdly with them, lest they multiply, and, if war befall us, they join our enemies and fight against us and escape from the land." Gen 47:11 [11]Therefore they set taskmasters over them to afflict them with heavy burdens; and they built for Pharaoh store-cities, Pithom and

---

speaks of the "people [of the sons] of Israel" (v. 9). The sacred book counterposes two peoples—the people of the pharaoh, cruel and oppressive, and the people of Israel, the victims of oppression. Over the course of their struggle to leave Egypt, the children of Israel will gradually become conscious of this—that they form a people chosen by God and released from bondage in order to fulfil an important historical mission. They are not a motley collection of tribes or families, but a people. "God, with loving concern contemplating, and making preparation for, the salvation of the whole human race, in a singular undertaking chose for himself a people to whom he would entrust his promises" (Vatican II, *Dei Verbum*, 14). At the same time the religious framework of this inspired book is established: on one side stand the enemies of God, on the other the people of the children of the Covenant (cf. Acts 3:25; *Catechism of the Catholic Church*, 527).

1:8. We do not know who exactly this "new king" was. He was probably Rameses II (early 13th century BC), who belonged to the nineteenth dynasty. This pharaoh sought to restore imperial control over foreigners and invaders. The

phrase "did not know Joseph" indicates how helpless and alone the "sons of Israel" were. The people of Israel never did count for very much politically, and yet God wills them to have an essential place in his plans.

Many Fathers of the Church saw in this pharaoh a personification of those who are opposed to the establishment of the Kingdom of Christ. St Bede, for example, reminds the Christian that if, having been baptized and having listened to the teachings of the faith, he goes back to living in a worldly way, "another king who knows not Joseph" will come to birth in him, that is, the selfishness which opposes the plans of God (cf. *Commentaria in Pentateuchum*, 2,1).

1:11. Pithom and Raamses are called "store-cities" because provisions for the frontier garrisons were stored in the silos of their temples. Reliable archeological studies identify Pithom (which in Egyptian means "dwelling of Athon") with some ruins a few kilometres from present-day Ishmailia, not far from the Suez canal. A temple of Athon has been discovered there, and huge stores of bricks. It is more difficult to say where Raamses was. The balance of probability

---

Aegyptum, qui ignorabat Ioseph; [9]et ait ad populum suum: «Ecce, populus filiorum Israel multus et fortior nobis est: [10]venite, prudenter agamus cum eo, ne forte multiplicetur et, si ingruerit contra nos bellum, addatur inimicis nostris, expugnatisque nobis, egrediatur de terra». [11]Praeposuit itaque eis magistros operum, ut affligerent eos oneribus; aedificaveruntque urbes promptuarias pharaoni, Phithom et

Raamses. ¹²But the more they were oppressed, the more they ^{Deut 11:10} multiplied and the more they spread abroad. And the Egyptians were in dread of the people of Israel. ¹³So they made the people of Israel serve with rigour, ¹⁴and made their lives bitter with hard service, in mortar and brick, and in all kinds of work in the field; in all their work they made them serve with rigour.

¹⁵Then the king of Egypt said to the Hebrew midwives, one of whom was named Shiphrah and the other Puah, ¹⁶"When you ^{Mt 2:16}

---

is that it was the earlier city of Avaris, a capital during the dynasties of invader pharaohs. It would later be called Tanis, and nowadays it is just a series of big ruins near a fishing village, San el-Hagar, near Port Said, on the eastern part of the Nile delta. Archeologists have discovered there the remains of an elaborate temple built by Rameses II (1279–1212 BC), probably the pharaoh mentioned here.

1:14. In ancient Egypt it was normal for people, particularly foreigners, to work for the pharaoh. This was not regarded as a form of slavery or "oppression"; we know, for example, there were towns or entire cities which accommodated the workers engaged in building the tombs or temples of the pharaohs. The oppression the sacred writer refers to lay in the fact that the Egyptians imposed particularly hard tasks on the Israelites—such as brick-making, building and agricultural labour—and treated them cruelly.

St Isidore of Seville, commenting on this passage, compares it with the situation of mankind which, after original sin, is subject to the tyranny of the devil, who often manages to turn work into slavery.

Just as the pharaoh imposed the hard labour of mortar and brick, so too the devil forces sinful man to engage in "earthly, dusty tasks which are moreover mixed with straw, that is to say, with frivolous and irrational acts" (cf. *Quaestiones in Exodum,* 3).

1:15–21. The situation of the Israelites was worse than slavery. The most serious thing was that they saw no future before them because the pharaoh had ordered all male children to be killed. As a kind of echo of this, the evangelists point out that Herod "sent and killed all the male children who were two years old or under" (Mt 2:16).

God shows his revulsion towards infanticide by protecting the midwives and making the chosen people fruitful. The brave action of the midwives has been praised by commentators in every age. The Targum, an Aramaic version which reflects ancient Hebrew oral traditions, translates v. 21 by saying that God gave them houses (descendants), the royal house and the house of the high priest. Apropos of this episode, Christian writers comment that God always rewards good actions. St Thomas says that the midwives were rewarded not

---

Ramesses. ¹²Quantoque opprimebant eos, tanto magis multiplicabantur et crescebant. ¹³Formidaveruntque filios Israel Aegyptii et in servitutem redegerunt eos ¹⁴atque ad amaritudinem perducebant vitam eorum operibus duris luti et lateris omnique famulatu, quo in terrae operibus premebantur. ¹⁵Dixit autem rex Aegypti obstetricibus Hebraeorum, quarum una vocabatur Sephra, altera Phua, ¹⁶praecipiens eis: «Quando obstetricabitis Hebraeas, et partus tempus advenerit, si masculus fuerit, interficite

serve as midwife to the Hebrew women, and see them upon the birthstool, if it is a son, you shall kill him; but if it is a daughter, she shall live." [17]But the midwives feared God, and did not do as the king of Egypt commanded them, but let the male children live. [18]So the king of Egypt called the midwives, and said to them, "Why have you done this, and let the male children live?" [19]The midwives said to Pharaoh, "Because the Hebrew women are not like the Egyptian women; for they are vigorous and are delivered before the midwife comes to them." [20]So God dealt well with the midwives; and the people multiplied and grew very strong. [21]And because the midwives feared God he gave them families. [22]Then Pharaoh commanded all his people, "Every son that is born to the Hebrews[a] you shall cast into the Nile, but you shall let every daughter live."

Acts 7:19

Acts 7:19

---

because they lied to the pharaoh but because they showed reverence to God (cf. *Summa theologiae,* 2–2, 110, 3 ad 2).

1:16. The Hebrew text says literally "see the two stones" for "see them upon the birthstool". Apparently, Hebrew women, when about to give birth, used to sit on two stones; the Targum translates it as "see the chairs". In any event, the point is that the midwives were told to be alert at the moment of childbirth, to see if it was a girl or a boy.

1:20. The people of Israel multiplied and grew strong despite difficulties and persecution, thanks to God's favour. The helpful part played by the midwives (who were probably Egyptians) serves to show God's great love. Women, Israelite and

Egyptian, play a key role in the early stages of Israel's salvation.

St Cyril of Alexandria, applying this episode generally, comments that our situation is like that of the Israelites: "we were overwhelmed, by sin from the very beginning, from our first parents onwards; we were oppressed by a lack of good things, and in our unhappiness we found ourselves also, against our will, subject to the yoke of Satan, the prince of all evil. [. . .] There was no pain or suffering that we did not have, when God had mercy on us, set us free from the position we were in, and saved us" (*Glaphyra in Exodum,* 1, 3).

1:22. The original text always refers to "the River" because the entire life of ancient Egypt depended on it. Obviously it is referring to the Nile.

---

eum; si femina, reservate». [17]Timuerunt autem obstetrices Deum et non fecerunt iuxta praeceptum regis Aegypti, sed conservabant mares. [18]Quibus ad se accersitis rex ait: «Quidnam est hoc, quod facere voluistis, ut pueros servaretis?». [19]Quae responderunt: «Non sunt Hebraeae sicut Aegyptiae mulieres; ipsae enim robustae sunt et, priusquam veniamus ad eas, pariunt». [20]Bene ergo fecit Deus obstetricibus, et crevit populus confortatusque est nimis; [21]et, quia timuerunt obstetrices Deum, aedificavit illis domos. [22]Praecepit ergo pharao omni populo suo dicens: «Quidquid masculini sexus natum fuerit, in flumen proicite; quidquid feminei, reservate». [1]Egressus est vir de domo Levi et accepit uxorem stir-

a. Sam Gk Tg: Heb lacks *to the Hebrews*

2. THE CALL OF MOSES

The birth and early years of Moses*

2 ¹Now a man from the house of Levi went and took to wife a
daughter of Levi. ²The woman conceived and bore a son; and
when she saw that he was a goodly child, she hid him three
months. ³And when she could hide him no longer she took for
him a basket made of bulrushes, and daubed it with bitumen and
pitch; and she put the child in it and placed it among the reeds at
the river's brink. ⁴And his sister stood at a distance, to know what
would be done to him. ⁵Now the daughter of Pharaoh came down
to bathe at the river, and her maidens walked beside the river; she
saw the basket among the reeds and sent her maid to fetch it.
⁶When she opened it she saw the child; and lo, the babe was
crying. She took pity on him and said, "This is one of the
Hebrews' children." ⁷Then his sister said to Pharaoh's daughter,

Ex 6:20

Acts 7:30
Heb 11:23

Gen 6:14
Acts 7:21

Acts 7:21

---

*2:1–10. With lots of detail and good
psychological insight, the sacred text
recounts the birth and upbringing of
Moses, the man whom divine providence
had chosen to be the liberator and leader
of the chosen people. What we have here
is not so much chronological or topo-
graphical data as information which pro-
files the religious personality of the man
who was both the guide and the prototype of the people.

In a masterly way the sacred writer
highlights those aspects of his life and
personality which most clearly show
Moses to resemble the people and show
divine intervention to be at work. Moses
grew up during a period of severe persecution, but thanks to the good offices of
three women (his mother, his sister and
the pharaoh's daughter) he is received

into the Egyptian court and shown every
honour. His tranquil childhood reflects
the pleasant lifestyle of the sons of Israel
in Egypt prior to the onset of oppression
and persecution.

In this entire account of Moses' birth
there is no mention of the names of his
parents (Amram, according to Ex 6:20
his father, and Jochebed, his mother:
Num 26:59) or his sister, Miriam (Ex
15:20). The sacred writer prefers to con-
centrate on Moses, making it clear that
God takes care of him in birth and
infancy, as he will also do of the people.
Even the popular etymology of Moses'
name ("taken from the waters") is an
indication of God's intervention. The
name in fact is Egyptian, meaning "son"
or "born", as can be deduced from the
names of some pharaohs Tut-mosis (son

---

pis suae; ²quae concepit et peperit filium et videns eum elegantem abscondit tribus mensibus. ³Cumque
iam celare non posset, sumpsit fiscellam scirpeam et linivit eam bitumine ac pice; posuitque intus
infantulum et exposuit eum in carecto ripae fluminis, ⁴stante procul sorore eius et considerante even-
tum rei. ⁵Ecce autem descendebat filia pharaonis, ut lavaretur in flumine, et puellae eius gradiebantur
per crepidinem alvei. Quae cum vidisset fiscellam in papyrione, misit unam e famulabus suis; et
allatam ⁶aperiens cernensque in ea parvulum vagientem, miserta eius ait: «De infantibus Hebraeorum
est hic». ⁷Cui soror pueri: «Vis, inquit, ut vadam et vocem tibi mulierem Hebraeam, quae nutrire possit
tibi infantulum?». ⁸Respondit: «Vade». Perrexit puella et vocavit matrem infantis. ⁹Ad quam locuta filia

43

"Shall I go and call you a nurse from the Hebrew women to nurse the child for you?" [8]And Pharaoh's daughter said to her, "Go." So the girl went and called the child's mother. [9]And Pharaoh's daughter said to her, "Take this child away, and nurse him for me, and I will give you your wages." So the woman took the child and Acts 7:21 nursed him. [10]And the child grew, and she brought him to Pharaoh's daughter, and he became her son; and she named him Moses,[b] for she said, "Because I drew him out[c] of the water."

---

of the god Tut) or Ra-mses (son of the god Ra)—but that does not matter: the important thing is that Moses is "the first to be saved", just as the Hebrew people is the first people to be saved, and that God is taking great care of him with a view to the important mission he has planned for him.

2:1–3. The Hebrew term translated here as "basket" is the same one as used for the Noah's "ark" (cf. Gen 6:14–9, 18, where it occurs 27 times). What we are told about the basket links Moses to Noah and his salvation from the waves of the flood which occurred so much earlier and in such dramatic circumstances. After the flood, mankind was reborn; now a new people is being born.

2:10. According to Egyptian law an adopted son had the same status as any other son. The text stresses that the pharaoh's daughter made him her son. In this paradox we can once again see God's providence at work: the child whom the Egyptians should have put to death is raised to great dignity, given the best of educations and thereby groomed for his future mission. Extra-biblical documents show that during this period the

pharaohs trained select foreign youths for posts in their civil service. However, although Moses spent his early years in the pharaoh's palace, he received from his true mother not only physical nourishment but also the faith of his ancestors and love for his people.

Origen, whom many Fathers follow, interprets this wonderful story in an allegorical sense: Moses is the law of the Old Testament, the pharaoh's daughter is the Church of Gentile background, because her father was wicked and unjust; the water of the Nile is Baptism. The Church of the pagans leaves her father's house, that is, leaves sin behind, to receive cleansing water, that is Baptism, and in the water she finds the law of Moses, that is, the Commandments. Only in the Church, in the royal palace of Wisdom, does the Law acquire complete maturity. "So," the ancient Christian writer concludes, "even if the pharaoh were our father, even if the prince of this world had begotten us in works of evil, by coming to the waters we receive the divine law. [. . .] We have a Moses great and strong. Let us not see anything mean in him . . . , for everything in him is greatness, sublimity and beauty. [. . .] And let us ask our Lord Jesus Christ to

---

pharaonis: «Accipe, ait, puerum istum et nutri mihi; ego dabo tibi mercedem tuam». Suscepit mulier et nutrivit puerum adultumque tradidit filiae pharaonis. [10]Quem illa adoptavit in locum filii vocavitque nomen eius Moysen dicens: «Quia de aqua tuli eum». [11]In diebus illis, postquam creverat, Moyses

b. Heb *Mosheh*   **c.** Heb *mashah*

Moses in Midian

Acts 7:23–29
Heb 11:24–27

[11]One day, when Moses had grown up, he went out to his people and looked on their burdens; and he saw an Egyptian beating a Hebrew, one of his people. [12]He looked this way and that, and seeing no one he killed the Egyptian and hid him in the sand. [13]When he went out the next day, behold, two Hebrews were struggling together; and he said to the man that did the wrong, "Why do you strike your fellow?" [14]He answered, "Who made Acts 7:27f, 35

---

show us and make known to us this greatness and sublimity of Moses" (*Homiliae in Exodum*, 2,4).

2:11–15. This is Act One in the calling of Moses. Because he carries out God's will he has to leave the pharaoh's palace, where he had a comfortable and easy life, and go out into the unknown. In this he is doing what the patriarchs did: first Abraham and then his descendants had to leave their homeland and their family (cf. Gen 12:1ff). The leader-to-be of Israel kills an Egyptian who is beating a Hebrew; and later he tries to make peace between two Hebrews. Freeing his people from oppression and slavery, and bringing about peace and unity among them are two of the goals of Moses' mission. Here again the sacred writer, over and above the details of events (about which he makes no moral judgments) is building up his theological profile of Moses and indicating the scope of his mission.

The same points are made when Moses is referred to in the New Testament. For example, according to St Stephen's reconstruction of these events in the Acts of the Apostles, Moses was forty years of age at this time and "mighty in his words and deeds"; his intervention on behalf of a member of his

people was, presumably, inspired by high ideals: "He supposed that his brethren understood that God was giving them deliverance by his hand" (Heb 7:25). The Letter to the Hebrews adds that "by faith Moses [. . .] refused to be called the son of Pharaoh's daughter, choosing rather to share ill-treatment with the people of God than to enjoy the fleeting pleasures of sin. He considered abuse suffered for the Christ greater wealth than the treasures of Egypt, for he looked to the reward" (Heb 11:24–26). However, his own people rejected him, and the pharaoh condemned him to death, furious at the killing of one of his overseers and fearful lest it signal an uprising of Hebrew slaves. Another forty years had to pass before Moses was actually given his mission (cf. Acts 7:30). On the basis of all these testimonies, St Cyril of Alexandria goes as far as to compare this episode of Moses' life with the Incarnation of Christ: "Do we not say that the Word of God the Father, who took on our condition, that is, became man, in some way went away from himself and became anonymous? [. . .] He left therefore to see his brothers, that is, the sons of Israel. For to them belong the promises and the patriarchs to whom the promises were made. And so he said, 'I have been sent only to the lost sheep of

---

egressus est ad fratres suos; viditque afflictionem eorum et virum Aegyptium percutientem quendam de Hebraeis fratribus suis. [12]Cumque circumspexisset huc atque illuc et nullum adesse vidisset, percussum Aegyptium abscondit sabulo. [13]Et egressus die altero conspexit duos Hebraeos rixantes dix-

Gen 24:11; 25:1–4;
29:2; 37:36
Num 10:29–32
Is 60:6
Mt 2:13
Acts 7:29
Heb 11:27

you a prince and a judge over us? Do you mean to kill me as you killed the Egyptian?" Then Moses was afraid, and thought, "Surely the thing is known." [15]When Pharaoh heard of it, he sought to kill Moses.

But Moses fled from Pharaoh, and stayed in the land of Midian; and he sat down by a well. [16]Now the priest of Midian had seven daughters; and they came and drew water, and filled the troughs to water their father's flock. [17]The shepherds came and drove them away; but Moses stood up and helped them, and

---

Israel.' But, on seeing that they were subject to a heavy and intolerable tyranny, he chose to set them free and to make them see that they could hope for deliverance from pain of any kind" (*Glaphyra in Exodum,* 1, 7).

2:15 It is not at all clear where Midian was. The Bible often refers to Midianites, who were descendants of Abraham (cf. Gen 25:1–4) and were therefore related to the Israelites; we meet them as traders who used to travel from one place to another (cf. Gen 37:36; Num 10:29–32); who engage the Hebrews in battle (Num 25:6–18; 31:1–9) and are roundly defeated by Gideon (Judg 6–8). At the end of time, as the third part of the book of Isaiah announces, they will come to do homage before the Lord (Is 60:6). But none of this information tells us where exactly this place Midian was. Modern scholars are inclined to situate it somewhere in the Sinai peninsula, a desert region where people sought refuge who wanted to evade the Egyptian authorities.

Moses' flight into the wilderness is also part of his God-given mission,

according to the interpretation in the Letter to the Hebrews: "By faith he left Egypt, not being afraid of the anger of the king; for he endured as seeing him who is invisible" (Heb 11:27).

2:16–22. The ownership of wells and the right to use them caused frequent disputes. Moses' clear sense of justice leads him to take the part of the weaker side— once again showing him to be a liberator who "helps" (="saves", according to the Hebrew etymology of the word: v. 17) and "delivers" (v. 19) the daughters of the priest of Midian. The sacred writer stresses the religious dimension of the incident: the daughters of Reuel are *seven* in number; Reuel is a priest; and it is Moses who delivers them. Moses will eventually marry and have a family; but there is very little mention of it later.

In the years when Moses lived among the Midianites, he must have learned a lot about their customs and how they managed to cope with the great difficulties desert life involved; but there is no hard evidence that this Midianite priest taught Moses anything about their religious cult.

---

itque ei, qui faciebat iniuriam: «Quare percutis proximum tuum?». [14]Qui respondit: «Quis te constituit principem et iudicem super nos? Num occidere me tu vis, sicut occidisti Aegyptium?». Timuit Moyses et ait: «Quomodo palam factum est verbum istud?». [15]Audivitque pharao sermonem hunc et quaerebat occidere Moysen. Qui fugiens de conspectu eius moratus est in terra Madian; venit ergo in terram Madian et sedit iuxta puteum. [16]Erant autem sacerdoti Madian septem filiae, quae venerunt ad hauriendam aquam; et impletis canalibus adaquare cupiebant greges patris sui. [17]Supervenere pastores et

watered their flock. [18]When they came to their father Reuel, he said, "How is it that you have come so soon today?" [19]They said, "An Egyptian delivered us out of the hand of the shepherds, and even drew water for us and watered the flock." [20]He said to his daughters, "And where is he? Why have you left the man? Call him, that he may eat bread." [21]And Moses was content to dwell with the man, and he gave Moses his daughter Zipporah. [22]She bore a son, and he called his name Gershom; for he said, "I have been a sojourner[d] in a foreign land."

Num 10:29
Judg 1:16;
4:11

Ex 3:1; 4:18;
18:1f

I Chron 23:15
Acts 7:6, 29

[23]In the course of those many days the king of Egypt died. And the people of Israel groaned under their bondage, and cried out for

---

2:18. The priest of Midian (v. 16) and Moses' father-in-law have different names in different places: here he is called Reuel, and in Numbers 10:29 Moses' father-in-law is called Hobab the son of Reuel. In Judges 1:16 and 4:11, his father-in-law is not considered a Midianite: he is referred to as Heber the Kenite. In the book of Exodus, from chapter 3 on, he is called Jethro (cf. 3:1; 4:18; 18:1f). It may be that the sacred writer is using various traditions which he does not feel he should tamper with.

2:22. He called his son Gershom to show his gratitude towards a foreign land which accepted him as a guest and a sojourner (*ger*). The popular etymology given this name here and in 18:3 links Moses to Abraham and Jacob, who also had to live as exiles in a strange land (Deut 26:5): "A wandering Aramaean was my father; and he went down into Egypt and sojourned there, few in number" (cf. Gen 12:10). The term "sojourner" or "resident" is used in the sense of someone who settles down in a country that is not his own, with the intention of staying there permanently or for a long time.

The sacred writer normally gives the meaning of certain proper names either because they are important figures in the history of salvation (Eve, Abraham, Jacob, Moses, etc.) or because the name is relevant to some point he wants to make (as is the case here). However, it is always a matter of popular, rather than scholarly, etymology. Here the text is emphasizing that Moses realized he was a stranger abroad and that he had a mission to lead his people into their own land; that people will itself spend time as a sojourner prior to settling down in its final home in Canaan.

2:23–25. The chapter ends by summing up the background to the time of Moses' youth, linking up with what it says at the start of the book (1:1–5). Both passages probably come from the Priestly tradition, which tends to focus on the logic of events over and above anecdotal details or concrete facts. Thus, these verses give the history of those years in telegraphic

---

eiecerunt eas; surrexitque Moyses et, defensis puellis, adaquavit oves earum. [18]Quae cum revertissent ad Raguel patrem suum, dixit ad eas: «Cur velocius venistis solito?». [19]Responderunt: «Vir Aegyptius liberavit nos de manu pastorum; insuper et hausit aquam nobis potumque dedit ovibus». [20]At ille: «Ubi est?», inquit. «Quare dimisistis hominem? Vocate eum, ut comedat panem». [21]Consensit ergo Moyses habitare cum eo accepitque Sephoram filiam eius uxorem. [22]Quae peperit ei filium, quem vocavit

d. Heb *ger*

47

Lk 1:72 help, and their cry under bondage came up to God. [24]And God heard their groaning, and God remembered his covenant with Abraham, with Isaac, and with Jacob. [25]And God saw the people

Ex 6:2–13;
6:28–7:7
Acts 7:30–35
Acts 13:17 of Israel, and God knew their condition.

God appears to Moses in the burning bush*

Ex 19
1 Kings 19:8–19
Mk 12:26 **3** [1]Now Moses was keeping the flock of his father-in-law, Jethro, the priest of Midian; and he led his flock to the west

---

form: the death of the pharaoh who killed the Hebrew male children might be expected to augur improved conditions but in fact bondage remains the order of the day; the people petition God, and he cannot ignore them.

God's action is summed up with four characteristic verbs: he *heard* their cries, he *remembered* the Covenant, he *saw* them and *knew* their condition (vv. 24–25: see the next note). It is an excellent outline of what divine providence does, and it serves as an overture to the chapters that follow, in which God's direct intervention is going to be recounted. "the Lord saw the affliction of his people reduced to slavery, heard their cry, knew their sufferings and decided to deliver them (cf. Ex 3:7f). In this act of salvation by the Lord, the prophet perceived his love and compassion (cf. Is 63:9). This is precisely the grounds upon which the people and each of its members based their certainty of the mercy of God, which can be invoked whenever tragedy strikes" (John Paul II, *Dives in misericordia*, 4).

2:25. In the original Hebrew this verse is unfinished: "And God saw the people of Israel, and God knew. . ." The Greek and

New Vulgate read the last verb as being passive: "And God saw the people of Israel and he made himself known to them". These are matters of different nuances; really the original could be translated literally, because the action of "knowing" implies that God is listening and looking after the people known (as can be seen from Psalm 31:7–8).

*3:1—4:17. This account of the calling of Moses is charged with theological content; it gives the features of the two protagonists (Moses and God) and the bases of the liberation of the people by means of wondrous divine intervention.

In the dialogue between God and Moses after the theophany of the burning bush (vv. 1–10), the Lord endows Moses with all the gifts he needs to carry out his mission: he promises him help and protection (vv. 11–12), he makes his name known to him (vv. 13–22), he gives him the power to work wonders (4:1–9), and he designates his brother Aaron as his aide, who will be his spokesman (4:10–17).

This section shows how God brings about salvation by relying on the docility of a mediator whom he calls and trains

Gersam dicens: «Advena sum in terra aliena». [23]Post multum vero temporis mortuus est rex Aegypti; et ingemiscentes filii Israel propter opera vociferati sunt, ascenditque clamor eorum ad Deum ab operibus. [24]Et audivit gemitum eorum ac recordatus est foederis, quod pepigit cum Abraham, Isaac et Iacob; [25]et respexit Dominus filios Israel et apparuit eis. [1]Moyses autem pascebat oves Iethro soceri sui sacerdotis Madian; cumque minasset gregem ultra desertum, venit ad montem Dei Horeb. [2]Apparuitque ei angelus Domini in flamma ignis de medio rubi; et videbat quod rubus arderet et non

side of the wilderness, and came to Horeb, the mountain of God. ²And the angel of the Lord appeared to him in a flame of fire out of the midst of a bush; and he looked, and lo, the bush was burning, yet it was not consumed. ³And Moses said, "I will turn aside and see this great sight, why the bush is not burnt." ⁴When the Lord saw that he turned aside to see, God called to him out of

Gen 16:7; 2:11, 14; 31:11, 13
Ex 24:7
Lev 9:23–24
Ezra 1:17
Deut 33:16
Lk 20:37
Acts 7:30
Acts 7:31

---

for the purpose. But the initiative always stays with God. Thus, God himself designs the smallest details of the most important undertaking the Israelites will embark on—their establishment as a people and their passing from bondage to freedom and the possession of the promised land.

3:1–3. The mountain of God, Horeb, called in other traditions Sinai, probably lies in the south-east part of the Sinai peninsula. Even today shepherds in that region will leave the valleys scorched by the sun in search of better pasture in the mountains. Although we do not yet know exactly where Mount Horeb is, it still had primordial importance in salvation history. On this same mountain the Law will later be promulgated (chap. 19), in the context of another dramatic theophany. Elijah will come back here to meet God (1 Kings 19:8–19). It is the mountain of God *par excellence*.

The "angel of the Lord" is probably an expression meaning "God". In the most ancient accounts (cf., e.g., Gen 16:7; 22:11, 14; 31:11, 13), immediately after the angel comes on the scene it is God himself who speaks: since God is invisible he is discovered to be present and to be acting in "the angel of the Lord", who usually does not appear in human form. Later, in the period of the monarchy, the existence of heavenly

messengers distinct from God will begin to be recognized (cf. 2 Sam 19:28; 24:16; 1 Kings 19:5, 7; etc.).

Fire is often a feature of theophanies (cf., e.g., Ex 19:18; 24:17; Lev 9:23–24; Ezek 1:17), perhaps because it is the best symbol to convey the presence of things spiritual and the divine transcendence. The bush mentioned here would be one of the many thorny shrubs that grow in desert uplands in that region. Some Christian writers have seen in the burning bush an image of the Church which endures despite the persecutions and trials it undergoes. It is also seen as a figure of the Blessed Virgin, in whom the divinity always burned (cf. St Bede, *Commentaria in Pentateuchum*, 2,3).

All the details given in the passage help to bring out the simplicity and at the same time the drama of God's action; the scene is quite ordinary (grazing, a mountain, a bush . . .), but extraordinary things happen (the angel of the Lord, a flame which does not burn, a voice).

3:4–10. The calling of Moses is described in this powerful dialogue in four stages: God calls him by his name (v. 4); he introduces himself as the God of Moses' ancestors (v. 9); he makes his plan of deliverance known in a most moving way (vv. 7–9); and, finally, he imperiously gives Moses his mission (v. 10).

---

combureretur. ³Dixit ergo Moyses: «Vadam et videbo visionem hanc magnam, quare non comburatur rubus». ⁴Cernens autem Dominus quod pergeret ad videndum, vocavit eum Deus de medio rubi et ait: «Moyses, Moyses». Qui respondit: «Adsum». ⁵At ille: «Ne appropies, inquit, huc; solve calceamen-

Gen 28:16–17
Josh 5:5
Acts 7:33
Ex 19:12; 33:20
Mt 22:32
Mk 12:26
Lk 20:37
Acts 3:13; 7:32
Heb 11:16

the bush, "Moses, Moses!" And he said, "Here am I." ⁵Then he said, "Do not come near; put off your shoes from your feet, for the place on which you are standing is holy ground." ⁶And he said, "I am the God of your father, the God of Abraham, the God of Isaac, and the God of Jacob." And Moses hid his face, for he was afraid to look at God.

Acts 7:34
Lev 20:24
Num 13:27
Deut 7:1; 26:9, 15
Jer 11:5; 32:22
Ezra 20:15
Gen 15:19–21
Ex 3:17; 13:5;
22:23, 28; 32:2;
34:11

⁷Then the Lord said, "I have seen the affliction of my people who are in Egypt, and have heard their cry because of their taskmasters; I know their sufferings, ⁸and I have come down to deliver them out of the hand of the Egyptians, and to bring them up out of that land to a good and broad land, a land flowing with milk and honey, to the place of the Canaanites, the Hittites, the

---

The repetition of his name ("Moses, Moses!") stresses how important this event is (cf. Gen 22:11; Lk 22:31). Taking one's shoes off is a way of showing veneration in a holy place. In some Byzantine communities there was a custom for a long time of celebrating the liturgy barefoot or wearing different footwear from normal. Christian writers have seen this gesture as being an act of humility and detachment in the face of the presence of God: "no one can gain access to God or see him unless first he has shed every earthly attachment" (*Glossa ordinaria in Exodum*, 3,4).

The sacred writer makes it clear that the God of Sinai is the same as the God of Moses' ancestors; Moses, then, is not a founder of a new religion; he carries on the religious tradition of the patriarchs, confirming the election of Israel as people of God. Four very expressive verbs are used to describe this election, this choice of Israel by God: I have seen . . . , I have heard . . . , I know . . . , I have come down to deliver (v. 8). This sequence of action includes no human action: the people are oppressed, they

cry, theirs is a sorry plight. But God has a clear aim in sight—"to deliver them and to bring them up [. . .] to a good and broad land" (v. 8). These two terms will become keynotes of God's saving action. To bring up to the promised land will come to mean, not only a geographical ascent but also a journey towards plenitude. St Luke's Gospel will take up the same idea. God's imperative command is clear in the original text (v. 10): ". . . bring forth my people, the sons of Israel, out of Egypt". This is another way of referring to the salvific event which gives its name to this book; according to Greek and Latin traditions "exodus" means "going out".

3:8. This description of the promised land is meant to show that it is extensive and fertile. Its fertility can be seen from its basic products—milk and honey (Lev 20:24; Num 13:27; Deut 26:9, 15; Jer 11:5; 32:22; Ezek 20:15)—the ideal desert food; a land which produces them in abundance is a veritable paradise.

The number of nations inhabiting the

---

tum de pedibus tuis; locus enim, in quo stas, terra sancta est». ⁶Et ait: «Ego sum Deus patris tui, Deus Abraham, Deus Isaac et Deus Iacob». Abscondit Moyses faciem suam; non enim audebat aspicere contra Deum. ⁷Cui ait Dominus: «Vidi afflictionem populi mei in Aegypto et clamorem eius audivi propter duritiam exactorum eorum. ⁸Et sciens dolorem eius descendi, ut liberem eum de manibus

Amorites, the Perizzites, the Hivites, and the Jebusites. [9]And now, behold, the cry of the people of Israel has come to me, and I have seen the oppression with which the Egyptians oppress them. [10]Come, I will send you to Pharaoh that you may bring forth my   Acts 7:34 people, the sons of Israel, out of Egypt."

The divine name is revealed

[11]But Moses said to God, "Who am I that I should go to Pharaoh, and bring the sons of Israel out of Egypt?" [12]He said, "But I will   Gen 28:15 be with you; and this shall be the sign for you, that I have sent   1 Sam 14:10 you: when you have brought forth the people out of Egypt, you   Jer 1:6 shall serve God upon this mountain."   Acts 7:7

Gen 28:15
Josh 1:5
1 Sam 14:10
Jer 1:6
Lk 2:27
Acts 7:7

---

promised land and disputing over it gives an indication as to its extent and desirability. The Pentateuch often lists the pre-Israelite peoples (with small variations from one list to the other): cf. Gen 15:19–20; Ex 3:17; 13:5; 23:23, 28; 32:2; 34:11. Mentions like this probably act as a reminder of the difficulties the Israelites had in settling the land, and the countless ways in which God intervened on their behalf.

3:11–12. In reply to Moses' first objection about his sheer inability to do what God is asking of him, God assures him that he will be at his side and will protect him—as he will help all who have a difficult mission of salvation (cf. Gen 28:15; Josh 1:5; Jer 1:8). The Blessed Virgin will hear the same words at the Annunciation: "The Lord is with you" (Lk 1:27).

The sign which God gives Moses is linked to his faith, because it involves both a promise and a command: when they come out of Egypt, Moses and the people will worship God on this very mountain. When this actually happens, Moses will acknowledge the supernatural nature of his mission but, meanwhile, he has to obey faithfully the charge given him by God.

Moses' conversation with the Lord is a beautiful prayer and one worth imitating. By following his example, a Christian can dialogue personally and intimately with the Lord: "We ought to be seriously committed to dealing with God. We cannot take refuge in the anonymous crowd. If interior life doesn't involve personal encounter with God, it doesn't exist—it's as simple as that. There are few things more at odds with Christianity than superficiality. To settle down to routine in our Christian life is to dismiss the possibility of becoming a contemplative soul. God seeks us out, one by one. And we ought to answer him, one by one: 'Here I am, Lord, because you have called me' (1 Kings 3:5)" (St Josemaría Escrivá, *Christ Is Passing By*, 174; cf. *Catechism of the Catholic Church*, 2574–5).

Aegyptiorum et educam de terra illa in terram bonam et spatiosam, in terram, quae fluit lacte et melle, ad loca Chananaei et Hetthaei et Amorraei et Pherezaei et Hevaei et Iebusaei. [9]Clamor ergo filiorum Israel venit ad me, vidique afflictionem eorum, qua ab Aegyptiis opprimuntur; [10]sed veni, mittam te ad pharaonem, ut educas populum meum, filios Israel, de Aegypto». [11]Dixitque Moyses ad Deum: «Quis sum ego, ut vadam ad pharaonem et educam filios Israel de Aegypto?». [12]Qui dixit ei: «Ego ero tecum; et hoc habebis signum quod miserim te: cum eduxeris populum de Aegypto, servietis Deo super

Is 42:8
Jn 8:24;
17:6, 26
Heb 11:6
Rev 1:4
Acts 5:30
Mt 22:32
Mk 12:26
Lk 20:37
Acts 3:13;
7:32; 22:14

[13]Then Moses said to God, "If I come to the people of Israel and say to them, 'The God of your fathers has sent me to you,' and they ask me, 'What is his name?' what shall I say to them?" [14]God said to Moses, "I AM WHO I AM."[e]* And he said, "Say this to the people of Israel, 'I AM has sent me to you.'" [15]God also said to Moses, "Say this to the people of Israel, 'The Lord, the God of your fathers, the God of Abraham, the God of Isaac, and the God of Jacob, has sent me to you': this is my name for ever, and thus I am to be remembered throughout all generations.

3:13–15. Moses now raises another difficulty: he does not know the name of the God who is commissioning him. This gives rise to the revelation of the name "Yahweh" and the explanation of what it means—"I am who I am".

According to the tradition recorded in Genesis 4:26, a grandson of Adam, Enosh, was the first to call upon the name of the Lord (Yahweh). Thus, the biblical text is stating that a part of mankind knew the true God, whose name was revealed to Moses in this solemn way (Ex 35:15 and 6:2). The patriarchs invoked God under other names, to do with the divine attributes, such as the Almighty ("El-Shaddai": Gen 17:1; Ex 6:2-3). Other proper names of God which appear in very ancient documents lead one to think that the name Yahweh had been known from a long time back. The revelation of the divine name is important in salvation history because by that name God will be invoked over the course of the centuries.

All kinds of suggestions have been put forward as to the meaning of Yahweh; not all are mutually exclusive.

Here are some of the main ones: (a) God is giving an evasive answer here because he does not want those in ancient times, contaminated as they were by magical rites, to think that because they knew the name they would have power over the god. According to this theory, "I am who I am" would be equivalent to "I am he whom you cannot know", "I am the unnameable". This solution stresses the transcendence of God. (b) What God is revealing is his nature—that he is subsistent being; in which case "I am who I am" means I am he who exists *per sibi*, absolute be-ing. The divine name refers to what he is by essence; it refers to him whose essence it is to be. God is saying that he *is*, and he is giving the name by which he is to be called. This explanation is often to be found in Christian interpretation. (c) On the basis of the fact that Yahweh is a causative form of the ancient Hebrew verb *hwh* (to be), God is revealing himself as "he who causes to be", the creator, not so much in the fullest sense of the word (as creator of the universe) but above all the creator of the present situation—the one who gives

---

montem istum». [13]Ait Moyses ad Deum: «Ecce, ego vadam ad filios Israel et dicam eis: Deus patrum vestrorum misit me ad vos. Si dixerint mihi: 'Quod est nomen eius?', quid dicam eis?». [14]Dixit Deus ad Moysen: «Ego sum qui sum». Ait: «Sic dices filiis Israel: Qui sum misit me ad vos». [15]Dixitque iterum Deus ad Moysen: «Haec dices filiis Israel: Dominus, Deus patrum vestrorum, Deus Abraham, Deus Isaac et Deus Iacob, misit me ad vos; hoc nomen mihi est in aeternum, et hoc memoriale meum in generationem et generationem. [16]Vade et congrega seniores Israel et dices ad eos: Dominus, Deus

e. Or I AM WHAT I AM or I WILL BE WHAT I WILL BE

The mission of Moses

[16]Go and gather the elders of Israel together, and say to them, 'The LORD[f] the God of your fathers, the God of Abraham, of Isaac, and of Jacob, has appeared to me, saying, "I have observed you and what has been done to you in Egypt; [17]and I promise that I will bring you up out of the affliction of Egypt, to the land of the Canaanites, the Hittites, the Amorites, the Perizzites, the Hivites, and the Jebusites, a land flowing with milk and honey."' [18]And they will hearken to your voice; and you and the elders of Israel

Deut 7:1

---

the people its being and who always stays with it. Thus, calling upon Yahweh will always remind the good Israelite of his reason-for-being, as an individual and as a member of a chosen people.

None of these explanations is entirely satisfactory. "This divine name is mysterious just as God is mystery. It is at once a name revealed and something like the refusal of a name, and hence it better expresses God as what he is—infinitely above everything that we can understand or say: he is the 'hidden God' (Is 45:15), his name is ineffable, and he is the God who makes himself close to men (cf. Judg 13:18)" (*Catechism of the Catholic Church*, 206).

At a later time, around the 4th century BC, out of reverence for the name of Yahweh the use of the word was avoided; when it occurred in the sacred text it was read as "Adonai", my Lord. In the Greek version it is translated as "Kyrios" and in the Latin as "Dominus". "It is under this title that the divinity of Jesus will be acclaimed: 'Jesus is Lord'" (ibid., 209). The RSV always renders "Yahweh" as "the Lord". The medieval form *Jehovah* was the result of a misreading of the

Hebrew text into which vowels were inserted by the Massoretes; it is simply a mistake and there is no justification for the use of "Jehovah" nowadays (cf. ibid., 446).

3:16–22. The Lord comes back again to the subject of Moses' mission; despite all the obstacles, it will be a success. "The elders of Israel" (v. 16), that is, the chiefs of clans, representing the whole community, will be happy to hear what Moses has to say. The words "I have observed you" (v. 16: literally, "I have carried out an inspection among you") are significant because they indicate the key thing—God's is a friendly presence; but it is also a demanding presence which expects an account of the use we make of gifts received (cf. 32:34; Jer 9:24; Hos 4:14). The three days' journey (v. 18) would not take them to Sinai but it was enough to get them away from Egypt. Later, three days will become a number symbolizing divine action. See the note on 6:10–13.

The pharaoh, unlike the elders, will refuse to let the people go—making it clearer that the Israelites will attain their

patrum vestrorum, apparuit mihi, Deus Abraham, Deus Isaac et Deus Iacob, dicens: Visitans visitavi vos et vidi omnia, quae acciderunt vobis in Aegypto; [17]et dixi: Educam vos de afflictione Aegypti in terram Chananaei et Hetthaei et Amorraei et Pherezaei et Hevaei et Iebusaei, ad terram fluentem lacte et melle. [18] Et audient vocem tuam, ingredierisque tu et seniores Israel ad regem Aegypti, et dicetis ad

f. The word LORD, when spelled with capital letters, stands for the divine name, *YHWH*, which is here connected with the verb *hayah*, to be

shall go to the king of Egypt and say to him, 'The LORD, the God of the Hebrews, has met with us; and now, we pray you, let us go a three days' journey into the wilderness, that we may sacrifice to the LORD our God.' [19]I know that the king of Egypt will not let you go unless compelled by a mighty hand.[g] [20]So I will stretch out my hand and smite Egypt with all the wonders which I will do in it; after that he will let you go. [21]And I will give this people favor in the sight of the Egyptians; and when you go, you shall not go empty, [22]but each woman shall ask of her neighbour, and of her who sojourns in her house, jewelry of silver and of gold, and clothing, and you shall put them on your sons and on your daughters; thus you shall despoil the Egyptians."

Gen 15:14
Ex 11:2–3;
12:35–36
Wis 10:17

Moses is granted miraculous powers

Mt 13:57

Ex 7:9

4 [1]Then Moses answered, "But behold, they will not believe me or listen to my voice, for they will say, 'The LORD did not appear to you.'" [2]The LORD said to him, "What is that in your hand?" He said, "A rod." [3]And he said, "Cast it on the ground." So he cast it on the ground, and it became a serpent; and Moses fled from it. [4]But the LORD said to Moses, "Put out your hand, and take it by the tail"—so he put out his hand and caught it, and it became

---

freedom only if God comes to their rescue.

The "despoiling" of the Egyptians (v. 22) is by way of compensation for the years they have spent with nothing to show for it (cf. Gen 15:14; Wis 10:17) and also as a sort of booty of war (cf. Ex 11:2–3; 12:35–36): God comes out the victor in the struggle against the pharaoh, and he gives the sons of Israel a share in the booty. It may also be meant to signal festive joy: the Israelites are to dress up to celebrate the victory God has given them.

4:1–9. God replies to a new objection from Moses by working miracles; these are designed more to prove that God is intervening, not just to provide a spectacle: they are done that "they may believe that the Lord has appeared to you" (v. 5).

It is worth noting that the wonders worked here are tailor-made for the Egyptians, who were used to snake-charming or thought that only their own wise men knew how to cure leprosy. If Moses is more powerful than the wise men of Egypt, it is because he has been given divine power.

---

eum: Dominus, Deus Hebraeorum, occurrit nobis; et nunc eamus viam trium dierum in solitudinem, ut immolemus Domino Deo nostro. [19]Sed ego scio quod non dimittet vos rex Aegypti, ut eatis, nisi per manum validam. [20]Extendam enim manum meam et percutiam Aegyptum in cunctis mirabilibus meis, quae facturus sum in medio eius; post haec dimittet vos. [21]Daboque gratiam populo huic coram Aegyptiis, et, cum egrediemini, non exibitis vacui. [22]Sed postulabit mulier a vicina sua et ab hospita sua vasa argentea et aurea ac vestes; ponetisque eas super filios et filias vestras et spoliabitis Aegyptum». [1]Respondens Moyses ait: «Quid autem, si non credent mihi neque audient vocem meam,

g. Gk Vg: Heb *no, not by a mighty hand*

a rod in his hand—⁵"that they may believe that the LORD, the God of their fathers, the God of Abraham, the God of Isaac, and the God of Jacob, has appeared to you." ⁶Again, the LORD said to him, Lev 13:1 "Put your hand into your bosom." And he put his hand into his bosom; and when he took it out, behold, his hand was leprous, as white as snow. ⁷Then God said, "Put your hand back into your bosom." So he put his hand back into his bosom; and when he took it out, behold, it was restored like the rest of his flesh. ⁸"If they will not believe you," God said, "or heed the first sign, they may believe the latter sign. ⁹If they will not believe even these two signs or heed your voice, you shall take some water from the Nile and pour it upon the dry ground; and the water which you shall take from the Nile will become blood upon the dry ground."

Aaron, the mouthpiece of Moses

¹⁰But Moses said to the LORD, "Oh, my Lord, I am not eloquent, Jer 1:6 either heretofore or since thou hast spoken to thy servant; but I am slow of speech and of tongue." ¹¹Then the LORD said to him, "Who has made man's mouth? Who makes him dumb, or deaf, or seeing, or blind? Is it not I, the LORD? ¹²Now therefore go, and I Deut 18:18 will be with your mouth and teach you what you shall speak." Mt 10:19–20

4:10–17. Moses' last objection succeeds in irritating God. The sacred writer uses a nice anthropomorphism to show how patient God is and how determined he is to set the people free.

"He shall speak for you to the people; and he shall be a mouth for you, and you shall be to him as God" (v. 16). To speak in the name of God is the role of a prophet, quite independently of his qualities, whether he has or has not oratorical skills (cf. Jer 1:6). Moses is the prototype of the prophet (cf. Deut 18:9–22); all future prophets should look up to him and try to copy him (cf. Acts 7:22).

By associating Aaron with Moses as his spokesman, the sacred text is making the point that there should never be disputes between temple priests and prophets; the mission of teaching the people belongs also to those in charge of divine worship (cf. Lev 10:11; Deut 33:10).

---

sed dicent: 'Non apparuit tibi Dominus'?». ²Dixit ergo ad eum: «Quid est quod tenes in manu tua?». Respondit: «Virga». ³Dixitque Dominus: «Proice eam in terram!». Proiecit, et versa est in serpentem, ita ut fugeret Moyses. ⁴Dixitque Dominus: «Extende manum tuam et apprehende caudam eius!». Extendit et tenuit, versaque est in virgam. ⁵«Ut credant, inquit, quod apparuerit tibi Dominus, Deus patrum suorum, Deus Abraham, Deus Isaac et Deus Iacob». ⁶Dixitque Dominus rursum: «Mitte manum tuam in sinum tuum!». Quam cum misisset in sinum, protulit leprosam instar nivis. ⁷«Retrahe, ait, manum tuam in sinum tuum!». Retraxit et protulit iterum, et erat similis carni reliquae. ⁸«Si non crediderint, inquit, tibi, neque audierint sermonem signi prioris, credent verbo signi sequentis. ⁹Quod si nec duobus quidem his signis crediderint neque audierint vocem tuam, sume aquam fluminis et effunde eam super aridam, et, quidquid hauseris de fluvio, vertetur in sanguinem». ¹⁰Ait Moyses: «Obsecro, Domine, non sum eloquens ab heri et nudiustertius et ex quo locutus es ad servum tuum, nam impeditioris et tardioris linguae sum». ¹¹Dixit Dominus ad eum: «Quis fecit os hominis? Aut quis fabricatus est mutum vel surdum vel videntem vel caecum? Nonne ego? ¹²Perge igitur, et ego ero in

[Ex 7:12] ¹³But he said, "Oh, my Lord, send, I pray, some other person." ¹⁴Then the anger of the LORD was kindled against Moses and he said, "Is there not Aaron, your brother, the Levite? I know that he can speak well; and behold, he is coming out to meet you, and when he sees you he will be glad in his heart. ¹⁵And you shall speak to him and put the words in his mouth; and I will be with your mouth and with his mouth, and will teach you what you shall do. ¹⁶He shall speak for you to the people; and he shall be a mouth for you, and you shall be to him as God. ¹⁷And you shall take in your hand this rod, with which you shall do the signs."

[Heb 2:17]

Moses returns to Egypt

[Ex 2:18] ¹⁸Moses went back to Jethro his father-in-law and said to him, "Let me go back, I pray, to my kinsmen in Egypt and see whether they are still alive." And Jethro said to Moses, "Go in peace." ¹⁹And the LORD said to Moses in Midian, "Go back to Egypt; for all the men who were seeking your life are dead." ²⁰So Moses took his wife and his sons and set them on an ass, and went back to the land of Egypt; and in his hand Moses took the rod of God. ²¹And the LORD said to Moses, "When you go back to Egypt, see that you do before Pharaoh all the miracles which I have put

[Mt 2:20]

[Ex 7:3; 9:12; 10:1, 20, 27; 14:4, 8.17 Rom 9:18]

4:18-20. Moses' decision to return to Egypt immediately is recorded in two different ways—as something permitted by Jethro, the head of the clan (v. 18) and as something commanded by God (vv. 19-20). This may mean that there are two redactional sources, Elohistic and Yahwistic respectively, although it could also be that the sacred writer wants to put it on record that Moses is fulfilling a divine command without contravening family custom of the time, which required the permission of the chief of the tribe before one left like this. It is

worth noticing that Moses hid from Jethro his real motives for returning to Egypt; this is an indication that Moses did not learn the cult of Yahweh from the Midianites but that the initiative behind all these events is divine.

4:21-23. "I will harden his heart". This phrase comes up often (7:3; 9:12; 10:1, 20, 27; 9:12; 14:4, 8, 17) but it does not mean that the pharaoh is any less responsible for his actions (that, indeed, is specifically stated in the context: 8:11, 28; 9:34); rather, it emphasizes the man's

---

ore tuo; doceboque te quid loquaris». ¹³At ille: «Obsecro, inquit, Domine, mitte quem missurus es». ¹⁴Iratus Dominus in Moysen ait: «Aaron, frater tuus Levites, scio quod eloquens sit; ecce ipse egreditur in occursum tuum vidensque te laetabitur corde. ¹⁵Loquere ad eum et pone verba mea in ore eius; et ego ero in ore tuo et in ore illius et ostendam vobis quid agere debeatis. ¹⁶Ipse loquetur pro te ad populum et erit os tuum; tu autem eris ei ut Deus. ¹⁷Virgam quoque hanc sume in manu tua, in qua facturus es signa». ¹⁸Abiit Moyses et reversus est ad Iethro socerum suum dixitque ei: «Vadam, quaeso, et revertar ad fratres meos in Aegyptum, ut videam, si adhuc vivant». Cui ait Iethro: «Vade in pace». ¹⁹Dixit ergo Dominus ad Moysen in Madian: «Vade, revertere in Aegyptum; mortui sunt enim omnes, qui quaerebant animam tuam». ²⁰Tulit Moyses uxorem suam et filios suos et imposuit eos super asinum; reversusque est in Aegyptum portans virgam Dei in manu sua. ²¹Dixitque ei Dominus revertenti in

in your power; but I will harden his heart, so that he will not let the people go. ²²And you shall say to Pharaoh, 'Thus says the LORD, Israel is my first-born son, ²³and I say to you, "Let my son go that he may serve me"; if you refuse to let him go, behold, I will slay your first-born son.'"

Rom 9:4
Is 63:16; 64:8
Hos 11:1–4

Moses' son is circumcised

Gen 32:25–33

²⁴At a lodging place on the way the LORD met him and sought to kill him. ²⁵Then Zipporah took a flint and cut off her son's fore-skin, and touched Moses' feet with it, and said, "Surely you are a bridegroom of blood to me!" ²⁶So he let him alone. Then it was that she said, "You are a bridegroom of blood," because of the cir-cumcision.

Josh 5:2–3

---

obstinacy and blindness. It needs to be borne in mind that the Semitic mind attributes directly to God (the first cause) the actions of creatures (secondary causes). Moreover, by being contrasted against the intransigent Egyptian king, God's love stands out more; God uses the pharaoh's increasing hardness of heart to show by ever more amazing deeds his special love for the people of Israel.

"Israel is my first-born son" (v. 22). God's confrontation with the pharaoh will end up in the death of the Egyptian first-born. God has a greater love for Israel than the pharaoh has for his first-born. One of the most consoling things that God has revealed is his fatherhood (cf. Hos 11:1–4); this revelation is a sign of his special favour (cf. Is 63:16; 64:8) "In Israel, God is called 'Father' inasmuch as he is Creator of the world (cf. Deut 32:6; Mal 2:10). Even more, God is Father because of the covenant and the gift of the law to Israel 'his first-born son' (Ex 4:22). God is also called the Father of the

king of Israel. Most especially he is 'the Father of the poor', of the orphaned and the widowed, who are under his loving protection (cf. Sam 7:14; Ps 68:5)" (*Catechism of the Catholic Church*, 238). Divine fatherhood, which in the Old Testament simply meant that there was a particularly close relationship between God and his people, prepared the way for the consoling fact that Jesus revealed: "Jesus revealed that God is Father in an unheard-of sense: he is Father not only in being Creator; he is eternally Father by his relationship to his only Son who, reciprocally, is Son only in relation to his Father: 'No one knows the Son except the Father, and no one knows the Father except the Son and any one to whom the Son chooses to reveal him' (Mt 11:27)" (ibid., 240; cf. nos. 2778–2782).

4:24–26. This is a puzzling episode because it concerns superstitious healing practices which are unknown nowadays: Moses falls gravely ill (this is what it

Aegyptum: «Vide, ut omnia ostenta, quae posui in manu tua, facias coram pharaone; ego indurabo cor eius, et non dimittet populum. ²²Dicesque ad eum: Haec dicit Dominus: Filius meus primogenitus Israel. ²³Dico tibi: Dimitte filium meum, ut serviat mihi; si autem non vis dimittere eum, ecce ego inter-ficiam filium tuum primogenitum». ²⁴Cumque esset in itinere, in deversorio, occurrit ei Dominus et volebat occidere eum. ²⁵Tulit ilico Sephora acutissimam petram et circumcidit praeputium filii sui; tetigitque pedes eius et ait: «Sponsus sanguinum tu mihi es». ²⁶Et dimisit eum, postquam dixerat:

Moses meets Aaron

²⁷The LORD said to Aaron, "Go into the wilderness to meet Moses." So he went, and met him at the mountain of God and kissed him. ²⁸And Moses told Aaron all the words of the LORD with which he had sent him, and all the signs which he had charged him to do. ²⁹Then Moses and Aaron went and gathered together all the elders of the people of Israel. ³⁰And Aaron spoke all the words which the LORD had spoken to Moses, and did the signs in the sight of the people. ³¹And the people believed; and when they heard that the LORD had visited the people of Israel and that he had seen their affliction, they bowed their heads and worshipped.

Ex 14:31
Lk 1:68

Moses' first audience with the pharaoh

Ex 23:14–17

5 ¹Afterward Moses and Aaron went to Pharaoh and said, "Thus says the LORD, the God of Israel, 'Let my people go, that they

---

means when it says the Lord "met him and sought to kill him") and Zipporah interprets this as meaning that he has committed some fault. So she proceeds to circumcise the boy and also Moses himself (the mention of Moses' "feet" seems an obvious euphemism). So, this circumcision seems to be a religious rite, propiatory in character and somehow connected with marital relations, since his wife refers to him as "a bridegroom of blood". Many theories based on what circumcision meant to the Midianites have been put forward to explain this expression and the whole ritual; but so far none of them is very satisfactory. The Fathers tended to comment on the passage allegorically, saying that Moses blessed his wife and children by means of this rite, to give them a share in the fruits of his salvific mission. Anyway, it does seem as though the sacred writer included this episode in order to show

that Moses, the leader and lawgiver of the people, himself underwent circumcision before all the sons of Israel had to.

4:27–31. Moses meets no opposition from his brother Aaron, the elders or the people themselves. This docility is in sharp contrast to the pharaoh's reaction (v. 21). Whereas the Egyptians proved obstinate, "the people believed" (v. 21): God's plan for their deliverance can be put into action only if men are ready to believe in it; this first act of faith on the part of the people will suffer many ups and downs.

"The mountain of God" (v. 27) is Mount Horeb. The mention of the holy mountain in this context underlines the sacred character of Aaron's mission (cf. the note on 3:1–3). The Bible often reports important events as having happened on a mountain; this has led many writers to reflect on the spiritual meaning of mountain. Origen, for example, says:

«Sponsus sanguinum», ob circumcisionem. ²⁷Dixit autem Dominus ad Aaron: «Vade in occursum Moysi in desertum». Qui perrexit obviam ei in montem Dei et osculatus est eum. ²⁸Narravitque Moyses Aaron omnia verba Domini, quibus miserat eum, et signa, quae mandaverat. ²⁹Veneruntque simul et congregaverunt cunctos seniores filiorum Israel. ³⁰Locutusque est Aaron omnia verba, quae dixerat Dominus ad Moysen, et fecit signa coram populo. ³¹Et credidit populus, audieruntque quod visitasset Dominus filios Israel et quod respexisset afflictionem eorum; et proni adoraverunt. ¹Post haec ingressi

may hold a feast to me in the wilderness.'" ²But Pharaoh said,
"Who is the LORD, that I should heed his voice and let Israel go?
I do not know the LORD, and moreover I will not let Israel go."
³Then they said, "The God of the Hebrews has met with us; let us
go, we pray, a three days' journey into the wilderness, and sacrifice to the LORD our God, lest he fall upon us with pestilence or
with the sword." ⁴But the king of Egypt said to them, "Moses and
Aaron, why do you take the people away from their work? Get to
your burdens." ⁵And Pharaoh said, "Behold, the people of the land
are now many and you make them rest from their burdens!"

The Hebrews' work is made heavier
⁶The same day Pharaoh commanded the taskmasters of the people
and their foremen, ⁷"You shall no longer give the people straw to

"Peter, James and John also went up the
mountain of God to merit the vision of
Jesus when he was transfigured and to
see him talking to Moses and Elijah in
heaven. And you too: if you do not climb
the mountain of God, that is, if you do
not attain the heights of spiritual knowledge, the Lord will be unable to open
your mouth " (*Homiliae in Exodum*, 3,2).

5:1–5. This first confrontation with the
pharaoh lets us see the difference between
God's plans for salvation and the
pharaoh's elaborate projects, whose only
purpose is to immortalize his name. The
pharaoh does not yet go directly against
the Lord (whom he does not know: v. 2);
he does not give any anti-religious reasons for not acceding to Moses' request.
The objections he raises are social and
economic: there is work to be done and it
must not be delayed (v. 5). But his new
commands are very hard on the Hebrews:

their bondage will worsen and the chance
of deliverance will seem to diminish.

"To hold a feast" (v. 1)—a religious
pilgrimage ending in a popular celebration. The three great pilgrimages to
Jerusalem which Israelites were obliged
to attend in later times (cf. 23:14–17)
were called "feasts". The Israelites later
came to appreciate the importance of this
divine command, as also their duty to
take part in the prescribed "feasts".

"The people of the land" (v. 5): in
this context a reference to the fact that
the Israelites belonged to the lower
classes. Elsewhere in the Old Testament
it is used with other meanings such as
"autonomous grouping" or even freemen
with a say in the election of a king (cf. 2
Kings 11:14, 18, 20).

5:6–9. "Taskmasters and foremen" (v. 6):
the former must have been Egyptian officials overseeing the building work, while

sunt Moyses et Aaron et dixerunt pharaoni: «Haec dicit Dominus, Deus Israel: Dimitte populum meum,
ut sacrificet mihi in deserto». ²At ille respondit: «Quis est Dominus, ut audiam vocem eius et dimittam
Israel? Nescio Dominum et Israel non dimittam». ³Dixeruntque: «Deus Hebraeorum occurrit nobis;
eamus, quaeso, viam trium dierum in solitudinem et sacrificemus Domino Deo nostro, ne forte accidat
nobis pestis aut gladius». ⁴Ait ad eos rex Aegypti: «Quare, Moyses et Aaron, sollicitatis populum ab
operibus suis? Ite ad onera vestra». ⁵Dixitque pharao: «Multus nimis iam est populus terrae; videtis
quod turba succreverit; quanto magis si dederitis eis requiem ab operibus?». ⁶Praecepit ergo in die

59

make bricks, as heretofore; let them go and gather straw for themselves. ⁸But the number of bricks which they made heretofore you shall lay upon them, you shall by no means lessen it; for they are idle; therefore they cry, 'Let us go and offer sacrifice to our God.' ⁹Let heavier work be laid upon the men that they may labour at it and pay no regard to lying words."

¹⁰So the taskmasters and the foremen of the people went out and said to the people, "Thus says Pharaoh, 'I will not give you straw. ¹¹Go yourselves, get your straw wherever you can find it; but your work will not be lessened in the least.'" ¹²So the people were scattered abroad throughout all the land of Egypt, to gather stubble for straw. ¹³The taskmasters were urgent, saying, "Complete your work, your daily task, as when there was straw." ¹⁴And the foremen of the people of Israel, whom Pharaoh's taskmasters had set over them, were beaten, and were asked, "Why have you not done all your task of making bricks today, as hitherto?"

¹⁵Then the foremen of the people of Israel came and cried to Pharaoh, "Why do you deal thus with your servants? ¹⁶No straw is given to your servants, yet they say to us, 'Make bricks!' And behold, your servants are beaten; but the fault is in your own people." ¹⁷But he said, "You are idle, you are idle; therefore you

---

the latter would have been Israelites in charge of a group of workers of their own ethnic background.

"Bricks" (v. 7): the usual building material in a region where stone was scarce; the Egyptians used the clay deposited by the Nile in flood, mixed it with straw and then left the bricks to harden in the heat of the sun.

5:10–18. This is a detailed account of the growing pressure on the sons of Israel; in addition to the physical demands being

made on them, the pharaoh was accusing them of being lazy. Perhaps there is a lesson here that those whom God chooses undergo all kinds of trials and misunderstanding but they should put their trust in God alone.

As Origen observes, history bears out that often "everything (they think) goes well for those who yield to the demands of the 'prince of this world', while the servants of God lack even modest means of subsistence" (*Homiliae in Exodum*, 3,3).

---

illo exactoribus populi et praefectis eius dicens: ⁷«Nequaquam ultra dabitis paleas populo ad conficiendos lateres sicut prius, sed ipsi vadant et colligant stipulas. ⁸Et mensuram laterum, quam prius faciebant, imponetis super eos; nec minuetis quidquam. Vacant enim et idcirco vociferantur dicentes: 'Eamus et sacrificemus Deo nostro'. ⁹Opprimantur operibus et expleant ea, ut non acquiescant verbis mendacibus». ¹⁰Igitur egressi exactores populi et praefecti eius dixerunt ad populum: «Sic dicit pharao: 'Non do vobis paleas. ¹¹Ite et colligite, sicubi invenire poteritis, nec minuetur quidquam de opere vestro'». ¹²Dispersusque est populus per omnem terram Aegypti ad colligendas paleas. ¹³Exactores quoque instabant dicentes: «Complete opus vestrum cotidie, ut prius facere solebatis, quando dabantur vobis paleae». ¹⁴Flagellatique sunt praefecti filiorum Israel, quos constituerant super eos exactores pharaonis dicentes: «Quare non implestis mensuram laterum sicut prius, nec heri nec hodie?». ¹⁵Veneruntque praefecti filiorum Israel et vociferati sunt ad pharaonem dicentes: «Cur ita agis contra

say, 'Let us go and sacrifice to the LORD.' [18]Go now, and work; for no straw shall be given you, yet you shall deliver the same number of bricks."

Moses intercedes with the pharaoh

[19]The foremen of the people of Israel saw that they were in evil plight, when they said, "You shall by no means lessen your daily number of bricks." [20]They met Moses and Aaron, who were waiting for them, as they came forth from Pharaoh; [21]and they said to them, "The LORD look upon you and judge, because you have made us offensive in the sight of Pharaoh and his servants, and have put a sword in their hand to kill us."

[22]Then Moses turned again to the LORD and said, "O LORD, why hast thou done evil to this people? Why didst thou ever send me? [23]For since I came to Pharaoh to speak in thy name, he has done evil to this people, and thou hast not delivered thy people at all."

Ex 17:4;
32:11–13
Deut 9:26–29

6 [1]But the LORD said to Moses, "Now you shall see what I will do to Pharaoh; for with a strong hand he will send them out, yea, with a strong hand he will drive them out of his land."

Acts 13:17

5:19–23. Moses is the intermediary between God and the people. In this simple and tense exchange we see how the people feel, and the kind of obstacles Moses meets in performing his mission. By emphasizing the difficulties involved in leaving Egypt, the sacred writer is preparing the reader to appreciate how great God's intervention was. The people's obstinacy was one of the things that most tested Moses' faith.

Moses' prayer is sincere and simple; he is not being rebellious, but he is uneasy (cf. 17:4; 32:11–13; Deut 9:26–29), because he does not yet understand the ways of God. But it is a trusting prayer, because he knows that only God can provide a lasting solution, as indeed he will (cf. Ex 6:1). The way Moses relates to the Lord is a fine example of mediatory prayer.

6:2–9. The narrative picks up again on the revelation of the divine name and the calling of Moses, an episode which was dealt with amply in chapter 3 (cf. 3:1—4:17). The Priestly tradition, from which this account is probably taken, usually concentrates more on doctrinal aspects than on the details of incidents. Here it is easy to see where the accent is being put—on the name of Yahweh (v.

servos tuos? [16]Paleae non dantur nobis, et lateres similiter imperantur; en famuli tui flagellis caedimur, et populus tuus est in culpa». [17]Qui ait: «Vacatis otio et idcirco dicitis: 'Eamus et sacrificemus Domino'. [18]Ite ergo et operamini; paleae non dabuntur vobis, et reddetis consuetum numerum laterum». [19]Videbantque se praefecti filiorum Israel in malo, eo quod diceretur eis: «Non minuetur quidquam de lateribus per singulos dies»; [20]occurreruntque Moysi et Aaron, qui stabant ex adverso egredientibus a pharaone, [21]et dixerunt ad eos: «Videat Dominus et iudicet, quoniam foetere fecistis odorem nostrum coram pharaone et servis eius; et praebuistis ei gladium, ut occideret nos». [22]Reversusque est Moyses ad Dominum et ait: «Domine, cur afflixisti populum istum? Quare misisti me? [23]Ex eo enim quo ingressus sum ad pharaonem, ut loquerer in nomine tuo, afflixit populum tuum; et non liberasti eos». [1]Dixitque Dominus ad Moysen: «Nunc videbis quae facturus sim pharaoni; per

Ex 3:1–4, 23 **A new call to Moses**

Gen 17:1 ²And God said to Moses, "I am the LORD. ³I appeared to Abraham, to Isaac, and to Jacob, as God Almighty,[h] but by my name the LORD I did not make myself known to them. ⁴I also established my covenant with them, to give them the land of Canaan, the land in which they dwelt as sojourners. ⁵Moreover I have heard the groaning of the people of Israel whom the Egyptians hold in bondage and I have remembered my covenant.

Acts 13:17 ⁶Say therefore to the people of Israel, 'I am the LORD, and I will bring you out from under the burdens of the Egyptians, and I will deliver you from their bondage, and I will redeem you with an outstretched arm and with great acts of judgment, ⁷and I will take you for my people, and I will be your God; and you shall know that I am the LORD your God, who has brought you out from

Gen 15; 24:7 under the burdens of the Egyptians. ⁸And I will bring you into the

---

2); on the fact that he is the same as the God of the patriarchs (v. 3); on the Covenant established in ancient times (v. 4); on the theological meaning of the Exodus ("I will bring you out", "I will deliver you": v. 6); on the profound wording of the Covenant ("I will take you for my people, and I will be your God": v. 7); and on his giving the Land to the patriarchs under oath (v. 8).

The doctrinal centre in the Priestly tradition is the Covenant, which God initially made with Noah (Gen 9:8ff) after the flood, and which he later ratified with Abraham (Gen 17:1ff) and definitively inaugurated with the entire chosen people (Ex 19:24). Pacts ensure peace when they are made between equals, as perhaps was the case with pacts between nomadic tribes in the desert; or else they formalize

a relationship between unequals when they are made, at the end of a war, between winner and loser (there are Hittite documents of that sort). In both cases the contracting parties come out as beneficiaries. In the divine Covenant things are different: God (and only he) is the one who takes the initiative; the people (and only they) derive benefit; God always does whatever he commits himself to do in the Covenant, even when the people break its main commandment—to follow him. The Covenant is, therefore, that act which best reveals God's unconditional love, first to the chosen people, and later to all men who in Christ share in the New and eternal Covenant.

6:6. "I will redeem you with an outstretched arm": here, for the first time a

---

manum enim fortem dimittet eos et in manu robusta eiciet illos de terra sua». ²Locutusque est Dominus ad Moysen dicens: «Ego Dominus, ³qui apparui Abraham, Isaac et Iacob ut Deus omnipotens; et nomen meum Dominum non indicavi eis. ⁴Pepigique cum eis foedus, ut darem illis terram Chanaan, terram peregrinationis eorum, in qua fuerunt advenae. ⁵Ego audivi gemitum filiorum Israel, quia Aegyptii oppresserunt eos, et recordatus sum pacti mei. ⁶Ideo dic filiis Israel: Ego Dominus, qui educam vos de ergastulo Aegyptiorum; et eruam de servitute ac redimam in brachio excelso et iudiciis magnis. ⁷Et assumam vos mihi in populum et ero vester Deus; et scietis quod ego sum Dominus Deus vester, qui eduxerim vos de ergastulo Aegyptiorum ⁸et induxerim in terram, super quam levavi manum

h. Heb *El Shaddai*

land which I swore to give to Abraham, to Isaac, and to Jacob; I will give it to you for a possession. I am the LORD.'" [9]Moses spoke thus to the people of Israel; but they did not listen to Moses, because of their broken spirit and their cruel bondage.

[10]And the LORD said to Moses, [11]"Go in, tell Pharaoh king of Egypt to let the people of Israel go out of his land." [12]But Moses said to the LORD, "Behold, the people of Israel have not listened to me; how then shall Pharaoh listen to me, who am a man of uncircumcised lips?" [13]But the LORD spoke to Moses and Aaron, and gave them a charge to the people of Israel and to Pharaoh king of Egypt to bring the people of Israel out of the land of Egypt.

Ex 3:11; 4:10

The genealogy of Aaron and Moses

Num 26:57–61; 3:1–10

[14]These are the heads of their fathers' houses: the sons of Reuben, the first-born of Israel: Hanoch, Pallu, Hezron, and Carmi; these

Gen 46:9
Num 26:5–14

---

key word in salvation history is used— "redemption". A redeemer (in Hebrew, *go'el*) was the person or family who for reasons of blood-relationship had an obligation to re-assert the infringed rights of an offended family member, be it getting him out of bondage, recovering a field or some other piece of property unjustly taken from him, or ensuring that reprisals were taken against a murderer. By taking this role of redeemer, God is committing himself to wipe out any injustices against the people—in the first instance setting it free from the bondage of slavery, as a symbol of liberation from the deeper bondage of sin, devil and death (cf. the note on Lev 25:23–24).

The anthropomorphism of the "outstretched arm" occurs often in the Bible; it is used to show the power of God's action. It is a graphic image which anyone can understand; it is used nowadays, for example, in the phrase "the arm of the law".

6:10–13. This account about Moses' exchange with the Lord over his lack of eloquence covers the same ground as 3:11 and 4:10, but the style is more formal. According to this "Priestly tradition" account Moses has to win the total freedom of the people, not just get permission for a three-day pilgrimage (cf. 3:18; 5:1).

"Uncircumcised lips" (v. 12): using a religious metaphor to make it clear that his limited facility for speech got worse when it was things of God he had to deal with.

6:14–27. Genealogies (which usually come from the Priestly tradition) are not meant to be historically very accurate but are designed to show that there is continuity in the mission God entrusted to each of the tribes of Israel. The genealogy given here is important because it culminates in Aaron, the ancestor of the

---

meam, ut darem eam Abraham, Isaac et Iacob; daboque illam vobis possidendam, ego Dominus».
[9]Narravit ergo Moyses omnia filiis Israel; qui non acquieverunt ei propter angustiam spiritus et opus durissimum. [10]Locutusque est Dominus ad Moysen dicens: [11]«Ingredere et loquere ad pharaonem regem Aegypti, ut dimittat filios Israel de terra sua». [12]Respondit Moyses coram Domino: «Ecce, filii Israel non audiunt me, et quomodo audiet me pharao, praesertim cum incircumcisus sim labiis?».
[13]Locutusque est Dominus ad Moysen et Aaron et dedit mandatum ad filios Israel et ad pharaonem

are the families of Reuben. ¹⁵The sons of Simeon: Jemuel, Jamin, Ohad, Jachin, Zohar, and Shaul, the son of a Canaanite woman; these are the families of Simeon. ¹⁶These are the names of the sons of Levi according to their generations: Gershon, Kohath, and Merari, the years of the life of Levi being a hundred and thirty-seven years. ¹⁷The sons of Gershon: Libni and Shime-i, by their families. ¹⁸The sons of Kohath: Amram, Izhar, Hebron, and Uzziel, the years of the life of Kohath being a hundred and thirty-three years. ¹⁹The sons of Merari: Mahli and Mushi. These are the families of the Levites according to their generations. ²⁰Amram took to wife Jochebed his father's sister and she bore him Aaron and Moses, the years of the life of Amram being one hundred and thirty-seven years. ²¹The sons of Izhar: Korah, Nepheg, and Zichri. ²²And the sons of Uzziel: Misha-el, Elzaphan, and Sithri. ²³Aaron took to wife Elisheba, the daughter of Amminadab and the sister of Nahshon; and she bore him Nadab, Abihu, Eleazar, and Ithamar. ²⁴The sons of Korah: Assir, Elkanah, and Abiasaph; these are the families of the Korahites. ²⁵Eleazar, Aaron's son, took to wife one of the daughters of Puti-el; and she bore him Phinehas. These are the heads of the fathers' houses of the Levites by their families.

Gen 46:11
Num 3:17ff
1 Chron 6:1

Ex 2:1–2
Num 26:59

Lk 1:5

Num 25:6–13

---

priestly class; it is repeated word for word in Numbers 3:1–10 and 26:57–61.

6:28—7:7. In this new discourse of the Lord the first person singular is used in an emphatic way ("I make you as God", "all I command you", "I will harden Pharaoh's heart") to underline the religious character of the Exodus; it is not a human enterprise but rather the start of a key stage in salvation history, and the initiative always lies with God.

"Aaron your brother shall be your prophet" (v. 1): Moses as leader of the people enjoys an authority received from God, but Aaron has been given a charge to speak on Moses' behalf, which is the equivalent of speaking in God's name. A prophet is a man chosen by God to proclaim the will of God and his plans of salvation. Therefore, foretelling the future is not what typifies a prophet, except when that future plays a part in God's salvific plan.

---

regem Aegypti, ut educerent filios Israel de terra Aegypti. ¹⁴Isti sunt principes domorum per familias suas. Filii Ruben primogeniti Israelis: Henoch et Phallu, Hesron et Charmi; hae cognationes Ruben. ¹⁵Filii Simeon: Iamuel et Iamin et Ahod et Iachin et Sohar et Saul filius Chananitidis; hae progenies Simeon. ¹⁶Et haec nomina filiorum Levi per cognationes suas: Gerson et Caath et Merari; anni autem vitae Levi fuerunt centum triginta septem. ¹⁷Filii Gerson: Lobni et Semei per cognationes suas. ¹⁸Filii Caath: Amram et Isaar et Hebron et Oziel; anni quoque vitae Caath centum triginta tres. ¹⁹Filii Merari: Moholi et Musi; hae cognationes Levi per familias suas. ²⁰Accepit autem Amram uxorem Iochabed amitam suam, quae peperit ei Aaron et Moysen; fueruntque anni vitae Amram centum triginta septem. ²¹Filii quoque Isaar: Core et Napheg et Zechri. ²²Filii quoque Oziel: Misael et Elisaphan et Sethri. ²³Accepit autem Aaron uxorem Elisabeth filiam Aminadab sororem Naasson, quae peperit ei Nadab et Abiu et Eleazar et Ithamar. ²⁴Filii quoque Core: Asir et Elcana et Abiasaph; hae sunt cognationes Coritarum. ²⁵At vero Eleazar filius Aaron accepit uxorem de filiabus Phutiel, quae peperit ei Phinees;

²⁶These are the Aaron and Moses to whom the LORD said: "Bring out the people of Israel from the land of Egypt by their hosts." ²⁷It was they who spoke to Pharaoh king of Egypt about bringing out the people Israel from Egypt, this Moses and this Aaron.

The announcement of the plagues

Ex 6:2–13

²⁸On the day when the LORD spoke to Moses in the land of Egypt, ²⁹the LORD said to Moses, "I am the LORD; tell Pharaoh king of Egypt all that I say to you." ³⁰But Moses said to the LORD, "Behold, I am of uncircumcised lips; how then shall Pharaoh listen to me?"

7 ¹And the LORD said to Moses, "See, I make you as God to Pharaoh; and Aaron your brother shall be your prophet. ²You shall speak all that I command you; and Aaron your brother shall tell Pharaoh to let the people of Israel go out of his land. ³But I will harden Pharaoh's heart, and though I multiply my signs and wonders in the land of Egypt, ⁴Pharaoh will not listen to you; then I will lay my hand upon Egypt and bring forth my hosts, my people the sons of Israel, out of the land of Egypt by great acts of judgment. ⁵And the Egyptians shall know that I am the LORD, when I stretch forth my hand upon Egypt and bring out the people of Israel from among them." ⁶And Moses and Aaron did so; they did as the LORD commanded them. ⁷Now Moses was eighty years old, and Aaron eighty-three years old, when they spoke to Pharaoh.

Ex 4:16
Jn 10:34

Ex 4:21
Ps 135:9
Acts 7:36
Rom 9:18

7:7. The ages given for Moses and Aaron are more symbolic than real. The sacred writer probably uses the figure forty to stand for a generation, and sees Moses' life as covering three stages or generations—the first spent at the pharaoh's court (cf. Acts 7:23), the second in Midian, and the third and most important leading the people to the promised land; his death comes then when he reaches one hundred and twenty. So even, in his chronology Moses is depicted as someone whom God takes perfect care of.

hi sunt principes familiarum Leviticarum per cognationes suas. ²⁶Iste est Aaron et Moyses, quibus praecepit Dominus, ut educerent filios Israel de terra Aegypti per turmas suas. ²⁷Hi sunt qui loquuntur ad pharaonem regem Aegypti, ut educant filios Israel de Aegypto; iste est Moyses et Aaron ²⁸in die, qua locutus est Dominus ad Moysen in terra Aegypti. ²⁹Et locutus est Dominus ad Moysen dicens: «Ego Dominus loquere ad pharaonem regem Aegypti omnia, quae ego loquor tibi». ³⁰Et ait Moyses coram Domino: «En incircumcisus labiis sum. Quomodo audiet me pharao?». ¹Dixitque Dominus ad Moysen: «Ecce constitui te deum pharaonis, et Aaron frater tuus erit propheta tuus. ²Tu loqueris omnia, quae mando tibi; et ille loquetur ad pharaonem, ut dimittat filios Israel de terra sua. ³Sed ego indurabo cor eius et multiplicabo signa et ostenta mea in terra Aegypti. ⁴Et non audiet vos; immittamque manum meam super Aegyptum et educam exercitum et populum meum, filios Israel, de terra Aegypti per iudicia maxima. ⁵Et scient Aegyptii quia ego sum Dominus, qui extenderim manum meam super Aegyptum et eduxerim filios Israel de medio eorum». ⁶Fecit itaque Moyses et Aaron, sicut praeceperat Dominus; ita egerunt. ⁷Erat autem Moyses octoginta annorum et Aaron octoginta trium, quando locuti

Ex 4:1–5
Ps 78; 105
Wis 11:14–20;
16–18

3. THE PLAGUES*

Moses' miraculous rod

⁸And the LORD said to Moses and Aaron, ⁹"When Pharaoh says to you, 'Prove yourselves by working a miracle,' then you shall say to Aaron, 'Take your rod and cast it down before Pharaoh, that it may become a serpent.'" ¹⁰So Moses and Aaron went to Pharaoh and did as the LORD commanded; Aaron cast down his rod before Pharaoh and his servants, and it became a serpent. ¹¹Then Pharaoh

2 Tim 3:8

*7:8—11:10. The ten plagues are actions God takes to prepare the mind of the pharaoh and the heart of the people for the massive Exodus from Egypt.

The stylistic and doctrinal richness of this whole section indicates how deeply etched its content was on the social and religious memory of the people of Israel. The sacred writer has produced an account based on information in the old traditions, and he makes a point of spelling out the theological meaning of every event. Thus, he gives importance to order: there are ten plagues here, whereas Psalms 78:45–51 and 105:27–36 mention only seven. The magicians appear up to the third plague, when they are roundly defeated by Moses. The seventh plague, the storm, is something of a theophany (visible manifestation of God to man), given that it is explained in such detail and ends with the pharaoh admitting that he is at fault (9:27-28). In the three last plagues the pharaoh yields bit by bit until with the death of the first-born he gives in completely.

The plagues, as they come, do increasing damage: the first four are merely nuisances, though serious ones; the next four affect people and their property; the ninth plunges the Egyptians in a mysterious darkness which prevents all movement; the tenth inflicts terrible loss on families and forces the pharaoh to let the people of Israel go.

The narrative is written in an epic style which makes God's victory over the king even more pronounced: God begins by acting through Moses and Aaron who use the rod as a thaumaturgical tool, but he gradually uses them less and less until it is he alone who is involved in the final catastrophe affecting the first-born. Some of the plagues are rather like the natural phenomena which occur from time to time in Egypt; but their being reported as marvels serves to highlight profound basic teaching—that God, the Lord of nature and of history, is intervening in a supernatural way to save his people from bondage and lead them to a new state of freedom and well-being.

7:8–13. The miraculous rod (closely connected with the story told in 4:1–5) further emphasizes the importance of Aaron, who is the one who actually wields the thaumaturgical power.

sunt ad pharaonem. ⁸Dixitque Dominus ad Moysen et Aaron: ⁹«Cum dixerit vobis pharao: 'Ostendite signum', dices ad Aaron: Tolle virgam tuam et proice eam coram pharaone, ac vertetur in colubrum». ¹⁰Ingressi ita que Moyses et Aaron ad pharaonem fecerunt, sicut praeceperat Dominus; proiecitque Aaron virgam coram pharaone et servis eius, quae versa est in colubrum. ¹¹Vocavit autem pharao sapientes et maleficos, et fecerunt etiam ipsi magi Aegypti per incantationes suas similiter. ¹²Proiecteruntque singuli virgas suas, quae versae sunt in colubros; sed devoravit virga Aaron virgas eorum.

summoned the wise men and the sorcerers; and they also, the magicians of Egypt, did the same by their secret arts. [12]For every man cast down his rod, and they became serpents. But Aaron's rod swallowed up their rods. [13]Still Pharaoh's heart was hardened, and he would not listen to them; as the LORD had said.

The first plague: the water turns to blood

Wis 11:68

[14]*Then the LORD said to Moses, "Pharaoh's heart is hardened, he refuses to let the people go. [15]Go to Pharaoh in the morning, as he

---

The "wise men", "sorcerers" and "magicians" (v. 11) were the pharaoh's circle of advisers. Magical rites and snake-charming were held in high regard in the cultural and religious life of Egypt (cf. Gen 41:8).

God is shown to be more powerful than the pharaoh and his magicians not so much by his ability to work wonders as by his sovereign power: God is the Lord, the only Lord; all other powers are subject to him. The Fathers saw the rod as a figure of the cross, for, as St Paul says, Christ on the cross is the "power of God and the wisdom of God" (1 Cor 1:24: cf. Origen, *Homiliae in Exodum*, 4, 6).

Jewish tradition has conserved the names of two of the magicians of Egypt; St Paul, making this tradition his own, mentions them as being the prototype of obstinate people who deny even the most obvious truth: "As Jannes and Jambres opposed Moses, so these men also oppose the truth, men of corrupt mind and counterfeit faith" (2 Tim 3:8).

7:13. The pharaoh's obstinacy is a refrain which is repeated up to the last plague (cf. 7;14; 8:11, 15, 28; 9:7, 12, 35). Insistence on this piece of information

helps the reader to see time and time again that God alone can overcome the huge obstacles being raised against the deliverance of the sons of Israel, as can be seen in the key statement in the plague account, "By this you shall know that I am the Lord" (cf. 7:17; 8:6, 18; 9:14; 10:2).

7:14–24. The first scourge used against the pharaoh is the water turned to blood. Being an epic account, it is not surprising that it should reflect a phenomenon with which the Egyptians were familiar: the Nile in springtime takes on a reddish, bloody colour, due to the mud which it brings down from Abyssinia; the natives call it the Red Nile. Nor should we be surprised to find small inconsistencies in this account: sometimes it is Moses who carries the rod, sometimes Aaron; the Egyptian magicians also turn water into blood even though *all* the water of Egypt has already become blood. In gathering together these ancient traditions the sacred writer's aim is to recount the pharaoh's direct confrontation with God, showing it as taking place on the Nile, which Egyptian literature mythologized as the country's source of life and wealth. The book of Wisdom interprets this first

---

[13]Induratumque est cor pharaonis, et non audivit eos, sicut dixerat Dominus. [14]Dixit autem Dominus ad Moysen: «Ingravatum est cor pharaonis: non vult dimittere populum. [15]Vade ad eum mane. Ecce egredietur ad aquas; et stabis in occursum eius super ripam fluminis. Et virgam, quae conversa est in serpentem, tolles in manu tua [16]dicesque ad eum: Dominus, Deus Hebraeorum, misit me ad te dicens:

is going out to the water; wait for him by the river's brink, and take in your hand the rod which was turned into a serpent. [16]And you shall say to him, 'The LORD, the God of the Hebrews, sent me to you, saying, "Let my people go, that they may serve me in the wilderness; and behold, you have not yet obeyed." [17]Thus says the LORD, "By this you shall know that I am the LORD: behold, I will strike the water that is in the Nile with the rod that is in my hand, and it shall be turned to blood, [18]and the fish in the Nile shall die, and the Nile shall become foul, and the Egyptians will loathe to drink water from the Nile."'" [19]And the LORD said to Moses, "Say to Aaron, 'Take your rod and stretch out your hand over the waters of Egypt, over their rivers, their canals, and their ponds, and all their pools of water, that they may become blood; and there shall be blood throughout all the land of Egypt, both in vessels of wood and in vessels of stone.'"

[20]Moses and Aaron did as the LORD commanded; in the sight of Pharaoh and in the sight of his servants, he lifted up the rod and struck the water that was in the Nile, and all the water that was in the Nile turned to blood. [21]And the fish in the Nile died; and the Nile became foul, so that the Egyptians could not drink water from the Nile; and there was blood throughout all the land of Egypt. [22]But the magicians of Egypt did the same by their secret arts; so Pharaoh's heart remained hardened, and he would not listen to them; as the LORD had said. [23]Pharaoh turned and went into his house, and he did not lay even this to heart. [24]And

Margin references:
Rev 11:6; 16:3-4
Rev 11:6; 16:4
Ps 78:44; 105:29 Rev 8:8
2 Tim 3:8

---

plague as God's just response to the killing of Hebrew children by drowning in the Nile: "in rebuke for the decree to slay the infants" (Wis 11:7).

7:25—8:15. The second plague is described as an invasion by frogs and, probably, other types of amphibians. It is the immense quantity of these animals and the fact that they appear and disappear at Moses' say-so that shows the hand of God to be at work. The purpose of this

Dimitte populum meum, ut sacrificet mihi in deserto; et usque ad praesens audire noluisti. [17]Haec igitur dicit Dominus: In hoc scies quod sim Dominus: ecce percutiam virga, quae in manu mea est, aquam fluminis; et vertetur in sanguinem. [18]Pisces quoque, qui sunt in fluvio, morientur, et computrescent aquae, et taedebit Aegyptios bibere aquam fluminis». [19]Dixit quoque Dominus ad Moysen: «Dic ad Aaron: Tolle virgam tuam et extende manum tuam super aquas Aegypti, super fluvios eorum et rivos ac paludes et omnes lacus aquarum, ut vertantur in sanguinem; et sit cruor in omni terra Aegypti, tam in ligneis vasis quam in saxeis». [20]Feceruntque ita Moyses et Aaron, sicut praeceperat Dominus. Et elevans virgam percussit aquam fluminis coram pharaone et servis eius; quae versa est in sanguinem. [21]Et pisces, qui erant in flumine, mortui sunt, computruitque fluvius, et non poterant Aegyptii bibere aquam fluminis; et fuit sanguis in tota terra Aegypti. [22]Feceruntque similiter malefici Aegyptiorum incantationibus suis; et induratum est cor pharaonis, nec audivit eos, sicut dixerat Dominus. [23]Avertitque se et ingressus est domum suam nec ad hoc apposuit cor suum. [24]Foderunt autem omnes Aegyptii per circuitum fluminis aquam, ut biberent; non enim poterant bibere de aqua fluminis. [25]Impletique sunt

all the Egyptians dug round about the Nile for water to drink, for they could not drink the water of the Nile.

The second plague: the frogs

[25]Seven days passed after the LORD had struck the Nile.

8 [1i]Then the LORD said to Moses, "Go in to Pharaoh and say to him, 'Thus says the LORD "Let my people go, that they may serve me. [2]But if you refuse to let them go, behold, I will plague all your country with frogs; [3]the Nile shall swarm with frogs which shall come up into your house, and into your bedchamber and on your bed, and into the houses of your servants and of your people,[j] and into your ovens and your kneading bowls; [4]the frogs shall come up on you and on your people and on all your servants."'" [5k]And the LORD said to Moses, "Say to Aaron, 'Stretch out your hand with your rod over the rivers, over the canals, and over the pools, and cause frogs to come upon the land of Egypt!'" [6]So Aaron stretched out his hand over the waters of Egypt; and the frogs came up and covered the land of Egypt. [7]But the magicians did the same by their secret arts, and brought frogs upon the land of Egypt.

[8]Then Pharaoh called Moses and Aaron, and said, "Entreat the LORD to take away the frogs from me and from my people; and I will let the people go to sacrifice to the LORD." [9]Moses said to Pharaoh, "Be pleased to command me when I am to entreat, for you and for your servants and for your people, that the frogs be

Ps 78:45; 105:30

Rev 16:13

Acts 8:24

---

wondrous phenomenon is to show that "there is no one like the Lord our God" (v. 10). Moreover, Moses' authority comes out enhanced, because he is seen to be the one who is able to intercede successfully with God (v. 9). It is worth noting also that the pharaoh for the first time entertains the idea of letting the people go, even though for selfish reasons, but he soon changes his mind (v. 8).

septem dies, postquam percussit Dominus fluvium. [26]Dixit quoque Dominus ad Moysen: «Ingredere ad pharaonem et dices ad eum: Haec dicit Dominus: Dimitte populum meum, ut sacrificet mihi. [27]Sin autem nolueris dimittere, ecce ego percutiam omnes terminos tuos ranis. [28]Et ebulliet fluvius ranas, quae ascendent et ingredientur domum tuam et cubiculum lectuli tui et super stratum tuum et in domos servorum tuorum et in populum tuum et in furnos tuos et in pistrina tua; [29]et ad te et ad populum tuum et ad omnes servos tuos intrabunt ranae». [1]Dixitque Dominus ad Moysen: «Dic ad Aaron: Extende manum tuam cum baculo tuo super fluvios, super rivos ac paludes et educ ranas super terram Aegypti». [2]Et extendit Aaron manum super aquas Aegypti, et ascenderunt ranae operueruntque terram Aegypti. [3]Fecerunt autem et malefici per incantationes suas similiter eduxeruntque ranas super terram Aegypti. [4]Vocavit autem pharao Moysen et Aaron et dixit: «Orate Dominum, ut auferat ranas a me et a populo meo, et dimittam populum, ut sacrificet Domino». [5]Dixitque Moyses ad pharaonem: «Constitue mihi, quando deprecer pro te et pro servis et pro populo tuo, ut abigantur ranae a te et a domo tua et tantum

---

i. Ch 7.26 in Heb [and in New Vulgate]   j. Gk: Heb *upon your people*   k. Ch 8.1 in Heb [and in New Vulgate]

destroyed from you and your houses and be left only in the Nile."
[10]And he said, "Tomorrow." Moses said, "Be it as you say, that
you may know that there is no one like the LORD our God. [11]The
frogs shall depart from you and your houses and your servants
and your people; they shall be left only in the Nile." [12]So Moses
and Aaron went out from Pharaoh; and Moses cried to the LORD
concerning the frogs, as he had agreed with Pharaoh.[1] [13]And the
LORD did according to the word of Moses; the frogs died out of
the houses and courtyards and out of the fields. [14]And they gathered them together in heaps, and the land stank. [15]But when
Pharaoh saw that there was a respite, he hardened his heart, and
would not listen to them; as the LORD had said.

The third plague: the gnats

[16]Then the LORD said to Moses, "Say to Aaron, 'Stretch out your
rod and strike the dust of the earth, that it may become gnats
Ps 105:31 throughout all the land of Egypt.'" [17]And they did so; Aaron
stretched out his hand with his rod, and struck the dust of the
earth, and there came gnats on man and beast; all the dust of the
Wis 17:1 earth became gnats throughout all the land of Egypt. [18]The magicians tried by their secret arts to bring forth gnats, but they could
Lk 11:20 not. So there were gnats on man and beast. [19]And the magicians
said to Pharaoh, "This is the finger of God." But Pharaoh's heart

---

8:16–19. This account is usually attributed
to the Priestly tradition on the grounds that
the protagonist is Aaron. The climax of
this prodigy is the fact that the Egyptian
magicians cannot match it and they have
to admit that "the finger of God" (far more
powerful than their magical arts) is present. Thus, the account of the plagues is
showing that people are gradually coming
to see the almighty power of God. With
the plague of gnats the magicians' defeat
is irreversible; no longer will they venture
to use their skills against the plagues. But
the pharaoh still refuses to yield.

---

in flumine remaneant». [6]Qui respondit: «Cras». At ille: «Iuxta verbum, inquit, tuum faciam, ut scias
quoniam non est sicut Dominus Deus noster. [7]Et recedent ranae a te et a domo tua et a servis tuis et a
populo tuo; tantum in flumine remanebunt». [8]Egressique sunt Moyses et Aaron a pharaone; et clamavit
Moyses ad Dominum pro sponsione ranarum, quam condixerat pharaoni. [9]Fecitque Dominus iuxta
verbum Moysi, et mortuae sunt ranae de domibus et de villis et de agris; [10]Congregaveruntque eas in
immensos aggeres, et computruit terra. [11]Videns autem pharao quod data esset requies, ingravavit cor
suum et non audivit eos, sicut dixerat Dominus. [12]Dixitque Dominus ad Moysen: «Loquere ad Aaron:
Extende virgam tuam et percute pulverem terrae, et sint scinifes in universa terra Aegypti».
[13]Feceruntque ita; et extendit Aaron manum virgam tenens percussitque pulverem terrae. Et facti sunt
scinifes in hominibus et in iumentis; omnis pulvis terrae versus est in scinifes per totam terram
Aegypti. [14]Feceruntque similiter malefici incantationibus suis, ut educerent scinifes; et non potuerunt.
Erantque scinifes tam in hominibus quam in iumentis; [15]et dixerunt malefici ad pharaonem: «Digitus
Dei est hic». Induratumque est cor pharaonis et non audivit eos, sicut praeceperat Dominus. [16]Dixit

l. Or *which he had brought upon Pharaoh*

was hardened, and he would not listen to them; as the LORD had said.

The fourth plague: the flies

[20]Then the LORD said to Moses, "Rise up early in the morning and wait for Pharaoh, as he goes out to the water, and say to him, 'Thus says the LORD, "Let my people go, that they may serve me. [21]Else, if you will not let my people go, behold, I will send swarms of flies on you and your servants and your people, and into your houses; and the houses of the Egyptians shall be filled with swarms of flies, and also the ground on which they stand. [22]But on that day I will set apart the land of Goshen, where my people dwell, so that no swarms of flies shall be there; that you may know that I am the LORD in the midst of the earth. [23]Thus I will put a division[m] between my people and your people. By tomorrow shall this sign be."'" [24]And the LORD did so; there came great swarms of flies into the house of Pharaoh and into his servants' houses, and in all the land of Egypt the land was ruined by reason of the flies.

[25]Then Pharaoh called Moses and Aaron, and said, "Go, sacrifice to your God within the land." [26]But Moses said, "It would not be right to do so; for we shall sacrifice to the LORD our God offer-

Ps 78:45
Ex 7:15
Wis 16:9

Gen 47:1f

8:20–32. The description of the plague of the gadflies may come from the Yahwistic tradition (witness its colour and richness of detail); in fact, some authors think that this account may be a variant of the previous one (the gnats).

Moses has to meet the pharaoh again when the latter goes to the Nile in the early morning (cf. 7:15), either to bathe or to worship the God of the River. As in the previous plague, the insects obey Moses, this time to infest the houses of

the Egyptians. God's special protection of the people of Israel is underlined.

The conversation between Moses and the pharaoh is interesting. Moses cannot modify the plans of God; therefore he cannot agree to the restriction that the people's sacrifice take place within the boundaries of Egypt. The excuse Moses offers shows his astuteness: the Egyptians would be affronted if they saw the Israelites sacrificing lambs (cf. v. 26). Throughout this

quoque Dominus ad Moysen: «Consurge diluculo et sta coram pharaone. Egredietur enim ad aquas, et dices ad eum: Haec dicit Dominus: Dimitte populum meum, ut sacrificet mihi. [17]Quod si non dimiseris eum, ecce ego immittam in te et in servos tuos et in populum tuum et in domos tuas omne genus muscarum; et implebuntur domus Aegyptiorum muscis et etiam humus, in qua fuerint. [18]Et segregabo in die illa terram Gessen, in qua populus meus est, ut non sint ibi muscae, et scias quoniam ego Dominus in medio terrae; [19]ponamque divisionem inter populum meum et populum tuum; cras erit signum istud». [20]Fecitque Dominus ita; et venit musca gravissima in domos pharaonis et servorum eius et in omnem terram Aegypti, corruptaque est terra ab huiuscemodi muscis. [21]Vocavitque pharao Moysen et Aaron et ait eis: «Ite, sacrificate Deo vestro in terra». [22]Et ait Moyses: «Non potest ita fieri: abom-

m. Gk Vg: Heb *set redemption*

ings abominable to the Egyptians. If we sacrifice offerings abominable to the Egyptians before their eyes, will they not stone us? ²⁷We must go three days' journey into the wilderness and sacrifice to the LORD our God as he will command us." ²⁸So Pharaoh said, "I will let you go, to sacrifice to the LORD your God in the wilderness; only you shall not go very far away. Make entreaty for me." ²⁹Then Moses said, "Behold, I am going out from you and I will pray to the LORD that the swarms of flies may depart from Pharaoh, from his servants, and from his people, tomorrow; only let not Pharaoh deal falsely again by not letting the people go to sacrifice to the LORD." ³⁰So Moses went out from Pharaoh and prayed to the LORD. ³¹And the LORD did as Moses asked, and removed the swarms of flies from Pharaoh, from his servants, and from his people; not one remained. ³²But Pharaoh hardened his heart this time also, and did not let the people go.

The fifth plague: the livestock epidemic

9 ¹Then the LORD said to Moses, "Go in to Pharaoh, and say to him, 'Thus says the LORD, the God of the Hebrews, "Let my people go, that they may serve me. ²For if you refuse to let them go and still hold them, ³behold, the hand of the LORD will fall with a very severe plague upon your cattle which are in the field, the horses, the asses, the camels, the herds, and the flocks. ⁴But the

Ps 78:48

---

account the sacred writer emphasizes the separateness of the people of Israel: it is not like other peoples, for God has segregated it, has chosen it for a special mission (cf. 19:1–5). The pharaoh continues to refuse; but his obstinacy is weakening.

9:1–7. The cattle epidemic is a much more serious scourge than the previous plagues because it affects possessions necessary to people's livelihood. Brief though it is, the account has features which suggest it comes from the Yahwistic tradition, such as the listing of types of domestic animals

inationes enim Aegyptiorum immolabimus Domino Deo nostro; quod si mactaverimus ea, quae colunt Aegyptii, coram eis, lapidibus nos obruent. ²³Viam trium dierum pergemus in solitudinem et sacrificabimus Domino Deo nostro, sicut praecepit nobis». ²⁴Dixitque pharao: «Ego dimittam vos, ut sacrificetis Domino Deo vestro in deserto, verumtamen longius ne abeatis; rogate pro me». ²⁵Et ait Moyses: «Egressus a te, orabo Dominum, et recedet musca a pharaone et a servis suis et a populo eius cras; verumtamen noli ultra fallere, ut non dimittas populum sacrificare Domino». ²⁶Egressusque Moyses a pharaone oravit Dominum; ²⁷qui fecit iuxta verbum illius et abstulit muscas a pharaone et a servis suis et a populo eius; non superfuit ne una quidem. ²⁸Et ingravatum est cor pharaonis, ita ut ne hac quidem vice dimitteret populum. ¹Dixit autem Dominus ad Moysen: «Ingredere ad pharaonem et loquere ad eum: Haec dicit Dominus, Deus Hebraeorum: Dimitte populum meum, ut sacrificet mihi. ²Quod si adhuc renuis et retines eos, ³ecce manus Domini erit super possessionem tuam in agris, super equos et asinos et camelos et boves et oves, pestis valde gravis; ⁴et distinguet Dominus inter possessiones Israel et possessiones Aegyptiorum, ut nihil omnino pereat ex his, quae pertinent ad filios Israel. ⁵Constituitque Dominus tempus dicens: Cras faciet Dominus verbum istud in terra». ⁶Fecit ergo Dominus verbum hoc altera die, mortuaque sunt omnia animantia Aegyptiorum; de animalibus vero

LORD will make a distinction between the cattle of Israel and the cattle of Egypt, so that nothing shall die of all that belongs to the people of Israel."'" ⁵And the LORD set a time, saying, "Tomorrow the LORD will do this thing in the land." ⁶And on the morrow the LORD did this thing; all the cattle of the Egyptians died, but of the cattle of the people of Israel not one died. ⁷And Pharaoh sent, and behold, not one of the cattle of the Israelites was dead. But the heart of Pharaoh was hardened, and he did not let the people go.

The sixth plague: the boils

⁸And the LORD said to Moses and Aaron, "Take handfuls of ashes from the kiln, and let Moses throw them toward heaven in the sight of Pharaoh. ⁹And it shall become fine dust over all the land of Egypt, and become boils breaking out in sores on man and beast throughout all the land of Egypt." ¹⁰So they took ashes from the kiln, and stood before Pharaoh, and Moses threw them toward heaven, and it became boils breaking out in sores on man and beast. ¹¹And the magicians could not stand before Moses because of the boils, for the boils were upon the magicians and upon all the Egyptians. ¹²But the LORD hardened the heart of Pharaoh, and he did not listen to them; as the LORD had spoken to Moses.

Rev 16:2

Mt 27:10

The seventh plague: the hail

¹³Then the LORD said to Moses, "Rise up early in the morning and stand before Pharaoh, and say to him, 'Thus says the LORD, the

Ps 78:47ff;
105:32
Rev 16:21

(v. 3) and the hyperbole that "all" the cattle succumbed. It stresses the distinction God makes between the Egyptians and the Israelites, and points out that God sets a time limit on the plague.

9:8–12. This plague, too, is narrated in few words; the account may come from the Priestly tradition. The severity of the scourge is worse again: it affects people as well as livestock. Indeed, even the magicians (who have said and done nothing since the plague of gnats) are themselves affected. By showing the worsening plague, the sacred writer manages to make the reader feel increasing hostility towards the obstinate and foolish pharaoh, and to identify with the Lord, who does not impose himself by force but takes action to gradually bend the tyrant's will.

filiorum Israel nihil omnino periit. ⁷Et misit pharao ad videndum; nec erat quidquam mortuum de his, quae possidebat Israel. Ingravatumque est cor pharaonis, et non dimisit populum. ⁸Et dixit Dominus ad Moysen et Aaron: «Tollite plenas manus cineris de camino, et spargat illum Moyses in caelum coram pharaone; ⁹sitque pulvis super omnem terram Aegypti; erunt enim in hominibus et iumentis ulcera et vesicae turgentes in universa terra Aegypti». ¹⁰Tuleruntque cinerem de camino et steterunt coram pharaone, et sparsit illum Moyses in caelum; factaque sunt ulcera vesicarum turgentium in hominibus et iumentis. ¹¹Nec poterant malefici stare coram Moyse propter ulcera, quae in illis erant et in omni terra Aegypti. ¹²Induravitque Dominus cor pharaonis, et non audivit eos, sicut locutus est Dominus ad Moysen. ¹³Dixitque Dominus ad Moysen: «Mane consurge et sta coram pharaone et dices ad eum:

God of the Hebrews, "Let my people go, that they may serve me. [14]For this time I will send all my plagues upon your heart, and upon your servants and your people, that you may know that there is none like me in all the earth. [15]For by now I could have put forth my hand and struck you and your people with pestilence, Rom 9:17 and you would have been cut off from the earth; [16]but for this purpose have I let you live, to show you my power, so that my name may be declared throughout all the earth. [17]You are still exalting Mk 13:19 yourself against my people, and will not let them go. [18]Behold, tomorrow about this time I will cause very heavy hail to fall, such as never has been in Egypt from the day it was founded until now. [19]Now therefore send, get your cattle and all that you have in the field into safe shelter; for the hail shall come down upon every man and beast that is in the field and is not brought home, and they shall die." ' " [20]Then he who feared the word of the LORD among the servants of Pharaoh made his slaves and his cattle flee into the houses; [21]but he who did not regard the word of the LORD left his slaves and his cattle in the field.

9:13–35. The seventh plague, the hailstorm, knows no limits: affects the entire land of Egypt—plants, animals and men.

In the Bible a storm accompanied by hail, thunder and lightning is a sign that God is making himself manifest (cf. 19:18; Ps 18:9–14; 29:3–9); this theophany is meant to show that there is none greater than God (vv. 14–16). St Paul refers to this passage of Exodus (cf. Rom 9:17), pointing out that the pharaoh himself had an important role in God's designs: his blindness made God's power and wisdom plainer to see.

All those living in Egypt were witnesses to God's intervention and they reacted by more or less acknowledging the Lord: the Israelites, who were living in Goshen, presumably realized the special protection they were enjoying; the pharaoh's ministers for the first time "feared the word of the Lord" (v. 20); the pharaoh himself began to admit his fault in his suit against God: "The Lord is in the right, and I and my people are in the wrong" (v. 27).

The sacred writer has seen in the scourge of hailstones a clearer manifestation of God's saving plan; this plague is recalled forcefully in Psalms 78:47f and 105:32, and, later on, the book of Revelation refers to it as an eschatological sign (Rev 16:21).

Haec dicit Dominus, Deus Hebraeorum: Dimitte populum meum, ut sacrificet mihi; [14]quia in hac vice mittam omnes plagas meas super cor tuum et super servos tuos et super populum tuum, ut scias quod non sit similis mei in omni terra. [15]Nunc enim extendens manum si percussissem te et populum tuum peste, perisses de terra. [16]Idcirco autem servavi te, ut ostendam in te fortitudinem meam, et narretur nomen meum in omni terra. [17]Adhuc retines populum meum et non vis dimittere eum? [18]En pluam cras, hac ipsa hora, grandinem multam nimis, qualis non fuit in Aegypto a die, qua fundata est, usque in praesens tempus. [19]Mitte ergo iam nunc et congrega iumenta tua et omnia, quae habes in agro; homines enim et iumenta universa, quae inventa fuerint foris nec congregata de agris, cadet super ea grando, et morientur». [20]Qui timuit verbum Domini de servis pharaonis, fecit confugere servos suos et iumenta in domos; [21]qui autem neglexit sermonem Domini, dimisit servos suos et iumenta in agris. [22]Et dixit Dominus ad Moysen: «Extende manum tuam in caelum, ut fiat grando in universa terra Aegypti super

²²And the LORD said to Moses, "Stretch forth your hand toward heaven, that there may be hail in all the land of Egypt, upon man and beast and every plant of the field, throughout the land of Egypt." ²³Then Moses stretched forth his rod toward heaven; and the LORD sent thunder and hail, and fire ran down to the earth. And the LORD rained hail upon the land of Egypt; ²⁴there was hail, and fire flashing continually in the midst of the hail, very heavy hail, such as had never been in all the land of Egypt since it became a nation. ²⁵The hail struck down everything that was in the field throughout all the land of Egypt, both man and beast; and the hail struck down every plant of the field, and shattered every tree of the field. ²⁶Only in the land of Goshen, where the people of Israel were, there was no hail.

²⁷Then Pharaoh sent, and called Moses and Aaron, and said to them, "I have sinned this time; the LORD is in the right, and I and my people are in the wrong. ²⁸Entreat the LORD; for there has been enough of this thunder and hail; I will let you go, and you shall stay no longer." ²⁹Moses said to him, "As soon as I have gone out of the city, I will stretch out my hands to the LORD; the thunder will cease, and there will be no more hail, that you may know that the earth is the LORD's. ³⁰But as for you and your servants, I know that you do not yet fear the LORD God." ³¹(The flax and the barley were ruined, for the barley was in the ear and the flax was in bud. ³²But the wheat and the spelt were not ruined, for they are late in coming up.) ³³So Moses went out of the city from Pharaoh, and stretched out his hands to the LORD; and the thunder and the hail ceased, and the rain no longer poured upon the earth. ³⁴But when Pharaoh saw that the rain and the hail and the thunder had ceased, he sinned yet again, and hardened his heart, he and his servants. ³⁵So the heart of Pharaoh was hardened, and he did not let the people of Israel go; as the LORD had spoken through Moses.

Ps 78:47;
105:32
Wis 16:6
Rev 16:21; 8:7
Rev 11:19;
16:18

Acts 8:24

Deut 10:14
Ps 24:1

homines et super iumenta et super omnem herbam agri in terra Aegypti». ²³Extenditque Moyses virgam in caelum, et Dominus dedit tonitrua et grandinem ac discurrentia fulgura super terram; pluitque Dominus grandinem super terram Aegypti. ²⁴Et grando et ignis immixta pariter ferebantur; tantaeque fuit magnitudinis, quanta ante numquam apparuit in universa terra Aegypti, ex quo gens illa condita est. ²⁵Et percussit grando in omni terra Aegypti cuncta, quae fuerunt in agris, ab homine usque ad iumentum; cunctamque herbam agri percussit grando et omne lignum regionis confregit. ²⁶Tantum in terra Gessen, ubi erant filii Israel, grando non cecidit. ²⁷Misitque pharao et vocavit Moysen et Aaron dicens ad eos: «Nunc peccavi; Dominus iustus, ego et populus meus rei». ²⁸Orate Dominum, ut desinant tonitrua Dei et grando, et dimittam vos, et nequaquam hic ultra manebitis». ²⁹Ait Moyses: «Cum egressus fuero de urbe, extendam palmas meas ad Dominum; et cessabunt tonitrua, et grando non erit, ut scias quia Domini est terra. ³⁰Novi autem quod et tu et servi tui necdum timeatis Dominum Deum». ³¹Linum ergo et hordeum laesum est, eo quod hordeum iam spicas et linum iam folliculos germinaret; ³²triticum autem et far non sunt laesa, quia serotina erant. ³³Egressusque Moyses a pharaone ex urbe tetendit manus ad Dominum; et cessaverunt tonitrua et grando, nec ultra effundebatur pluvia super terram. ³⁴Videns autem pharao quod cessasset pluvia et grando et tonitrua, auxit peccatum; ³⁵et ingra-

The eighth plague: the locusts

Joel 1:2–10

10 ¹Then the LORD said to Moses, "Go in to Pharaoh; for I have hardened his heart and the heart of his servants, that I

Ex 12:26; 13:8
Deut 4:9;
6:20–25

may show these signs of mine among them, ²and that you may tell in the hearing of your son and of your son's son how I have made sport of the Egyptians and what signs I have done among them; that you may know that I am the LORD."

³So Moses and Aaron went in to Pharaoh, and said to him, "Thus says the LORD, the God of the Hebrews, 'How long will you refuse to humble yourself before me? Let my people go, that

Wis 16:9

they may serve me. ⁴For if you refuse to let my people go, behold, tomorrow I will bring locusts into your country, ⁵and they shall cover the face of the land, so that no one can see the land; and they shall eat what is left to you after the hail, and they shall eat every tree of yours which grows in the field, ⁶and they shall fill your houses, and the houses of all your servants and of all the Egyptians; as neither your fathers nor your grandfathers have seen, from the day they came on earth to this day.'" Then he turned and went out from Pharaoh.

⁷And Pharaoh's servants said to him, "How long shall this man be a snare to us? Let the men go, that they may serve the LORD

10:1–20. Plagues of locusts often affected north Africa, including Egypt; borne by the wind, they can descend on a region in vast numbers and leave farmland devastated. However, this particular plague is, we are told, a severe punishment sent by God (cf. Joel 1:2–10). The sacred writer once again says things which indicate the deep meaning of all the prodigies which preceded the

Exodus—particularly the religious meaning of the plagues (their main object is to make known that "I am the Lord": v. 2); the intervention of the pharaoh's servants who, although they do not know the Lord, are at least ready to let the Israelites go (v. 7); the pharaoh's readiness to let the men go, while holding the women and children hostage (vv. 8–11); and his admission of his sin.

---

vatum est cor eius et servorum illius et induratum nimis; nec dimisit filios Israel, sicut dixerat Dominus per manum Moysi. ¹Et dixit Dominus ad Moysen: «Ingredere ad pharaonem: ego enim induravi cor eius et servorum illius, ut faciam signa mea haec in medio eorum, ²et narres in auribus filii tui et nepotum tuorum, quotiens contriverim Aegyptios et signa mea fecerim in eis; et sciatis quia ego Dominus». ³Introierunt ergo Moyses et Aaron ad pharaonem et dixerunt ei: «Haec dicit Dominus, Deus Hebraeorum: Usquequo non vis subici mihi? Dimitte populum meum, ut sacrificet mihi. ⁴Sin autem resistis et non vis dimittere eum, ecce ego inducam cras locustam in fines tuos, ⁵quae operiat superficiem terrae, ne quidquam eius appareat, sed comedatur, quod residuum fuerit grandini; corrodet enim omnia ligna, quae germinant in agris. ⁶Et implebunt domos tuas et servorum tuorum et omnium Aegyptiorum, quantam non viderunt patres tui et avi, ex quo orti sunt super terram usque in praesentem diem». Avertitque se et egressus est a pharaone. ⁷Dixerunt autem servi pharaonis ad eum: «Usquequo patiemur hoc scandalum? Dimitte homines, ut sacrificent Domino Deo suo; nonne vides quod perierit Aegyptus?». ⁸Revocaveruntque Moysen et Aaron ad pharaonem, qui dixit eis: «Ite, sacrificate Domino Deo vestro. Quinam sunt qui ituri sunt?». ⁹Ait Moyses: «Cum parvulis nostris et

their God; do you not yet understand that Egypt is ruined?" [8]So Moses and Aaron were brought back to Pharaoh; and he said to them, "Go, serve the LORD your God; but who are to go?" [9]And Moses said, "We will go with our young and our old; we will go with our sons and daughters and with our flocks and herds, for we must hold a feast to the LORD." [10]And he said to them, "The LORD be with you, if ever I let you and your little ones go! Look, you have some evil purpose in mind.[n] [11]No! Go, the men among you, and serve the LORD, for that is what you desire." And they were driven out from Pharaoh's presence.

[12]Then the LORD said to Moses, "Stretch out your hand over the land of Egypt for the locusts, that they may come upon the land of Egypt, and eat every plant in the land, all that the hail has left." [13]So Moses stretched forth his rod over the land of Egypt, and the Lord brought an east wind upon the land all that day and all that night; and when it was morning the east wind had brought the locusts. [14]And the locusts came up over all the land of Egypt, and settled on the whole country of Egypt, such a dense swarm of locusts as had never been before, nor ever shall be again. [15]For they covered the face of the whole land, so that the land was darkened, and they ate all the plants in the land and all the fruit of the trees which the hail had left; not a green thing remained, neither tree nor plant of the field, through all the land of Egypt. [16]Then Pharaoh called Moses and Aaron in haste, and said, "I have sinned against the LORD your God, and against you. [17]Now therefore, forgive my sin, I pray you, only this once, and entreat the LORD your God only to remove this death from me." [18]So he went out from Pharaoh, and entreated the LORD. [19]And the LORD turned

Ps 78:46;
105:34
Rev 9:3

Lk 15:18

Acts 8:24

senioribus pergemus, cum filiis et filiabus, cum ovibus et armentis; est enim sollemnitas Domini nobis». [10]Et respondit eis: «Sic Dominus sit vobiscum, quomodo ego dimittam vos et parvulos vestros. Cui dubium est quod pessime cogitetis? [11]Non fiet ita, sed ite tantum viri et sacrificate Domino; hoc enim et ipsi petistis». Statimque eiecti sunt de conspectu pharaonis. [12]Dixit autem Dominus ad Moysen: «Extende manum tuam super terram Aegypti, ut veniat locusta et ascendat super eam et devoret omnem herbam, quidquid residuum fuerit grandini». [13]Et extendit Moyses virgam super terram Aegypti, et Dominus induxit ventum urentem tota die illa et nocte. Et mane facto, ventus urens levavit locustas; [14]quae ascenderunt super universam terram Aegypti et sederunt in cunctis finibus Aegyptiorum innumerabiles, quales ante illud tempus non fuerant nec postea futurae sunt. [15]Operueruntque universam superficiem terrae, et obscurata est terra. Devoraverunt igitur omnem herbam terrae et, quidquid pomorum in arboribus fuit, quae grando dimiserat; nihilque omnino virens relictum est in lignis et in herbis terrae in cuncta Aegypto. [16]Quam ob rem festinus pharao vocavit Moysen et Aaron et dixit eis: «Peccavi in Dominum Deum vestrum et in vos. [17]Sed nunc dimittite peccatum mihi tantum hac vice et rogate Dominum Deum vestrum, ut auferat a me saltem mortem istam». [18]Egressusque Moyses de conspectu pharaonis oravit Dominum, [19]qui flare fecit ventum ab occidente vehementissimum et arreptam locustam proiecit in mare Rubrum; non remansit ne una quidem in cunc-

n. Heb *before your face*

a very strong west wind, which lifted the locusts and drove them into the Red Sea; not a single locust was left in all the country of Egypt. [20]But the LORD hardened Pharaoh's heart, and he did not let the children of Israel go.

Wis 17:1–18:4 **The ninth plague: the darkness**

Rev 8:12 [21]Then the LORD said to Moses, "Stretch out your hand toward heaven that there may be darkness over the land of Egypt, a dark-
Ps 105:28 ness to be felt." [22]So Moses stretched out his hand toward heaven,
Rev 16:10 and there was thick darkness in all the land of Egypt three days; [23]they did not see one another, nor did any rise from his place for three days; but all the people of Israel had light where they dwelt. [24]Then Pharaoh called Moses, and said, "Go, serve the LORD; your children also may go with you; only let your flocks and your herds remain behind." [25]But Moses said, "You must also let us have sacrifices and burnt offerings, that we may sacrifice to the LORD our God. [26]Our cattle also must go with us; not a hoof shall be left behind, for we must take of them to serve the LORD our God, and we do not know with what we must serve the LORD until we arrive there." [27]But the LORD hardened Pharaoh's heart, and he

---

10:21–29. In springtime Egypt sometimes gets a warm desert wind so laden with sand particles as to produce a cloud that reduces visibility. Although there is a climatic basis to it, this ninth plague is particularly ominous. The book of Wisdom interprets darkness as a terrible abandonment of man by God. The sacred writer here points out that dialogue with the pharaoh has broken down: the other plagues were usually preceded by an announcement or a threat; not so this time, and after a tense interview the pharaoh and Moses regard their dealings as over.

Yet, we now glimpse that this is the beginning of the end: the pharaoh would allow the sons of Israel to leave, provided they left their flocks behind. But Moses will not accept this condition either; he openly talks about how they have to offer God sacrifices and burnt offerings—a clear allusion to the Passover sacrifice.

At the start of v. 24, in only a few Hebrew manuscripts, it says, "Then Pharaoh called Moses and Aaron"; but this reference to Aaron is found in all the Greek and Latin versions. His presence alongside Moses serves to emphasize how this plague is a figure of them all.

---

tis finibus Aegypti. [20]Et induravit Dominus cor pharaonis, nec dimisit filios Israel. [21]Dixit autem Dominus ad Moysen: «Extende manum tuam in caelum, et sint tenebrae super terram Aegypti tam densae ut palpari queant». [22]Extenditque Moyses manum in caelum, et factae sunt tenebrae horribiles in universa terra Aegypti tribus diebus. [23]Nemo vidit fratrem suum nec movit se de loco, in quo erat. Ubi, cumque autem habitabant filii Israel, lux erat. [24]Vocavitque pharao Moysen et Aaron et dixit eis: «Ite, sacrificate Domino; oves tantum vestrae et armenta remaneant, parvuli vestri eant vobiscum». [25]Ait Moyses: «Etiamsi tu hostias et holocausta dares nobis, quae offeramus Domino Deo nostro, [26]tamen et greges nostri pergent nobiscum; non remanebit ex eis ungula, quoniam ex ipsis sumemus, quae necessaria sunt in cultum Domini Dei nostri; praesertim cum ignoremus quid debeat immolari,

would not let them go. ²⁸Then Pharaoh said to him, "Get away from me; take heed to yourself; never see my face again; for in the day you see my face you shall die." ²⁹Moses said, "As you say! I will not see your face again."

The tenth plague is announced

11 ¹The LORD said to Moses, "Yet one plague more I will bring upon Pharaoh and upon Egypt; afterwards he will let you go hence; when he lets you go, he will drive you away completely. ²Speak now in the hearing of the people, that they ask, every man of his neighbor and every woman of her neighbour, jewelry of silver and of gold." ³And the LORD gave the people favor in the sight of the Egyptians. Moreover, the man Moses was very great in the land of Egypt, in the sight of Pharaoh's servants and in the sight of the people.

⁴And Moses said, "Thus says the LORD: About midnight I will go forth in the midst of Egypt; ⁵and all the first-born in the land of Egypt shall die, from the first-born of Pharaoh who sits upon his throne, even to the first-born of the maidservant who is behind the mill; and all the first-born of the cattle. ⁶And there shall be a great

Ex 3:22
Ex 13:11ff
Ex 12:35
Sir 45:1
Acts 7:22

11:1–10. The account of the plagues ends with the announcement of the last one, the death of the first-born, whose fulfilment forms part of the institution of the Passover sacrifice described in the two chapters that follow. This chapter once again explains the reason behind all that has taken place so far. It is a preparation for the prodigies which will occur in the Passover and the departure from Egypt: *that* will be the most marvellous of the Lord's doings.

In the first place, we are told that there is "one plague more" (v. 1) to come—the first time the term "plague" appears—indicating that the previous ones were a sort of prelude to the definitive punishment. Then it tells us that Moses and the people gained the esteem of the Egyptians (v. 3), which serves to stress that the dispute is between the pharaoh alone, who regarded himself as a god, and the Lord, the only true God. Finally, the announcement of the slaying of the first-born sons (vv. 5–8) has profound significance: Israel alone is the first-born son and heir, in God's plan (cf. 4:23). Moreover, if Egypt loses its first-born, its survival is endangered; whereas Israel's

---

donec ad ipsum locum perveniamus». ²⁷Induravit autem Dominus cor pharaonis, et noluit dimittere eos. ²⁸Dixitque pharao ad eum: «Recede a me. Cave, ne ultra videas faciem meam; quocumque die apparueris mihi, morieris». ²⁹Respondit Moyses: «Ita fiet, ut locutus es; non videbo ultra faciem tuam». ¹Et dixit Dominus ad Moysen: «Adhuc una plaga tangam pharaonem et Aegyptum, et post haec dimittet vos utique, immo et exire compellet. ²Dices ergo omni plebi, ut postulet vir ab amico suo et mulier a vicina sua vasa argentea et aurea; ³dabit autem Dominus gratiam populo coram Aegyptiis». Fuitque Moyses vir magnus valde in terra Aegypti coram servis pharaonis et omni populo. ⁴Et ait Moyses: «Haec dicit Dominus: Media nocte egrediar in Aegyptum; ⁵et morietur omne primogenitum in terra Aegyptiorum, a primogenito pharaonis, qui sedet in solio eius, usque ad primogenitum ancillae, quae est ad molam, et omnia primogenita iumentorum. ⁶Eritque clamor magnus in universa terra Aegypti,

cry throughout all the land of Egypt, such as there has never been, nor ever shall be again. 7But against any of the people of Israel, either man or beast, not a dog shall growl; that you may know that the LORD makes a distinction between the Egyptians and Israel. 8And all these your servants shall come down to me, and bow down to me, saying, 'Get you out, and all the people who follow you.' And after that I will go out." And he went out from Pharaoh in hot anger. 9Then the LORD said to Moses, "Pharaoh will not listen to you; that my wonders may be multiplied in the land of Egypt."

10Moses and Aaron did all these wonders before Pharaoh; and the LORD hardened Pharaoh's heart, and he did not let the people of Israel go out of his land.

Ex 12:21–28;
34:18
Lev 23:5–8
Num 28: 16–25
Deut 16:1–8
Ezek 45:21–24
Mt 26:17ff
Lk 22:15–16
1 Cor 5:7

4. THE PASSOVER

The institution of the Passover*

12 1*The Lord said to Moses and Aaron in the land of Egypt, 2"This month shall be for you the beginning of months; it

---

survival and identity is assured. In Christ Jesus, the "first-born of all creation", the life of all believers is for ever assured (cf. Col 1:15–20).

*12:1–14. This discourse of the Lord contains a number of rules for celebrating the Passover and the events commemorated in it; it is a kind of catechetical-liturgical text which admirably summarizes the profound meaning of that feast.

The Passover probably originated as a shepherds' feast held in springtime, when lambs are born and the migration to summer pastures was beginning; a new-born lamb was sacrificed and its

blood used to perform a special rite in petition for the protection and fertility of the flocks. But once this feast became connected with the history of the Exodus it acquired a much deeper meaning, as did the rites attaching to it.

Thus, the "congregation" (v. 3) comprises all the Israelites organized as a religious community to commemorate the most important event in their history, deliverance from bondage.

The victim will be a lamb, without blemish (v. 5) because it is to be offered to God. Smearing the doorposts and lintel with the blood of the victim (vv. 7, 13), an essential part of the rite, signifies protection from dangers. The Passover is

---

qualis nec ante fuit nec postea futurus est. 7Apud omnes autem filios Israel non mutiet canis contra hominem et pecus, ut sciatis quanto miraculo dividat Dominus Aegyptios et Israel. 8Descendentque omnes servi tui isti ad me et adorabunt me dicentes: 'Egredere tu et omnis populus, qui sequitur te'. Post haec egrediar». Et exivit a pharaone iratus nimis. 9Dixit autem Dominus ad Moysen: «Non audiet vos pharao, ut multa signa fiant in terra Aegypti». 10Moyses autem et Aaron fecerunt omnia ostenta haec coram pharaone; et induravit Dominus cor pharaonis, nec dimisit filios Israel de terra sua. 1Dixit

shall be the first month of the year for you. ³Tell all the congregation of Israel that on the tenth day of this month they shall take
every man a lamb according to their fathers' houses, a lamb for a
household; ⁴and if the household is too small for a lamb, then a
man and his neighbour next to his house shall take according to
the number of persons; according to what each can eat you shall
make your count for the lamb. ⁵Your lamb shall be without blem- Lev 22:19
ish, a male a year old; you shall take it from the sheep or from the
goats; ⁶and you shall keep it until the fourteenth day of this
month, when the whole assembly of the congregation of Israel
shall kill their lambs in the evening.ᵒ ⁷Then they shall take some

essentially sacrificial from the very start.

The meal (v. 11) is also a necessary part, and the manner in which it is held is a very appropriate way of showing the urgency imposed by circumstances: there is no time to season it (v. 9); no other food is eaten with it, except for the bread and desert herbs (a sign of indigence); the dress and posture of those taking part (standing, wearing sandals and holding a staff) show that they are on a journey. In the later liturgical commemoration of the Passover, these things indicate that the Lord is passing among his people.

The rules laid down for the Passover are evocative of very ancient nomadic desert rites, where there was no priest or temple or altar. When the Israelites had settled in Palestine, the Passover continued to be celebrated at home, always retaining the features of a sacrifice, a family meal and, very especially, a memorial of the deliverance the Lord brought about on that night.

Our Lord chose the context of the Passover Supper to institute the Eucharist: "By celebrating the Last Supper with his apostles in the course of the Passover meal, Jesus gave the Jewish Passover its definitive meaning. Jesus' passing over to his Father by his death and Resurrection, the new Passover, is anticipated in the Supper and celebrated in the Eucharist, which fulfils the Jewish Passover and anticipates the final Passover of the Church in the glory of the kingdom" (*Catechism of the Catholic Church*, 1340).

12:2. This event is so important that it is going to mark the starting point in the reckoning of time. In the history of Israel there are two types of calendar, both based on the moon—one which begins the year in the autumn, after the feast of Weeks (cf. 23:16; 34:22), and the other beginning it in spring, between March and April. This second calendar probably

Dominus ad Moysen et Aaron in terra Aegypti: ²«Mensis iste vobis principium mensium, primus erit in mensibus anni. ³Loquimini ad universum coetum filiorum Israel et dicite eis: Decima die mensis huius tollat unusquisque agnum per familias et domos suas. ⁴Sin autem minor est numerus, ut sufficere possit ad vescendum agnum, assumet vicinum suum, qui iunctus est domui suae, iuxta numerum animarum, quae sufficere possunt ad esum agni. ⁵Erit autem vobis agnus absque macula, masculus, anniculus; quem de agnis vel haedis tolletis ⁶et servabitis eum usque ad quartam decimam diem mensis huius; immolabitque eum universa congregatio filiorum Israel ad vesperam. ⁷Et sument de sanguine eius ac ponent super utrumque postem et in superliminaribus domorum, in quibus comedent illum; ⁸et

o. Heb *between the two evenings*

of the blood, and put it on the two doorposts and the lintel of the houses in which they eat them. [8]They shall eat the flesh that night, roasted; with unleavened bread and bitter herbs they shall eat it. [9]Do not eat any of it raw or boiled with water, but roasted, its head with its legs and its inner parts. [10]And you shall let none of it remain until the morning, anything that remains until the morning

Lk 12:35 you shall burn. [11]In this manner you shall eat it: your loins girded, your sandals on your feet, and your staff in your hand; and you

Num 33:4 shall eat it in haste. It is the LORD'S passover. [12]For I will pass through the land of Egypt that night, and I will smite all the first-born in the land of Egypt, both man and beast; and on all the gods

Lev 1:5 of Egypt I will execute judgments: I am the LORD. [13]The blood shall be a sign for you, upon the houses where you are; and when I see the blood, I will pass over you, and no plague shall fall upon you to destroy you, when I smite the land of Egypt.

---

held sway for quite a long time, for we know that the first month, known as Abib (spring)—cf. 13:4; 23:18; 34:18—was called, in the post-exilic period (from the 6th century BC onwards) by the Babylonian name of Nisan (Neh 2:1; Esther 3:7). Be that as it may, the fact that this month is called the first month is a way of highlighting the importance of the event which is going to be commemorated (the Passover).

12:11. Even now it is difficult to work out the etymology of the word "Passover".

In other Semitic languages it means "joy" or "festive joy" or also "ritual and festive leap". In the Bible the same root means "dancing or limping" in an idolatrous rite (cf. 1 Kings 18:21, 26) and

"protecting" (cf. Is 31:5), so it could mean "punishment, lash" and also "salvation, protection". In the present text the writer is providing a popular, non-scholarly etymology, and it is taken as meaning that "the Lord passes through", slaying Egyptians and sparing the Israelites.

In the New Testament it will be applied to Christ's passage to the Father by death and resurrection, and the Church's "passage" to the eternal Kingdom: "The Church will enter the glory of the kingdom only through this final Passover, when she will follow her Lord in his death and Resurrection" (*Catechism of the Catholic Church*, 677).

12:14. The formal tone of these words gives an idea of the importance the Pass-

---

edent carnes nocte illa assas igni et azymos panes cum lactucis amaris. [9]Non comedetis ex eo crudum quid nec coctum aqua, sed tantum assum igni; caput cum pedibus eius et intestinis vorabitis. [10]Nec remanebit quidquam ex eo usque mane; si quid residuum fuerit, igne comburetis. [11]Sic autem comedetis illum: renes vestros accingetis, calceamenta habebitis in pedibus, tenentes baculos in manibus, et comedetis festinanter; est enim Pascha (*id est Transitus*) Domini! [12]Et transibo per terram Aegypti nocte illa percutiamque omne primogenitum in terra Aegypti ab homine usque ad pecus; et in cunctis diis Aegypti faciam iudicia, ego Dominus. [13]Erit autem sanguis vobis in signum in aedibus, in quibus eritis; et videbo sanguinem et transibo vos, nec erit in vobis plaga disperdens, quando percussero terram Aegypti. [14]Habebitis autem hanc diem in monumentum et celebrabitis eam sollemnem Domino

[14]"This day shall be for you a memorial day, and you shall keep it as a feast to the LORD; throughout your generations you shall observe it as an ordinance for ever.

Ex 12:3–10;
23:15; 34:18
Deut 26:9
Lk 22:19
Mt 26:17
Mk 14:12

The feast of the unleavened bread

[15]Seven days you shall eat unleavened bread; on the first day you shall put away leaven out of your houses, for if any one eats what is leavened, from the first day until the seventh day, that person shall be cut off from Israel. [16]On the first day you shall hold a holy assembly, and on the seventh day a holy assembly; no work shall be done on those days; but what everyone must eat, that only may be prepared by you. [17]And you shall observe the feast of unleavened bread, for on this very day I brought your hosts out of the land of Egypt: therefore you shall observe this day, throughout your generations, as an ordinance for ever. [18]In the first

1 Cor 5:7
Lk 2:43

Lk 23:56

Lk 22:7

---

over always had. If the historical books (Joshua, Judges, Samuel and Kings) hardly mention it, the reason is that they allude only to sacrifices in the temple, and the Passover was always celebrated in people's homes. When the temple ceased to be (6th century BC), the feast acquired more prominence, as can be seen from the post-exilic biblical texts (cf. Ezra 6:19–22; 2 Chron 30:1–27; 35:1–19) and extrabiblical texts such as the famous "Passover papyrus of Elephantine" (Egypt) of the 5th century BC. In Jesus' time a solemn passover sacrifice was celebrated in the temple and the passover meal was held at home.

12:15–20. The feast of the Azymes, or unleavened bread, seems to date back to earliest times in Canaan. It betokens an agricultural background (Deut 26:9) and it marked the start of the barley harvest.

Given that it is recorded here, it must have been celebrated from very early times along with the Passover. So, the feast of the unleavened bread, which would originally have simply been an offering of the first-fruits of the harvest, now acquires the same meaning as the Passover, that is, it commemorates the deliverance of the people of God, the "first-fruits", as it were, of the nations.

Unleavened bread was, and still is among the Bedouin, the norm in the desert. When the people eventually settled down in the promised land, the idea was kept that fermentation of any kind implied some impurity; which was why in the offering of sacrifices (cf. Lev 2:11; 6:10) and even more so in the passover meal, only unleavened bread was used. Jesus availed himself of this notion when he advised his disciples to "beware of the leaven of the Pharisees" (Mk 8:15), that

---

in generationibus vestris cultu sempiterno. [15]Septem diebus azyma comedetis. Iam in die primo non erit fermentum in domibus vestris; quicumque comederit fermentatum, a primo die usque ad diem septimum, peribit anima illa de Israel. [16]Dies prima erit sancta atque sollemnis, et dies septima eadem festivitate venerabilis. Nihil operis facietis in eis, exceptis his, quae ad vescendum pertinent. [17]Et observabitis azyma, in eadem enim ipsa die eduxi exercitum vestrum de terra Aegypti; et custodietis diem istum in generationes vestras ritu perpetuo. [18]Primo mense, quarta decima die mensis ad vesperam comedetis azyma; usque ad diem vicesimam primam eiusdem mensis ad vesperam. [19]Septem

month, on the fourteenth day of the month at evening, you shall
eat unleavened bread, and so until the twenty-first day of the
1 Cor 5:7 month at evening. [19]For seven days no leaven shall be found in
your houses; for if any one eats what is leavened, that person
shall be cut off from the congregation of Israel, whether he is a
sojourner or a native of the land. [20]You shall eat nothing leavened; in all your dwellings you shall eat unleavened bread."

Ex 10:2; 12:1–14
1 Cor 5:7 **Instructions relating to the Passover**

[21]Then Moses called all the elders of Israel, and said to them,
"Select lambs for yourselves according to your families, and kill
Heb 11:28 the passover lamb. [22]Take a bunch of hyssop and dip it in the
blood which is in the basin, and touch the lintel and the two
doorposts with the blood which is in the basin; and none of you
shall go out of the door of his house until the morning. [23]For the
LORD will pass through to slay the Egyptians; and when he sees
the blood on the lintel and on the two doorposts, the LORD will

---

is, of their evil dispositions. In the Latin
rite the Church uses unleavened bread in
the Eucharist, to imitate Jesus, who celebrated the Last Supper with this type of
bread.

12:21–28. This section parallels 12:1–14
but, possibly because it comes from a different tradition, it omits many of the rites
that appear there and instead adds some
details not previously mentioned—like
the hyssop, the basin for holding the
blood, and the instruction that no one is
to leave the house. But the most significant thing is the insistence on and details
given about the rite of the blood, as if it
were more important than the passover
meal as such. This is another hint that the

Passover, in its origin, may have been a
nomadic sacrifice designed very much to
ward off every kind of evil.

The mention of the "destroyer" (v.
23) seems to come from an ancient tradition, because this unpleasant name is
given to God or to an angel in order to
enhance the drama of that night: God will
be the cause of death for the Egyptians
and of deliverance for the Hebrews.

The children's question about the
meaning of the rite (v. 26) shows the
importance that oral transmission of
Tradition always had. Successive generations will learn the profound meaning of
the Passover not from written documents
but by word of mouth from their elders
(cf. Rom 10:17).

---

diebus fermentum non invenietur in domibus vestris. Qui comederit fermentatum, peribit anima eius
de coetu Israel, tam de advenis quam de indigenis terrae. [20]Omne fermentatum non comedetis; in cunctis habitaculis vestris edetis azyma». [21]Vocavit autem Moyses omnes seniores filiorum Israel et dixit ad
eos: «Ite tollentes animal per familias vestras et immolate Pascha. [22]Fasciculumque hyssopi tingite in
sanguine, qui est in pelvi, et aspergite ex eo superliminare et utrumque postem. Nullus vestrum egrediatur ostium domus suae usque mane. [23]Transibit enim Dominus percutiens Aegyptios; cumque viderit
sanguinem in super liminari et in utroque poste, transcendet ostium et non sinet percussorem ingredi
domos vestras et laedere. [24]Custodite verbum istud legitimum tibi et filiis tuis usque in aeternum.
[25]Cumque introieritis terram, quam Dominus daturus est vobis, ut pollicitus est, observabitis caeremo-

pass over the door, and will not allow the destroyer to enter your houses to slay you. [24]You shall observe this rite as an ordinance for you and for your sons for ever. [25]And when you come to the land which the LORD will give you, as he has promised, you shall keep this service. [26]And when your children say to you, 'What do you mean by this service?' [27]you shall say, 'It is the sacrifice of the LORD's passover, for he passed over the houses of the people of Israel in Egypt, when he slew the Egyptians but spared our houses.'" And the people bowed their heads and worshiped.

[28]Then the people of Israel went and did so; as the LORD had commanded Moses and Aaron, so they did.

Ex 13:8–14

The tenth plague: death of the first-born

[29]At midnight the LORD smote all the first-born in the land of Egypt, from the first-born of Pharaoh who sat on his throne to the first-born of the captive who was in the dungeon, and all the first-born of the cattle. [30]And Pharaoh rose up in the night, he, and all his servants, and all the Egyptians; and there was a great cry in Egypt, for there was not a house where one was not dead. [31]And he summoned Moses and Aaron by night, and said, "Rise up, go forth from among my people, both you and the people of Israel; and go, serve the LORD, as you have said. [32]Take your flocks and your herds, as you have said, and be gone; and bless me also!"

Ex 11:4–8; 13:11
Ps 78:51; 105:36;
135:8;136:10
Wis 18:6–19

12:29–36. After this detailed description of the Passover, the narrative picks up the thread and recounts very quickly the death of the first-born of Egypt. The sacred text gives hardly any details about this tragedy that afflicts the Egyptians, whereas it gives much more detailed information about the long-awaited permission from the pharaoh for the Israelites to leave—giving the impression that their departure-deliverance is much more important than the last plague, however terrible we may find it today. The people leave in haste, but they leave victorious. The very Egyptians readily give them presents, to show that they acknowledge the dignity of Israel and of the God who gives them protection. Here is fulfilled to the letter the promise God made to Moses when he first entrusted him with his mission (cf. 3:21–22 and note).

---

nias istas; [26]et, cum dixerint vobis filii vestri: 'Quae est ista religio?', [27]dicetis eis: 'Victima Paschae Domino est, quando transivit super domos filiorum Israel in Aegypto percutiens Aegyptios et domos nostras liberans'». Incurvatusque populus adoravit; [28]et egressi filii Israel fecerunt, sicut praeceperat Dominus Moysi et Aaron. [29]Factum est autem in noctis medio, percussit Dominus omne primogenitum in terra Aegypti, a primogenito pharaonis, qui in solio eius sedebat, usque ad primogenitum captivi, qui erat in carcere, et omne primogenitum iumentorum. [30]Surrexitque pharao nocte et omnes servi eius cunctaque Aegyptus, et ortus est clamor magnus in Aegypto, neque enim erat domus, in qua non iaceret mortuus. [31]Vocatisque pharao Moyse et Aaron nocte, ait: «Surgite, egredimini a populo meo, vos et filii Israel; ite, immolate Domino, sicut dicitis. [32]Oves vestras et armenta assumite, ut petieratis, et

Ex 3:21–22; 11:2
Wis 10:17 **Provisions for the Exodus**

³³And the Egyptians were urgent with the people, to send them out of the land in haste; for they said, "We are all dead men." ³⁴So the people took their dough before it was leavened, their kneading bowls being bound up in their mantles on their shoulders. ³⁵The people of Israel had also done as Moses told them, for they had asked of the Egyptians jewelry of silver and of gold, and clothing; ³⁶and the LORD had given the people favour in the sight of the Egyptians, so that they let them have what they asked. Thus they despoiled the Egyptians.

Num 33:3–5 **The sons of Israel leave Egypt**

Num 1:46; ³⁷And the people of Israel journeyed from Rameses to Succoth, 26:51 about six hundred thousand men on foot, besides women and children. ³⁸A mixed multitude also went up with them, and very many cattle, both flocks and herds. ³⁹And they baked unleavened cakes of the dough which they had brought out of Egypt, for it Gen 15:13 was not leavened, because they were thrust out of Egypt and

---

12:37–42. Here we are given concrete details about the departure from Egypt. They headed towards Succoth, a city which modern excavations locate some 15kms (nine miles) south-east of Rameses, in the Nile delta. It seems to make sense that they should have avoided trade routes, which would have been quieter but busier and patrolled by Egyptian armies—the coast road to the country of the Philistines (cf. 13:17), the road through the southern desert, which led to Beer-sheba, or the trading route linking Egypt and Arabia. Even in this little thing one can see God's special providence at work: he has no need of beaten tracks to show his people where to go.

The figure of 600,000 is an idealized one (cf. Num 1:46; 26:51), for it would imply a total population of three million people, women and children included. Maybe for the hagiographer's contemporaries this figure had a significance which escapes us today; or perhaps it is just a way of indicating that there were very many people—part of the epic style of the account, to highlight the power of God.

The figure of 430 years for the time the sons of Israel had been in Egypt (v. 40) is slightly different from the 400 years which appears more often in the Bible (cf. Gen 15:13; Acts 7:6; Gal 3:16–17). In the Pentateuch numbers

---

abeuntes benedicite mihi». ³³Urgebantque Aegyptii populum de terra exire velociter dicentes: «Omnes moriemur». ³⁴Tulit igitur populus conspersam farinam, antequam fermentaretur; et ligans pistrina in palliis suis posuit super umeros suos. ³⁵Feceruntque filii Israel, sicut praeceperat Moyses, et petierunt ab Aegyptiis vasa argentea et aurea vestemque plurimam. ³⁶Dominus autem dedit gratiam populo coram Aegyptiis, ut commodarent eis; et spoliaverunt Aegyptios. ³⁷Profectique sunt filii Israel de Ramesse in Succoth, sescenta fere milia peditum virorum absque parvulis. ³⁸Sed et vulgus promiscuum innumerabile ascendit cum eis, oves et armenta, animantia multa nimis. ³⁹Coxeruntque farinam, quam dudum de Aegypto conspersam tulerant, et fecerunt subcinericios panes azymos; neque enim poterant fermentari, cogentibus exire Aegyptiis et nullam facere sinentibus moram; nec pulmenti quidquam

could not tarry, neither had they prepared for themselves any provisions.

[40]The time that the people of Israel dwelt in Egypt was four Gal 3:16–17
hundred and thirty years. [41]And at the end of four hundred and
thirty years, on that very day, all the hosts of the LORD went out
from the land of Egypt. [42]It was a night of watching by the LORD, Acts 13:17
to bring them out of the land of Egypt; so this same night is a
night of watching kept to the LORD by all the people of Israel
throughout their generations.

Further instructions about the Passover

[43]And the LORD said to Moses and Aaron, "This is the ordinance
of the passover: no foreigner shall eat of it; [44]but every slave that
is bought for money may eat of it after you have circumcised him.
[45]No sojourner or hired servant may eat of it. [46]In one house shall Num 9:13
it be eaten; you shall not carry forth any of the flesh outside the Jn 19:36
1 Cor 5:7
house; and you shall not break a bone of it. [47]All the congregation
of Israel shall keep it. [48]And when a stranger shall sojourn with Num 9:14
Heb 11:28

---

often have a more symbolic than chronological meaning (cf. the note on Gen
5:1–32). The 400 years would mean that
the chosen people lived in Egypt for ten
generations (forty years per generation:
cf. the note on Ex 7:9), that is, a complete period of the history of Israel.

"Night of watching" (v. 42): if the
darkness causes any misgiving, God will
transform it into a time of salvation.
Because God looks out for them, the
Israelites will also commemorate the night
of their deliverance by keeping watch.
Christian liturgy celebrates the Lords' resurrection with a solemn vigil, commemorating the deliverance of the Israelites, the
redemption of Christians, and Christ's

victory over death—three stages in God's
intervention to save souls; as the Church
sings: "This is the night when first you
saved our fathers: you freed the people of
Israel from their slavery. [. . .] This is the
night when Christians everywhere (are)
washed clean of sin and freed from all
defilement. [. . .] This is the night when
Jesus Christ broke the chains of death and
rose triumphant from the grave" (*Roman
Missal*, Exultet).

12:43–51. Here are new rules for the
Passover which make its meaning more
explicit. Only members of the people
may eat it, for it will be the rite which
marks the unity of the sons of Israel and

---

[40]occurrerant praeparare. [40]Habitatio autem filiorum Israel, qua manserant in Aegypto, fuit quadringen-
torum triginta annorum. [41]Quibus expletis, eadem die egressus est omnis exercitus Domini de terra
Aegypti. [42]Nox ista vigiliarum Domino, quando eduxit eos de terra Aegypti: hanc observare debent
Domino omnes filii Israel in generationibus suis. [43]Dixitque Dominus ad Moysen et Aaron: «Haec est
religio Paschae: Omnis alienigena non comedet ex eo; [44]omnis autem servus empticius circumcidetur
et sic comedet; [45]advena et mercennarius non edent ex eo. [46]In una domo comedetur, nec efferetis de
carnibus eius foras nec os illius confringetis. [47]Omnis coetus filiorum Israel faciet illud. [48]Quod si quis
peregrinorum in vestram voluerit transire coloniam et facere Pascha Domini, circumcidetur prius omne
masculinum eius, et tunc rite celebrabit eritque sicut indigena terrae; si quis autem circumcisus non

you and would keep the passover to the LORD, let all his males be circumcised, then he may come near and keep it; he shall be as a native of the land. But no uncircumcised person shall eat of it. ⁴⁹There shall be one law for the native and for the stranger who sojourns among you."

Ex 13:11–16;
22:28–29; 34:19–20
Lev 27:26
Num 3:11–13,
40–51; 8:16–18;
18:15
Deut 15:19–23
Lk 2:22–24

⁵⁰Thus did all the people of Israel; as the LORD commanded Moses and Aaron, so they did. ⁵¹And on that very day the LORD brought the people of Israel out of the land of Egypt by their hosts.

The law about the first-born

Lk 2:23

13 ¹The LORD said to Moses, ²"Consecrate to me all the first-born; whatever is the first to open the womb among the people of Israel, both of man and of beast, is mine."

---

shows that they are special. It is the rite to be performed with maximum purity: those partaking must be circumcised and not a bone of the victim is to be broken (v. 46). This last requirement is used by St John to show that the passover lamb is a figure of Christ immolated on the cross (cf. Jn 19:36; cf. also 1 Cor 5:7).

13:1–2. The sacred text links to the events of the Exodus the ancient custom of consecrating all the first-born to God. Among the Phoenicians this custom went as far as immolating first-born children: but in Israel the sacrifice of infants was never permitted, as can be seen from the account of the sacrifice of Isaac (Gen 22:1–14), for whom a ram was substituted at the last minute. The legislation handed down in all the traditions recorded in the Pentateuch (Ex 22:28–29; Num 3:11–13; 3:40–45; Deut 15:19–23) commanded that every first-born should be sacrificed, but children were to be redeemed (Ex 13:13; 34:19–20; Num 18:15). Nor should unclean animals be

sacrificed; of domestic animals only the donkey was considered unclean and therefore its blood should not be shed (that is, it should not be sacrificed); instead it should have its neck broken or a lamb should be sacrificed instead of it. But the first-born child should always be redeemed. As the years went by, laws and rites developed concerning the consecration of the first-born to the Lord and about their redemption by means of an animal or even some payment (Ex 34:20; Num 3:40–51). We also know that later on Levites were consecrated to God as substitutes for the first-born (Num 3:12–13; 8:16–18).

This law, which is an acknowledgement that children are a gift from God and belong to him, stayed in place virtually unchanged up to the time of the New Testament. Jesus himself submitted to it in a profound act of humility (cf. Lk 2:22–24).

13:3–16. Just as more precise rules were given for the celebration of the Passover

---

⁴⁹fuerit, non vescetur ex eo. ⁴⁹Eadem lex erit indigenae et colono, qui peregrinatur apud vos». ⁵⁰Feceruntque omnes filii Israel, sicut praeceperat Dominus Moysi et Aaron; ⁵¹et in eadem die eduxit Dominus filios Israel de terra Aegypti per turmas suas. ¹Locutusque est Dominus ad Moysen dicens: ²«Sanctifica mihi omne primogenitum, quod aperit vulvam in filiis Israel, tam de hominibus quam de iumentis: mea sunt enim omnia». ³Et ait Moyses ad populum: «Mementote diei huius, in qua egressi

Instructions about the feast of the unleavened bread

Ex 12:1; 12:
15–20; 34:18

³And Moses said to the people, "Remember this day, in which you came out from Egypt, out of the house of bondage, for by strength of hand the LORD brought you out from this place; no leavened bread shall be eaten. ⁴This day you are to go forth, in the month of Abib. ⁵And when the LORD brings you into the land of the Canaanites, the Hittites, the Amorites, the Hivites, and the Jebusites, which he swore to your fathers to give you, a land flowing with milk and honey, you shall keep this service in this month. ⁶Seven days you shall eat unleavened bread, and on the seventh day there shall be a feast to the LORD. ⁷Unleavened bread shall be eaten for seven days; no leavened bread shall be seen with you, and no leaven shall be seen with you in all your territory. ⁸And you shall tell your son on that day, 'It is because of what the LORD did for me when I came out of Egypt.' ⁹And it shall be to you as a sign on your hand and as a memorial between your eyes, that the law of the LORD may be in your mouth; for with a strong hand the LORD has brought you out of Egypt. ¹⁰You shall therefore keep this ordinance at its appointed time from year to year.

1 Cor 5:7

Ex 12:26; 13:14

Mt 23:5

(12:44–51), the same is now done for the feast of the unleavened bread (vv. 3–10) and the consecration of the first-born (vv. 11–16). These are the three rites which the Israelites used to commemorate their deliverance from bondage.

The main feature of this new set of rules is its liturgical-catechetical character, involving the obligation to explain the rite to one's son (12:26; 13:8, 14), thereby keeping alive the memory of God's intervention. "In the sense of Sacred Scripture the *memorial* is not merely the recollection of past events but the proclamation of the mighty works wrought by God for men (cf. Ex 13:3). In

the liturgical celebration of these events, they become in a certain way present and real. This is how Israel understands its liberation from Egypt: every time Passover is celebrated the Exodus events are made present to the memory of believers so that they may conform their lives to them" (*Catechism of the Catholic Church*, 1363).

Verses 9 and 16 show that the two rites will be the distinguishing mark of the Israelite people. We do not know if they interpreted it as an external sign or whether this was the origin of the later custom of wearing phylacteries, that is, tiny rolls of parchment tied to the forehead

estis de Aegypto et de domo servitutis, quoniam in manu forti eduxit vos Dominus de loco isto, ut non comedatis fermentatum panem. ⁴Hodie egredimini, mense Abib (*id est novarum Frugum*). ⁵Cumque introduxerit te Dominus in terram Chananaei et Hetthaei et Amorraei et Hevaei et Iebusaei, quam iuravit patribus tuis, ut daret tibi, terram fluentem lacte et melle; celebrabis hunc morem sacrorum mense isto. ⁶Septem diebus vesceris azymis, et in die septimo erit sollemnitas Domini. ⁷Azyma comedetis septem diebus: non apparebit apud te aliquid fermentatum nec in cunctis finibus tuis. ⁸Narrabisque filio tuo in die illo dicens: 'Propter hoc, quod fecit mihi Dominus, quando egressus sum de Aegypto'. ⁹Et erit quasi signum in manu tua et quasi monumentum inter oculos tuos, ut lex Domini semper sit in ore tuo; in manu enim forti eduxit te Dominus de Aegypto. ¹⁰Custodies huiuscemodi

Ex 13:1–2 **Instructions about redeeming the first-born**

¹¹"And when the LORD brings you into the land of the Canaanites,
Gen 22:1 as he swore to you and your fathers, and shall give it to you, ¹²you
Lk 2:23 shall set apart to the LORD all that first opens the womb. All the
firstlings of your cattle that are males shall be the LORD'S. ¹³Every
firstling of an ass you shall redeem with a lamb, or if you will not
redeem it you shall break its neck. Every first-born of man among
Ex 12:26; 13:8 your sons you shall redeem. ¹⁴And when in time to come your son
asks you, 'What does this mean?' you shall say to him, 'By
strength of hand the LORD brought us out of Egypt, from the
Lk 2:23 house of bondage. ¹⁵For when Pharaoh stubbornly refused to let
us go, the LORD slew all the first-born in the land of Egypt, both
the first-born of man and the first-born of cattle. Therefore I sacrifice to the LORD all the males that first open the womb; but all
Deut 6:8; 11:18 the first-born of my sons I redeem.' ¹⁶It shall be as a mark on your
hand or frontlets between your eyes; for by a strong hand the
LORD brought us out of Egypt."

5. THE DEPARTURE FROM EGYPT

A roundabout way

¹⁷When Pharaoh let the people go, God did not lead them by way
Gen 50:25 of the land of the Philistines, although that was near; for God said,

---

and arm, on which were written the words
of Deuteronomy 6:4–9 and 11:13–21.

13:17–18. The geographical information
given in the book of Exodus is insuffi-
cient to enable us to say exactly what
route the Israelites took through the Sinai
peninsula. The sacred author probably
did not intend to give a detailed chronicle, but to describe the places and events

which help to show God's constant presence among his people. We do know that
they did not take any of the normal routes
but used a roundabout way through the
desert (v. 18), in the direction of the Red
Sea. This sea goes round the Sinai, form-
ing the gulf of Akabah to the east and the
gulf of Suez to the west. The construction
of the Suez canal had a considerable
impact on the topography, but we do

---

cultum statuto tempore a diebus in dies. ¹¹Cumque introduxerit te Dominus in terram Chananaei, sicut
iuravit tibi et patribus tuis, et dederit tibi eam, ¹²separabis omne, quod aperit vulvam, Domino et quod
primitivum est in pecoribus tuis; quidquid habueris masculini sexus, consecrabis Domino.
¹³Primogenitum asini mutabis ove; quod, si non redemeris, interficies. Omne autem primogenitum
hominis de filiis tuis pretio redimes. ¹⁴Cumque interrogaverit te filius tuus cras dicens: 'Quid est hoc?',
respondebis ei: 'In manu forti eduxit nos Dominus de Aegypto, de domo servitutis. ¹⁵Nam, cum indura-
tus esset pharao et nollet nos dimittere, occidit Dominus omne primogenitum in terra Aegypti, a primogenito hominis usque ad primogenitum iumentorum; idcirco immolo Domino omne, quod aperit
vulvam, masculini sexus, et omnia primogenita filiorum meorum redimo'. ¹⁶Erit igitur quasi signum

"Lest the people repent when they see war, and return to Egypt." ^{Josh 24:32}
¹⁸But God led the people round by the way of the wilderness ^{Num 33:5–6}
toward the Red Sea. And the people of Israel went up out of the
land of Egypt equipped for battle. ¹⁹And Moses took the bones of
Joseph with him; for Joseph had solemnly sworn the people of ^{Ex 40:36}
Israel, saying, "God will visit you; then you must carry my bones ^{Num 14:14}
with you from here." ²⁰And they moved on from Succoth, and ^{Deut 1:33} ^{Ps 78:14; 105:39}
encamped at Etham, on the edge of the wilderness. ²¹And the ^{Neh 9:19}
LORD went before them by day in a pillar of cloud to lead them ^{Wis 10:17–18; 18:3}
along the way, and by night in a pillar of fire to give them light, ^{Is 4:5}
that they might travel by day and by night; ²²the pillar of cloud by ^{Jn 8:12; 10:4} ^{1 Cor 10:1}
day and the pillar of fire by night did not depart from before the ^{Rev 10:1}
people.

---

know that, between the gulf of Suez and the Mediterranean there was a series of lakes and marshes which were affected by tides, which gave those waters a reddish hue; this is the reason why this whole area is also called the Red Sea; the Septuagint Greek (and with it the New Testament: Acts 7:36 and Heb 11:29) speaks here of the Eritrean Sea (*erythrós* means "red"). The Hebrew text, on the other hand, calls it the "Sea of Reeds" on account of the large amount of papyrus reeds on its banks. It is more than likely that the Israelites led by Moses crossed one of these marshy areas, and not the sea itself.

13:19. This piece of information is important because it serves to identify the Israelites who left Egypt with those of the patriarchal period.

Joseph made his brothers swear that they would not leave his bones in Egypt (cf. Gen 50:25). When they are leaving the country, the sons of Israel bring his remains with them and, according to the book of Joshua (24:32), those who settled in the land promised to the patriarchs buried them in Shechem. In this way, the memory of Joseph is a further link between the patriarchal traditions, those of the Exodus and those to do with taking possession of the Land.

13:21–22. The cloud and the fire are the sign that shows God is with them. The sacred writer gives all these details to make it clear that the entire people saw with their eyes that God himself had brought them out of Egypt, was leading them, was protecting them, and was making himself manifest to them.

---

in manu tua et quasi appensum quid ob recordationem inter oculos tuos, eo quod in manu forti eduxit nos Dominus de Aegypto». ¹⁷Igitur cum emisisset pharao populum, non eos duxit Deus per viam terrae Philisthim, quae vicina est, reputans ne forte paeniteret populum, si vidisset adversum se bella consurgere, et reverteretur in Aegyptum, ¹⁸sed circumduxit per viam deserti, quae est iuxta mare Rubrum. Et armati ascenderunt filii Israel de terra Aegypti. ¹⁹Tulit quoque Moyses ossa Ioseph secum, eo quod adiurasset filios Israel dicens: «Visitabit vos Deus; efferte ossa mea hinc vobiscum». ²⁰Profectique de Succoth castrametati sunt in Etham, in extremis finibus solitudinis. ²¹Dominus autem praecedebat eos ad ostendendam viam per diem in columna nubis et per noctem in columna ignis, ut dux esset itineris utroque tempore. ²²Nunquam defuit columna nubis per diem nec columna ignis per noctem coram populo. ¹Locutus est autem Dominus ad Moysen dicens: ²«Loquere filiis Israel: Reversi castrameten-

The Lord shapes events*

14 ¹Then the LORD said to Moses, ²"Tell the people of Israel to turn back and encamp in front of Pi-ha-hiroth, between Migdol and the sea, in front of Baal-zephon; you shall encamp over against it, by the sea. ³For Pharaoh will say of the people of Israel, 'They are entangled in the land; the wilderness has shut them in.' ⁴And I will harden Pharaoh's heart, and he will pursue them and I will get glory over Pharaoh and all his host; and the Egyptians shall know that I am the LORD." And they did so.

Ex 16:2–3; 17:3
Num 11:1–6;
14:1–4; 20:2;
21:4–5
Ps 78:40

The Egyptians in pursuit

⁵When the king of Egypt was told that the people had fled, the mind of Pharaoh and his servants was changed toward the

---

*14:1–31. The passage of the Red Sea, a great feat of God and his people against the pharaoh and his men, is something the Old Testament harks back to constantly. Just as the death of the first-born is the last of the prodigies prior to the Exodus, so the passage of the Red Sea is the first on the people's pilgrimage in the wilderness. But it is of such importance that it came to be seen as the zenith and obligatory reference-point of God's manifestation of his might and of his love for the people. To mention the passage of the Red Sea is to speak of God's deliverance of the Israelites from bondage. When they eventually enter the promised land, the crossing of the Jordan will be recounted in similar terms (cf. Josh 3–4) and both events will be sung in tribute to the liberating power of God (cf., e.g., Ps 66:6; 74:13–15; 78:15, 53; 114:1–4).

This account bears traces of the great Jewish traditions—which suggests that each of them kept these events very much in mind. One tradition depicts the crossing of the sea as an epic event in which a series of natural elements combined spectacularly (strong winds, wheels sticking in the mud, etc.). Another puts the accent more on the miraculous side of things: the angel of God intervenes, the waters divide to form two walls through which the Israelites pass; the waters fall back into place to drown the pharaoh's chariots and cavalry, etc. Both traditions evidence the portentous action of God. Using all these elements, the writer has produced a masterly account, a veritable epic: he describes the geography of the place (v. 2); he includes God's speeches, which contain a command and an oracle (vv. 3–4, 15–18, 26); he inserts lively dialogues between Moses and the people (vv. 11–12) or Moses and God (v. 15); and above all he stresses the miraculous nature of the whole event: the pharaoh goes out with *all* his chariots (v. 7); the Lord himself gives *direct* help to the Israelites (v. 14); the Lord *looked down* on the Egyptians (v. 24)—which is

---

tur e regione Phihahiroth, quae est inte Magdolum et mare contra Beelsephon; in conspectu eius castra ponetis super mare. ³Dicturusque est pharao super filiis Israel: 'Errant in terra, conclusit eos desertum'. ⁴Et indurabo cor eius, ac persequetur eos, et glorificabor in pharaone et in omni exercitu eius; scientque Aegyptii quia ego sum Dominus». Feceruntque ita. ⁵Et nuntiatum est regi Aegyptiorum quod fugisset populus; immutatumque est cor pharaonis et servorum eius super populo, et dixerunt: «Quid hoc fecimus, ut dimitteremus Israel, ne servirent nobis?». ⁶Iunxit ergo currum et omnem populum

people, and they said, "What is this we have done, that we have let Israel go from serving us?" ⁶So he made ready his chariot and took his army with him, ⁷and took six hundred picked chariots and all the other chariots of Egypt with officers over all of them. ⁸And the LORD hardened the heart of Pharaoh king of Egypt and he pursued the people of Israel as they went forth defiantly. ⁹The Egyptians pursued them, all Pharaoh's horses and chariots and his horsemen and his army, and overtook them encamped at the sea, by Pi-ha-hiroth, in front of Baal-zephon.

¹⁰When Pharaoh drew near, the people of Israel lifted up their eyes, and behold, the Egyptians were marching after them; and they were in great fear. And the people of Israel cried out to the LORD; ¹¹and they said to Moses, "Is it because there are no graves

---

enough to frighten them (v. 24); etc. The end result is a real conviction that God has brought about the deliverance of his people. That is why, over the history of Israel, the Israelites will always look back to this event whenever they need to strengthen their hope of receiving further divine help at times of misfortune, or when they want to sing God's praises in times of prosperity. St Paul sees in the passage of the sea a figure of Christian Baptism. Baptism marks the start of salvation, and the start also of a persevering effort on the Christian's part to respond to it (cf. 1 Cor 10:1–5).

14:1–4. The positions of these cities has not yet been accurately established; it seems certain that they were situated in the marshy region north of the Bitter Lakes. They may have been small villages or even places of worship known to people when the book was first written.

In this dramatic salvation event the initiative lies with God: he planned it, he

gives the orders, he makes the Egyptians turn tail (v. 25) and see "the great work of the Lord" (v. 31). All these wondrous events have a theological purpose—to make known not only to the Israelites but even to the Gentiles, the Egyptians, the basic message: He is the Lord (vv 14–18).

14:10–14. The Eygptians get so close that the Israelites are terrified; this produces their first crisis of faith: the liberty they seek means giving up a quiet life in Egypt. Moses begins to reveal himself not just as a charismatic leader but as a mediator between the people and God. The words of v. 13 underlie the theological virtue of hope: God is the one who acts, man has to stand firm in faith; he has no reason to fear. As the Letter to the Hebrews teaches, Jesus is the model of faithfulness and hope: "Therefore [. . .] let us run with perseverance the race that is set before us, looking to Jesus the pioneer and perfecter of our faith, who for the joy that was set before him endured

---

suum assumpsit secum; ⁷tulitque sescentos currus electos et quidquid in Aegypto curruum fuit et bellatores in singulis curribus. ⁸Induravitque Dominus cor pharaonis regis Aegypti, et persecutus est filios Israel; at illi egressi erant in manu excelsa. ⁹Cumque persequerentur Aegyptii vestigia praecedentium, reppererunt eos in castris super mare; omnes equi et currus pharaonis, equites et exercitus eius erant in Phihahiroth contra Beelsephon. ¹⁰Cumque appropinquasset pharao, levantes filii Israel oculos viderunt

in Egypt that you have taken us away to die in the wilderness? What have you done to us, in bringing us out of Egypt? [12]Is not this what we said to you in Egypt, 'Let us alone and let us serve the Egyptians'? For it would have been better for us to serve the Egyptians than to die in the wilderness." [13]And Moses said to the people, "Fear not, stand firm, and see the salvation of the LORD, which he will work for you today; for the Egyptians whom you see today, you shall never see again. [14]The LORD will fight for you, and you have only to be still."

Josh 3–4
Ps 66:6; 74:
13–15; 78:15,
53; 105; 106;
114:1–4
Wis 10:18–19
1 Cor 10:1–5

Crossing the Red Sea

[15]The LORD said to Moses, "Why do you cry to me? Tell the people of Israel to go forward. [16]Lift up your rod, and stretch out your hand over the sea and divide it, that the people of Israel may go on dry ground through the sea. [17]And I will harden the hearts of the Egyptians so that they shall go in after them, and I will get glory over Pharaoh and all his host, his chariots, and his horsemen. [18]And the Egyptians shall know that I am the LORD, when I have gotten glory over Pharaoh, his chariots, and his horsemen."

Gen 16:7
Is 43:1–3
Wis 19:6–9

[19]Then the angel of God who went before the host of Israel moved and went behind them; and the pillar of cloud moved from

---

the cross, despising the shame, and is seated at the right hand of the throne of God" (Heb 12:12).

14:17–18. The military language and the depiction of God as a warrior should cause no surprise: it is a daring anthropomorphism which shows that God is almighty and therefore can deliver the elect from any danger that threatens: "You, too, if you distance yourself from the Egyptians and flee far from the power

of demons," Origen comments, "will see what great helps will be provided to you each day and what great protection is available to you. All that is asked of you is that you stand firm in the faith and do not let yourself be terrified by either the Egyptian cavalry or the noise of their chariots" (*Homiliae in Exodum*, 5, 4).

14:19–22. At the wonderful moment of the crossing of the sea, God, man and the forces of nature play the leading role. In

---

Aegyptios post se et timuerunt valde clamaveruntque ad Dominum [11]et dixerunt ad Moysen: «Forsitan non erant sepulcra in Aegypto? Ideo tulisti nos, ut moreremur in solitudine. Quid hoc fecisti, ut educeres nos ex Aegypto? [12]Nonne iste est sermo, quem loquebamur ad te in Aegypto, dicentes: Recede a nobis, ut serviamus Aegyptiis? Multo enim melius erat servire eis quam mori in solitudine». [13]Et ait Moyses ad populum: «Nolite timere; state et videte salutem Domini, quam facturus est vobis hodie; Aegyptios enim, quos nunc videtis, nequaquam ultra videbitis usque in sempiternum. [14]Dominus pugnabit pro vobis, et vos silebitis». [15]Dixitque Dominus ad Moysen: «Quid clamas ad me? Loquere filiis Israel, ut proficiscantur. [16]Tu autem eleva virgam tuam et extende manum tuam super mare et divide illud, ut gradiantur filii Israel in medio mari per siccum. [17]Ego autem indurabo cor Aegyptiorum, ut persequantur eos; et glorificabor in pharaone et in omni exercitu eius, in curribus et in equitibus illius. [18]Et scient Aegyptii quia ego sum Dominus, cum glorificatus fuero in pharaone, in curribus atque

before them and stood behind them, [20]coming between the host of Egypt and the host of Israel. And there was the cloud and the darkness; and the night passed[p] without one coming near the other all night.

[21]Then Moses stretched out his hand over the sea; and the LORD drove the sea back by a strong east wind all night, and made the sea dry land, and the waters were divided. [22]And the people of Israel went into the midst of the sea on dry ground, the waters being a wall to them on their right hand and on their left. [23]The Egyptians pursued, and went in after them into the midst of the sea, all Pharaoh's horses, his chariots, and his horsemen. [24]And in the morning watch the LORD in the pillar of fire and of cloud looked down upon the host of the Egyptians, and discomfited the host of the Egyptians, [25]clogging[q] their chariot wheels so that they drove heavily; and the Egyptians said, "Let us flee from before Israel; for the LORD fights for them against the Egyptians."

[26]Then the LORD said to Moses, "Stretch out your hand over the sea, that the water may come back upon the Egyptians, upon their chariots, and upon their horsemen." [27]So Moses stretched forth his hand over the sea, and the sea returned to its wonted flow when the morning appeared; and the Egyptians fled into it, and the LORD

Ps 77:16–19
Jn 14:1
1 Cor 10:1
Heb 11:29
Deut 11:4
Heb 11:29

---

the person of the angel of the Lord, God becomes more visible; he directs operations; he plays a direct part. Moses' part consists in doing as the Lord commands; he is his vicar. The sons of Israel have no active part; they benefit from what happens. Even the forces of nature come into play: the pillar of cloud which marked the route by day now blocks the Egyptians' way; night, the symbol of evil, has become, as in the Passover, the time of

God's visitation; the warm west wind, always feared for its harmful effects, now proves a great help; and the waters of the sea, so often the symbol of the abyss and of evil, allow the victorious passage of the sons of Israel.

The prophets see this event as an instance of the creative power of God (cf. Is 43:1–3), and Christian writers comment along the same lines. Thus, Origen will say: "See the goodness of God the

in equitibus eius». [19]Tollensque se angelus Dei, qui praecedebat castra Israel, abiit post eos; et cum eo pariter columna nubis, priora dimittens, post tergum. [20]Stetit inter castra Aegyptiorum et castra Israel; et erat nubes tenebrosa et illuminans noctem, ita ut ad se invicem toto noctis tempore accedere non valerent. [21]Cumque extendisset Moyses manum super mare, reppulit illud Dominus, flante vento vehementi et urente tota nocte, et vertit in siccum; divisaque est aqua. [22]Et ingressi sunt filii Israel per medium maris sicci; erat enim aqua quasi murus a dextra eorum et laeva. [23]Persequentesque Aegyptii ingressi sunt post eos, omnis equitatus pharaonis, currus eius et equites per medium maris. [24]Iamque advenerat vigilia matutina, et ecce respiciens Dominus super castra Aegyptiorum per columnam ignis et nubis perturbavit exercitum eorum; [25]et impedivit rotas curruum, ita ut difficile moverentur. Dixerunt ergo Aegyptii: «Fugiamus Israelem! Dominus enim pugnat pro eis contra nos». [26]Et ait Dominus ad Moysen: «Extende manum tuam super mare, ut revertantur aquae ad Aegyptios super currus et equi-

p. Gk: Heb *and it lit up the night*   **q.** Or *binding*. Sam Gk Syr: Heb *removing*

routed[r] the Egyptians in the midst of the sea. [28]The waters returned and covered the chariots and the horsemen and all the host[s] of Pharaoh that had followed them into the sea; not so much as one of them remained. [29]But the people of Israel walked on dry ground through the sea, the waters being a wall to them on their right hand and on their left.

[30]Thus the LORD saved Israel that day from the hand of the Egyptians; and Israel saw the Egyptians dead upon the seashore.

Ex 4:31   [31]And Israel saw the great work which the LORD did against the Egyptians, and the people feared the LORD; and they believed in the LORD and in his servant Moses.

Song of victory*

Wis 10:20
Rev 15:3

15 [1]Then Moses and the people of Israel sang this song to the LORD, saying,

---

Creator: if you submit to his will and follow his Law, he will see to it that created things cooperate with you, against their own nature if necessary" (*Homiliae in Exodum*, 5,5).

The book of Wisdom turns the account of the crossing of the sea into a hymn of praise to the Lord who delivered Israel (cf. Wis 19:6–9), and St Paul sees the waters as a figure of baptismal water: "All were baptized into Moses in the cloud and in the sea" (1 Cor 10:2).

14:31. The main effect the miraculous crossing of the sea had on the Israelites was the faith it gave them in the power of God and in the authority of Moses. This section of the account of the escape from Egypt ends as it began—that is, showing that the people's faith (4:31) is now

strengthened. So, too, Christian faith is strengthened when we do what God desires: "Following Jesus on his way. You have understood what our Lord was asking from you and you have decided to accompany him on his way. You are trying to walk in his footsteps, to clothe yourself in Christ's clothing, to be Christ himself: well, your faith, your faith in the light our Lord is giving you, must be both operative and full of sacrifice" (St Josemaría Escrivá, *Friends of God*, 198).

***15:1–21.** This victory anthem, along with that of Deborah (Judg 5), is one of the oldest hymns of Israel. It probably goes as far back as the 13th century BC, long before the redactor of this book decided to include it as a colophon to his Exodus account. It is called the "Song of

---

tes eorum». [27]Cumque extendisset Moyses manum contra mare, reversum est primo diluculo ad priorem locum; fugientibusque Aegyptiis occurrerunt aquae, et involvit eos Dominus in mediis fluctibus. [28]Reversaeque sunt aquae et operuerunt currus et equites cuncti exercitus pharaonis, qui sequentes ingressi fuerant mare; ne unus quidem superfuit ex eis. [29]Filii autem Israel perrexerunt per medium sicci maris, et aquae eis erant quasi pro muro a dextris et a sinistris. [30]Liberavitque Dominus in die illo Israel de manu Aegyptiorum. Et viderunt Aegyptios mortuos super litus maris [31]et manum magnam, quam exercuerat Dominus contra eos; timuitque populus Dominum et crediderunt Domino et Moysi servo eius. [1]Tunc cecinit Moyses et filii Israel carmen hoc Domino, et dixerunt: «Cantemus Domino, / gloriose enim magnificatus est: / equum et ascensorem eius / deiecit in mare! / [2]Fortitudo mea et robur

r. Heb *shook off*   **s.** Gk Syr: Heb *to all the host*

"I will sing to the LORD, for he has triumphed gloriously;
    the horse and his rider[t] he has thrown into the sea.
[2]The LORD is my strength and my song,   Is 12:2
    and he has become my salvation;
this is my God, and I will praise him,
    my father's God, and I will exalt him.
[3]The LORD is a man of war;   Gen 3:14
    the LORD is his name.

[4]"Pharaoh's chariots and his host he cast into the sea;   Acts 7:36
    and his picked officers are sunk in the Red Sea.

Miriam" (v. 21) because, as we know from Ugarit poems of the period (13th–9th centuries BC) it was the practice to put at the end (not the start) the reason why the poem was written, the author's name and the poem's title (vv. 18–21). It is very likely that this canticle was recited in the liturgy and that the entire people said the response (vv. 1, 21) after each stanza was said or sung by the choir.

It is a hymn of praise and thanksgiving in which the three stages of the deliverance of Israel are remembered—the prodigies of the Red Sea (vv. 4–10), the triumphal pilgrimage in the desert (vv. 14–16) and the taking possession of the land of Canaan (vv. 17–18).

In this poetic re-creation of these events the divine attributes are extolled one by one (might, military power, redemption, etc); they reflect the theological implications of exodus, wilderness and land: it is God who has done all these wondrous things; he has done them because he has chosen the people to be his very own; he himself requires that they respond by acknowledging him to be God, Lord of all, the only deliverer.

15:1–3. Victory over the Egyptians has revealed the glory and might of God. Strength, power, salvation can be taken as meaning the same thing, for the sacred author does not regard the divine attributes as abstract qualities but as particular actions: only God could truly save the people.

"The Lord is a man of war": this daring description indicates that this is a very ancient poem. Some translations, possibly because they thought it might be misunderstood, toned it down a little: the Samaritan Pentateuch has "powerful in combat" and the Septuagint "he who breaks through battles". The Spanish version coincides with the RSV and the New Vulgate, retaining the blunt military imagery, which is very descriptive of the almighty power of God: "He is the Lord of the Universe [. . .]. He is master of history, governing hearts and events in keeping with his will" (*Catechism of the Catholic Church*, 269).

"The Lord is his name": literally, "his name is Yah", using an abbreviation of Yahweh which may have been customary in more ancient times. It may well be that there is an echo of this name in the "Alleluia" of the Psalms.

meum Dominus, / et factus est mihi in salutem. / Iste Deus meus, / et glorificabo eum; / Deus patris mei, / et exaltabo eum! / [3]Dominus quasi vir pugnator; / Dominus nomen eius! / [4]Currus pharaonis et exercitum eius / proiecit in mare, / electi bellatores eius / submersi sunt in mari Rubro. / [5]Abyssi ope-

t. Or *its chariot*

⁵The floods cover them;
    they went down into the depths like a stone.

⁶Thy right hand, O LORD, glorious in power,
    thy right hand, O LORD, shatters the enemy.

⁷In the greatness of thy majesty thou overthrowest thy
    adversaries;
    thou sendest forth thy fury, it consumes them like stubble.

⁸At the blast of thy nostrils the waters piled up,
    the floods stood up in a heap;
    the deeps congealed in the heart of the sea.

⁹The enemy said, 'I will pursue, I will overtake,
    I will divide the spoil, my desire shall have its fill of them.
    I will draw my sword, my hand shall destroy them.'

¹⁰Thou didst blow with thy wind, the sea covered them;
    they sank as lead in the mighty waters.

¹¹"Who is like thee, O LORD, among the gods?
    Who is like thee, majestic in holiness,
    terrible in glorious deeds, doing wonders?

¹²Thou didst stretch out thy right hand,
    the earth swallowed them.

¹³"Thou hast led in thy steadfast love
    the people whom thou hast redeemed,

Margin references:
Jer 51:63
Rev 18:21
Is 5:24
Obad 18
Nahum 1:10

Lev 19:2
Rev 13:4

15:4–12. The crossing of the Red Sea is viewed as a sort of dyptych: on the one hand, the defeat of the Egyptians (vv. 4–5) leads to praise of God as the victor ("thy right hand", "thy majesty", "the blast of thy nostrils": vv. 6–8); on the other hand, the machinations of the enemy and God's intervening to punish them (vv. 9–10) leads to an act of faith in God: "Who is like thee, O Lord?" (vv. 11–13).

Faith in God, according to the Bible, is not something theoretical or based on philosophical reasoning; it is something practical and based on experience: one believes in God because one has experienced his powerful protection, one knows that he alone saves in a loving way.

15:8. "The deeps congealed in the heart of the sea": that is, the bottom of the sea was filled with the dead bodies of the enemy.

15:13–18. The image of the Red Sea is used to look ahead to the conquest of Canaan: the peoples there are so afraid

---

ruerunt eos, / descenderunt in profundum quasi lapis. / ⁶Dextera tua, Domine, / magnifice in fortitudine, / dextera tua, Domine, / percussit inimicum. / ⁷Et in multitudine gloriae tuae / deposuisti adversarios tuos; / misisti iram tuam, / quae devoravit eos sicut stipulam. / ⁸Et in spiritu furoris tui / congregatae sunt aquae; / stetit ut agger / unda fluens, / coagulatae sunt abyssi / in medio mari. / ⁹Dixit inimicus: / 'Persequar, comprehendam; / dividam spolia, / implebitur anima mea: / evaginabo gladium meum, / interficiet eos manus mea!'. / ¹⁰Flavit spiritus tuus, / et operuit eos mare; / submersi sunt quasi plumbum / in aquis vehementibus. / ¹¹Quis similis tui / in diis, Domine? / Quis similis tui, / magnificus in sanctitate, / terribilis atque laudabilis, / faciens mirabilia? / ¹²Extendisti manum tuam, / devoravit eos

thou hast guided them by thy strength to thy holy abode.

¹⁴The peoples have heard, they tremble;   Rev 11:18

    pangs have seized on the inhabitants of Philistia.

¹⁵Now are the chiefs of Edom dismayed;   Num 20:21;

    the leaders of Moab, trembling seizes them;   21:4–13

                             Deut 2:1–9

    all the inhabitants of Canaan have melted away.

¹⁶Terror and dread fall upon them;   Is 11:11

    because of the greatness of thy arm, they are as still as a stone, Ps 74:2

till thy people, O LORD, pass by,   I Kings 8:13

                             Rev 11:11

    till the people pass by whom thou hast purchased.   Eph 1:14

¹⁷Thou wilt bring them in, and plant them on thy own mountain,

    the place, O LORD, which thou hast made for thy abode,

    the sanctuary, LORD, which thy hands have established.

¹⁸The LORD will reign for ever and ever."

¹⁹For when the horses of Pharaoh with his chariots and his horsemen went into the sea, the LORD brought back the waters of the

---

that they act as the ways of the sea did: they become immobile, as if made of stone, while the Israelites pass through their lands in triumph.

Since this is a poetic re-creation, the author does not want to limit himself to what exactly did happen when the Land was conquered: he just sketches in a few lines the peoples whom Israel will find there, on "thy own mountain", where the Lord's sanctuary is to be built. This does not mean that this part must necessarily have been written after the conquest of Palestine; it could be that the writer visualized that the Land would be conquered in this wonderful way, proving that it was the work of the Lord and showing his almighty power over all things, as the last verse puts it: "The Lord will reign for ever" (v. 18). The Vulgate translated

these words as "God reigns over all eternity and more", and some medieval philosophers used this to argue that it was not quite correct to say that God is eternal, for it would seem that some created things are also eternal. St Thomas replies, with his usual precision, saying that on the one hand God in his be-ing surpasses any imaginable duration, and on the other "even if something else were to exist forever, as certain philosophers believed the rotation of the heavens to do, the Lord would still reign beyond it, because his reign is instantaneously whole" (*Summa theologiae* 1, 10, 2 ad 2).

15:19–21. It was customary among the Israelites for women to celebrate victory in song and dance (cf. Judg 11:34; 1 Sam 18:6–7). This epilogue once more recalls

terra. / ¹³Dux fuisti in misericordia tua / populo, quem redemisti, / et portasti eum in fortitudine tua / ad habitaculum sanctum tuum. / ¹⁴Attenderunt populi et commoti sunt, / dolores obtinuerunt habitatores Philisthaeae. / ¹⁵Tunc conturbati sunt principes Edom, / potentes Moab obtinuit tremor, / obriguerunt omnes habitatores Chanaan. / ¹⁶Irruit super eos / formido et pavor; / in magnitudine brachii tui / fiunt immobiles quasi lapis, / donec pertranseat populus tuus, Domine, / donec pertranseat populus tuus iste, / quem possedisti. / ¹⁷Introduces eos et plantabis / in monte hereditatis tuae, / firmissimo habitaculo tuo, / quod operatus es, Domine, / sanctuario, Domine, / quod firmaverunt manus tuae. / ¹⁸Dominus regnabit / in aeternum et ultra!». ¹⁹Ingressi sunt enim equi pharaonis cum curribus et equi-

99

Num 26:59
Judg 11:34
1 Sam 18:6–7

sea upon them; but the people of Israel walked on dry ground in the midst of the sea. ²⁰Then Miriam, the prophetess, the sister of Aaron, took a timbrel in her hand; and all the women went out after her with timbrels and dancing. ²¹And Miriam sang to them:

"Sing to the LORD, for he has triumphed gloriously;
the horse and his rider he has thrown into the sea."

6. ISRAEL IN THE DESERT*

The bitter water of Marah

Ex 17:5–6
Num 20:7–11;
33:8

²²Then Moses led Israel onward from the Red Sea, and they went into the wilderness of Shur; they went three days in the wilderness

---

the epic crossing of the Red Sea, the festive dancing and the refrain of the canticle.

Miriam (*Miryam* in Hebrew) is described as a prophetess (v. 20) because, together with Aaron, she is portrayed as being a spokesperson of God (cf. Num 12:2) and, as we see here, the composer of this hymn. Deborah is also described as a prophetess (cf. Judg 4:4) and to her is attributed another of the most ancient canticles (cf. Judg 5:1–31). The prophets say that it will be a sign of the messianic age that "your sons and daughters shall prophesy" (Joel 2:28).

*15:22—18:27. During the first stage of their sojourn in the wilderness, the sons of Israel became gradually more aware of themselves as being a people, chosen by God to carry out a special mission. Their experiences in the desert (chaps. 16–18) and the promulgation of the laws (chaps 19–24) will give them a clear hierarchical structure and reassure them of God's special protection.

In this stage of consolidation of their national identify, God first puts them to

the test through the rigours of desert life—unvaried diet (chap. 16) and shortage of water (17:1–7). After a while Moses' leadership, already clear since the time they left Egypt, is strengthened and widened in scope: he is now their mediator (17:8–16) and a judge along with the elders (chap. 18).

15:22–27. Once they start to travel through the desert the first difficulty they meet is a shortage of water; this is going to happen more than once (cf. 17:5–6; Num 20:7–11). It is difficult to say where Marah and Elim were; most scholars accept that Marah is Ayun Mûsa (Fountain of Moses) a few kilometres/ miles from where the crossing of the sea took place; Elim may be present-day Wadi Garandel, about 80 kilometers (50 miles) from Marah. Naturally, desert caravans encamped near wells or natural springs which gave rise to small leafy oases.

This episode contains a number of things which are reminiscent of important events or truths—the discovery that the water is undrinkable (the popular ety-

---

tibus eius in mare, et reduxit super eos Dominus aquas maris; filii autem Israel ambulaverunt per siccum in medio eius. ²⁰Sumpsit ergo Maria prophetissa soror Aaron tympanum in manu sua; egressaeque sunt omnes mulieres post eam cum tympanis et choris, ²¹quibus praecinebat dicens: «Cantemus Domino, / gloriose enim magnificatus est: / equum et ascensorem eius / deiecit in mare!». ²²Tulit autem Moyses Israel de mari Rubro, et egressi sunt in desertum Sur; ambulaveruntque tribus diebus per soli-

and found no water. [23]When they came to Marah, they could not drink the water of Marah because it was bitter; therefore it was named Marah.[u] [24]And the people murmured against Moses, saying, "What shall we drink?" [25]And he cried to the LORD; and the LORD showed him a tree, and he threw it into the water, and the water became sweet.

There the LORD[v] made for them a statute and an ordinance and there he proved them, [26]saying, "If you will diligently hearken to the voice of the LORD your God, and do that which is right in his eyes, and give heed to his commandments and keep all his statutes, I will put none of the diseases upon you which I put upon the Egyptians; for I am the LORD, your healer."

[27]Then they came to Elim, where there were twelve springs of water and seventy palm trees; and they encamped there by the water.

The manna and the quails*

16 [1]They set out from Elim, and all the congregation of the people of Israel came to the wilderness of Sin, which is

Margin references:
Heb 38
Rev 8:11
Ex 14:11
Sir 38:5
Num 11
Deut 8:3, 16
Josh 5:10–12
Ps 78
Wis 16:20–29
Jn 6:26–58

---

mology of Marah is "bitter" or "bitterness"), which recalls the first plague of Egypt (v. 26); the people's complaints, so often repeated (cf. 16:2; 17:3; Num 14:2; 20:3; etc.); Moses' intercession; the first mention of a divine ordinance or law; the promise of divine protection and the description of God as "healer"; and the arrival at Elim, a place where there were trees and plenty of water. All this combines to convey an essential teaching: because of the special love God has shown his people, he will look after their welfare, as long as they obey him.

The first Christian commentators saw in this account symbols of things to do with the New Covenant: in the tree that Moses threw into the waters to purify them, they see a prefigurement of the cross by which we are all healed (St Justin, Origen, St Cyril of Alexandria); in the twelve springs and seventy palm trees, the seventy disciples sent out by our Lord, and the twelve Apostles (Origen, St Gregory of Nyssa).

*16:1–36. The prodigy of the manna and the quails was a very important sign of God's special providence towards his people while they were in the desert. It is recounted here and in Numbers 11, but in both accounts facts are interwoven with

---

tudinem et non inveniebant aquam. [23]Et venerunt in Mara, nec poterant bibere aquas de Mara, eo quod essent amarae; unde vocatum est nomen eius Mara (*id est Amaritudo*). [24]Et murmuravit populus contra Moysen dicens: «Quid bibemus?». [25]At ille clamavit ad Dominum, qui ostendit ei lignum; quod cum misisset in aquas, in dulcedinem versae sunt. Ibi constituit ei praecepta atque iudicia et ibi tentavit eum [26]dicens: «Si audieris vocem Domini Dei tui et, quod rectum est coram eo, feceris et oboedieris mandatis eius custodierisque omnia praecepta illius, cunctum languorem, quem posui in Aegypto, non inducam super te: Ego enim Dominus sanator tuus». [27]Venerunt autem in Elim, ubi erant duodecim fontes aquarum et septuaginta palmae; et castrametati sunt iuxta aquas. [1]Profectique sunt de Elim, et venit

u. That is *Bitterness* **v.** Heb *he*

between Elim and Sinai, on the fifteenth day of the second month
_{I Cor 10:10} after they had departed from the land of Egypt. ²And the whole
congregation of the people of Israel murmured against Moses and
_{Ex 14:11} Aaron in the wilderness, ³and said to them, "Would that we had
died by the hand of the LORD in the land of Egypt, when we sat by
the fleshpots and ate bread to the full; for you have brought us out
into this wilderness to kill this whole assembly with hunger."

---

interpretation of same and with things to do with worship and ethics.

Some scholars have argued that the manna is the same thing as a sweet secretion that comes from the tamarisk (*tamarix mannifera*) when punctured by a particular insect commonly found in the mountains of Sinai. The drops of this resin solidify in the coldness of the night and some fall to the ground. They have to be gathered up early in the morning because they deteriorate at twenty-four degrees temperature Celsius (almost seventy-five degrees Fahrenheit). Even today desert Arabs collect them and use them for sucking and as a sweetener in confectionery.

As we know, quails cross the Sinai peninsula on their migrations back and forth between Africa and Europe or Asia. In May or June, when they return from Africa they usually rest in Sinai, exhausted after a long sea crossing; they can be easily trapped at this point.

Although these phenomenon can show where the manna and the quail come from, the important thing is that the Israelites saw them as wonders worked by God. The sacred writer stops to describe the impact the manna had on the sons of Israel. They are puzzled by it, as can be seen from their remarks when it comes for the first time: "What is it?" they ask, which in Hebrew sounds like "man hû", that is, manna (v. 15), which is how the Greek translation puts it. Indeed, the need to collect it every day gave rise to complaints about some people being greedy (v. 20) and who did not understand the scope of God's gift (v. 15). And just as manna is a divine gift to meet a basic human need (nourishment), so too the divine precepts, specifically that of the sabbath, are a free gift from the Lord (v. 28). So, obedience is not a heavy burden but the exercise of a capacity to receive the good things that God gives to those who obey him.

The prodigy of the manna will resound right through the Bible: in the "Deuteronomic" tradition it is a test that God gives his people to show them that "man does not live by bread alone, but [. . .] by everything that proceeds from the mouth of the Lord" (Deut 8:3). The psalmist discovers that manna is "the bread of the strong" ("of angels", says the Vulgate and the RSV), which God sent in abundance (Ps 78:23ff; cf. Ps 105:40). The book of Wisdom spells out the features of this bread from heaven "ready to eat, providing every pleasure and suited to every taste" (Wis 16:20–29). And the New Testament reveals the full depth of this "spiritual" food (1 Cor 10:3), for, as the *Catechism* teaches, "manna in the desert prefigured

omnis congregatio filiorum Israel in desertum Sin, quod est inter Elim et Sinai, quinto decimo die mensis secundi postquam egressi sunt de terra Aegypti. ²Et murmuravit omnis congregatio filiorum Israel contra Moysen et Aaron in solitudine, ³dixeruntque filii Israel ad eos: «Utinam mortui essemus

⁴Then the LORD said to Moses, "Behold, I will rain bread from
heaven for you; and the people shall go out and gather a day's
portion every day, that I may prove them, whether they will walk
in my law or not. ⁵On the sixth day, when they prepare what they
bring in, it will be twice as much as they gather daily." ⁶So Moses
and Aaron said to all the people of Israel, "At evening you shall
know that it was the LORD who brought you out of the land of
Egypt, ⁷and in the morning you shall see the glory of the LORD,
because he has heard your murmurings against the LORD. For
what are we, that you murmur against us?" ⁸And Moses said,

Jn 6:32
1 Cor 10:3

2 Cor 3:18

the Eucharist, 'the true bread from
heaven' (Jn 6:32)" (*Catechism of the
Catholic Church*, 1094).

16:1. From the Byzantine period
onwards, Christian tradition has identified Sinai with the range of mountains in
the south of the Sinai peninsula; these
mountains go as high as 2,500 metres
(8,200 feet) above sea level.

The main mountains are Djébel
Serbal, Djébel Katerina and Djébel
Mûsa, the last mentioned of which tradition regards as Mount Sinai or Horeb. At
the foot of this mountain lies the
monastery of St Catherine. The desert of
Sin (different from the desert of the same
name running along the side of the Dead
Sea: cf. the note on Num 20:1–19), is
very near to this; people involved in
mining the copper and turquoise that is
found there used to camp there temporar-
ily.

16:2–3. The complaining that usually
precedes the desert prodigies (cf. 14:11;
15:24; 17:3; Num 11:1, 4; 14:2; 20:2;
21:4–5) brings into focus the chosen

people's lack of faith and hope, and (by
contrast) the faithfulness of God, who
time and again alleviates their needs even
though they do not deserve it. At the
same time, just as Moses and Aaron listened patiently to complaints, God too is
always ready to dialogue with the sinner,
sometimes listening to his complaints
and sorting them out, and sometimes
simply giving him a chance to repent:
"Although God could inflict punishment
on those whom he condemns without
saying anything, he does not do so; on
the contrary, up to the point when he
does condemn, he speaks with the guilty
person and lets him talk, so as to help
him avoid condemnation" (Origen,
Homiliae in Ieremiam, 1,1).

16:6–7. The manna and the quails not
only alleviate the people's hunger; they
are, above all, a sign of the triple presence of God: the Lord who brought them
out of Egypt (v. 7) is not going to aban-
don them; he manifests his glory by
dominating nature; he has not brought
them out to die, but to make sure that
they survive in spite of difficulties.

per manum Domini in terra Aegypti, quando sedebamus super ollas carnium et comedebamus panem
in saturitate. Cur eduxistis nos in desertum istud, ut occideretis omnem coetum fame?». ⁴Dixit autem
Dominus ad Moysen: «Ecce ego pluam vobis panes de caelo; egrediatur populus et colligat, quae suf-
ficiunt per singulos dies, ut tentem eum, utrum ambulet in lege mea an non. ⁵Die autem sexta parabunt
quod intulerint, et duplum erit quam colligere solebant per singulos dies». ⁶Dixeruntque Moyses et
Aaron ad omnes filios Israel: «Vespere scietis / quod Dominus eduxerit vos / de terra Aegypti; / ⁷et

"When the LORD gives you in the evening flesh to eat and in the morning bread to the full, because the LORD has heard your murmurings which you murmur against him—what are we? Your murmurings are not against us but against the LORD."

⁹And Moses said to Aaron, "Say to the whole congregation of the people of Israel, 'Come near before the LORD, for he has heard your murmurings.'" ¹⁰And as Aaron spoke to the whole congregation of the people of Israel, they looked toward the wilderness, and behold, the glory of the LORD appeared in the cloud. ¹¹And the LORD said to Moses, ¹²"I have heard the murmurings of the people of Israel; say to them, 'At twilight you shall eat flesh, and in the morning you shall be filled with bread; then you shall know that I am the LORD your God.'"

¹³In the evening quails came up and covered the camp; and in the morning dew lay round about the camp. ¹⁴And when the dew had gone up, there was on the face of the wilderness a fine, flake-like thing, fine as hoar frost on the ground.* ¹⁵When the people of Israel saw it, they said to one another, "What is it?"ʷ For they did not know what it was. And Moses said to them, "It is the bread which the LORD has given you to eat. ¹⁶This is what the LORD has

Rom 9:4
2 Cor 3:18

Jn 6:32
1 Cor 10:2

16:16–20. The people of God are made up of members who enjoy equality of rights. From the very start, from the very constitution of the nation, there is a sense of social responsibility which imposes limits on the ownership of property. Greed is symptomatic of a grave mistrust in the Lord who "each day" provides sufficient to meet one's needs. The episode of the manna confirms the need to trust in God alone; so, when someone tries to gather up more than he needs, it rots (vv. 20–21). The Bible, and the Church later

on, have tried to shed light on social questions and, specifically the right to and limitations on private property. "Christian tradition", John Paul II writes, "has never upheld this right as absolute and untouchable. On the contrary, it has always understood this right within the broader context of the right common to all to use the goods of the whole of creation: *the right to private property is subordinated to the right to common use*, to the fact that goods are meant for everyone" (*Laborem exercens*, 14).

mane videbitis / gloriam Domini. Audivit enim murmur vestrum contra Dominum. Nos vero quid sumus, quia mussitatis contra nos?». ⁸Et ait Moyses: «Dabit Dominus vobis / vespere carnes edere / et mane panes in saturitate, / eo quod audierit murmurationes vestras, quibus murmurati estis contra eum. Nos enim quid sumus? Nec contra nos est murmur vestrum, sed contra Dominum». ⁹Dixitque Moyses ad Aaron: «Dic universae congregationi filiorum Israel: Accedite coram Domino; audivit enim murmur vestrum». ¹⁰Cumque loqueretur Aaron ad omnem coetum filiorum Israel, respexerunt ad solitudinem, et ecce gloria Domini apparuit in nube. ¹¹Locutus est autem Dominus ad Moysen dicens: ¹²«Audivi murmurationes filiorum Israel. Loquere ad eos: Vespere comedetis carnes et mane saturabimini panibus scietisque quod ego sum Dominus Deus vester». ¹³Factum est ergo vespere, et ascendens coturnix operuit castra; mane quoque ros iacuit per circuitum castrorum. ¹⁴Cumque operuisset superficiem deserti,

w. Or *"It is manna."* Heb *man hu*

commanded: 'Gather of it, every man of you, as much as he can eat; you shall take an omer apiece, according to the number of the persons whom each of you has in his tent.'" ¹⁷And the people of Israel did so; they gathered, some more, some less. ¹⁸But when *2 Cor 8:15* they measured it with an omer, he that gathered much had nothing over, and he that gathered little had no lack; each gathered according to what he could eat. ¹⁹And Moses said to them, "Let *Mt 6:34* no man leave any of it till the morning." ²⁰But they did not listen to Moses; some left part of it till the morning, and it bred worms and became foul; and Moses was angry with them. ²¹Morning by morning they gathered it, each as much as he could eat; but when the sun grew hot, it melted.

²²On the sixth day they gathered twice as much bread, two *Gen 12:1–3* omers apiece; and when all the leaders of the congregation came *Ex 20:11* and told Moses, ²³he said to them, "This is what the LORD has *Deut 5:15* commanded: 'Tomorrow is a day of solemn rest, a holy sabbath to the LORD; bake what you will bake and boil what you will boil, and all that is left over lay by to be kept till the morning.'" ²⁴So they laid it by till the morning, as Moses bade them; and it did not become foul, and there were no worms in it. ²⁵Moses said, "Eat it

---

16:22–30. The sabbath is the day consecrated entirely to God; therefore, it is unlawful to do the tasks one does on other days. There are social reasons for rest on the seventh day: the calendar is arranged by weeks and work is so organized as to allow all in the household, animals included, to be given a day of rest each week. But it is the religious side of the sabbath that Holy Scripture emphasizes most, and there are two aspects to it—imitation of God, and commemoration of the deliverance-salvation obtained by the Exodus. To ground the idea that sabbath observance is an imitation of God (cf. the Ten Commandments in 20:11), the Priestly tradition's account of creation spans six days in such a way that God rested and blessed the seventh day (Gen 2:1–3). To show that each sabbath commemorated deliverance from Egypt (cf. Deut 5:15), the same tradition, when recounting the prodigy of the manna (in the passage we are discussing) stresses the observance of the sabbath rest.

---

apparuit minutum et squamatum in similitudinem pruinae super terram. ¹⁵Quod cum vidissent filii Israel, dixerunt ad invicem: «Manhu?» (*quod significat: «Quid est hoc?»*). Ignorabant enim quid esset. Quibus ait Moyses: «Iste est panis, quem dedit Dominus vobis ad vescendum. ¹⁶Hic est sermo, quem praecepit Dominus: 'Colligat ex eo unusquisque quantum sufficiat ad vescendum; gomor per singula capita iuxta numerum animarum vestrarum, quae habitant in tabernaculo, sic tolletis'». ¹⁷Feceruntque ita filii Israel; et collegerunt alius plus, alius minus. ¹⁸Et mensi sunt ad mensuram gomor; nec qui plus collegerat, habuit amplius, nec qui minus paraverat, repperit minus, sed singuli, iuxta id quod edere poterant, congregaverunt. ¹⁹Dixitque Moyses ad eos: «Nullus relinquat ex eo in mane». ²⁰Qui non audierunt eum, sed dimiserunt quidam ex eis usque mane, et scatere coepit vermibus atque computruit; et iratus est contra eos Moyses. ²¹Colligebant autem mane singuli, quantum sufficere poterat ad vescendum; cumque incaluisset sol, liquefiebat. ²²In die autem sexta collegerunt cibos duplices, id est duo

today, for today is a sabbath to the LORD; today you will not find it in the field. ²⁶Six days you shall gather it; but on the seventh day, which is a sabbath, there will be none." ²⁷On the seventh day some of the people went out to gather, and they found none. ²⁸And the LORD said to Moses, "How long do you refuse to keep my commandments and my laws? ²⁹See! The LORD has given you the sabbath, therefore on the sixth day he gives you bread for two days; remain every man of you in his place, let no man go out of his place on the seventh day." ³⁰So the people rested on the seventh day.

Num 11:7 ³¹Now the house of Israel called its name manna; it was like coriander seed, white, and the taste of it was like wafers made Rev 2:17 with honey. ³²And Moses said, "This is what the LORD has com-

---

Three basic ideas underlie this narrative. The main one is that, since the manna is the first wonder that God works for his people now that they have been established as a people, so too the sabbath is the first benefit and the first commandment that God gives them. Also, the precept specifies that the sabbath should be celebrated on the seventh day. And, no less important, its origin goes right back to Moses himself, who as God's spokesman explains the meaning of events (cf. 17:23–25, 28–29). As time goes by, the sons of Israel will become more aware of the sacred character of the sabbath and, particularly during the exile in Babylon, that day will acquire the importance we see reflected in the various biblical passages.

In New Testament times some Pharisees and adherents of other religious movements overburdened sabbath observance with many regulations, running the risk that its religious benefits would be lost sight of. Our Lord gives it back its true meaning when he says, "The sabbath was made for man, not man for the sabbath" (Mk 2:27).

From very early on, Christians realized that the sabbath, commemorating as it did God's role in creation and in delivering the Hebrew people from bondage, was a figure of God's supreme intervention in the resurrection of Jesus. And they began to celebrate the day on which Jesus rose as *dies dominica*, the day of the Lord. So, Sunday is not a transfer of the biblical sabbath; it is the great day which commemorates the definitive Redemption brought about by Christ, taking on the religious meaning which the sabbath had in the Old Testament (cf.

---

gomor per singulos homines. Venerunt autem omnes principes congregationis et narraverunt Moysi. ²³Qui ait eis: «Hoc est quod locutus est Dominus: Requies, sabbatum sanctum Domino cras; quodcumque torrendum est, torrete et, quae coquenda sunt, coquite; quidquid autem reliquum fuerit, reponite usque in mane». ²⁴Feceruntque ita, ut praeceperat Moyses, et non computruit, neque vermis inventus est in eo. ²⁵Dixitque Moyses: «Comedite illud hodie, quia sabbatum est Domino; non invenietur hodie in agro. ²⁶Sex diebus colligite; in die autem septimo sabbatum est Domino, idcirco non invenietur in eo». ²⁷Venitque septima dies; et egressi de populo, ut colligerent, non invenerunt. ²⁸Dixit autem Dominus ad Moysen: «Usquequo non vultis custodire mandata mea et legem meam? ²⁹Videte quo Dominus dederit vobis sabbatum et propter hoc die sexta tribuit vobis cibos duplices; maneat unusquisque apud semetipsum, nullus egrediatur de loco suo die septimo». ³⁰Et sabbatizavit populus die septimo. ³¹Appellavitque domus Israel nomen eius Man: quod erat quasi semen coriandri album,

manded: 'Let an omer of it be kept throughout your generations, that they may see the bread with which I fed you in the wilderness, when I brought you out of the land of Egypt.'" [33]And Moses said to Aaron, "Take a jar, and put an omer of manna in it, and place it before the LORD, to be kept throughout your generations." [34]As the LORD commanded Moses, so Aaron placed it before the testimony, to be kept. [35]And the people of Israel ate the manna forty years, till they came to a habitable land; they ate the manna, till they came to the border of the land of Canaan. [36](An omer is the tenth part of an ephah.)

Heb 9:4

Num 21:5
Josh 5:10–12
Neh 9:21
Acts 13:18
1 Cor 10:3

The water from the rock

Num 20:1–13;
20:24

17 [1]All the congregation of the people of Israel moved on from the wilderness of Sin by stages, according to the

Num 33:12–14
Heb 3:16

Acts 20:7; 1 Cor 16:2; Rev 1:10). "In Christ's Passover, Sunday fulfils the spiritual truth of the Jewish sabbath and announces man's eternal rest in God" (*Catechism of the Catholic Church*, 2175). See also John Paul II, Apostolic Letter, *Dies Domini* (31 May 1998).

16:32–36. Later generations need to remember the importance of this event, by being able to see alongside the tables of the Decalogue (the Testimony v. 34) an urn containing manna (and probably made of gold: cf. Heb 9:4). The tradition about the manna being kept inside the ark may have been a later one, because when the ark was solemnly enthroned in the temple of Solomon (cf. 1 Kings 8:9) it contained only the tables of the Law. Be that as it may, the religious meaning of the manna was something never forgotten—this food which

God gave Israel in the desert for forty years (cf. Josh 5:10–11; Ps 78:24–25; Wis 16:20–21).

"Omer" means literally "sheaf". Here we are told it was a tenth of an ephah. An ephah was both a receptacle and the content of same, so it became a unit of volume; it was the equivalent of 21 litres (about five gallons).

17:1–7. The severity of desert life (notably hunger and thirst) leads God to help the Israelites in various ways, all of them full of theological implications. The miracle of the manna, which was preceded by that of the water which Moses made drinkable (15:22–25), is followed by a new work of wonder to do with water: Moses causes water to flow from a rock. This happened at Rephidim, probably what is now Wadi Refayid, some 13 km (8 miles) from Djébel Mûsa.

gustusque eius quasi similae cum melle. [32]Dixit autem Moyses: «Iste est sermo, quem praecepit Dominus: 'Imple gomor ex eo, et custodiatur in generationes vestras, ut noverint panem, quo alui vos in solitudine, quando educti estis de terra Aegypti'». [33]Dixitque Moyses ad Aaron: «Sume vas unum et mitte ibi man, quantum potest capere gomor; et repone coram Domino ad servandum in generationes vestras». [34]Sicut praecepit Dominus Moysi, posuit illud Aaron coram testimonio reservandum. [35]Filii autem Israel comederunt man quadraginta annis, donec venirent in terram habitabilem; hoc cibo aliti sunt, usquequo tangerent fines terrae Chanaan. [36]Gomor autem decima pars est ephi. [1]Igitur profecta omnis congregatio filiorum Israel de deserto Sin per mansiones suas iuxta sermonem Domini, cas-

commandment of the LORD, and camped at Reph'idim; but there was no water for the people to drink. ²Therefore the people found fault with Moses, and said, "Give us water to drink." And Moses said to them, "Why do you find fault with me? Why do you put the LORD to the proof?" ³But the people thirsted there for water, and the people murmured against Moses, and said, "Why did you bring us up out of Egypt, to kill us and our children and our cattle with thirst?" ⁴So Moses cried to the LORD, "What shall I do with this people? They are almost ready to stone me." ⁵And the LORD said to Moses, "Pass on before the people, taking with you some of the elders of Israel; and take in your hand the rod with which you struck the Nile, and go. ⁶Behold, I will stand before you there on the rock at Horeb; and you shall strike the rock, and water shall come out of it, that the people may drink." And Moses did so, in the sight of the elders of Israel. ⁷And he called the name of the place Massah[x] and Meribah,[y] because of the

Marginal references:
Ex 14:11
Deut 16:6
1 Cor 10:4
Jn 7:38; 19:34
Deut 6:16; 9 22–24; 32:51; 33:8
Ps 78: 15–16; 95: 8–9; 105:41; 106:32
Wis 11:4

The sons of Israel's faith in God and Moses has been strengthening little by little; but they often doubt whether God is there at all (v. 7). They begin to murmur and to seek proofs of his presence: have they been brought out of Egypt to die, or to attain salvation? The water which Moses causes to come out of the rock is a further sign to bolster their faith.

This episode names two places—Meribah, which in popular etymology means "contention", "dispute", "lawsuit", and Massah, which is "proof", "test", "temptation". Many biblical passages recall this sin (cf. Deut 6:16; 9:22–24; 33:8; Ps 95:8–9), even adding that Moses himself lacked faith and struck the rock twice (cf. Num 20:1–13;

Deut 32:51; Ps 106:32). Lack of trust in the goodness and power of God means tempting God and it is a grave sin against faith—even more so in the case of Moses, who had experienced God's special love and who ought to have given good example. When man meets some contradiction or some difficulty he cannot immediately solve, his faith may waver but he should never doubt, because "if deliberately cultivated, doubt can lead to spiritual blindness" (*Catechism of the Catholic Church*, 2008).

There is a rabbinical tradition which says that the rock stayed with the Israelites throughout their sojourn in the desert; St Paul refers to this legend when he says "the Rock was Christ" (1 Cor

---

trametati sunt in Raphidim, ubi non erat aqua ad bibendum populo. ²Qui iurgatus contra Moysen ait: «Da nobis aquam, ut bibamus». Quibus respondit Moyses: «Quid iurgamini contra me? Cur tentatis Dominum?». ³Sitivit ergo ibi populus prae aquae penuria et murmuravit contra Moysen dicens: «Cur fecisti nos exire de Aegypto, ut occideres nos ac liberos nostros ac iumenta siti?». ⁴Clamavit autem Moyses ad Dominum dicens: «Quid faciam populo huic? Adhuc paululum et lapidabunt me». ⁵Et ait Dominus ad Moysen: «Antecede populum et sume tecum de senioribus Israel, et virgam, qua percussisti fluvium, tolle in manu tua et vade. ⁶En ego stabo coram te ibi super petram Horeb; percutiesque petram, et exibit ex ea aqua, ut bibat populus». Fecit Moyses ita coram senioribus Israel. ⁷Et vocavit nomen loci illius Massa et Meriba, propter iurgium filiorum Israel et quia tentaverunt Dominum

x. That is *Proof* **y.** That is *Contention*

faultfinding of the children of Israel, and because they put the
LORD to the proof by saying, "Is the LORD among us or not?"

Is 43:20
Heb 3:8
Gen 14:7;
36:12, 16
Num 24:20
Judg 1:16
Josh 1:1
Wis 11:3

A battle against the Amalekites

⁸Then came Amalek and fought with Israel at Rephidim. ⁹And
Moses said to Joshua, "Choose for us men, and go out, fight with
Amalek; tomorrow I will stand on the top of the hill with the rod
of God in my hand." ¹⁰So Joshua did as Moses told him, and
fought with Amalek; and Moses, Aaron, and Hur went up to the
top of the hill. ¹¹Whenever Moses held up his hand, Israel prevailed; and whenever he lowered his hand, Amalek prevailed.
¹²But Moses' hands grew weary; so they took a stone and put it
under him, and he sat upon it, and Aaron and Hur held up his
hands, one on one side, and the other on the other side; so his
hands were steady until the going down of the sun. ¹³And Joshua
mowed down Amalek and his people with the edge of the sword.

10:4). On the basis of biblical references
to the wondrous nature of waters (cf. Ps
78:15–16; 105:4; Wis 11:4–14) the
Fathers said this episode prefigures the
wonderful effects of Baptism: "See the
mystery: 'Moses' is the Prophet; the rod
is the word of God; the priest touches the
rock with the word of God, and water
flows, and the people of God drink" (St
Ambrose, *De sacramentis*, 8, 5, 1, 3).

17:8–16 In addition to shortages of food
and water the Israelites also had to cope
with attacks from other groups in the
desert over rights to wells and pastures.
Their confrontation with the Amalekites
shows that the same God as alleviated
their more pressing needs (hunger and
thirst) will protect them from enemy
attack.

The Amalekites were an ancient
people (cf. Num 24:20; Gen 14:7; 36:12,
16; Judg 1:16) who were spread all over
the north of the Sinai peninsula, the
Negeb, Seir and the south of Canaan;
they controlled the caravan routes
between Arabia and Egypt. In the Bible
they appear as a perennial enemy of
Israel (cf. Deut 25:17–18; 1 Sam 15:3;
27:8; 30) until in the time of Hezekiah (1
Chron 4:41–43) the oracle about blotting
out their memory finds fulfilment (v. 14).
The mention of Joshua leading the battle
and of Aaron and Hur helping Moses to
pray point to the fact that after Moses
political-military and religious authority
will be split, with the priests taking over
the latter.

With the rod in his hand, Moses
directs the battle from a distance, but his

---

dicentes: «Estne Dominus in nobis an non?». ⁸Venit autem Amalec et pugnabat contra Israel in
Raphidim. ⁹Dixitque Moyses ad Iosue: «Elige nobis viros et egressus pugna contra Amalec; cras ego
stabo in vertice collis habens virgam Dei in manu mea». ¹⁰Fecit Iosue, ut locutus erat ei Moyses, et
pugnavit contra Amalec; Moyses autem et Aaron et Hur ascenderunt super verticem collis. ¹¹Cumque
levaret Moyses manus, vincebat Israel; sin autem remisisset, superabat Amalec. ¹²Manus autem Moysi
erant graves; sumentes igitur lapidem posuerunt subter eum, in quo sedit; Aaron autem et Hur sus-
tentabant manus eius ex utraque parte. Et factum est ut manus eius non lassarentur usque ad occasum
solis. ¹³Vicitque Iosue Amalec et populum eius in ore gladii. ¹⁴Dixit autem Dominus ad Moysen:

1 Chron
4:41–43

¹⁴And the LORD said to Moses, "Write this as a memorial in a book and recite it in the ears of Joshua, that I will utterly blot out the remembrance of Amalek from under heaven." ¹⁵And Moses built an altar and called the name of it, The LORD is my banner, ¹⁶saying, "A hand upon the banner of the LORD![z] The LORD will have war with Amalek from generation to generation."

Deut 25:17–18

1 Sam 15:3f;
27:8, 30

The meeting of Jethro and Moses*

Ex 2:18

18 ¹Jethro, the priest of Midian, Moses' father-in-law, heard of all that God had done for Moses and for Israel his people, how the LORD had brought Israel out of Egypt. ²Now Jethro, Moses' father-in-law, had taken Zipporah, Moses' wife, after he had sent her away, ³and her two sons, of whom the name of the one was Gershom (for he said, "I have been a sojourner[a] in

Ex 2:22
Acts 7:29

---

main involvement is by interceding for his people, asking God to give them victory. The Fathers read this episode as a figure of the action of Christ who, on the cross (symbolized by the rod), won victory over the devil and death (cf. Tertullian, *Adversus Marcionem*, 3, 18; St Cyprian, *Testimonia*, 2, 21).

17:14. This command given by Moses to record the battle in a book is one of the reasons for the traditional attribution of the Pentateuch to him. However, there are very strong motives for thinking that Moses did not write the five books (cf. "Introduction to the Pentateuch", pp 19f, above).

*18:1–27. Moses' meeting with his father-in-law Jethro and the institution of the Judges are the last two events in the

desert prior to the appearance of God on Sinai (chaps. 19–24). In the first, Jethro and the Midianites, who here stand for the Gentiles, celebrate with Israel its deliverance and share in a communion sacrifice. In the second, Moses, acting in the name of God, institutes the legal system. The book of Deuteronomy recounts this event after the Israelites leave Sinai (Deut 1:9–18). By situating it here, the sacred writer wants to show that God himself willed that the Israelites should have the structure of a people before the revelation on Sinai took place. The fact that the Israelites who came out of Egypt should form a people (with all that that meant in terms of authority, laws, common good etc.) is very important for seeing the way God chose to bring about man's salvation. "He has, however, willed to make men holy and

---

«Scribe hoc ob monumentum in libro et trade auribus Iosue; delebo enim memoriam Amalec sub caelo». ¹⁵Aedificavitque Moyses altare et vocavit nomen eius Dominus Nissi (*Dominus vexillum meum*) ¹⁶dicens: «Quia manus contra solium Domini: / bellum Domino erit contra Amalec / a generatione in generationem». ¹Cumque audisset Iethro sacerdos Madian socer Moysi omnia, quae fecerat Deus Moysi et Israel populo suo, eo quod eduxisset Dominus Israel de Aegypto, ²tulit Sephoram uxorem Moysi, quam remiserat, ³et duos filios eius, quorum unus vocabatur Gersam, dicente patre:

z. Cn: Heb obscure   **a.** Heb *ger*

a foreign land"), ⁴and the name of the other, Eliezerᵇ (for he said,   Acts 12:11
"The God of my father was my help, and delivered me from the
sword of Pharaoh"). ⁵And Jethro, Moses' father-in-law, came   Ex 19:1
with his sons and his wife to Moses in the wilderness where he
was encamped at the mountain of God. ⁶And when one told
Moses, "Lo,ᶜ your father-in-law Jethro is coming to you with
your wife and her two sons with her," ⁷Moses went out to meet
his father-in-law, and did obeisance and kissed him; and they
asked each other of their welfare, and went into the tent. ⁸Then
Moses told his father-in-law all that the LORD had done to
Pharaoh and to the Egyptians for Israel's sake, all the hardship
that had come upon them in the way, and how the LORD had
delivered them. ⁹And Jethro rejoiced for all the good which the
LORD had done to Israel, in that he had delivered them out of the
hand of the Egyptians.

---

save them, not as individuals without any
bond or link between them, but rather to
make them into a people who might
acknowledge him and serve him in holiness. He therefore chose the Israelite race
to be his own people and established a
covenant with it. He gradually instructed
this people—in its history manifesting
both himself and the decree of his will—
and made it holy unto himself" (Vatican
II, *Lumen gentium*, 9).

18:1–12. In the first part of this book
Moses' father-in-law was mentioned
(under the name of Reuel: 2:18), as was
his wife Zipporah (4:20, 24–26). The
sacred writer seems to see in this episode
many very significant details: the names
of his two sons sum up the two last stages
in Moses' life, first as a stranger among

the Midianites (*Gershom* means "guest":
v. 3) and then later when he experiences
God's protection in his leadership of the
people (*Eliezer* means "God is my protection": v. 4). In this formal meeting (vv.
5–7) it is Jethro who is the visitor (thus
acknowledging the superior status of
Moses). At the centre of their conversation is the deliverance brought about by
the Lord: this gives joy to all who hear it
(vv. 8–11). The Midianites and in them all
the Gentile nations will come to acknowledge the Lord as the true God and will
share in his worship through appreciating
the wonders that the Lord has worked (v.
12). Finally, the fact that the leaders of
Israel partake of Jethro's sacrificial meal
indicates that all the sacrifices and rites
which are celebrated will have clear reference to the events of the Exodus.

«Advena fui in terra aliena», ⁴alter vero Eliezer: «Deus enim, ait, patris mei adiutor meus, et eruit me
de gladio pharaonis». ⁵Venit ergo Iethro socer Moysi et filii eius et uxor eius ad Moysen in desertum,
ubi erat castrametatus iuxta montem Dei; ⁶et mandavit Moysi dicens: «Ego socer tuus Iethro venio ad
te et uxor tua et duo filii tui cum ea». ⁷Qui egressus in occursum soceri sui adoravit et osculatus est
eum, salutaveruntque se mutuo verbis pacificis. Cumque intrasset tabernaculum, ⁸narravit Moyses
socero suo cuncta, quae fecerat Dominus pharaoni et Aegyptiis propter Israel, universumque laborem,
qui accidisset eis in itinere, et quod liberaverat eos Dominus. ⁹Laetatusque est Iethro super omnibus

b. Heb *Eli*, my god, *'eser*, help   **c.** Sam Gk Syr: Heb *I*

[10]And Jethro said, "Blessed be the LORD, who has delivered you out of the hand of the Egyptians and out of the hand of Pharaoh. [11]Now I know that the LORD is greater than all gods, because he delivered the people from under the hand of the Egyptians,[d] when they dealt arrogantly with them." [12]And Jethro, Moses' father-in-law, offered[e] a burnt offering and sacrifices to God; and Aaron came with all the elders of Israel to eat bread with Moses' father-in-law before God.

Deut 1:9–18 **The appointment of judges**

[13]On the morrow Moses sat to judge the people, and the people stood about Moses from morning till evening. [14]When Moses' father-in-law saw all that he was doing for the people, he said, "What is this that you are doing for the people? Why do you sit alone, and all the people stand about you from morning till evening?"

Ex 33:7   [15]And Moses said to his father-in-law, "Because the people come to me to inquire of God; [16]when they have a dispute, they come to me and I decide between a man and his neighbor, and I make them know the statutes of God and his decisions."

Acts 6:2f [17]Moses' father-in-law said to him, "What you are doing is not Num 11:14 good. [18]You and the people with you will wear yourselves out,

---

18:13–27. As the people's leader Moses personally held all authority, religious, legislative and legal. But the history of the Israelites shows that, although all authority had a sacred character, a separation gradually developed between strictly religious matters and political affairs. In various places in the Bible there are indications that the judicial arrangements of Israel were almost always copied from the neighbouring peoples. According to the present text, the institution of the judges was taken from the Midianites, who were governed along the lines of the people of Tyre, Carthage and many other places. Samuel's time saw the birth of the monarchy, with the Israelites themselves asking for "a king to govern us like all the nations" (1 Sam 8:5). The people of Israel were no different from the rest as far as their political structure was con-

---

bonis, quae fecerat Dominus Israel, eo quod eruisset eum de manu Aegyptiorum, [10]et ait: «Benedictus Dominus, qui liberavit vos de manu Aegyptiorum et de manu pharaonis. [11]Nunc cognovi quia magnus Dominus super omnes deos, eo quod eruerit populum de manu Aegyptiorum, qui superbe egerunt contra illos». [12]Obtulit ergo Iethro socer Moysi holocausta et hostias Deo; veneruntque Aaron et omnes seniores Israel, ut comederent panem cum eo coram Deo. [13]Altero autem die sedit Moyses, ut iudicaret populum, qui assistebat Moysi de mane usque ad vesperam. [14]Quod cum vidisset socer eius, omnia scilicet, quae agebat in populo, ait: «Quid est hoc, quod facis in plebe? Cur solus sedes, et omnis populus praestolatur de mane usque ad vesperam?». [15]Cui respondit Moyses: «Venit ad me populus quaerens sententiam Dei. [16]Cumque acciderit eis aliqua disceptatio, veniunt ad me, ut iudicem inter

d. Transposing the last clause of v. 10 to v. 11   **e.** Syr Tg Vg: Heb *took*

for the thing is too heavy for you; you are not able to perform it alone. [19]Listen now to my voice; I will give you counsel, and Heb 5:1 God be with you! You shall represent the people before God, and bring their cases to God; [20]and you shall teach them the statutes and the decisions, and make them know the way in which they must walk and what they must do. [21]Moreover choose able men Num 11:16–17 from all the people, such as fear God, men who are trustworthy and who hate a bribe; and place such men over the people as rulers of thousands, of hundreds, of fifties, and of tens. [22]And let them judge the people at all times; every great matter they shall bring to you, but any small matter they shall decide themselves; so it will be easier for you, and they will bear the burden with you. [23]If you do this, and God so commands you, then you will be able to endure, and all this people also will go to their place in peace."

[24]So Moses gave heed to the voice of his father-in-law and did all that he had said. [25]Moses chose able men out of all Israel, and made them heads over the people, rulers of thousands, of hundreds, of fifties, and of tens. [26]And they judged the people at all times; hard cases they brought to Moses, but any small matter they decided themselves. [27]Then Moses let his father-in-law Num 10:30 depart, and he went his way to his own country.

---

cerned; its originality lay in their religious mission and in the fact that they were the chosen people; they would always have someone to "teach them the statutes and the decisions" and "make them know the way in which they must walk and what they must do" (v. 20).

This account sheds light on the human and at the same time transcendent extent of political authority: "It is clear that the political community and public authority are based on human nature, and therefore that they need belong to an order established by God; nevertheless, the choice of political régime and the appointment of rulers are left to the free decision of the citizens (cf. Rom 13:1–5)" (Vatican II, *Gaudium et spes*, 74).

---

eos et ostendam praecepta Dei et leges eius». [17]At ille: «Non bonam, inquit, rem facis. [18]Consumeris et tu et populus iste, qui tecum est. Ultra vires tuas est negotium; solus illud non poteris sustinere. [19]Sed audi verba mea atque consilia, et erit Deus tecum: Esto tu populo in his, quae ad Deum pertinent, ut referas causas ad Deum [20]ostendasque populo praecepta et leges viamque, per quam ingredi debeant, et opus, quod facere debeant. [21]Provide autem de omni plebe viros strenuos et timentes Deum, in quibus sit veritas et qui oderint avaritiam, et constitue ex eis tribunos et centuriones et quinquagenarios et decanos, [22]qui iudicent populum omni tempore. Quidquid autem maius fuerit, referant ad te, et ipsi minora tantummodo iudicent; leviusque sit tibi, partito cum aliis onere. [23]Si hoc feceris, implebis imperium Dei et praecepta eius poteris sustentare, et omnis hic populus revertetur ad loca sua cum pace». [24]Quibus auditis, Moyses fecit omnia, quae ille suggesserat; [25]et, electis viris strenuis de cuncto Israel, constituit eos principes populi, tribunos et centuriones et quinquagenarios et decanos, [26]qui iudicabant plebem omni tempore. Quidquid autem gravius erat, referebant ad eum, faciliora tantummodo iudicantes. [27]Dimisitque socerum suum, qui reversus abiit in terram suam. [1]Mense tertio egressionis

PART TWO

The People of Israel

7. IN THE DESERT OF SINAI*

The Israelites arrive in Sinai*

Num 33:15

19 [1]On the third new moon after the people of Israel had gone forth out of the land of Egypt, on that day they came into

---

*19:1—24:18. These chapters deal with the central events of the book of Exodus—the encounter with the Lord, and the Covenant established between God and his people. They provide an excellent summary of the theological message of the Old Testament. On the one hand, there is God's revelation that in his plan for the salvation of men he has chosen a people from among all others and established a special relationship with it—the Covenant: "After the patriarchs, God formed Israel as his people by freeing them from slavery in Egypt. He established with them the covenant of Mount Sinai and, through Moses, gave them his law so that they would recognize him and serve him as the one living and true God, the provident Father and just judge, and so that they would look for the promised Saviour" (*Catechism of the Catholic Church*, 62). On the other hand, the events of Sinai clearly show Israel's destiny as the chosen people: "By this election, Israel is to be the sign of the future gathering of all nations" (ibid., 762). Thus, Israel is a figure of the new people of God, the Church.

This entire section has a degree of literary unity which binds together narratives and laws, all with much solemnity, because the sacred writer wants to emphasize that in the theophany at Sinai God offered Israel the Covenant and the Law. We could say the section breaks down as follows: (a) prologue (chap. 19); (b) legislative part, which includes the Ten Commandments (20:1–21) and the document of the Covenant (20:22—23:19); (c) exhortatory appendix (23:20–33); (d) the rite of the Covenant (24:1–18).

*19:1–25. This chapter is written as part of a magnificent liturgy in which the events of Sinai are re-enacted for the reader. The sacred author, then, does not seek to provide an exact, scholarly report on what happened there; what he is providing, rather, is a theological interpretation of the real contact which took place between God and his people.

As in other important sections of this book, it draws on the great traditions of Israel but combines them so skilfully that they have become inseparable; only now and then can one identify traces of particular traditions. The text as it now stands

---

Israel de terra Aegypti, in die hac venerunt in solitudinem Sinai. [2]Nam profecti de Raphidim et pervenientes usque in desertum Sinai, castrametati sunt in eodem loco, ibique Israel fixit tentoria e regione

the wilderness of Sinai. ²And when they set out from Rephidim and came into the wilderness of Sinai, they encamped in the wilderness; and there Israel encamped before the mountain.

God promises a Covenant

³And Moses went up to God, and the LORD called to him out of the mountain, saying, "Thus you shall say to the house of Jacob, and tell the people of Israel:* ⁴You have seen what I did to the Egyptians, and how I bore you on eagles' wings and brought you to myself. ⁵Now therefore, if you will obey my voice and keep my covenant, you shall be my own possession among all peoples; for all the earth is mine, ⁶and you shall be to me a kingdom of priests

Acts 7:38
Deut 4:34;
29:2; 32:11
Rev 12:14
Deut 7:6: 10:14–
15; 26:17–19
Ps 135:4
Mal 3:17
Tit 2:14
Heb 8:9

---

is all of a piece. In this chapter there is a prologue (v. 9), summing up what follows, and the theophany proper (vv. 10–25).

19:1–2. This method of calculating time (v. 1) is one of the traces of the Priestly tradition, always keen to give dates a symbolic meaning (cf. 16:1 and 17:1). Three months is a very brief stage in the prolonged sojourn in the Sinai: in this way time becomes a sign of the religious importance of the events.

19:3–9. This passage summarizes the meaning of the Covenant that is going to be established. So, it contains the idea of *election*, though it does not use the term, and the idea of *demands* being made by God. Furthermore, we can see here the new status of the people (it is *God's own property*) and the basis of its *hope* (in the sense that Israel attains its dignity as a people to the extent that it is faithful to the divine will).

All the basic teachings are contained herein: (a) The basis of the Covenant is

Israel's deliverance from bondage (this has already happened: v. 4): the people are the object of God's preferential love; God made them a people by bringing about that deliverance. (b) If they keep the Covenant, they will become a very special kind of people. This offer will take effect the moment they take on their commitments, but Israel will develop towards its full maturity only to the extent that it listens to/obeys the will of God. (c) What God is offering the people is specified in three complementary expressions—"My own possession", "holy nation", "kingdom of priests".

The first of these expressions means private property, personally acquired and carefully conserved. Of all the nations of the earth Israel is to be "God's property" because he has chosen it and he protects it with special care. This new status is something which will be stressed frequently (cf. Deut 7:6; 26:17–19; Ps 135:4; Mal 3:17).

By being God's possession Israel shares in his holiness, it is a "holy nation", that is, a people separated out from among

---

montis. ³Moyses autem ascendit ad Deum, vocavitque eum Dominus de monte et ait: «Haec dices domui Iacob / et annuntiabis filiis Israel: / ⁴Vos ipsi vidistis, quae fecerim Aegyptiis, / quomodo portaverim vos super alas aquilarum / et adduxerim ad me. / ⁵Si ergo audieritis vocem meam / et custodieritis pactum meum, / eritis mihi in peculium de cunctis populis; / mea est enim omnis terra. / ⁶Et vos eritis mihi regnum sacerdotum / et gens sancta. / Haec sunt verba, quae loqueris ad filios Israel».

Lev 19:2
1 Pet 2:5, 9
Rev 1:6;
5:9–10; 20:6
and a holy nation. These are the words which you shall speak to the children of Israel."

Josh 24:16–24
Deut 5:27
Ex 13:22;
14:31
Sir 45:5
Deut 4:10–12;
5:2–5, 25–32
Ps 18:7–8
29:3–4;
77:16–17;
97:2ff
Rev 7:14

⁷So Moses came and called the elders of the people, and set before them all these words which the LORD had commanded him. ⁸And all the people answered together and said, "All that the LORD has spoken we will do." And Moses reported the words of the people to the LORD. ⁹And the LORD said to Moses, "Lo, I am coming to you in a thick cloud, that the people may hear when I speak with you, and may also believe you for ever."

Then Moses told the words of the people to the Lord.

The theophany on Sinai

¹⁰And the LORD said to Moses, "Go to the people and consecrate them today and tomorrow, and let them wash their garments, ¹¹and

the nations so as to keep a close relationship with God; in other passages we are told more—that this is the relationship of "a son of God" (cf. 4:22; Deut 14:1). This new way of being means that there is a moral demand on the members of the people to show by their lives what they are by God's election: "You shall be holy; for I the Lord your God am holy" (Lev 19:2).

And the expression "kingdom of priests" does not mean that that they will be ruled by priests, or that the entire people will exercise the role of priest (which is in fact reserved to the tribe of Levi); rather, it reflects the fact that God gives Israel the privilege of being the only nation in his service. Israel alone has been chosen to be a "kingdom for the Lord", that is, to be the sphere where he dwells and is recognized as the only Sovereign. Israel's acknowledgment of God is shown by the service the entire people renders to the Lord.

This section (vv. 7–8) ends with Moses' proposal of God's plans to the people and their acceptance of these plans by the elders and by all the people: "All that the Lord has spoken we will do" (v. 8). The same wording will be used twice again in the ceremony to ratify the Covenant (cf. 24:3, 7).

In the New Testament (1 Pet 2:5; Rev 1:6; 5:9–10) what happened here will be picked up again with the very same words, applying it to the new situation of the Christian in the Church, the new people of God and the true Israel (cf. Gal 3:29): every Christian shares in Christ's priesthood through his incorporation into Christ and is "called to serve God by his activity in the world, because of the common priesthood of the faithful, which makes him share in some way in the priesthood of Christ. This priesthood—though essentially distinct from the ministerial priesthood—gives him the

⁷Venit Moyses et, convocatis maioribus natu populi, exposuit omnes sermones, quos mandaverat Dominus. ⁸Responditque universus populus simul: «Cuncta, quae locutus est Dominus, faciemus». Cumque retulisset Moyses verba populi ad Dominum, ⁹ait ei Dominus: «Ecce ego veniam ad te in caligine nubis, ut audiat me populus loquentem ad te et tibi quoque credat in perpetuum». Nuntiavit ergo Moyses verba populi ad Dominum, ¹⁰qui dixit ei: «Vade ad populum et sanctifica illos hodie et cras; laventque vestimenta sua ¹¹et sint parati in diem tertium. In die enim tertio descendet Dominus coram omni plebe super montem Sinai. ¹²Constituesque terminos populo per circuitum et dices:

be ready by the third day; for on the third day the LORD will come
down upon Mount Sinai in the sight of all the people. [12]And you Heb 12:18:20
shall set bounds for the people round about, saying, 'Take heed
that you do not go up into the mountain or touch the border of it;
whoever touches the mountain shall be put to death; [13]no hand
shall touch him, but he shall be stoned or shot; whether beast or
man, he shall not live.' When the trumpet sounds a long blast, they
shall come up to the mountain." [14]So Moses went down from the Rev 7:14
mountain to the people, and consecrated the people; and they
washed their garments. [15]And he said to the people, "Be ready by Lev 15:16ff
the third day; do not go near a woman."

[16]On the morning of the third day there were thunders and Deut 4:10–12
lightnings, and a thick cloud upon the mountain, and a very loud Heb 12:19
trumpet blast, so that all the people who were in the camp trem- Rev 1:10; 4:5

---

capacity to take part in the worship of the Church and to help other men in their journey to God, with the witness of his word and his example, through his prayer and work of atonement" (St Josemaría Escrivá, *Christ Is Passing By*, 120).

19:10–25. This description of the theopany on Sinai contains features of a solemn liturgy in order to highlight the majesty and transcendence of God. Verses 10–15 cover as it were the preparation for the great event, and vv. 16–20 the event itself.

The preparation is very detailed: ritual purification in the days previous, ablutions and everything possible done to ensure that the participants have the right dispositions, even a ban on sexual intercourse (cf. Lev 15:16ff) as a sign of exclusive concentration on God who is coming to visit. Also, the fact that the people have to keep within bounds is a tangible way of show-

ing the transcendence of God. Once Jesus Christ, God made man, comes, no barrier will any longer be imposed.

The manifestation of God took place on the third day. The smoke, the fire and the earthquake are external signs of the presence of God, who is the master of nature. The two trumpet blasts (vv. 16, 19), the people's march to the foot of the mountain and then standing to attention—all give a liturgical tone to their acknowledgement of the Lord as their only Sovereign. All these things and even the voice of God in the thunder convey the idea that this awesome storm was something quite unique, for what was happening, this special presence of God on Sinai, could never happen again.

Israel will never forget this religious experience, as we can see from the Psalms (cf. Ps 18:7–8; 29:3–4; 77:16–17; 97:2ff). In the New Testament, extraordinary divine manifestations will carry

---

Cavete, ne ascendatis in montem nec tangatis fines illius; omnis, qui tetigerit montem, morte morietur. [13]Manus non tanget eum, sed lapidibus opprimetur aut confodietur iaculis; sive iumentum fuerit, sive homo, non vivet. Cum coeperit clangere bucina, tunc ascendant in montem». [14]Descenditque Moyses de monte ad populum et sanctificavit eum; cumque lavissent vestimenta sua, [15]ait ad eos: «Estote parati in diem tertium; ne appropinquetis uxoribus vestris». [16]Iamque advenerat tertius dies, et mane inclaruerat; et ecce coeperunt audiri tonitrua ac micare fulgura et nubes densissima operire montem, clangorque bucinae vehementius perstrepebat; et timuit populus, qui erat in castris. [17]Cumque eduxis-

bled. [17]Then Moses brought the people out of the camp to meet
Rev 9:2 God; and they took their stand at the foot of the mountain. [18]And
Mount Sinai was wrapped in smoke, because the LORD descended
upon it in fire; and the smoke of it went up like the smoke of a
Heb 12:19 kiln, and the whole mountain quaked greatly. [19]And as the sound
of the trumpet grew louder and louder, Moses spoke, and God
answered him in thunder. [20]And the LORD came down upon Mount
Sinai, to the top of the mountain; and the LORD called Moses to the
Ex 33:20 top of the mountain, and Moses went up. [21]And the LORD said to
Moses, "Go down and warn the people, lest they break through to
the LORD to gaze and many of them perish. [22]And also let the
priests who come near to the LORD consecrate themselves, lest the
LORD break out upon them." [23]And Moses said to the LORD, "The
people cannot come up to Mount Sinai; for thou thyself didst
charge us, saying, 'Set bounds about the mountain, and consecrate
Rev 4:1 it.'" [24]And the LORD said to him, "Go down, and come up bringing
Aaron with you; but do not let the priests and the people break
through to come up to the LORD, lest he break out against them."
[25]So Moses went down to the people and told them.

echoes of this theophany (cf. Mt 27:45;
51; Acts 2:2–4).

19:21–25. These verses, which repeat the
instructions about the people keeping
within fixed bounds, come from another
tradition, probably the Priestly tradition
given that priests are mentioned (and
their obligation to purify themselves
carefully: cf. 28:41). Verse 25 is an unfinished sentence; the redactor probably left
the phrase in the air to give more emphasis to the reading of the Decalogue, that
is, to make it appear as belonging to the
message Moses was given on the top of
the mountain.

*20:1–21. "Decalogue" comes from the
Greek, meaning "ten words" (cf. the literal sense of Deut 4:13). It consists of the
Ten Commandments or moral code,
recorded here and in Deuteronomy
5:6–21. The Decalogue is dealt with in a
very special way here: for one thing, it is
embedded in the account of the theophany, slotted in between 19:19 and
20:18; for another, attached to the concise commandments (identical in Exodus
and Deuteronomy) are other more elaborate commandments (giving reasons and
explanations) which differ as between the
two versions. The fact that the Decalogue
(and not any other legal code of the

set eos Moyses in occursum Dei de loco castrorum, steterunt ad radices montis. [18]Totus autem mons
Sinai fumabat, eo quod descendisset Dominus super eum in igne, et ascenderet fumus ex eo quasi de
fornace. Et tremuit omnis mons vehementer. [19]Et sonitus bucinae paulatim crescebat in maius; Moyses
loquebatur, et Deus respondebat ei cum voce. [20]Descenditque Dominus super montem Sinai in ipso
montis vertice et vocavit Moysen in cacumen eius. Quo cum ascendisset, [21]dixit ad eum: «Descende et
contestare populum, ne velit transcendere terminos ad videndum Dominum, et pereat ex eis plurima
multitudo. [22]Sacerdotes quoque, qui accedunt ad Dominum, sanctificentur, ne percutiat eos». [23]Dixitque
Moyses ad Dominum: «Non poterit vulgus ascendere in montem Sinai, tu enim testificatus es et ius-
sisti dicens: 'Pone terminos circa montem et sanctifica illum'». [24]Cui ait Dominus: «Vade, descende;

The ten commandments*

Deut 5:6–22
Mt 5
Ex 34:10–27
Mt 9:16–22

20 ¹And God spoke all these words, saying,* ²"I am the LORD your God, who brought you out of the land of Egypt, out of the house of bondage.

Pentateuch) is repeated practically verbatim in Exodus and Deuteronomy and has from ancient times been reproduced separately, as the Nash papyrus (2nd century BC) shows, indicates the importance the Decalogue always had among the people of Israel as a moral code.

On the supposition that the versions in Exodus and Deuteronomy can be reduced to a single original text, the variations between them can be explained in terms of the applications of the commandments to the circumstances of the period when each version was made; the final redaction, which we have here, is the one held to be inspired. The apodictic form (future imperative, second person: "You shall not kill") is that proper to biblical commandments and it differs from the casuistical type of wording that Israel shares with other Semitic people, as can be seen from the Code of the Covenant (chaps 21–23).

The ten commandments are the core of Old Testament ethics and they retain their value in the New Testament. Jesus often reminds people about them (cf. Lk 18:20) and he fills them out (cf. Mt 5:17ff). The Fathers and Doctors of the Church have commented on them at length because, as St Thomas points out, all the precepts of the natural law are contained in the Decalogue: the universal precepts, such as "Do good and avoid evil", "which are primary and general, are contained therein as principles in their proximate conclusions, while con-

versely, those which are mediated by the wise are contained in them as conclusions in their principles" (*Summa theologiae*, 1–2, 100, 3).

The commandments tend to be divided up in two different ways: thus, Jews and many Christian confessions divide the first commandment into two— the precept to adore only one God (vv. 2–3) and that of not making images (vv. 3–6); whereas Catholics and Lutherans (following St Augustine) make these commandments one and divide into two the last commandments (not to covet one's neighbour's wife: the ninth; and not to covet his goods: the tenth).

There is nothing sacrosanct about these divisions (their purpose is pedagogical); whichever way the commandments are divided, the Decalogue stands. In our commentary we follow St Augustine's division and make reference to the teaching of the Church, because the Ten Commandments contain the core of Christian morality (cf. the notes on Deut 5:1–22).

20:2. Hittite peoples (some of whose political and social documents have survived) used to begin peace treaties with an historical introduction, that is, by recounting the victory of a king over a vassal on whom specific obligations were being imposed. In a similar sort of way, the Decalogue begins by recalling the Exodus. However, what we have here is something radically different from a

---

ascendesque tu et Aaron tecum, sacerdotes autem et populus ne transeant terminos, nec ascendant ad Dominum, ne interficiat illos». ²⁵Descenditque Moyses ad populum et omnia narravit eis. ¹Locutusque est Deus cunctos sermones hos: ²«Ego sum Dominus Deus tuus, qui eduxi te de terra Aegypti, de domo

Deut 6:4–5
Mk 12:28–31

Lev 19:4
Deut 14:15–20
Rev 5:3

Ex 34:7; 34:14
Jn 2:17; 9:2
Deut 4:24

Gen 2:2–3
Ex 16:22–30;
23:12; 31:12–17;
34:21; 35:1–3
Deut 5:15
Lev 19:3; 23:3
Lk 13:14

³"You shall have no other gods before me.ᶠ

⁴"You shall not make for yourself a graven image, or any likeness of anything that is in heaven above, or that is in the earth beneath, or that is in the water under the earth; ⁵you shall not bow down to them or serve them; for I the LORD your God am a jealous God, visiting the iniquity of the fathers upon the children to the third and the fourth generation of those who hate me, ⁶but showing steadfast love to thousands of those who love me and keep my commandments.

Hittite pact, because the obligation that the commandments imply is not based on a defeat but on a deliverance. God is offering the commandments to the people whom he has delivered from bondage, whereas human princes imposed their codes on peoples whom they had reduced to vassalage. The commandments are therefore an expression of the Covenant. Acceptance of them is a sign that man has attained maturity in his freedom. "Man becomes free when he enters into the Covenant of God" (Aphraates, *Demonstrationes*, 12). Jesus stressed the same idea: "My yoke is easy, and my burden is light" (Mt 11:30).

20:3–6 "You shall love God above all things" is the wording of the first commandment given in most catechisms (cf. *Catechism of the Catholic Church*, 2083) summarizing the teaching of Jesus (cf. Mk 12:28–31, which quotes the text of Deuteronomy 6:4–5). In the ten commandments this precept covers two aspects—monotheism (v. 3) and the obligation not to adore idols or images of the Lord (vv. 4–6).

Belief in the existence of only one

God is the backbone of the entire Bible message. The prophets will openly teach monotheism, holding that God is the sovereign Lord of the universe and of time; but this ban on other gods itself implies the sure conviction that there is only one true God. "You shall have no other Gods before [or, besides] me", implies a belief in one God, that is, monotheism.

The ban on images was something that marked Israel as different from other peoples. The ban not only covered idols or images of other gods, but also representations of the Lord.

The one true God is spiritual and transcendent: he cannot be controlled or manipulated (unlike the gods of Israel's neighbours). On the basis of the mystery of the incarnate Word, Christians began to depict scenes from the Gospel and in so doing they knew that this was not at odds with God's freedom nor did it make for idolatry. The Church venerates images because they are representations either of Jesus who, being truly man, had a body, or of saints, who as human beings were portrayable and worthy of veneration. The Second Vatican Council recommended the veneration of sacred

servitutis. ³Non habebis deos alienos coram me. ⁴Non facies tibi sculptile neque omnem similitudinem eorum, quae sunt in caelo desuper et quae in terra deorsum et quae in aquis sub terra. ⁵Non adorabis ea neque coles, quia ego sum Dominus Deus tuus, Deus zelotes visitans iniquitatem patrum in filiis in tertiam et quartam generationem eorum, qui oderunt me, ⁶et faciens misericordiam in milia his, qui dili-

f. Or *besides*

7"You shall not take the name of the Lord your God in vain; for the LORD will not hold him guiltless who takes his name in vain.

8"Remember the sabbath day, to keep it holy. 9Six days you shall labour, and do all your work; 10but the seventh day is a sabbath to the LORD your God; in it you shall not do any work, you, or your son, or your daughter, your manservant, or your maidservant, or your cattle, or the sojourner who is within your gates; 11for in six days the LORD made heaven and earth, the sea, and all

Deut 5:12–15
Mt 12:2
Mk 2:27
Lk 23:56
Acts 4:24; 14;
15; 17:24
Rev 10:6
Deut 27:16;
20:20; 23:22;
30:17
Mt 15:4; 19:18ff
Mk 7:10; 10:19
Lk 18:20
Dan 6:2–3

images, while calling for sobriety and beauty: "The practice of placing sacred images in churches so that they be venerated by the faithful is to be maintained. Nevertheless their number should be moderate and their relative positions should reflect right order. For otherwise the Christian people may find them incongruous and they may foster devotion of doubtful orthodoxy" (*Sacrosanctum Concilium*, 125).

20:5–6. "A jealous God": an anthropomorphism emphasizing the uniqueness of God. Since he is the only true God, he cannot abide either the worship of other gods (cf. 34:14) or worship of idols. Idolatry is the gravest and most condemned sin in the Bible (cf. *Catechism of the Catholic Church*, 2113). Those in charge of worship in the temple are described as being "jealous" for the Lord (cf. Num 25:13; 1 Kings 19:10, 14), because they have to watch to ensure that no deviations occur. When expelling the money-changers from the temple (Jn 2:17), Jesus refers to this aspect of priests' responsibility: "Zeal for thy house has consumed me" (Ps 69:9).

On the Lord's merciful retribution, cf. the note on Ex 34:6–7.

20:7. Respect for God's name is respect for God himself. Hence this prohibition on invoking the name of the Lord to gain credence for evil, be it at a trial (by committing perjury), or by swearing to do something evil, or by blasphemy (cf. Sir 23:7–12). In ancient times, Israel's neighbours used the names of their gods in magical conjuration; in such a situation the invoking of the Lord's name is idolatrous. In general, this commandment forbids any abuse, any disrespect, any irreverent use of the name of God. And, to put it positively, "The second commandment *prescribes respect for the Lord's name*. Like the first commandment, it belongs to the virtue of religion and more particularly it governs our use of speech in sacred matters" (*Catechism of the Catholic Church*, 2142).

20:8–11 Israel's history evidently influenced the formulation of the sabbath precept, given that the usual apodictic mode is not used and that the prescriptions concerning this day are very well developed.

The commandment includes three ideas: the sabbath is a holy day, dedicated to the Lord; work is forbidden on it; one reason for it is to imitate God, who rested from creation on the seventh day.

gunt me et custodiunt praecepta mea. 7Non assumes nomen Domini Dei tui in vanum, nec enim habebit insontem Dominus eum, qui assumpserit nomen Domini Dei sui frustra. 8Memento, ut diem sabbati sanctifices. 9Sex diebus operaberis et facies omnia opera tua; 10septimus autem dies sabbatum Domino Deo tuo est; non facies omne opus tu et filius tuus et filia tua, servus tuus et ancilla tua, iumentum tuum

Lev 19:3
Eph 6:2
Gen 4:10; 9:6
Mt 5:21
Jas 2:11
Rom 13:9
Rev 9:21

that is in them, and rested the seventh day; therefore the LORD blessed the sabbath day and hallowed it.

¹²"Honour your father and your mother, that your days may be long in the land which the LORD your God gives you.

The sabbath is a holy day, that is, different from ordinary days (cf. Lev 23:3) because it is dedicated to God. No special rites are prescribed but the word "remember" (different from "observe" in Deuteronomy 5:10) is a word with cultic associations. Whatever the etymology or social origin of the sabbath was, in the Bible it is always something holy (cf. 16:22–30).

Sabbath rest implies that there is an obligation to work on the previous six days (v. 9). Work is the only justification for rest. The Hebrew word *shabbat* actually means "sabbath" and "rest". But on this day rest acquires a cultic value, for no special sacrifices or rites are prescribed for the sabbath: the whole community, and even animals, render homage to God by ceasing from their labours.

20:12 The fourth is the first commandment to do with inter-personal relationships (the subject of the second "table" as ancient Christian writers used to term these commandments: cf. *Catechism of the Catholic Church*, 2197). Like the sabbath precept, it is couched in a positive way; its direct reference is to family members. The fact that it comes immediately after the precepts that refer to God shows its importance. Parents, in effect, represent God within the family circle.

The commandment has to do not only with young children (cf. Prov 19:26; 20:20; 23:22; 30:17), who have a duty to remain subject to their parents (Deut 21:18–21), but to all children whatever their age, because it is offences committed by older children that incur a curse (cf. Deut 17:16).

The promise of a long life to those who keep this commandment shows how important it is for the individual, and also the importance the family has for society. The Second Vatican Council summed up the value of the family by calling it the "domestic church" (*Lumen gentium*, 11; cf. John Paul II, *Familiaris consortio*, 21).

20:13. The fifth commandment directly forbids vengeful killing of one's enemy, that is, murder; so it protects the sacredness of human life. The prohibition on murder already comes across in the account of the death of Abel (cf. Gen 4:10) and the precepts given to Noah (cf. Gen 9:6): life is something that belongs to God alone.

Revelation and the teaching of the Church tell us more about the scope of this precept: it is only in very specific circumstances (such as social or personal self-defence) that a person may be deprived of his or her life. Obviously, the killing of weaker members of society (abortion, direct euthanasia) is a particularly grave sin.

The encyclical *Evangelium vitae* spells out the Church's teaching on this commandment which "has absolute value when it refers to the *innocent person*. [. . .] Therefore, by the authority which Christ conferred upon Peter and

et advena, qui est intra portas tuas. ¹¹Sex enim diebus fecit Dominus caelum et terram et mare et omnia, quae in eis sunt, et requievit in die septimo; idcirco benedixit Dominus diei sabbati et sanctificavit eum. ¹²Honora patrem tuum et matrem tuam, ut sis longaevus super terram, quam Dominus Deus tuus dabit

13"You shall not kill.
14"You shall not commit adultery.
15"You shall not steal.

Lev 20:10
Deut 22:23ff
Prov 7:8–27;
23:27–28
Mt 5:27

his Successors, and in communion with the Bishops of the Catholic Church, *I confirm that the direct and voluntary killing of an innocent human being is always gravely immoral*" (John Paul II, *Evangelium vitae*, 57).

Our Lord taught that the positive meaning of this commandment was the obligation to practise charity (cf. Mt 5:21-26): "In the Sermon on the Mount, the Lord recalls the commandment, 'You shall not kill' (Mt 5:21), and adds to it the proscription of anger, hatred and vengeance. Going further, Christ asks his disciples to turn the other cheek, to love their enemies (cf. Mt 5:22–28). He did not defend himself and told Peter to leave his sword in its sheath (cf. Mt 26:52)" (*Catechism of the Catholic Church*, 2262).

20:14. The sixth commandment is orientated to safeguarding the holiness of marriage. In the Old Testament there were very severe penalties for those who committed adultery (cf. Deut 22:23ff; Lev 20:10). As Revelation progresses, it will become clear that not only is adultery grave, because it damages the rights of the other spouse, but every sexual disorder degrades the dignity of the person and is an offence against God (cf., e.g., Prov 7:8–27; 23:27–28). Jesus Christ, by his life and teaching, showed the positive thrust of this precept (cf. Mt 5:27–32): "Jesus came to restore creation to the purity of its origins. In the Sermon on the Mount, he interprets God's plan strictly: 'You have heard that it was said, "You shall not commit adultery."' But I say to

you that every one who looks at a woman lustfully has already committed adultery with her in his heart' (Mt 5:27–28). What God has joined together, let not man put asunder (cf. Mt 19:6). The tradition of the Church has understood the sixth commandment as encompassing the whole of human sexuality" (*Catechism of the Catholic Church*, 2336).

20:15. Because the Decalogue is regulating inter-personal relationships, this commandment condemns firstly the abducting of persons in order to sell them into slavery (cf. Deut 24:7) but obviously it covers unjust appropriation of another's goods. The Church continues to remind us that every violation of the right to property is unjust (cf. *Catechism of the Catholic Church*, 2409); but this is particularly true if actions of that type lead to the enslavement of human beings, or to depriving them of their dignity, as happens in traffic in children, trade in human embryos, the taking of hostages, arbitrary arrest or imprisonment, racial segregation, concentration camps, etc. "The seventh commandment forbids acts or enterprises that for any reason—selfish or ideological, commercial or totalitarian—lead to the *enslavement of human beings*, to their being bought, sold and exchanged like merchandise, in disregard for their personal dignity. It is a sin against the dignity of persons and their fundamental rights to reduce them by violence to their productive value or to a source of profit. St Paul directed a Christian master to treat his Christian slave 'no longer as a slave but more than

tibi. 13Non occides. 14Non moechaberis. 15Non furtum facies. 16Non loqueris contra proximum tuum

Sir 7:12–13
Jas 3:1–12
Lev 19:12
Acts 6:13
Mt 5:28
Rom 7:7
1 Jn 2:16
Mic 2:2
Deut 5:23–31
Heb 12:19
Ex 33:20

[16]"You shall not bear false witness against your neighbour. [17]"You shall not covet your neighbour's house; you shall not covet your neighbour's wife, or his manservant, or his maidservant, or his ox, or his ass, or anything that is your neighbour's." [18]Now when all the people perceived the thunderings and the lightnings and the sound of the trumpet and the mountain smoking, the people were afraid and trembled; and they stood afar off, [19]and said to Moses, "You speak to us, and we will hear; but let not God speak to us, lest we die." [20]And Moses said to the people, "Do not fear; for God has come to prove you, and that the fear of him may be before your eyes, that you may not sin."

---

a slave, as a beloved brother . . . both in the flesh and in the Lord' (Philem 16)" (*Catechism of the Catholic Church*, 2414).

20:16. Giving false testimony in court can cause one's neighbour irreparable damage because an innocent person may be found guilty. But, given that truth and fidelity in human relationships is the basis of social life (cf. Vatican II, *Gaudium et spes*, 26), this commandment prohibits lying, defamation (cf. Sir 7:12–13), calumny and the saying of anything that might detract from a neighbour's dignity (cf. Jas 3:1–12). "This moral prescription flows from the vocation of the holy people to bear witness to their God who is the truth and wills the truth. Offences against the truth express by word or deed a refusal to commit oneself to moral uprightness: they are fundamental infidelities to God and, in this sense, they undermine the foundations of the covenant" (*Catechism of the Catholic Church*, 2464).

20:17. The wording of this precept is different from that in Deuteronomy: there the distinction is made between coveting one's neighbour's wife and coveting his goods (cf. Deut 5:21). "St John distinguishes three kinds of covetousness or concupiscence: lust of the flesh, lust of the eyes and pride of life (cf. 1 Jn 2:16). In the Catholic catechetical tradition, the ninth commandment forbids carnal concupiscence; the tenth forbids coveting another's goods" (*Catechism of the Catholic Church*, 2514).

20:18–21. The account of the theophany (interrupted at 19:24) continues here, at the end of the Decalogue. Once more attention is focused on the transcendence of God, so much so that the people are fearful not only of the physical presence of God but even of his words. They ask Moses to speak to them on God's behalf, rather than hear God himself speaking.

"Do not fear" (v. 20): Moses tells them that it is God that they should fear, not the storm that has made him present. The "holy fear of God" is acknowledgement of his transcendence and also the ready acceptance of the offer of his Covenant as spelled out in the command-

---

falsum testimonium. [17]Non concupisces domum proximi tui: non desiderabis uxorem eius, non servum, non ancillam, non bovem, non asinum nec omnia, quae illius sunt». [18]Cunctus autem populus videbat voces et lampades et sonitum bucinae montemque fumantem; et perterriti ac pavore concussi steterunt procul [19]dicentes Moysi: «Loquere tu nobis, et audiemus; non loquatur nobis Deus, ne moriamur». [20]Et ait Moyses ad populum: «Nolite timere; ut enim probaret vos, venit Deus, et ut timor illius esset in

[21]And the people stood afar off, while Moses drew near to the thick darkness where God was.

8. THE BOOK OF THE COVENANT*

Laws concerning worship

[22]And the LORD said to Moses, "Thus you shall say to the people of Israel: 'You have seen for yourselves that I have talked with

---

ments. Fearing God means accepting the challenge of cooperating with him in the work of salvation, while being conscious of the fact that our weakness may prevent us from achieving what God expects of us. This explains the biblical proverb: "The fear of the Lord is the beginning of wisdom" (Prov 9:10). Within the sphere of the fear of God is to be found love for God, not only in the sense of feeling but particularly in the sense of doing, showing one's love with deeds and avoiding all evil (v. 20).

*20:22—23:19. This collection of laws is usually described as the "Book of the Covenant" on account of what is said in 24:7, or the "Code of the Covenant", because many of these laws are similar to those to be found in legal codes of Semitic peoples, such as the Sumerian code of Ur-Nammu (c.2050 BC), that of Esnunna (c.1950 BC), that of Lipit-Istar (c.1850 BC) and (the most famous) code of Hammurabi (c.1700 BC), which is conserved on a dioritic stone in the Louvre Museum, Paris.

The laws collected here probably existed earlier in a similar or even identical wording, but by being inserted into the Book of the Covenant in the context of the events of Sinai they acquire extra weight and authority. They become as it

were the "basic laws" of the people, ratified by God himself.

Within this corpus of law there are laws specific to Israel (such as the absolute or apodictic laws: e.g. 22:17, 27, 28), whereas others are casuistic laws, to be found in all the above-mentioned codes: they allow of different assumptions and reflect their own specific jurisprudence on particular cases (e.g. 21:2–11, 18–26). Also, the Code of the Covenant covers the various areas of social life: it contains laws about worship (20:22–26; 22:28–30; 23:10–19), moral laws (22:16–27; 23:1–9) and, mainly, civil and penal laws (21:1–22:14). Some clearly derive from nomadic life in the desert, where livestock is more important than land; others imply a settled life where agriculture is the more important.

The sacred text presents these regulations as something sanctioned by God himself and as part of the obligations of the Covenant. The point is thereby made that the people of Israel has to be seen, in all aspects of its life, to be the chosen people: politics, social and family life, worship and institutions generally—all have a religious character.

20:22–26. These are very early prescriptions concerning worship, because there is as yet no mention of temple (v. 25) or

---

vobis, ne peccaretis». [21]Stetitque populus de longe; Moyses autem accessit ad caliginem, in qua erat Deus. [22]Dixit praeterea Dominus ad Moysen: «Haec dices filiis Israel: Vos vidistis quod de caelo locu-

you from heaven. ²³You shall not make gods of silver to be with
Lev 1:1–17;
3:1–17 me, nor shall you make for yourselves gods of gold. ²⁴An altar of
earth you shall make for me and sacrifice on it your burnt offer-
ings and your peace offerings, your sheep and your oxen; in every
place where I cause my name to be remembered I will come to
Ex 27:1–8 you and bless you. ²⁵And if you make me an altar of stone, you
Deut 27:5–6 shall not build it of hewn stones; for if you wield your tool upon
Ex 28:43 it you profane it. ²⁶And you shall not go up by steps to my altar,
2 Sam 6:20–23 that your nakedness be not exposed on it.'

Lev 25:39–46 **Laws concerning slaves**
Deut 15:12–18
21 ¹"Now these are the ordinances which you shall set before
Jer 34:8–18 them. ²When you buy a Hebrew slave, he shall serve six
years, and in the seventh he shall go out free, for nothing. ³If he
comes in single, he shall go out single; if he comes in married,

---

altar (v. 24) or priests, or sacred vestments (v. 26). However, it is already
possible to glimpse the theological background: the Lord is the only true God,
who must not be confused with human
idols; divine worship has to be conducted
with special care (this applies both to the
objects used in it and the people who
take part in it).

The sacred altar has to be simple and
natural, because if it were made of
worked stone there would be a risk of
impurity. Later (cf. 27:18) there came an
instruction that the altar of sacrifice
should be made of acacia wood. But at
all times simplicity and sobriety will
imbue everything to do with worship.

Only two types of offerings are mentioned (v. 24), the burnt offering in which
the entire victim is burned (in recognition
of the sovereignty of God), and the communion or peace offering (more specific
to Israel) in which is burned the part

regarded as most noble (blood and fat),
the rest being served as a sacrificial meal.
The peace offering puts more stress on
communion of the offerers with one
another and with God. In Leviticus (cf.
Lev 1–7) the ritual of offerings will be
dealt with in full detail.

Since there is no mention of priests,
one supposes that it was the father of the
family who made the offering; but he has
a religious character, as can be seen from
the prescription that he should be mod-
estly dressed (cf. 2 Sam 6:20). In that
period men wore only a short wrap-
around, Egyptian style; this practice will
change when the rules on priestly vestments come into force (28:40–42).

21:1–11. Slavery was part of the way
society was organized at that time. The
rules collected here are designed to avoid
abuses regarding slaves. In the parallel
text of Deuteronomy 15:12–18, Israel's

tus sim vobis. ²³Non facietis praeter me deos argenteos, nec deos aureos facietis vobis. ²⁴Altare de terra
facietis mihi et offeretis super eo holocausta et pacifica vestra, oves vestras et boves; in omni loco, in
quo memoriam fecero nominis mei, veniam ad te et benedicam tibi. ²⁵Quod si altare lapideum feceris
mihi, non aedificabis illud de sectis lapidibus; si enim levaveris cultrum super eo, polluetur. ²⁶Non
ascendes per gradus ad altare meum, ne reveletur turpitudo tua. ¹Haec sunt iudicia, quae propones eis:
²Si emeris servum Hebraeum, sex annis serviet tibi; in septimo egredietur liber gratis. ³Si solus

then his wife shall go out with him. ⁴If his master gives him a wife and she bears him sons or daughters, the wife and her children shall be her master's and he shall go out alone. ⁵But if the slave plainly says, 'I love my master, my wife, and my children; I will not go out free,' ⁶then his master shall bring him to God, and he shall bring him to the door or the doorpost; and his master shall bore his ear through with an awl; and he shall serve him for life.

⁷"When a man sells his daughter as a slave, she shall not go out as the male slaves do. ⁸If she does not please her master, who has designated her[g] for himself, then he shall let her be redeemed; he shall have no right to sell her to a foreign people, since he has dealt faithlessly with her. ⁹If he designates her for his son, he shall deal with her as with a daughter. ¹⁰If he takes another wife to himself, he shall not diminish her food, her clothing, or her marital rights. ¹¹And if he does not do these three things for her, she shall go out for nothing, without payment of money.

---

bondage in Egypt is recalled to justify kindly treatment of slaves.

"Hebrew" (v. 2): this is the second time this term appears in the Bible (cf. Gen 14:13); it may possibly refer to a particular social class, the disinherited; but it is almost certain that it is a word for a member of the people of God, the brothers (cf. Deut 15:12).

The rite of boring a hole in the ear (which might seem barbaric nowadays) was used to show that a person now had a right to share in all the privileges of the family. It needs to be remembered that slavery in Israel always took account of the dignity of the person; it cannot be equated to Roman slavery or the enslavement of Africans in the Americas.

"He shall deal with her as with a daughter" (v. 9): literally, "in accordance with the statute of daughters". It seems that women had certain rights of inheritance and honour within the family. The rules in vv. 7–11 clearly tend to favour the status of women, who were frequently disadvantaged in that part of the world.

The New Testament contains clear pointers to the abolition of slavery, such as St Paul's advice to Philemon to treat his slave "as a beloved brother" (Philem 16).

---

intraverit, solus exeat; si habens uxorem, et uxor egredietur simul. ⁴Sin autem dominus dederit illi uxorem, et pepererit filios et filias, mulier et liberi eius erunt domini sui; ipse vero exibit solus. ⁵Quod si dixerit servus: 'Diligo dominum meum et uxorem ac liberos, non egrediar liber', ⁶afferet eum dominus ad Deum et applicabit eum ad ostium vel postes perforabitque aurem eius subula; et erit ei servus in saeculum. ⁷Si quis vendiderit filiam suam in famulam, non egredietur sicut servi exire consueverunt. ⁸Si displicuerit oculis domini sui, cui tradita fuerat, faciat eam redimi; populo autem alieno vendendi non habebit potestatem, quia fraudavit eam. ⁹Sin autem filio suo desponderit eam, iuxta morem filiarum faciet illi. ¹⁰Quod si alteram sibi acceperit, cibum et vestimentum et concubitum non negabit. ¹¹Si tria ista non fecerit ei, egredietur gratis absque pretio. ¹²Qui percusserit hominem, et ille mortuus

g. Another reading is *so that he has not designated her*

Ex 10:12, 13, 15
Lev 24:17
Num 35:11–34
Deut 4:41–43;
19:1–3
Josh 20:1–9
Mt 5:21
1 Kings 2:28–34

Laws concerning homicide

12"Whoever strikes a man so that he dies shall be put to death. 13But if he did not lie in wait for him, but God let him fall into his hand, then I will appoint for you a place to which he may flee. 14But if a man willfully attacks another to kill him treacherously, you shall take him from my altar, that he may die.

15"Whoever strikes his father or his mother shall be put to death.

Lev 20:9
Deut 27:16
Sir 3:16
Mt 15:4
Mk 7:10

16"Whoever steals a man, whether he sells him or is found in possession of him, shall be put to death.

17"Whoever curses his father or his mother shall be put to death.

Laws concerning violence

18"When men quarrel and one strikes the other with a stone or with his fist and the man does not die but keeps his bed, 19then if

---

21:12–17. The very grave crimes condemned here (homicide, abduction, and cursing of parents) are punishable by death with no appeal. The wording of these laws, which are usually called apodictic, is specific to Israel and shows their special gravity: witness the way the delinquent is described ("he who strikes . . .") and the use of a very Semitic expression to indicate the penalty (literally, "he shall die the death").

By repeating so severely the fourth, fifth and seventh precepts of the moral Decalogue (cf. 20:12, 13, 15) the importance of these laws in the religious and social life of Israel is being underlined.

A person who killed another could obtain asylum only when he caused the death unintentionally, by accident and without fault (cf. Num 35:11–34; Deut 4:41–43; 19:1–3; Josh 20:1–9).

21:18–32. Less serious crimes against persons are regulated by the classic "law of vengeance" (the punishment to fit the crime exactly), formally enunciated in vv. 23–25 (cf. Lev 24:19–20; Deut 19:21). This marks a considerable development in the history of law among nomadic peoples, because family members' desire for revenge often led to abuses (cf. Gen 4:23–24): no one will be able to go too far, seeking twice or six or ten times more than the harm done; the punishment is to equal the offence. Jesus will correct this harsh and unsophisticated law by means of the precept of charity (cf. Mt 5:38–42).

In these laws a distinction is made between a free person and a slave. The law of vengeance applied more to the former; that is why the law goes into greater detail in regard to slaves, because

---

fuerit, morte moriatur. 13Qui autem non est insidiatus, sed Deus illum tradidit in manus eius, constituam tibi locum, in quem fugere debeat. 14Si quis de industria occiderit proximum suum et per insidias, ab altari meo evelles eum, ut moriatur. 15Qui percusserit patrem suum aut matrem, morte moriatur. 16Qui furatus fuerit hominem sive vendiderit eum sive inventus fuerit in manu eius, morte moriatur. 17Qui maledixerit patri suo vel matri, morte moriatur. 18Si rixati fuerint viri, et percusserit alter proximum suum lapide vel pugno, et ille mortuus non fuerit, sed iacuerit in lectulo, 19si surrexerit et ambulaverit foris super baculum suum, impunitus erit, qui percusserit, ita tamen, ut operas eius

the man rises again and walks abroad with his staff, he that s.
him shall be clear; only he shall pay for the loss of his time,
shall have him thoroughly healed.

[20]"When a man strikes his slave, male or female, with a rc
and the slave dies under his hand, he shall be punished. [21]But i.
the slave survives a day or two, he is not to be punished; for the
slave is his money.

[22]"When men strive together, and hurt a woman with child, so
that there is a miscarriage, and yet no harm follows, the one who
hurt her shall[h] be fined, according as the woman's husband shall
lay upon him; and he shall pay as the judges determine. [23]If any
harm follows, then you shall give life for life, [24]eye for eye, tooth
for tooth, hand for hand, foot for foot, [25]burn for burn, wound for
wound, stripe for stripe.

Lev 2.
Deut 1.

[26]"When a man strikes the eye of his slave, male or female,
and destroys it, he shall let the slave go free for the eye's sake. [27]If

---

their rights were more open to abuse. In the Bible, more than in the codes of neighbouring peoples, the rights of slaves are defended: their status as persons is given more emphasis. In the context of God's gradual way of teaching, one could not expect much more, given the period in which this law was issued; one would have to wait until the New Testament to find clear condemnation of exploitation or marginalization (cf. Gal 3:28; Col 3:11), and open defence of the dignity of the person (cf. *Catechism of the Catholic Church*, 1929–1933).

Thirty coins, the payment for a slave (v. 32), was the price paid for the handing over of Jesus (cf. Mt 26:15).

21:22–23. This is the only passage in the Bible which mentions abortion

caused indirectly. Although it is a very bald legal statement, it could be interpreted as meaning that someone should pay with his life if he has done (mortal) harm to the foetus or to the mother (v. 23); however, it seems that only when it was the mother who died was the death penalty enjoined; if it was the foetus that was killed, there was only a monetary fine. Although it cannot be deduced from this text that the foetus was regarded as a human person with all a person's rights, it is also true that the offence was severely punished if a blow provoked an abortion. What one may deduce is that, since there is no biblical law about directly provoked abortion, this never in fact happened, because the child was valued as such from the moment of conception. Moreover, spon-

---

deperditas et impensas pro medela restituat. [20]Qui percusserit servum suum vel ancillam virga, et mortui fuerint in manibus eius, ultioni subiacetur. [21]Sin autem uno die vel duobus supervixerit, non subiacebit poenae, quia pecunia illius est. [22]Si rixati fuerint viri, et percusserit quis mulierem praegnantem et abortivum quidem fecerit, sed aliud quid adversi non acciderit, subiacebit damno, quantum maritus mulieris expetierit, et arbitri iudicaverint. [23]Sin autem quid adversi acciderit, reddet animam pro anima, [24]oculum pro oculo, dentem pro dente, manum pro manu, pedem pro pede, [25]adustionem

h. Heb *he shall*

he knocks out the tooth of his slave, male or female, he shall let the slave go free for the tooth's sake.

28"When an ox gores a man or a woman to death, the ox shall be stoned, and its flesh shall not be eaten; but the owner of the ox shall be clear. 29But if the ox has been accustomed to gore in the past, and its owner has been warned but has not kept it in, and it kills a man or a woman, the ox shall be stoned, and its owner also shall be put to death. 30If a ransom is laid on him, then he shall give for the redemption of his life whatever is laid upon him. 31If it gores a man's son or daughter, he shall be dealt with according to this same rule. 32If the ox gores a slave, male or female, the owner shall give to their master thirty shekels of silver, and the ox shall be stoned.

Mt 26:15

Laws concerning restitution

33"When a man leaves a pit open, or when a man digs a pit and does not cover it, and an ox or an ass falls into it, 34the owner of the pit shall make it good; he shall give money to its owner, and the dead beast shall be his.

35"When one man's ox hurts another's, so that it dies, then they shall sell the live ox and divide the price of it; and the dead beast also they shall divide. 36Or if it is known that the ox has been accustomed to gore in the past, and its owner has not kept it in, he shall pay ox for ox, and the dead beast shall be his.

2 Sam 12:6
Lk 19:8

---

taneous abortion was regarded as a misfortune (cf. 23:26).

21:33–36. The rules about damage to property are couched as casuistical laws, that is in terms of concrete cases which frequently occurred. For the most part they are applications of the law of vengeance, specifying the compensation to be made by the person who did the damage. There is an obligation to compensate even if what happened was an accident; but if imprudence or negligence was involved, the compensation required is greater.

pro adustione, vulnus pro vulnere, livorem pro livore. 26Si percusserit quispiam oculum servi sui aut ancillae et luscos eos fecerit, dimittet eos liberos pro oculo. 27Dentem quoque si excusserit servo vel ancillae suae, dimittet eos liberos pro dente. 28Si bos cornu percusserit virum aut mulierem et mortui fuerint, lapidibus obruetur, et non comedentur carnes eius; dominus autem bovis innocens erit. 29Quod si bos cornupeta fuerit ab heri et nudiustertius, et contestati sunt dominum eius, nec recluserit eum, occideritque virum aut mulierem: et bos lapidibus obruetur, et dominum illius occident. 30Quod si pretium ei fuerit impositum, dabit pro anima sua, quidquid fuerit postulatus. 31Filium quoque vel filiam si cornu percusserit, simili sententiae subiacebit. 32Si servum vel ancillam invaserit, triginta siclos argenti dabit domino; bos vero lapidibus opprimetur. 33Si quis aperuerit cisternam vel foderit et non operuerit eam, cedideritque bos vel asinus in eam, 34dominus cisternae reddet pretium iumentorum; quod autem mortuum est, ipsius erit. 35Si bos alienus bovem alterius vulneraverit, et ille mortuus fuerit, vendent bovem vivum et dividet pretium; cadaver autem mortui inter se disperdient. 36Sin autem notum erat quod bos cornupeta esset ab heri et nudiustertius, et non custodivit eum dominus suus,

22 ¹ⁱ"If a man steals an ox or a sheep, and kills it or sells it, he shall pay five oxen for an ox, and four sheep for a sheep.ʲ He shall make restitution; if he has nothing, then he shall be sold for his theft. ⁴If the stolen beast is found alive in his possession, whether it is an ox or an ass or a sheep, he shall pay double.

²ᵏ"If a thief is found breaking in, and is struck so that he dies, there shall be no blood guilt for him; ³but if the sun has risen upon him, there shall be blood guilt for him.

⁵"When a man causes a field or vineyard to be grazed over, or lets his beast loose and it feeds in another man's field, he shall make restitution from the best in his own field and in his own vineyard.

⁶"When fire breaks out and catches in thorns so that the stacked grain or the standing grain or the field is consumed, he that kindled the fire shall make full restitution.

⁷"If a man delivers to his neighbour money or goods to keep, Lev 5:21–26 and it is stolen out of the man's house, then, if the thief is found,

---

22:1–2. In these cases to do with theft, the law of vengeance is applied both to the thief and to anyone who tried to kill him. Thus, the thief always has to make restitution, either with his goods (22:1) or by being sold into slavery (22:2). On the other hand, if the thief is killed in the dark, so be it—perhaps because it is difficult to know whether the intruder intended simply to steal or also to kill. The principle of lawful defence underlies this precept. But if the thief is killed in the act of stealing in daylight, there is guilt on the person who kills him,

because he could see the person was only a thief; stealing property and killing a person are different levels of crime. This law seeks to obviate the kind of excesses vengeance can lead to.

22:5–14. In all the cases mentioned here, the person who causes the damage has to compensate the owner. Even in that period it was common practice to leave money or objects of value on deposit. It was also common for lawsuits to be solved by recourse to religious methods (v. 7), although it is not said here whether

---

reddet bovem pro bove et cadaver integrum accipiet. ³⁷Si quis furatus fuerit bovem aut ovem et occiderit vel vendiderit, quinque boves pro uno bove restituet et quattuor oves pro una ove. ¹Si effringens fur domum sive suffodiens fuerit inventus et, accepto vulnere, mortuus fuerit, percussor non erit reus sanguinis. ²Quod si orto sole hoc fecerit, erit reus sanguinis. Fur plene restituet. Si non habuerit, quod reddat, venumdabitur pro furto. ³Si inventum fuerit apud eum, quod furatus est, vivens sive bos sive asinus sive ovis, duplum restituet. ⁴Si quispiam depasci permiserit agrum vel vineam et dimiserit iumentum suum, ut depascatur agrum alienum, restituet plene ex agro suo secundum fruges eius; si autem totum agrum depastum fuerit, quidquid optimum habuerit in agro suo vel in vinea, restituet. ⁵Si egressus ignis invenerit spinas et comprehenderit acervos frugum sive stantes segetes sive agrum, reddet damnum, qui ignem succenderit. ⁶Si quis commendaverit amico pecuniam aut vasa in custo-

---

i. Ch 21.37 in Heb [and New Vulgate]   **j.** Restoring the second half of verse 3 and the whole of verse 4 to their place immediately following verse 1   **k.** Ch 22.1 in Heb [and New Vulgate]

he shall pay double. [8]If the thief is not found, the owner of the house shall come near to God, to show whether or not he has put his hand to his neighbour's goods.

[9]"For every breach of trust, whether it is for ox, for ass, for sheep, for clothing, or for any kind of lost thing, of which one says, 'This is it,' the case of both parties shall come before God; he whom God shall condemn shall pay double to his neighbour.

[10]"If a man delivers to his neighbour an ass or an ox or a sheep or any beast to keep, and it dies or is hurt or is driven away, without anyone seeing it, [11]an oath by the LORD shall be between them both to see whether he has not put his hand to his neighbour's property; and the owner shall accept the oath, and he shall not make restitution. [12]But if it is stolen from him, he shall make restitution to its owner. [13]If it is torn by beasts, let him bring it as evidence; he shall not make restitution for what has been torn.

[14]"If a man borrows anything of his neighbour, and it is hurt or dies, the owner not being with it, he shall make full restitution. [15]If the owner was with it, he shall not make restitution; if it was hired, it came for its hire.[1]

Heb 6:16

---

this was done through oaths, oracles or rites of ordeal, or by means of the sacred lots of the Urim and Thummin, which the high priest used for consulting the Lord (cf. 28:20; Num 27:21).

22:16–17. An unmarried girl belongs to the family of her father. The case described could be regarded as a legitimate procedure, though not the normal way, for getting married. But the father has the right to withhold consent. This protected the rights of young women and their families. The payment of the *mohar*, money given to the bride's father (cf. Gen 34:12; 1 Sam 18:25), was in line with a marriage custom followed among Semitic peoples; it would be an anachronism to think that marriage at that time was a kind of buying-selling contract in

---

diam, et ab eo, qui susceperat, furto ablata fuerint, si invenitur fur, duplum reddet. [7]Si latet fur, dominus domus applicabitur ad Deum et iurabit quod non extenderit manum in rem proximi sui. [8]In omni causa fraudis tam de bove quam de asino et ove ac vestimento et, quidquid damnum inferre potest, si quis dixerit: «Hoc est!», ad Deum utriusque causa perveniet, et, quem Deus condemnaverit, duplum restituet proximo suo. [9]Si quis commendaverit proximo suo asinum, bovem, ovem vel omne iumentum ad custodiam, et mortuum fuerit aut fractum vel captum ab hostibus, nullusque hoc viderit, [10]iusiurandum per Dominum erit in medio quod non extenderit manum ad rem proximi sui; suscipietque dominus iuramentum, et ille reddere non cogetur. [11]Quod si furto ablatum fuerit, restituet damnum domino; [12]si dilaceratum a bestia, deferat, quod occisum est, in testimonium et non restituet. [13]Qui a proximo suo quidquam horum mutuo postulaverit, et fractum aut mortuum fuerit, domino non praesente, reddere compelletur. [14]Quod si impraesentiarum dominus fuerit, non restituet. Si mercennarius

---

l. Or *it is reckoned in* (Heb *comes into*) *its hire*

Violation of a virgin

Gen 34:12
Deut 22:23–29
1 Sam 18:25

[16]"If a man seduces a virgin who is not betrothed, and lies with her, he shall give the marriage present for her, and make her his wife.

[17]If her father utterly refuses to give her to him, he shall pay money equivalent to the marriage present for virgins.

Social laws

Lev 20:6, 27
Deut 18:10–14
Lev 18:23–25

[18]"You shall not permit a sorceress to live.

[19]"Whoever lies with a beast shall be put to death.

[20]"Whoever sacrifices to any god, save to the LORD only, shall be utterly destroyed.

Deut 27:21

[21]"You shall not wrong a stranger or oppress him, for you were strangers in the land of Egypt. [22]You shall not afflict any widow or orphan. [23]If you do afflict them, and they cry out to me, I will surely hear their cry; [24]and my wrath will burn, and I will kill you with the sword, and your wives shall become widows and your children fatherless.

Deut 10:18–19;
24:17–18
Lev 19:33ff
Is 1:17
Jer 7:6
Mk 12:40
Lk 18:3
Jas 1:27
Deut 24:17ff; 27:19
Is 1:17

[25]"If you lend money to any of my people with you who is poor, you shall not be to him as a creditor, and you shall not exact interest from him. [26]If ever you take your neighbour's garment in pledge,

Lev 25:35–37
Deut 23:20–21

---

which the woman was regarded as a "thing". Rather it seems clear that a marriage ceremony was a commitment made between families and that the family gaining this new couple in some way compensated the family which was deprived of it.

22:18–31 This passage contains a number of laws on social matters, in no particular order; some are apodictic, some religious, others are work-associated—but all deal with serious offences.

Sorcery, which only women used to engage in (v. 18) was punished by death (cf. Lev 20:6, 27; Deut 18:10–14), being a form of idolatry (cf. *Catechism of the Catholic Church*, 2117). It was also forbidden by Assyrian laws and by the Code of Hammurabi.

Bestiality (v. 19) was a perversion more often found in pastoral and nomadic life (cf. Lev 18:23–25); it too was punishable by death.

Sacrificing to false gods was a temptation ever-present to Israelites because they were surrounded by wealthy and powerful, but polytheistic, nations such

---

est, venit in mercedem operis sui. [15]Si seduxerit quis virginem necdum desponsatam dormieritque cum ea, pretio acquiret eam sibi uxorem. [16]Si pater virginis eam dare noluerit, appendet ei pecuniam iuxta pretium pro virginibus dandum. [17]Maleficam non patieris vivere. [18]Qui coierit cum iumento, morte moriatur. [19]Qui immolat diis, occidetur, praeter Domino soli. [20]Advenam non opprimes neque affliges eum; advenae enim et ipsi fuistis in terra Aegypti. [21]Viduae et pupillo non nocebitis. [22]Si laeseritis eos, vociferabuntur ad me, et ego audiam clamorem eorum; [23]et indignabitur furor meus, percutiamque vos gladio, et erunt uxores vestrae viduae et filii vestri pupilli. [24]Si pecuniam mutuam dederis in populo meo pauperi, qui habitat tecum, non eris ei quasi creditor; non imponetis ei usuram. [25]Si pignus a proximo tuo acceperis pallium, ante solis occasum reddes ei; [26]ipsum enim est solum, quo operitur, indumentum carnis eius, nec habet aliud, in quo dormiat; si clamaverit ad me, exaudiam eum, quia

Deut
24:10–13, 17

you shall restore it to him before the sun goes down; 27for that is his only covering, it is his mantle for his body; in what else shall he sleep? And if he cries to me, I will hear, for I am compassionate.

Lev 24:15

28"You shall not revile God, nor curse a ruler of your people.

Acts 23:5
Jn 10:34; 18:22

29"You shall not delay to offer from the fulness of your harvest and from the outflow of your presses.

"The first-born of your sons you shall give to me. 30You shall do likewise with your oxen and with your sheep: seven days it shall be with its dam; on the eighth day you shall give it to me.

Lev 17:15–16
Deut 14:21

31"You shall be men consecrated to me; therefore you shall not eat any flesh that is torn by beasts in the field; you shall cast it to the dogs.

Duties of justice

Lev 5:22; 19:16
Deut 19:15
Lev 19:15
Deut 16:18–20

23 1"You shall not utter a false report. You shall not join hands with a wicked man, to be a malicious witness. 2You shall not follow a multitude to do evil; nor shall you bear witness

---

as Egypt, Babylonia, Assyria and, especially, Canaan; ". . . shall be utterly destroyed" (v. 20): or "shall be put under the ban" or "shall be anathema".

Strangers who (due to war, disease or famine) found themselves forced to leave their country, widows without a family to support them, and orphans were typical marginalized or poor people in that tribal society. In its laws (e.g., Deut 10:17–18; 24:17) and in its prophetic message (e.g. Is 1:17; Jer 7;6), the Bible constantly speaks out on behalf of people most in need (cf. Jas 1:27). The oppression of the weak and of those on the margin of society is one of the sins that cry out to heaven (cf. *Catechism of Catholic Church*, 1867).

Blasphemy against God (v. 28) was punishable by death (cf. Lev 24:15); blasphemy against the person on supreme authority in the nation was no less serious, because he was God's representative. In the time of St Paul this text was applied to offences against the high priest (cf. Acts 23:5).

On the law covering the first-born, cf. the note on 13:12. First-born sons had to be redeemed by means of an offering. Therefore, the very bald rule given in v. 29 needs to be interpreted in the light of others which describe how first-born sons were to be consecrated—for the sacrifice of human beings was never countenanced in Israel.

23:1–3. Offences against justice, especially if they occurred in the context of a lawsuit, were subject to severe penalties. Equity is to be the rule in lawsuits, which usually take place at the gates of the city. Verse 3 sounds rather shocking

---

misericors sum. 27Deo non detrahes et principi populi tui non maledices. 28Abundantiam areae tuae et torcularis tui non tardabis reddere. Primogenitum filiorum tuorum dabis mihi. 29De bobus quoque et ovibus similiter facies: septem diebus sit cum matre sua, die octavo reddes illum mihi. 30Viri sancti eritis mihi; carnem animalis in agro dilacerati non comedetis, sed proicietis canibus. 1Non suscipies famam falsam nec iunges manum tuam cum impio, ut dicas falsum testimonium. 2Non sequeris turbam ad faciendum malum; nec in iudicio plurimorum acquiesces sententiae, ut a vero devies. 3Pauperis

in a suit, turning aside after a multitude, so as to pervert justice;
³nor shall you be partial to a poor man in his suit.

⁴"If you meet your enemy's ox or his ass going astray, you   Deut 22:1–4
shall bring it back to him. ⁵If you see the ass of one who hates you
lying under its burden, you shall refrain from leaving him with it,
you shall help him to lift it up.ᵐ

⁶"You shall not pervert the justice due to your poor in his suit.   Deut 1:17;
⁷Keep far from a false charge, and do not slay the innocent and   16:19
righteous, for I will not acquit the wicked. ⁸And you shall take no   Deut 16:19
bribe, for a bribe blinds the officials, and subverts the cause of
those who are in the right.

⁹"You shall not oppress a stranger; you know the heart of a   Ex 22:20
stranger, for you were strangers in the land of Egypt.

The sabbatical year and the sabbath

Lev 25:1–7

¹⁰"For six years you shall sow your land and gather in its yield;   Deut 15:1–3
¹¹but the seventh year you shall let it rest and lie fallow, that the   Deut 24:19;
26:12–13

---

but it is really a call for judges to be impartial: they should not lean towards a rich man by accepting bribes, or towards a poor man on grounds of compassion (cf. Deut 16:19). Some commentators think that the original text said *gadol* (powerful), not *dal* (poor), in other words, that it should read "nor shall you be partial to a powerful man in his suit", similar to what Leviticus 19:15 says. But there is no Hebrew text or early translation that justifies changing the reading; therefore, it should be left as it is, even though it is difficult to explain.

St Augustine comments that this law does not lessen the value of mercy: "mercy is good, but never if it goes against justice" (*Quaestiones in Heptateuchum*, 2, 88).

23:4–9. Love of enemies is one of the new features in Christ's message (Mt 5:43–48), but the Old Testament prepared the ground for this great commandment by establishing laws which suppressed excesses of enmity (cf. Deut 22:1–4).

In v. 7 the New Vulgate translates this along these lines: "keep far away from lies". But the context in which this rule applies (trials: vv. 60–8) justifies the translation given ("a false charge"). For v. 8 also, the New Vulgate has a very literal translation: "bribery . . . corrupts the words of the just"; however, given the context (legal trials), the translation given is more correct.

23:10–13. The Code of the Covenant, which began with a set of laws dealing

---

quoque non misereberis in iudicio. ⁴Si occurreris bovi inimici tui aut asino erranti, reduc ad eum. ⁵Si videris asinum odientis te iacere sub onere suo, non pertransibis, sed sublevabis cum eo. ⁶Non pervertes iudicium pauperis in lite eius. ⁷Mendacium fugies. Insontem et iustum non occides, quia aversor impium. ⁸Nec accipies munera, quae excaecant etiam prudentes et subvertunt verba iustorum. ⁹Peregrinum non opprimes; scitis enim advenarum animas, quia et ipsi peregrini fuistis in terra

m. Gk: Heb obscure

poor of your people may eat; and what they leave the wild beasts may eat. You shall do likewise with your vineyard, and with your olive orchard.

Ex 20:8
Mk 2:27
Josh 23:7

[12]"Six days you shall do your work, but on the seventh day you shall rest; that your ox and your ass may have rest, and the son of your bondmaid, and the alien, may be refreshed. [13]Take heed to all that I have said to you; and make no mention of the names of other gods, nor let such be heard out of your mouth.

Ex 34:18–23
Lev 23
Deut 16:1–16
Lk 2:41

The great feasts

[14]"Three times in the year you shall keep a feast to me. [15]You shall keep the feast of unleavened bread; as I commanded you, you shall eat unleavened bread for seven days at the appointed time in the month of Abib, for in it you came out of Egypt. None

---

with religious matters (20:22–26), now ends with laws—dealing with worship on the sabbath and on pilgrimage feasts.

In Leviticus 25:2–7 and Deuteronomy 15:1–3 there is more elaborate legislation to do with sabbatical years. The purpose of such laws is predominantly religious.

23:14–17. This is one of the oldest cycles of religious feasts; it is very like that included in the Ritual Code (Ex 34:18–23) and that of the Deuteronomic Code (Deut 16:1–6); Leviticus also has its version (cf. Lev 23). The Hebrew word used for these feasts means "dance" or "dance in a ring", a reference to the processional form taken by pilgrimages to sanctuaries.

The three great pilgrimage feasts are described here succinctly and accurately: the feast of the unleavened bread was

held in spring, starting on the day after the Passover, although originally it had no connexion with the latter. It lasted a week, during which no unleavened bread was eaten, to indicate divine blessing on the first fruits; in Israel it marked the birth of the people, when delivered from bondage.

The harvest feast, sometimes called the feast of Weeks (34:22) was held fifty days after the Passover (seven weeks after the feast of the unleavened bread); hence its Greek name of Pentecost (cf. Thess 2:1). It celebrated the end of the grain harvest. Later on, probably as early as the 1st century BC, it also commemorated the handing down of the Law on Sinai.

The harvest feast, celebrated in autumn at the end of September, was also called the feast of Tents (or booths) or Tabernacles (cf. Deut 16:13; Lev 23:34)

Aegypti. [10]Sex annis seminabis terram tuam et congregabis fruges eius. [11]Anno autem septimo dimittes eam et requiescere facies, ut comedant pauperes populi tui; et quidquid reliquum fuerit, edant bestiae agri. Ita facies in vinea et in oliveto tuo. [12]Sex diebus operaberis; septima die cessabis, ut requiescat bos et asinus tuus, et refrigeretur filius ancillae tuae et advena. [13]Omnia, quae dixi vobis, custodite, et nomen externorum deorum non invocabitis, neque audietur ex ore tuo. [14]Tribus vicibus per singulos annos mihi festa celebrabitis. [15]Sollemnitatem Azymorum custodies: septem diebus comedes azyma, sicut praecepi tibi, tempore statuto mensis Abib, quando egressus es de Aegypto. Non apparebis in conspectu meo vacuus. [16]Et sollemnitatem Messis primitivorum operis tui, quaecumque seminaveris in

shall appear before me empty-handed. [16]You shall keep the feast of harvest, of the first fruits of your labor, of what you sow in the field. You shall keep the feast of in gathering at the end of the year, when you gather in from the field the fruit of your labour. [17]Three times in the year shall all your males appear before the LORD God.

[18]"You shall not offer the blood of my sacrifice with leavened bread, or let the fat of my feast remain until the morning.

[19]"The first of the first fruits of your ground you shall bring into the house of the LORD your God.

"You shall not boil a kid in its mother's milk.

Warnings and promises*

[20]"Behold, I send an angel before you, to guard you on the way and to bring you to the place which I have prepared. [21]Give heed

Margin references:
1 Kings 8:2
Tob 2:1
Ezra 45:25

Ex 34:26

Deut 7:1–26
Ex 14:19; 33:2
Mal 3:1
Is 63:9

---

after the huts that were built for it (similar to those used during the grape harvest and the harvest of the last fruits). It was mainly a thanksgiving feast and it eventually became so popular that it was simply "the feast" (cf. 1 Kings 8:2; Ezek 45:25). In Israel it commemorated the years spent in the desert, when they had to live in tents because they had neither land nor houses of their own (cf. Lev 23:43).

In addition to these feasts there were other less important ones, many of which eventually disappeared. Those that lasted longest were the Day of Atonement (cf. Lev 16 and 23:27) and those which developed much later, such as Purim, to celebrate the lifting of judgments against the Jews in Persia (cf. Esther 9:24) and the Dedication of the Temple or the feast of Lights (cf. 1 Mac 4:59). There is no evidence that the New Year was celebrated in any very special way, despite the possible reference in Leviticus 23:34.

The feasts laid down in the Bible,

especially the three pilgrimage feasts, commemorate salvific actions of God in favour of his people, even though among the Canaanites they were linked to agricultural seasons. So we can see that salvation history and God's actions in the past were kept before people's minds by these liturgical celebrations.

23:19. We now know more than we used to about the religious background to this last prohibition, "You shall not boil a kid in its mother's milk". According to a Canaanite document called "The birth of the gods" this dish was often made as a fertility rite: the milk in which a kid had been cooked was sprinkled on fields or on animals in order to improve their fertility. Since this was a product of magic or sorcery, it was forbidden in Israel (cf. 34:26).

*23:20–33. As an appendix and conclusion to the Code of the Covenant, the sacred writer put together these various

---

agro; sollemnitatem quoque Collectae in exitu anni, quando congregaveris omnes fruges tuas de agro. [17]Ter in anno apparebit omne masculinum tuum coram Domino Deo. [18]Non immolabis super fermento sanguinem victimae meae, nec remanebit adeps sollemnitatis meae usque mane. [19]Primitias primarum frugum terrae tuae deferes in domum Domini Dei tui. Non coques haedum in lacte matris suae. [20]Ecce

Mt 11:10
Mk 1:2
Lk 7:27

Deut 7:1
Ex 34:13
Deut 12:3;
16:22
2 Kings 17:10
Hos 4:10; 10:1
Mic 5:12–13

to him and hearken to his voice, do not rebel against him, for he will not pardon your transgression; for my name is in him.

²²"But if you hearken attentively to his voice and do all that I say, then I will be an enemy to your enemies and an adversary to your adversaries.

²³"When my angel goes before you, and brings you in to the Amorites, and the Hittites, and the Perizzites, and the Canaanites, the Hivites, and the Jebusites, and I blot them out, ²⁴you shall not bow down to their gods, nor serve them, nor do according to their works, but you shall utterly overthrow them and break their pil-

---

warnings or promises. Strictly speaking, this is not a formal epilogue of the type usually attached to the end of codes of laws (cf. Lev 26 for the Code of the Holiness, and Deut 28 for the Deuteronomic Code) because it contains no blessings or curses, and makes no specific reference to the preceding laws. It is more a collection of instructions based on the fact that God is close to his people; it is designed to fortify Israel's hope and encourage it to be faithful.

"I send an angel before you" (v. 20). The word "angel", according to St Augustine, refers to his office, not his nature. "If you enquire as to his nature, I will tell you that he is a spirit; if you ask what it is he does, I will tell you that he is an angel" (*Enarrationes in Psalmos*, 103, 1, 15). The expression "angel of the Lord" is equivalent to the presence of God himself or his direct intervention (cf. 3:2; 14:19 and also Gen 16:7; 22:11, 14). However, when Scripture speaks of an "angel" or "my angel" (cf. Ex 33:2; Num 20:16) it seems to refer rather to those spiritual beings who are attentive to the Lord's commands and are faithful doers of his word (cf. Ps 103:20). The role

assigned to them is that of guarding the people in the name of the Lord, just as they protected Lot (cf. Gen 19) or Hagar and her son (cf. Gal 21:17). On the basis of this biblical teaching, the Church holds that angels continue to lend men the same mysterious and powerful help. "Each member of the faithful has at his side an angel as a protector and shepherd to lead him towards life" (St Basil, *Adversus Eunomium*, 3,1; cf. *Catechism of the Catholic Church*, 334–336).

Whereas he sends an angel to the Israelites, he sends two scourges against their enemies—terror (v. 27) and a plague of hornets (v. 28). As usual when the Bible tells us this, it does not mean that God is wicked, but rather that, since he is the only Supreme Being, all blessings and all misfortunes are attributable to him. Furthermore, it is very much in the style of Semitic literature to make a play of contrasts—the misfortunes of enemies are a way of showing how well one is being treated oneself.

23:24–25. "Break their pillars in pieces": in general stelae (in Hebrew, *massebot*) were stones commemorating some spe-

ego mittam angelum, qui praecedat te et custodiat in via et introducat ad locum, quem paravi.
²¹Observa eum et audi vocem eius, nec contemnendum putes; quia non dimittet, cum peccaveritis, quia est nomen meum in illo. ²²Quod si audieris vocem eius et feceris omnia, quae loquor, inimicus ero inimicis tuis et affligam affligentes te. ²³Praecedet enim te angelus meus et introducet te ad Amorraeum et Hetthaeum et Pherezaeum Chananaeumque et Hevaeum et Iebusaeum, quos ego conteram. ²⁴Non

138

lars in pieces. [25]You shall serve the LORD your God, and I[n] will bless your bread and your water; and I will take sickness away from the midst of you. [26]None shall cast her young or be barren in your land; I will fulfil the number of your days. [27]I will send my terror before you, and will throw into confusion all the people against whom you shall come, and I will make all your enemies turn their backs to you. [28]And I will send hornets before you, which shall drive out Hivite, Canaanite, and Hittite from before you. [29]I will not drive them out from before you in one year, lest the land become desolate and the wild beasts multiply against you. [30]Little by little I will drive them out from before you, until you are increased and possess the land. [31]And I will set your bounds from the Red Sea to the sea of the Philistines, and from the wilderness to the Euphrates; for I will deliver the inhabitants of the land into your hand, and you shall drive them out before you. [32]You shall make no covenant with them or with their gods.

Lev 18:3
Num 33:52

Wis 12:3–10

Deut 7:20
Josh 24:12
Wis 12:8

Deut 7:22
Judg 2:6
Judg 20:1
1 Kings 5:1
Deut 11:24

---

cial event, erected as columns or obelisks (cf. Ex 24:4; 2 Kings 18:18). But in the Canaanite religion they were symbols of male gods (cf. Ex 34:13 and note). Both prophets (Hos 4:10; 10:1; Mic 5:12–13) and other books of the Bible (cf. Deut 16:22; 2 Kings 17:10; etc.) were severe in their condemnation of the idolatry implied in their presence in the holy land of Israel.

"I will bless" (v. 25): this is the translation also found in the Septuagint and the Vulgate. We prefer "He will bless".

23:27–30. This announcement that the conquest is going to take time is meant to be an explanation of what actually hap-pened. For one thing, it would take time for the Israelites to settle down and culti-vate the land: this is the most obvious reason for the delay. But there is a more theological reason, as the book of Wisdom implied (cf. Wis 12:3–10): God arranged to send a plague of hornets and other punishments in advance in order to give time to the pagan inhabitants of that land to repent, and to accept the true God.

23:31. The boundaries given here are those of the kingdom of Solomon (cf. 1 Kings 5:1; Judg 20:1), which ran from the Red Sea to the Mediterranean and from the Arabian desert to the Euph-rates.

---

adorabis deos eorum, nec coles eos; non facies secundum opera eorum, sed destrues eos et confringes lapides eorum. [25]Servietisque Domino Deo vestro, ut benedicam panibus tuis et aquis et auferam infir-mitatem de medio tui. [26]Non erit abortiens nec sterilis in terra tua; numerum dierum tuorum implebo. [27]Terrorem meum mittam in praecursum tuum et perturbabo omnem populum, ad quem ingredieris; cunctorumque inimicorum tuorum coram te terga vertam [28]emittens crabrones prius, qui fugabunt Hevaeum et Chananaeum et Hetthaeum, antequam introeas. [29]Non eiciam eos a facie tua anno uno, ne terra in solitudinem redigatur, et multiplicentur contra te bestiae agri. [30]Paulatim expellam eos de con-spectu tuo, donec augearis et possideas terram. [31]Ponam autem terminos tuos a mari Rubro usque ad mare Palaestinorum et a deserto usque ad Fluvium. Tradam manibus vestris habitatores terrae et eiciam eos de conspectu vestro. [32]Non inibis cum eis foedus nec cum diis eorum. [33]Non habitent in terra tua,

n. Gk Vg: Heb *he*

³³They shall not dwell in your land, lest they make you sin against me; for if you serve their gods, it will surely be a snare to you."

9. THE COVENANT IS RATIFIED*

A sacred meal and sprinkling with blood

Ex 6:23; 18:21–
26; 19:20; 28:1
Lev 10:1–2
Num 11:16
Lk 10:1

24 ¹And he said to Moses, "Come up to the LORD, you and Aaron, Nadab, and Abihu, and seventy of the elders of Israel, and worship afar off. ²Moses alone shall come near to the LORD; but the others shall not come near, and the people shall not come up with him."

---

*24:1–18. It was common practice for those peoples to ratify pacts by means of a rite or a meal. This section recounts a meal or rite whereby the Covenant was sealed. This event is very important for salvation history; it prefigures the sacrifice of Jesus Christ, which brought in the New Covenant.

The usual interpretation is that there were two stages in this ratification—first involving Moses and the elders, that is, the authorities (vv. 1–2, 9–11) and then the entire people (vv. 3–8). Other commentators think that there was only one ceremony, relayed by two different traditions. In both cases the final editor has tried to make it clear that both the leaders and the people themselves took part in and formally accepted the divine Covenant and all that it laid down.

24:1–11. Nabab and Abihu are priests of Aaron's line (cf. 6:33; 28:1; Lev 10:1–2); the elders represent the people on important matters. The ceremony takes place

on the top of the mountain, which all the leaders ascended—Moses; the priests, holders of religious authority; and the elders, that is, the civil and legal authorities (cf. 18:21–26).

Only Moses has direct access to God (v. 2), but all are able to see God without dying: what they see far outstrips in brilliance and luxury the great palaces and temples of the East (cf. the vision of Isaiah in Is 6:10). In fact, they all share the same table with God (v. 11): the description is reminiscent of a royal banquet, in which the guests are treated on a par with the host: thus, the king of Babylonia will show his benevolence to King Jehoiachin by having him as his dinner guest (cf. 2 Kings 25:27–30). But it is, above all, a ritual banquet in which sharing the same table shows the intimate relationship that exists between God and the leaders of the people, and shows too that both parties are mutually responsible for the Covenant now being sealed.

---

ne peccare te faciant in me, si servieris diis eorum; quod tibi certo erit in scandalum». ¹Moysi quoque dixit: «Ascende ad Dominum, tu et Aaron, Nadab et Abiu et septuaginta senes ex Israel, et adorabitis procul. ²Solusque Moyses ascendet ad Dominum, et illi non appropinquabunt, nec populus ascendet cum eo». ³Venit ergo Moyses et narravit plebi omnia verba Domini atque iudicia; responditque omnis populus una voce: «Omnia verba Domini, quae locutus est, faciemus». ⁴Scripsit autem Moyses universos sermones Domini; et mane consurgens aedificavit altare a radices montis et duodecim lapides

³Moses came and told the people all the words of the Lord and all the ordinances; and all the people answered with one voice, and said, "All the words which the Lord has spoken we will do." ⁴And Moses wrote all the words of the Lord. And he rose early in the morning, and built an altar at the foot of the mountain, and twelve pillars, according to the twelve tribes of Israel. ⁵And he sent young men of the people of Israel, who offered burnt offerings and sacrificed peace offerings of oxen to the Lord. ⁶And Moses took half of the blood and put it in basins, and half of the blood he threw against the altar. ⁷Then he took the book of the covenant, and read it in the hearing of the people; and they said, "All that the Lord has spoken we will do, and we will be obedient." ⁸And Moses took the blood and threw it upon the

Ex 19:8
Josh 24:16–24
Heb 9:19

Josh 4:3–9,
20–24;
24:26–27
1 Kings 18:31

Mt 26:28
Mk 14:24
Lk 22:20

24:3–8. The ceremony takes place on the slope of the mountain; Moses alone is the intermediary; but the protagonists are God and his people. The ceremony has two parts—the reading and accepting of the clauses of the Covenant (vv. 3–4), that is, the Words (Decalogue) and the laws (the so-called Code of the Covenant); then comes the offering which seals the pact.

The acceptance of the clauses is done with all due solemnity, using the ritual formula: "all the words which the Lord has spoken we will do". The people, who have already made this commitment (19:8), now repeat it after listening to Moses' address (v. 3) and just before being sprinkled with the blood of the offering. The binding force of the pact is thereby assured.

The offering has some very ancient features—the altar specially built for the occasion (v. 4; cf. 20:25); the twelve pillars, probably set around the altar; the young men, not priests, making the offerings; and particularly the sprinkling with

blood which is at the very core of the rite.

The dividing of the blood in two (one half for the altar which represents God, and the other for the people) means that both commit themselves to the requirements of the Covenant. There is evidence that nomadic peoples used to seal their pacts with the blood of sacrificed animals. But there are no traces in the Bible of blood being used in that way. This rite probably has deeper significance: given that blood, which stands for life (cf. Gen 4), belongs to God alone, it must only be poured on the altar or used to anoint people who are consecrated to God, such as priests (cf. Ex 29:19–22). When Moses sprinkled the blood of the offering on to the entire people, he was consecrating it, making it divine property and "a kingdom of priests" (cf. 19:3–6). The Covenant therefore is not only a commitment to obey its precepts but, particularly, the right to belong to the holy nation, which is God's possession. At the Last Supper, when instituting the

---

per duodecim tribus Israel. ⁵Misitque iuvenes de filiis Israel, et obtulerunt holocausta; immolaveruntque victimas pacificas Domino vitulos. ⁶Tulit itaque Moyses dimidiam partem sanguinis et misit in crateras; partem autem residuam respersit super altare. ⁷Assumensque volumen foederis legit, audiente populo, qui dixerunt: «Omnia, quae locutus est Dominus, faciemus et erimus oboedientes». ⁸Ille vero

1 Cor 11:25
Heb 9:20;
10:29; 13:20

people, and said, "Behold the blood of the covenant which the LORD has made with you in accordance with all these words."

⁹Then Moses and Aaron, Nadab, and Abihu, and seventy of the

Ex 33:20
Ezek 1–26
Rev 4:2–3

elders of Israel went up, ¹⁰and they saw the God of Israel; and there was under his feet as it were a pavement of sapphire stone, like the very heaven for clearness. ¹¹And he did not lay his hand on the chief men of the people of Israel; they beheld God, and ate and drank.

Ex 31:18;
32:15ff; 34:1,
28ff

Moses spends forty days on the mountain

Deut 4:13, 36;
5:22; 9:9, 15;
10:1–5
Josh 1:1

¹²The LORD said to Moses, "Come up to me on the mountain, and wait there; and I will give you the tables of stone, with the law and the commandment, which I have written for their instruction."

Mt 17:1

¹³So Moses rose with his servant Joshua, and Moses went up into the mountain of God. ¹⁴And he said to the elders, "Tarry here for us, until we come to you again; and, behold, Aaron and Hur are with you; whoever has a cause, let him go to them."

Ex 40:34–35
1 Kings 8:10
Mt 17:1
Mk 9:2

Eucharist, Jesus uses the very same terms, "blood of the Covenant", thereby indicating the nature of the new people of God who, having been redeemed, is fully "the holy people of God" (cf. Mt 26:27 and par.; 1 Cor 11:23–25).

The Second Vatican Council has this to say about the connexion between the New and Old Covenants, pointing out that the Church is the true people of God: "God chose the Israelite race to be his own people and established a covenant with it. He gradually instructed this people—in its history manifesting both himself and the decree of his will—and made it holy unto himself. All these things, however, happened as a preparation and figure of that new and perfect covenant which was to be ratified in Christ, and of the fuller revelation which

was to be given through the Word of God made flesh. [. . .] Christ instituted this new covenant, namely the new covenant in his blood (cf. 1 Cor 11:25); he called a race made up of Jews and Gentiles which would be one, not according to the flesh, but in the Spirit, and this race would be the new People of God" (*Lumen gentium*, 4 and 9).

24:12–18. Once more Moses goes up the mountain; this time it has to do with the tragic episode of the golden calf (cf. Ex 32). Laws were normally written on stone, not on clay tablets, perhaps to convey the idea of their perennial nature (this, for example, was true of the Code of Hammurabi, which was carved on a huge dioritic stone). St Paul, on the other hand, in order to stress, rather, the interi-

---

sumptum sanguinem respersit in populum et ait: «Hic est sanguis foederis, quod pepigit Dominus vobiscum super cunctis sermonibus his». ⁹Ascenderuntque Moyses et Aaron, Nadab et Abiu et septuaginta de senioribus Israel. ¹⁰Et viderunt Deum Israel, et sub pedibus eius quasi opus lapidis sapphirini et quasi ipsum caelum, cum serenum est. ¹¹Nec in electos filiorum Israel misit manum suam; videruntque Deum et comederunt ac biberunt. ¹²Dixit autem Dominus ad Moysen: «Ascende ad me in montem et esto ibi; daboque tibi tabulas lapideas et legem ac mandata, quae scripsi, ut doceas eos». ¹³Surrexerunt Moyses et Iosue minister eius; ascendensque Moyses in montem Dei ¹⁴senioribus ait:

[15]Then Moses went up on the mountain, and the cloud covered the mountain. [16]The glory of the LORD settled on Mount Sinai, and the cloud covered it six days; and on the seventh day he called to Moses out of the midst of the cloud. [17]Now the appearance of the glory of the LORD was like a devouring fire on the top of the mountain in the sight of the people of Israel. [18]And Moses entered the cloud, and went up on the mountain. And Moses was on the mountain forty days and forty nights.

Deut 4:36
2 Cor 3:18

Deut 9:9
Ex 34:28
Lk 9:34

10. INSTRUCTIONS FOR THE SANCTUARY*

Contributions for the sanctuary

25 [1]The LORD said to Moses, [2]"Speak to the people of Israel, that they take for me an offering; from every man whose

Ex 35:4–29
Lev 7:14
Num 15:19–21

ority of the law, will say that the Gospel message is inscribed on our hearts (cf. 2 Cor 3:3). In this narrative the tables of stone are the symbol of the faithfulness that the people failed to maintain and which God's mercy reconstituted (cf. the note on 32:1–6).

Verses 15–18, which probably come from the Priestly tradition, describe the theophany by using the language of worship, speaking of the "glory of the Lord". This is the divine presence made visible in the form of a bright, yet opaque, cloud (v. 16), the same cloud as will later cover the ark (cf. 40:34–35) and, later still, the temple (cf. 1 Kings 8:10–11). It is also a devouring fire, which nothing can resist (cf. Deut 4:36). Both images symbolize the transcendence of God. The Holy Spirit, too, will come in the form of tongues of fire (cf. Acts 2:3–4). On the profound meaning of the cloud, cf. *Catechism of the Catholic Church*, 697.

God made Moses go through a week of preparation before making himself visible to him on the seventh day; then Moses stayed on the mountain for forty days, in close contact with the Lord. These periods of time are not meant to be exact but rather to show how intense Moses' relationship with God was; they will be evoked when important events are narrated later: thus, Elijah walked for forty days in search of God (cf. 1 Kings 19:8) and Jesus will spend forty days in the desert before beginning his public life (cf. Mt 4:2).

*25:1—31:18. These chapters cover the very detailed rules about the building of the ark and the tabernacle, rules which will be applied later, as we are told at the end of the book, when the Lord has re-established the order broken by the Israelites' adoration of the golden calf (cf. chaps. 35–40). The Priestly tradi-

«Exspectate hic, donec revertamur ad vos. Habetis Aaron et Hur vobiscum; si quid natum fuerit quaestionis, referetis ad eos». [15]Cumque ascendisset Moyses in montem, operuit nubes montem; [16]et habitavit gloria Domini super Sinai tegens illum nube sex diebus; septimo autem die vocavit eum de medio caliginis. [17]Erat autem species gloriae Domini quasi ignis ardens super verticem montis in conspectu filiorum Israel. [18]Ingressusque Moyses medium nebulae ascendit in montem; et fuit ibi quadraginta diebus et quadraginta noctibus. [1]Locutusque est Dominus ad Moysen dicens: [2]«Loquere

heart makes him willing you shall receive the offering for me. [3]And this is the offering which you shall receive from them: gold, silver, and bronze, [4]blue and purple and scarlet stuff and fine twined linen, goats' hair, [5]tanned rams' skins, goatskins, acacia wood, [6]oil for the lamps, spices for the anointing oil and for the fragrant incense, [7]onyx stones, and stones for setting, for the ephod and for the breastpiece. [8]And let them make me a sanctuary, that I may dwell in their midst. [9]According to all that I show

Ex 25:40;
26:30; 27:8

---

tion, to whom both sections are attributed, has combined very ancient traditions about worship in the desert with other more recent ones; the construction of the temple of Zerubbabel (Ezek 40–48) will be built in line with the rules given here.

Thus, it is historically probable that the Israelite caravans in the desert set up a special tent for the purposes of worship—the tabernacle—in which was set the ark, a portable object which was specially venerated and in which were kept the three symbols of Israel's deliverance—Moses' rod, the urn with the manna (cf. Ex 16:33) and the tables of the Law. All the details regarding sizes, materials and design reflect later buildings, such as the temple of Shiloh and, particularly, Solomon's temple of Jerusalem.

The sacred writer has woven a number of doctrinal themes into the narrative: firstly, he is making it clear that the worship offered in the temple is perfectly orthodox, because everything about the temple goes right back to Moses; he is justifying the existence of a temple, and the meaning thereof: the tabernacle in the desert and, later on, the temple are a visible sign of the presence of God among his people; therefore, religious worship will always be an ack-

nowledgment of God's active presence among mankind. Finally, the building of the tabernacle is quite evocative of the account of creation (cf. Gen 1:1–2:4): there is a planned order, because God himself stipulates how everything is to be "made"; and, finally, Moses finishes his great work (Ex 40:33; cf. Gen 2:2) and blesses the craftsmen on that day (cf. Ex 39; 43; cf. Gen 2:3). In this way it is shown that the temple and its worship point to a new world.

With even more reason the Church is very careful to ensure that its liturgy and everything about it is done with dignity, for it is celebrating the mystery of Christ and prefiguring the heavenly liturgy: "In the earthly liturgy we take part in a foretaste of that heavenly liturgy which is celebrated in the Holy City of Jerusalem toward which we journey as pilgrims, where Christ is sitting at the right hand of God, Minister of the holies and of the true tabernacle. With all the warriors of the heavenly army we sing a hymn of glory to the Lord; venerating the memory of the saints, we hope for some part and fellowship with them; we eagerly await the Saviour, Our Lord Jesus Christ, until he, our life, shall appear and we too will appear with him in glory" (Vatican II, *Sacrosanctum Concilium*, 8).

---

filiis Israel, ut tollant mihi donaria; ab omni homine, qui offert ultroneus, accipietis ea. [3]Haec sunt autem, quae accipere debetis: aurum et argentum et aes, [4]hyacinthum et purpuram coccumque et byssum, pilos caprarum [5]et pelles arietum rubricatas pellesque delphini et ligna acaciae, [6]oleum ad luminaria concinnanda, aromata in unguentum et in thymiama boni odoris, [7]lapides onychinos et

you concerning the pattern of the tabernacle, and of all its furni- Num 8:4
ture, so you shall make it.

The ark

Ex 37:1–9

[10]"They shall make an ark of acacia wood; two cubits and a half
shall be its length, a cubit and a half its breadth, and a cubit and a
half its height. [11]And you shall overlay it with pure gold, within
and without shall you overlay it, and you shall make upon it a

---

25:1–9. The sanctuary will be built from
things freely offered by the Israelites. The
Hebrew word *terumáh*, here translated as
"offering" (v. 2), is a sort of tribute in the
sense that each person has to decide in
conscience how much to give; basically it
is a religious matter, to do with sacrifice
or offering (cf. Lev 7:14; Num 15:19–21).

Worship is such a worthy thing that
only precious metals and valuable
objects should be used; some of the
terms used here make little sense today
(cf. "goatskins": v. 5; literally, "porpoise
skins" or the skin of a kind of badger, or
of an animal now extinct, perhaps a kind
of dolphin found in the Red Sea). The
Church too has taken a lot of care over
the aesthetics of places of worship and
the objects used for worship. "Holy
Mother Church has always been the
patron of the fine arts and has ever
sought their noble ministry, to the end
especially that all things set apart for use
in divine worship should be worthy,
becoming, and beautiful signs and symbols of things supernatural" (Vatican II,
Sacrosanctum Concilium, 122).

Sanctuary or tabernacle (vv. 8-9) are
two terms meaning the same thing; they
refer to the holy tent, that is, the tent in
which the ark was kept and where God
made himself present to the Hebrews.
The terminology helps to highlight the

fact that God is transcendent and at the
same time he is near his people: God
dwells in heaven, but he communicates
with his people in this *shekináh*
(dwelling-place). St Stephen recalls the
true meaning of the sanctuary when he
cites Isaiah's words (66:1–2) to show that
"the Most High does not dwell in houses
made with hands" (Acts 7:48; cf. Heb
8:2; Rev 15:5).

25:10–22. The ark was a rectangular
chest, made of acacia wood and covered
with gold inside and out. A Hebrew cubit
was the distance between the elbow and
the tip of the middle finger; this means
the ark would have measured approxi-
mately 1.25 x .70 metres (4 x 2.3 feet).
The ark's accessories (rings and poles)
are designed to make it easier to carry
when moving from place to place in the
desert. The ark was of very great importance in the early history of Israel and
therefore it was given different names
according to where it was or the traditions which mention it. Thus, it is called
the Ark of God (in Joshua), the Ark of
the Lord (in 1 Samuel), the Ark of the
Law (in Deuteronomy), the Ark of
Witness. It was a memorial to the
Covenant between God and his people,
because it contained the tables of the
Covenant; but, first and foremost, it was

---

gemmas ad ornandum ephod ac pectorale. [8]Facientque mihi sanctuarium, et habitabo in medio eorum.
[9]Iuxta omnem similitudinem habitaculi, quam ostendam tibi, et omnium vasorum in cultum eius:
sicque facietis illud. [10]Arcam de lignis acaciae compingent; cuius longitudo habeat duos semis cubitos,

molding of gold round about. [12]And you shall cast four rings of gold for it and put them on its four feet, two rings on the one side of it, and two rings on the other side of it. [13]You shall make poles of acacia wood, and overlay them with gold. [14]And you shall put the poles into the rings on the sides of the ark, to carry the ark by them. [15]The poles shall remain in the rings of the ark; they shall not be taken from it. [16]And you shall put into the ark the testimony which I shall give you. [17]Then you shall make a mercy seat[o] of pure gold; two cubits and a half shall be its length, and a cubit and a half its breadth. [18]And you shall make two cherubim of gold; of hammered work shall you make them, on the two ends of the mercy seat. [19]Make one cherub on the one end, and one cherub on the other end; of one piece with the mercy seat shall you make the cherubim on its two ends. [20]The cherubim shall spread out their wings above, overshadowing the mercy seat with their wings, their faces one to another; toward the mercy seat shall the faces of the cherubim be. [21]And you shall put the mercy seat on the top of the ark; and in the ark you shall put the testimony that I shall give you. [22]There I will meet with you, and from above the mercy seat, from between the two cherubim that are upon the ark of the testimony, I will speak with you of all that I will give you in commandment for the people of Israel.

2 Sam 6:7
Ex 24:12
Heb 9:4
Lev 16:12–15
Rom 3:25
Heb 9:5

Heb 9:4

Ex 29:42
Num 7:89
1 Sam 4:4
2 Sam 6:2
2 Kings 19:15
Ps 99:1
Heb 9:5

---

a symbol of the presence of the Lord (v. 22; cf. 1 Sam 4:4; 2 Sam 6:2).

The ark was covered with a thick golden plate called the Mercy Seat, because on the Day of Atonement (cf. Lev 16:15–16) the priest used to sprinkle it with the blood of victims, imploring forgiveness of the people's sins. St Paul called Jesus Christ an "expiation" (from the same Hebrew word as "mercy seat")

because by Christ's blood man attains the remission of sins (cf. Rom 3:25).

On the two ends of the mercy seat were two cherubim, possibly two figures of winged animals which stood for the spiritual beings or angels who are ministers close to God. These figures, together with the mercy seat, formed a sort of majestic throne from which God would speak (v. 22; cf. Num 7: 89); hence the

latitudo cubitum et dimidium, altitudo cubitum similiter ac semissem. [11]Et deaurabis eam auro mundissimo intus et foris; faciesque supra coronam auream per circuitum [12]et conflabis ei quattuor circulos aureos, quos pones in quattuor arcae pedibus: duo circuli sint in latere uno et duo in altero. [13]Facies quoque vectes de lignis acaciae et operies eos auro; [14]inducesque per circulos, qui sunt in arcae lateribus, ut portetur in eis; [15]qui semper erunt in circulis nec umquam extrahentur ab eis. [16]Ponesque in arcam testimonium, quod dabo tibi. [17]Facies et propitiatorium de auro mundissimo; duos cubitos et dimidium tenebit longitudo eius, et cubitum ac semissem latitudo. [18]Duos quoque cherubim aureos et productiles facies ex utraque parte propitiatorii, [19]cherub unus sit in latere uno et alter in altero; ex propitiatorio facies cherubim in utraque parte eius. [20]Expandent alas sursum et operient alis suis propitiatorium; respicientque se mutuo, versis vultibus in propitiatorium, [21]quo operienda est arca, in qua pones

o. Or *cover*

The table for the offertory bread

Ex 37:10–16

²³"And you shall make a table of acacia wood; two cubits shall be Heb 9:2 its length, a cubit its breadth, and a cubit and a half its height. ²⁴You shall overlay it with pure gold, and make a molding of gold around it. ²⁵And you shall make around it a frame a handbreadth wide, and a molding of gold around the frame. ²⁶And you shall make for it four rings of gold, and fasten the rings to the four corners at its four legs. ²⁷Close to the frame the rings shall lie, as holders for the poles to carry the table. ²⁸You shall make the poles of acacia wood, and overlay them with gold, and the table shall be carried with these. ²⁹And you shall make its plates and dishes for Lev 24:5–9 incense, and its flagons and bowls with which to pour libations; Num 4:7
1 Sam 21:4–7 of pure gold you shall make them. ³⁰And you shall set the bread of the Presence on the table before me always. Heb 9:2

The lampstand

Ex 37:17–24
Lev 24:2–4

³¹"And you shall make a lampstand of pure gold. The base and the Rev 1:12 shaft of the lampstand shall be made of hammered work; its cups, its capitals, and its flowers shall be of one piece with it; ³²and

---

form of words, "the Lord who is enthroned on the cherubim" (1 Sam 4:4; 2 Kings 19:15; Ps 99:1).

25:23–30. The table of the bread of the Presence (cf. 37:10–16) was also made of acacia wood and covered with gold. Every sabbath twelve cakes of bread had to be placed on it separated from each other by bowls of incense (cf. Lev 24:5–9). They served to show that the bread of each day originates in the goodness of the Lord (cf. the Our Father). They were given the name "bread of the Presence" (1 Sam 21:7)

because they were placed on this table in front of the ark, but they were also called "holy" or "consecrated" bread (cf. 1 Sam 21:4–6) and "perpetual" bread (Num 4:7; not reflected in RSV). Only priests could eat them, although David when he was an outlaw had no qualms about eating them (1 Sam 21:4–7), a fact which our Lord made use of to talk about freedom of spirit as against sticking to the letter of the law (cf. Mt 2:23–28).

25:31–40. The seven-branched lampstand or *menoráh* (cf. 37:17–24) had to

testimonium, quod dabo tibi. ²²Et conveniam te ibi et loquar ad te supra propitiatorium de medio duorum cherubim, qui erunt super arcam testimonii, cuncta, quae mandabo per te filiis Israel. ²³Facies et mensam de lignis acaciae habentem duos cubitos longitudinis et in latitudine cubitum et in altitudine cubitum ac semissem. ²⁴Et inaurabis eam auro purissimo; faciesque illi coronam auream per circuitum. ²⁵Facies quoque ei limbum altum quattuor digitis per circuitum et super illum coronam auream. ²⁶Quattuor quoque circulos aureos praeparabis et pones eos in quattuor angulis eiusdem mensae per singulos pedes. ²⁷Iuxta limbum erunt circuli aurei, ut mittantur vectes per eos, et possit mensa portari. ²⁸Ipsosque vectes facies de lignis acaciae et circumdabis auro, et per ipsos subvehitur mensa. ²⁹Parabis et acetabula ac phialas, vasa et cyathos, in quibus offerenda sunt libamina, ex auro purissimo. ³⁰Et pones super mensam panes propositionis in conspectu meo semper. ³¹Facies et candelabrum ductile de auro mundissimo: basis et hastile eius, scyphi et sphaerulae ac flores in unum efformentur. ³²Sex calami

there shall be six branches going out of its sides, three branches of the lampstand out of one side of it and three branches of the lampstand out of the other side of it; ³³three cups made like almonds, each with capital and flower, on one branch, and three cups made like almonds, each with capital and flower, on the other branch—so for the six branches going out of the lampstand; ³⁴and on the lampstand itself four cups made like almonds, with their capitals and flowers, ³⁵and a capital of one piece with it under each pair of the six branches going out from the lampstand. ³⁶Their capitals and their branches shall be of one piece with it,

Rev 1:12   the whole of it one piece of hammered work of pure gold. ³⁷And you shall make the seven lamps for it; and the lamps shall be set up so as to give light upon the space in front of it. ³⁸Its snuffers

Heb 8:5   and their trays shall be of pure gold. ³⁹Of a talent of pure gold

Acts 7:44   shall it be made, with all these utensils. ⁴⁰And see that you make

Heb 8:5   them after the pattern for them, which is being shown you on the mountain.

Ex 33:7–11;
36:8–19
Heb 9:11–24   **The tabernacle**

26 ¹"Moreover you shall make the tabernacle with ten curtains of fine twined linen and blue and purple and scarlet stuff; with cherubim skilfully worked shall you make them. ²The length of each curtain shall be twenty-eight cubits, and the

---

be made of gold and weighed a talent (that is, about 32 kgs or 70 lbs). Its description is difficult to follow, but we can see that it was the item that involved most artistry. We do not know exactly what the seven branches symbolized; maybe the lampstand was meant to stand for a beautiful tree, another sign that the sanctuary was the place of the presence of God, who shel-

ters the faithful (see also the note on Num 8:1–4).

26:1–14. The sanctuary is described in minute detail, but it is not easy to visualize it exactly, due to the fact that it uses technical terms we are not familiar with nowadays. We can see that there were four curtains: the first, about 17 x 12 metres (56 x 40 feet), was made of linen

egredientur de lateribus, tres ex uno latere et tres ex altero. ³³Tres scyphi quasi in nucis modum in calamo uno sphaerulaeque simul et flores; et tres similiter scyphi instar nucis in calam altero sphaerulaeque simul et flores: hoc erit opus sex calamorum, qui producendi sunt de hastili. ³⁴In ipso autem hastili candelabri erunt quattuor scyphi in nucis modum sphaerulaeque et flores. ³⁵Singulae sphaerulae sub binis calamis per tria loca, qui simul sex fiunt, procedentes de hastili uno. ³⁶Sphaerulae igitur et calami unum cum ipso erunt, totum ductile de auro purissimo. ³⁷Facies et lucernas septem et pones eas super candelabrum, ut luceant in locum ex adverso. ³⁸Emunctoria quoque et vasa, in quibus emuncta condantur, fient de auro purissimo. ³⁹Omne pondus candelabri, cum universis vasis suis, habebit talentum auri purissimi. ⁴⁰Inspice et fac secundum exemplar, quod tibi in monte monstratum est. ¹Habitaculum vero ita facies: decem cortinas de bysso retorta et hyacintho ac purpura coccoque cum cherubim opere polymito facies. ²Longitudo cortinae unius habebit viginti octo cubitos, latitudo quat-

breadth of each curtain four cubits; all the curtains shall have one measure. ³Five curtains shall be coupled to one another; and the other five curtains shall be coupled to one another. ⁴And you shall make loops of blue on the edge of the outmost curtain in the first set; and likewise you shall make loops on the edge of the outmost curtain in the second set. ⁵Fifty loops you shall make on the one curtain, and fifty loops you shall make on the edge of the curtain that is in the second set; the loops shall be opposite one another. ⁶And you shall make fifty clasps of gold, and couple the curtains one to the other with the clasps, that the tabernacle may be one whole.

⁷"You shall also make curtains of goats' hair for a tent over the tabernacle; eleven curtains shall you make. ⁸The length of each curtain shall be thirty cubits, and the breadth of each curtain four cubits; the eleven curtains shall have the same measure. ⁹And you shall couple five curtains by themselves, and six curtains by themselves, and the sixth curtain you shall double over at the front of the tent. ¹⁰And you shall make fifty loops on the edge of the curtain that is outmost in one set, and fifty loops on the edge of the curtain which is outmost in the second set.

¹¹"And you shall make fifty clasps of bronze, and put the clasps into the loops, and couple the tent together that it may be one whole. ¹²And the part that remains of the curtains of the tent, the half curtain that remains, shall hang over the back of the taber-

---

and consisted of ten tapestries. The second (19 x 13 metres), was made of goatskin. Over these there were two further coverings, one made of goatskin, the other of fine leather, probably ramskin.

Although the sanctuary looked like the tents the Israelites used, it was clearly a very majestic sort of tent: the richness of the materials used in it highlighted the great regard in which the worship of God was held and the conviction that God always deserved the very best they could offer him.

---

tuor cubitorum erit. Unius mensurae fient universae cortinae. ³Quinque cortinae sibi iungentur mutuo, et aliae quinque nexu simili cohaerebunt. ⁴Ansulas hyacinthinas in latere facies cortinae unius in extremitate iuncturae et similiter facies in latere cortinae extremae in iunctura altera. ⁵Quinquaginta ansulas facies in cortina una et quinquaginta ansulas facies in summitate cortinae, quae est in iunctura altera, ita insertas, ut ansa contra ansam veniat. ⁶Facies et quinquaginta fibulas aureas, quibus cortinarum vela iungenda sunt, ut unum habitaculum fiat. ⁷Facies et saga cilicina undecim pro tabernaculo super habitaculum. ⁸Longitudo sagi unius habebit triginta cubitos et latitudo quattuor; aequa erit mensura sagorum omnium. ⁹E quibus quinque iunges seorsum et sex sibi mutuo copulabis, ita ut sextum sagum in fronte tecti duplices. ¹⁰Facies et quinquaginta ansas in ora sagi ultimi iuncturae unius et quinquaginta ansas in ora sagi iuncturae alterius. ¹¹Facies et quinquaginta fibulas aeneas, quibus iungantur ansae, ut unum ex omnibus tabernaculum fiat. ¹²Quod autem superfuerit in sagis, quae parantur tecto, id est unum sagum, quod amplius est, ex medietate eius operies posteriora habitaculi; ¹³et cubitus ex una parte pendebit, et alter ex altera, qui plus est in longitudine sagorum tabernaculi utrumque latus

nacle. [13]And the cubit on the one side, and the cubit on the other side, of what remains in the length of the curtains of the tent shall hang over the sides of the tabernacle, on this side and that side, to cover it. [14]And you shall make for the tent a covering of tanned rams' skins and goatskins.

Ex 25:40;
36:20–34

The framework for the tabernacle

[15]"And you shall make upright frames for the tabernacle of acacia wood. [16]Ten cubits shall be the length of a frame, and a cubit and a half the breadth of each frame. [17]There shall be two tenons in each frame, for fitting together; so shall you do for all the frames of the tabernacle. [18]You shall make the frames for the tabernacle: twenty frames for the south side; [19]and forty bases of silver you shall make under the twenty frames, two bases under one frame for its two tenons, and two bases under another frame for its two tenons; [20]and for the second side of the tabernacle, on the north side twenty frames, [21]and their forty bases of silver, two bases under one frame, and two bases under another frame; [22]and for the rear of the tabernacle westward you shall make six frames. [23]And you shall make two frames for corners of the tabernacle in the rear; [24]they shall be separate beneath, but joined at the top, at the first ring; thus shall it be with both of them; they shall form the two corners. [25]And there shall be eight frames, with their bases of silver, sixteen bases; two bases under one frame, and two bases under another frame.

26:15–30. The mounting for the sanctuary (cf. 36:20–34) was made up of huge planks (about 4.2 x .6 metres; or 12 feet x 2 feet). The whole thing would have been about 12 metres long by 5 metres wide by 4 metres high (40 x 16 x 13 feet).

So, the structure was similar to the temple to be rebuilt in due course in Jerusalem, but with the difference that the desert sanctuary could be dismantled and moved from place to place.

---

habitaculi protegens. [14]Facies et operimentum aliud pro tabernaculo de pellibus arietum rubricatis et super hoc rursum aliud operimentum de pellibus delphini. [15]Facies et tabulas stantes habitaculi de lignis acaciae, [16]quae singulae denos cubitos in longitudine habeant et in latitudine singulos ac semissem. [17]In tabula una duo pedes fient, quibus tabula alteri tabulae conectatur; atque in hunc modum cunctae tabulae habitaculi parabuntur. [18]Quarum viginti erunt in latere meridiano, quod vergit ad austrum; [19]quibus quadraginta bases argenteas fundes, ut binae bases singulis pedibus singularum tabularum subiciantur. [20]In latere quoque secundo habitaculi, quod vergit ad aquilonem, viginti tabulae erunt, [21]quadraginta habentes bases argenteas; binae bases singulis tabulis supponentur. [22]Ad occidentalem vero plagam in tergo habitaculi facies sex tabulas; [23]et rursum alias duas, quae in angulis erigantur, post tergum habita-culi. [24]Eruntque geminae a deorsum usque sursum in compaginem unam; ita erit duabus istis, pro duabus angulis erunt. [25]Et erunt simul tabulae octo, bases earum argenteae sedecim, duabus basibus per unam tabulam supputatis. [26]Facies et vectes de lignis acaciae, quinque ad continendas tabulas in uno latere habitaculi [27]et quinque alios in altero et eiusdem numeri in tergo ad occidentalem plagam;

²⁶"And you shall make bars of acacia wood, five for the frames of the one side of the tabernacle, ²⁷and five bars for the frames of the other side of the tabernacle, and five bars for the frames of the side of the tabernacle at the rear westward. ²⁸The middle bar, halfway up the frames, shall pass through from end to end. ²⁹You shall overlay the frames with gold, and shall make their rings of gold for holders for the bars; and you shall overlay the bars with gold. ³⁰And you shall erect the tabernacle according to the plan for it which has been shown you on the mountain.

The veil

³¹"And you shall make a veil of blue and purple and scarlet stuff and fine twined linen; in skilled work shall it be made, with cherubim; ³²and you shall hang it upon four pillars of acacia overlaid with gold, with hooks of gold, upon four bases of silver. ³³And you shall hang the veil from the clasps, and bring the ark of the testimony in thither within the veil; and the veil shall separate for you the holy place from the most holy. ³⁴You shall put the

Ex 36:35–38
1 Kings 6:16
Mt 27:51
Mk 15:38
Lk 23:45
Heb 6:19; 9:1–14, 24; 10:19ff

26:31–37. The holy of holies (or the most holy), *Sancta sanctorum*, and the holy place or *sanctum* were the two parts into which the space formed by the mounting was divided. The first, a room 4 x 4 metres, was the holiest place of all; in it was kept the ark, and was considered to be the place where the Lord dwelt. Only the high priest was permitted to enter this space—and even then only once a year on the Day of Atonement (cf. Lev 16); the Letter to the Hebrews portrays Christ as the only priest, who brings about the redemption of all mankind, once for all, by his sacrifice on the cross and his glorious entry into heaven (cf. Heb 9:1–14).

This way of isolating the most holy place helped to show the transcendence of God. The veil (v. 31) was retained in the temple of Solomon (cf. 1 Kings 6:15–16) and in that of Herod (this was the veil that was torn in two at the moment of Christ's death, as a sign that a new era of salvation was beginning (cf. Mt 27:51) in which all mankind has direct access to God).

In the area known as the "holy" (*hekal*), the table of the bread was kept, and in front of it the seven-branched lampstand. Ordinary Jews could not go in here either (as the entrance veil or screen positioned here showed). But the richly-worked screen or veil separating the most holy from the holy place was much the more important.

---

²⁸vectis autem medius transibit per medias tabulas a summo usque ad summum. ²⁹Ipsasque tabulas deaurabis et fundes eis anulos aureos, per quos vectes tabulata contineant, quos operies laminis aureis. ³⁰Et eriges habitaculum iuxta exemplar, quod tibi in monte monstratum est. ³¹Facies et velum de hyacintho et purpura coccoque et bysso retorta, opere polymito, cum cherubim intextis. ³²Quod appendes in quattuor columnis de lignis acaciae, quae ipsae quidem deauratae erunt et habebunt uncos aureos, sed bases argenteas. ³³Inseres autem velum subter fibulas, intra quod pones arcam testimonii et quo sanctum et sanctum sanctorum dividentur. ³⁴Pones et propitiatorium super arcam testimonii in

mercy seat upon the ark of the testimony in the most holy place. [35]And you shall set the table outside the veil, and the lampstand on the south side of the tabernacle opposite the table; and you shall put the table on the north side.

The screen at the entrance

[36]"And you shall make a screen for the door of the tent, of blue and purple and scarlet stuff and fine twined linen, embroidered with needlework. [37]And you shall make for the screen five pillars of acacia, and overlay them with gold; their hooks shall be of gold, and you shall cast five bases of bronze for them.

Ex 38:1–7
1 Kings 8:64
Ezra 43:13–17

The altar of holocaust

27 [1]"You shall make the altar of acacia wood, five cubits long and five cubits broad; the altar shall be square, and its height shall be three cubits. [2]And you shall make horns for it on its four corners; its horns shall be of one piece with it, and you shall overlay it with bronze. [3]You shall make pots for it to receive its ashes, and shovels and basins and forks and firepans; all its utensils you shall make of bronze. [4]You shall also make for it a grating, a network of bronze; and upon the net you shall make four bronze rings at its four corners. [5]And you shall set it under the ledge of the altar so that the net shall extend halfway down the altar. [6]And you shall make poles for the altar, poles of acacia wood, and overlay them with bronze; [7]and the poles shall be put

Ex 29:12
1 Kings 1:50;
2:28
Rev 9:13

27:1–8. The altar of offering (cf. 38:1–7) was a kind of altar of acacia wood measuring 2 metres wide by 2 metres long by 1.2 metres high. On the four corners there were four horns, which would be anointed with the blood of sacrificed victims (cf. 29:12); by clinging to these horns, fugitives could win the right to asylum (cf. 1 Kings 50; 2:28).

Apparently the victims were not burnt on the altar (because the altar was made of material which could not resist heat); so, probably the animals were burned elsewhere (in line with the system laid down in 20:24), and the flame on the altar was symbolic.

sancto sanctorum [35]mensamque extra velum et contra mensam candelabrum in latere habitaculi meridiano; mensa enim stabit in parte aquilonis. [36]Facies et velum in introitu tabernaculi de hyacintho et purpura coccoque et bysso retorta opere plumarii. [37]Et quinque columnas deaurabis lignorum acaciae, ante quas ducetur velum, quarum erunt unci aurei et bases aeneae. [1]Facies et altare de lignis acaciae, quod habebit quinque cubitos in longitudine et totidem in latitudine, id est quadrum, et tres cubitos in altitudine. [2]Cornua autem per quattuor angulos ex ipso erunt, et operies illud aere. [3]Faciesque in usus eius lebetes ad suscipiendos cineres et vatilla et pateras atque fuscinulas et ignium receptacula; omnia vasa ex aere fabricabis. [4]Craticulamque facies ei in modum retis aeneam, per cuius quattuor angulos erunt quattuor anuli aenei, [5]et pones eam subter marginem altaris; eritque craticula usque ad altaris medium. [6]Facies et vectes altaris de lignis acaciae duos, quos operies laminis aeneis, [7]et induces per anulos; eruntque ex utroque latere altaris ad portandum. [8]Cavum ex tabulis facies illud; sicut tibi in monte

through the rings, so that the poles shall be upon the two sides of the altar, when it is carried. ⁸You shall make it hollow, with boards; as it has been shown you on the mountain, so shall it be made.

The court of the tabernacle

Ex 38:9–20
1 Kings 6:36
Ezek 40:17–49

⁹"You shall make the court of the tabernacle. On the south side the court shall have hangings of fine twined linen a hundred cubits long for one side; ¹⁰their pillars shall be twenty and their bases twenty, of bronze, but the hooks of the pillars and their fillets shall be of silver. ¹¹And likewise for its length on the north side there shall be hangings a hundred cubits long, their pillars twenty and their bases twenty, of bronze, but the hooks of the pillars and their fillets shall be of silver. ¹²And for the breadth of the court on the west side there shall be hangings for fifty cubits, with ten pillars and ten bases. ¹³The breadth of the court on the front to the east shall be fifty cubits. ¹⁴The hangings for the one side of the gate shall be fifteen cubits, with three pillars and three bases. ¹⁵On the other side the hangings shall be fifteen cubits, with three pillars and three bases. ¹⁶For the gate of the court there shall be a screen twenty cubits long, of blue and purple and scarlet stuff and fine twined linen, embroidered with needlework; it shall have four pillars and with them four bases. ¹⁷All the pillars around the court shall be filleted with silver; their hooks shall be of silver, and their bases of bronze. ¹⁸The length of the court shall be a hundred

---

27:9–21. The courtyard of the sanctuary (cf. 38:9–20) was an ample rectangular space some 42 metres (138 ft) long by 20 metres wide. There were curtains all round this sacred space hung from posts; they separated it from the rest of the encampment. In the temple of Solomon and in the second temple built after the Exile, this area formed the courtyards (cf. 1 Kings 6:36) out of which Jesus had to expel the money changers for profaning the holy place (Mt 21:12–17).

The use of pure olive oil (vv. 20–21) is a further small indication of the value and quality of all the items used in worship.

---

monstratum est, sic facient. ⁹Facies et atrium habitaculi, in cuius plaga australi contra meridiem erunt tentoria de bysso retorta: centum cubitos unum latus tenebit in longitudine ¹⁰et columnas viginti et bases totidem aeneas et uncos columnarum anulosque earum argenteos. ¹¹Similiter in latere aquilonis: per longum erunt tentoria centum cubitorum, columnae viginti et bases aeneae eiusdem numeri et unci columnarum anulique earum argentei. ¹²In latitudine vero atrii, quae respicit ad occidentem, erunt tentoria per quinquaginta cubitos et columnae decem basesque totidem. ¹³In ea quoque atrii latitudine, quae respicit ad orientem, quinquaginta cubiti erunt, ¹⁴in quibus quindecim cubitorum tentoria lateri uno deputabuntur columnaeque tres et bases totidem; ¹⁵et in latere altero erunt tentoria, cubitos obtinentia quindecim, columnae tres et bases totidem. ¹⁶In introitu vero atrii fiet velum cubitorum viginti, ex hyacintho et purpura coccoque et bysso retorta opere plumarii; columnas habebit quattuor cum basibus totidem. ¹⁷Omnes columnae atrii per circuitum cinctae erunt anulis argenteis et unci earum erunt

cubits, the breadth fifty, and the height five cubits, with hangings of fine twined linen and bases of bronze. [19]All the utensils of the tabernacle for every use, and all its pegs and all the pegs of the court, shall be of bronze.

Lev 24:2–4 **The oil for the lamps**

[20]"And you shall command the people of Israel that they bring to you pure beaten olive oil for the light, that a lamp may be set up Ex 30:7–8 to burn continually. [21]In the tent of meeting, outside the veil which 1 Sam 3:3 is before the testimony, Aaron and his sons shall tend it from evening to morning before the LORD. It shall be a statute for ever to be observed throughout their generations by the people of Israel.

Lev 8:10
Heb 5:4 **The priests' vestments**

28 [1]"Then bring near to you Aaron your brother, and his sons with him, from among the people of Israel, to serve me as priests—Aaron and Aaron's sons, Nadab and Abihu, Eleazar and Ithamar. [2]And you shall make holy garments for Aaron your brother, for glory and for beauty. [3]And you shall speak to all who have ability, whom I have endowed with an able mind, that they make Aaron's garments to consecrate him for my priesthood.

28:1–5. After these regulations about the sanctuary and its content the text now gives us the rules about priests. Priesthood in Israel was hereditary; it was the province of the sons of Aaron, and later on of the tribe of Levi; but the latter always regarded Aaron as their model, because God himself had made him priest (cf. 29:4–7). The priestly class will perform an important role, not only as those who maintain and perform the liturgy but also as defenders of the faith and transmitters of doctrine, especially from the Babylonian exile onwards. And from the time of the Maccabees the priests will be prominent in political history too.

The vestments worn by the priests show the importance that worship has: they have to be made of rich material and by expert craftspeople.

argentei et bases aeneae. [18]In longitudine occupabit atrium cubitos centum, in latitudine quinquaginta, altitudo quinque cubitorum erit; fietque de bysso retorta, et habebit bases aeneas. [19]Cuncta vasa habitaculi in omnes usus eius et omnes paxillos eius et omnes paxillos atrii ex aere facies. [20]Praecipe filiis Israel, ut afferant tibi oleum de arboribus olivarum purissimum piloque contusum, ut ardeat lucerna semper [21]in tabernaculo conventus, extra velum, quod oppansum est testimonio. Et parabunt eam Aaron et filii eius, ut a vespere usque mane luceat coram Domino. Perpetuus erit cultus per successiones eorum a filiis Israel. [1]Applica quoque ad te Aaron fratrem tuum cum filiis suis de medio filiorum Israel, ut sacerdotio fungantur mihi: Aaron, Nadab et Abiu, Eleazar et Ithamar. [2]Faciesque vestes sanctas Aaron fratri tuo in gloriam et decorem; [3]et loqueris cunctis sapientibus corde, quos replevi spiritu prudentiae, ut faciant vestes Aaron, in quibus sanctificatus ministret mihi. [4]Haec autem erunt vestimenta, quae facient: pectorale et ephod, tunicam et subuculam textam, tiaram et balteum. Facient vestimenta sancta Aaron fratri tuo et filiis eius, ut sacerdotio fungantur mihi; [5]accipientque aurum et hyacinthum

⁴These are the garments which they shall make: a breastpiece, an ephod, a robe, a coat of checker work, a turban, and a girdle; they shall make holy garments for Aaron your brother and his sons to serve me as priests.

⁵"They shall receive gold, blue and purple and scarlet stuff, and fine twined linen.

The ephod

⁶And they shall make the ephod of gold, of blue and purple and scarlet stuff, and of fine twined linen, skilfully worked. ⁷It shall have two shoulder-pieces attached to its two edges, that it may be joined together. ⁸And the skilfully woven band upon it, to gird it on, shall be of the same workmanship and materials, of gold, blue and purple and scarlet stuff, and fine twined linen. ⁹And you shall take two onyx stones, and engrave on them the names of the sons of Israel, ¹⁰six of their names on the one stone, and the names of the remaining six on the other stone, in the order of their birth. ¹¹As a jeweller engraves signets, so shall you engrave the two stones with the names of the sons of Israel; you shall enclose them in settings of gold filigree. ¹²And you shall set the two stones upon the shoulder-pieces of the ephod, as stones of remembrance for the sons of Israel; and Aaron shall bear their names

Ex 39:2–7
1 Sam 2:18
2 Sam 6:14

Ex 30:16
Num 31:54

28:6–30. The ephod (cf. 39:2–7) was the garment specific to priests (cf. 1 Kings 2:18) and those who had a direct role in divine worship (for example, David: cf. 2 Kings 6:14). The same word was used for a receptacle used in the early sanctuaries of the north to hold the lots for divining the will of God (cf. 1 Kings 2:28; 14:18–20); it even came to mean an idolatrous object (cf. Judg 8:26–27). As a priestly vestment the ephod was distinctive of the high priest; it was a kind of apron which was held in place by a belt and two shoulder-pads; these latter each

had on it an onyxstone engraved with the names of the tribes (six and six).

The breastpiece of judgment was a richly-embroidered square piece of fabric placed over the chest and fixed to the shoulder pads and the belt. At the time when the sacred author wrote this, priestly vestments had undergone many changes; so it is not easy to work out what form they originally took. However, it does seem that the breastpiece had a kind of bag inside it where the Urim and Tummim were kept; these were devices used for ascertaining the will of God and

---

et purpuram coccumque et byssum. ⁶Facient autem ephod de auro et hyacintho ac purpura coccoque bysso retorta opere polymito. ⁷Duas fascias umerales habebit et in utroque latere summitatum suarum copulabitur cum eis. ⁸Et balteus super ephod ad constringendum, eiusdem operis et unum cum eo, erit ex auro et hyacintho et purpura coccoque et bysso retorta. ⁹Sumesque duos lapides onychinos et sculpes in eis nomina filiorum Israel: ¹⁰sex nomina in lapide uno et sex reliqua in altero, iuxta ordinem nativitatis eorum. ¹¹Opere sculptoris et caelatura gemmarii sculpes eos nominibus filiorum Israel, inclusos textura aurea; ¹²et pones duos lapides super fascias umerales ephod, lapides memorialis filiorum

before the LORD upon his two shoulders for remembrance. [13]And you shall make settings of gold filigree, [14]and two chains of pure gold, twisted like cords; and you shall attach the corded chains to the settings.

Ex 39:8–21 **The breastpiece**

[15]"And you shall make a breastpiece of judgment, in skilled work; like the work of the ephod you shall make it; of gold, blue and purple and scarlet stuff, and fine twined linen shall you make it. [16]It shall be square and double, a span its length and a span its

Ex 39:10–13 breadth. [17]And you shall set in it four rows of stones. A row of
Ezek 28:13 sardius, topaz, and carbuncle shall be the first row; [18]and the sec-
Rev 21:19 ond row an emerald, a sapphire, and a diamond; [19]and the third row a jacinth, an agate, and an amethyst; [20]and the fourth row a beryl, an onyx, and a jasper; they shall be set in gold filigree.

Rev 21:12, 19 [21]There shall be twelve stones with their names according to the names of the sons of Israel; they shall be like signets, each engraved with its name, for the twelve tribes. [22]And you shall make for the breastpiece twisted chains like cords, of pure gold; [23]and you shall make for the breastpiece two rings of gold, and put the two rings on the two edges of the breastpiece. [24]And you shall put the two cords of gold in the two rings at the edges of the breastpiece; [25]the two ends of the two cords you shall attach to the two settings of filigree, and so attach it in front to the shoulder-pieces of the ephod. [26]And you shall make two rings of gold, and put them at the two ends of the breastpiece, on its inside edge next to the ephod. [27]And you shall make two rings of gold, and attach them in front to the lower part of the two shoulder-pieces of the ephod, at its joining above the skilfully woven band of the ephod. [28]And they shall bind the breastpiece by its rings to the rings of

---

Israel. Portabitque Aaron nomina eorum coram Domino super utrumque umerum ob recordationem. [13]Facies ergo margines textas ex auro [14]et duas catenulas ex auro purissimo quasi funiculos opus tortile et inseres catenulas tortas marginibus. [15]Pectorale quoque iudicii facies opere polymito, iuxta texturam ephod, ex auro, hyacintho et purpura coccoque et bysso retorta. [16]Quadrangulum erit et duplex; mensuram palmi habebit tam in longitudine quam in latitudine. [17]Ponesque in eo quattuor ordines lapidum: in primo versu erit lapis sardius et topazius et smaragdus; [18]in secundo carbunculus, sapphirus et iaspis; [19]in tertio hyacinthus, achates et amethystus; [20]in quarto chrysolithus, onychinus et beryllus. Inclusi auro erunt per ordines suos. [21]Habebuntque nomina filiorum Israel: duodecim nominibus caelabuntur, singuli lapides nominibus singulorum per duodecim tribus. [22]Facies in pectorali catenas quasi funiculos, opus tortile, ex auro purissimo; [23]et duos anulos aureos, quos pones in utraque pectoralis summitate; [24]catenasque aureas iunges anulis, qui sunt in marginalibus eius; [25]et ipsarum catenarum extrema duobus copulabis marginibus in fasciis umeralibus ephod in parte eius anteriore. [26]Facies et duos anulos aureos, quos pones in summitatibus pectoralis in ora interiore, quae respicit ephod. [27]Necnon et alios duos anulos aureos, qui ponendi sunt in utraque fascia umerali ephod deorsum, versus partem anteriorem eius iuxta iuncturam eius supra balteum ephod, [28]et stringatur pectorale anulis suis

the ephod with a lace of blue, that it may lie upon the skilfully woven band of the ephod, and that the breastpiece shall not come loose from the ephod. [29]So Aaron shall bear the names of the sons of Israel in the breastpiece of judgment upon his heart, when he goes into the holy place, to bring them to continual remembrance before the LORD. [30]And in the breastpiece of judgment you shall put the Urim and the Thummim, and they shall be upon Aaron's heart, when he goes in before the LORD; thus Aaron shall bear the judgment of the people of Israel upon his heart before the LORD continually.

Jn 11:51

The robe

Ex 39:22–26

[31]"And you shall make the robe of the ephod all of blue. [32]It shall have in it an opening for the head, with a woven binding around the opening, like the opening in a garment,[p] that it may not be torn. [33]On its skirts you shall make pomegranates of blue and purple and scarlet stuff, around its skirts, with bells of gold between them, [34]a golden bell and a pomegranate, a golden bell and a pomegranate, roundabout on the skirts of the robe. [35]And it shall be upon Aaron when he ministers, and its sound shall be heard when he goes into the holy place before the LORD, and when he comes out, lest he die.

Sir 45:9

---

the fate of the sons of Israel (v. 30). This garment too had twelve stones on it with the names of the tribes, to show that the high priest's main function was to represent the people before God at the most solemn liturgical ceremonies.

28:31–35 The robe of the ephod (cf. 39:22–26) was an ample garment rather like a dalmatic which reached as far as the knees; it was all one piece and had an opening for the head. It was very richly worked, with pomegranates embroidered on the edges, and bells. The tingling of these bells (we do not know their origin) was later to become "a reminder to the sons of his people" (Sir 45:9) of the splendour of the glory of the Lord.

cum anulis ephod vitta hyacinthina, ut maneat supra balteum ephod, et a se invicem pectorale et ephod nequeant separari. [29]Portabitque Aaron nomina filiorum Israel in pectorali iudicii super cor suum, quando ingredietur sanctuarium: memoriale coram Domino in aeternum. [30]Pones autem in pectorali iudicii Urim et Tummim, quae erunt super cor Aaron, quando ingredietur coram Domino; et gestabit iudicium filiorum Israel super cor suum in conspectu Domini semper. [31]Facies et pallium ephod totum hyacinthinum, [32]in cuius medio supra erit capitium et ora per gyrum eius textilis, sicut in capitio loricae, ne rumpatur. [33]Deorsum vero, ad pedes eiusdem pallii per circuitum, quasi mala punica facies ex hyacintho et purpura et cocco, mixtis in medio tintinnabulis aureis; [34]ita ut sit tintinnabulum aureum inter singula mala punica. [35]Et vestietur eo Aaron in officio ministerii, ut audiatur sonitus, quando ingreditur et egreditur sanctuarium in conspectu Domini, et non moriatur. [36]Facies et laminam de auro purissimo, in qua sculpes opere caelatoris: «Sanctum Domino». [37]Ligabisque eam vitta hyacinthina, et

p. The Hebrew word is of uncertain meaning

Ex 39:27–31 **The tiara or turban**

Rev 13:16 ³⁶"And you shall make a plate of pure gold, and engrave on it, like the engraving of a signet, 'Holy to the LORD.' ³⁷And you shall fasten it on the turban by a lace of blue; it shall be on the front of the turban. ³⁸It shall be upon Aaron's forehead, and Aaron shall take upon himself any guilt incurred in the holy offering which the people of Israel hallow as their holy gifts; it shall always be upon his forehead, that they may be accepted before the LORD.

³⁹"And you shall weave the coat in checker work of fine linen, and you shall make a turban of fine linen, and you shall make a girdle embroidered with needlework.

Ex 20:26
2 Sam 6:20–23 **The vestments of the priests**

⁴⁰"And for Aaron's sons you shall make coats and girdles and caps; you shall make them for glory and beauty. ⁴¹And you shall put them upon Aaron your brother, and upon his sons with him, and shall anoint them and ordain them and consecrate them, that they may serve me as priests. ⁴²And you shall make for them linen breeches to cover their naked flesh; from the loins to the thighs they shall reach; ⁴³and they shall be upon Aaron, and upon his

---

28:36–39. The headpiece (cf. 39:27–31 and Lev 8:9) comprised of a magnificent turban or tiara at the centre of which was gold plate probably shaped like a flower (as the Hebrew root of the word suggests: cf. Num 17:23), symbol of life and health, inscribed with the words "Holy to the Lord", that is, separated out from others to attend to the things of God. This motto came to be understood by the people as meaning that involuntary ritual sins were expiated for in the person of the high priest. The expiatory role of the priest will receive increasing emphasis as time goes on, until eventu-

ally it is his main role: "He [the high priest] is bound to offer sacrifice for his own sins as well as for those of the people" (Heb 5:3).

28:40–43. The other priests will also wear suitably rich vestments but much less elaborate than the high priest's. The last stipulation (vv. 42–43) is connected to the precept of Exodus 20:26 and shows the importance given to the smallest details of cult, avoiding any trace of immodesty (cf. 2 Sam 6:20–23).

On the meaning of ordination (v. 21) see the note on Ex 29:9.

---

erit super tiaram ³⁸super frontem Aaron. Portabitque Aaron iniquitatem contra sancta, quae sanctificabunt filii Israel in cunctis muneribus et donariis suis. Eritque lamina semper in fronte eius, ut placatus eis sit Dominus. ³⁹Texesque tunicam bysso et tiaram byssinam facies et balteum opere plumarii. ⁴⁰Porro filiis Aaron tunicas lineas parabis et balteos ac mitras in gloriam et decorem; ⁴¹vestiesque his omnibus Aaron fratrem tuum et filios eius cum eo. Et unges eos et implebis manus eorum sanctificabisque illos, ut sacerdotio fungantur mihi. ⁴²Facies eis et feminalia linea, ut operiant carnem turpitudinis suae a renibus usque ad femora; ⁴³et utentur eis Aaron et filii eius, quando ingredientur tabernaculum conventus, vel quando appropinquant ad altare, ut ministrent in sanctuario, ne iniquitatis

sons, when they go into the tent of meeting, or when they come
near the altar to minister in the holy place; lest they bring guilt
upon themselves and die. This shall be a perpetual statute for him
and for his descendants after him.

The ordination of priests*

Lev 8
Heb 7:26–28

29 [1]"Now this is what you shall do to them to consecrate
them, that they may serve me as priests. Take one young
bull and two rams without blemish, [2]and unleavened bread,
unleavened cakes mixed with oil, and unleavened wafers spread
with oil. You shall make them of fine wheat flour. [3]And you shall
put them in one basket and bring them in the basket, and bring the
bull and the two rams. [4]You shall bring Aaron and his sons to the
door of the tent of meeting, and wash them with water. [5]And you
shall take the garments, and put on Aaron the coat and the robe of
the ephod, and the ephod, and the breastpiece, and gird him with
the skilfully woven band of the ephod; [6]and you shall set the

Lev 2:4

Ex 30:18–21
Heb 10:22

Ex 28:36ff;
39:30

---

*29:1–9. The rite of consecration of
priests is described in great detail: more
information on some of the ritual is given
in Leviticus 8. This ceremony presup-
poses that the priesthood was exercised
only by members of the tribe of Levi—
which did not happen until after the exile
in Babylon. Prior to that, priestly func-
tions were on occasions performed by
non-Levites such as Micah (cf. Judg
17:5), Eleazar (cf. 1 Sam 7:1), and David
himself (cf. 2 Sam 8:18). So, this ritual
includes ancient elements as well as
others which did not come in until the
temple of Zerubbabel was built.

There were two stages in the consecration—anointing and offering. The
anointing with oil showed that the man
was being dedicated exclusively to the
service of the Lord.

It seems that only the high priest had
to be anointed (cf. Lev 16:32; 21:10),
despite the allusions to the anointing of
all priests (cf. Ex 28:41; 30:30; 40:15).
Before being anointed he had to be
rewashed all over and carefully dressed
in priestly garments. All this shows the
complete ritual purity required of the
high priest (cf. the note on 30:22–33).

29:4. Ritual washing symbolized the
inner cleanliness of those officiating at
the ceremony. Each time they approached the altar they had to wash hands and
feet (cf. 30:18–21); but on the day of
consecration they had to be washed all
over.

In Christian liturgy there are simple
ablutions, meant to symbolize interior
contrition; for example, the *Lavabo* at

---

rei moriantur: legitimum sempiternum erit Aaron et semini eius post eum. [1]Sed et hoc facies eis, ut
mihi in sacerdotio consecrentur: tolle vitulum unum de armento et arietes duos immaculatos [2]panesque
azymos et crustulas absque fermento, quae conspersa sint oleo, lagana quoque azyma oleo lita; de
simila triticea cuncta facies [3]et posita in canistro offeres, vitulum quoque et duos arietes. [4]Aaron ac
filios eius applicabis ad ostium tabernaculi conventus. Cumque laveris patrem cum filiis suis aqua,
[5]indues Aaron vestimentis suis, id est subucula et tunica ephod et ephod et pectorali, quod constringes
ei cingulo ephod; [6]et pones tiaram in capite eius et diadema sanctum super tiaram [7]et oleum unctionis

Ex 28:41;
30:22–23;
30:30; 40:15
Lev 8:1ff; 21:10

turban on his head, and put the holy crown upon the turban. [7]And you shall take the anointing oil, and pour it on his head and anoint him. [8]Then you shall bring his sons, and put coats on them, [9]and you shall gird them with girdles[q] and bind caps on them; and the priesthood shall be theirs by a perpetual statute. Thus you shall ordain Aaron and his sons.

Sacrifices at ordination*

Lev 1:5; 4:1–12

[10]"Then you shall bring the bull before the tent of meeting. Aaron and his sons shall lay their hands upon the head of the bull, [11]and you shall kill the bull before the LORD, at the door of the tent of

Lev 4:7

meeting, [12]and shall take part of the blood of the bull and put it upon the horns of the altar with your finger, and the rest of[r] the blood you shall pour out at the base of the altar. [13]And you shall take all the fat that covers the entrails, and the appendage of the

---

Mass is, primarily, a sign of repentance, accompanied by some words taken from Psalm 51.

29:9. "Thus you shall ordain": literally, "you will fill their hands" (cf. 28:41; Lev 8:22-29; Judg 17:5, 12). This is a technical term which probably refers to the fact that they were being given for the first time part of the victims offered in the sacrifice. In the Christian rite of ordination of priests, the bishop gives the ordinand the chalice and paten as a sign of the ministry being conferred on him.

*29:10–37. The offerings or sacrifices at the consecration of priests were three in number—one expiatory (vv. 10–14), according to the ritual to be found in Leviticus 4:1–12); the second a burnt offering (vv. 14–18) in praise and thanksgiving to God (cf. Lev 1); the last a con-

secration sacrifice (vv. 19–37) which was a type of offering and which also involved the unleavened bread (v. 32); as well as having its own features, it was a communion offering (vv. 31–37).

The importance of the consecration of the high priest can be seen in the fact that it included the holding of the three most solemn kinds of sacrifice. In the Old Testament sacrifices were the key acts of worship, because they were an external expression of communion with God, his sovereignty over creation, and his mercy in forgiving sin. Communion with God is to be seen above all in the communion or peace offerings, probably the oldest sort of sacrifice, in which God accepts the victim offered and receives a part of it on the altar, while the rest is eaten by the offerers at a holy meal. God's sovereignty over creation is seen in the holocaust or burnt offering, in

---

fundes super caput eius; atque hoc ritu consecrabitur. [8]Filios quoque illius applicabis et indues tunicis lineis cingesque balteo [9]et impones eis mitras; eruntque sacerdotes mihi iure perpetuo. Postquam impleveris manus Aaron et filiorum eius, [10]applicabis et vitulum coram tabernaculo conventus; imponentque Aaron et filii eius manus super caput illius, [11]et mactabis eum in conspectu Domini, iuxta ostium tabernaculi conventus. [12]Sumptumque de sanguine vituli, pones super cornua altaris digito tuo,

q. Gk: Heb *girdles, Aaron and his sons* **r.** Heb *all*

liver, and the two kidneys with the fat that is on them, and burn them upon the altar. ¹⁴But the flesh of the bull, and its skin, and its dung, you shall burn with fire outside the camp; it is a sin offering. Lev 4:1ff

¹⁵"Then you shall take one of the rams, and Aaron and his sons shall lay their hands upon the head of the ram, ¹⁶and you shall slaughter the ram, and shall take its blood and throw it against the altar round about. ¹⁷Then you shall cut the ram into pieces, and wash its entrails and its legs, and put them with its pieces and its head, ¹⁸and burn the whole ram upon the altar; it is a burnt offering to the LORD; it is a pleasing odour, an offering by fire to the LORD

Lev 1:1–17
Eph 5:2
Phil 4:18

¹⁹"You shall take the other ram; and Aaron and his sons shall lay their hands upon the head of the ram, ²⁰and you shall kill the

---

which God accepts the entire victim, itself a gift from the offerer showing that he acknowledges the supreme dominion of the Lord: "All things come from thee, and of thy own have we been given them" (1 Chron 29:14). Expiatory sacrifices, sin offerings, express faith in God's mercy: the ceremony involving the blood is essential because it symbolizes the purification which God is bringing about; however, these sacrifices were never magical rites which produced results irrespective of the attitude of the offerers. Hence the prophets' constant condemnation of those who try to get away with their depraved behaviour by going through the formality of ritual sacrifice (cf. Hos 2:3–15; Amos 4:4–5; etc.).

These three offerings are, like the Passover, a figure of the one, true sacrifice of Christ on the cross, which is at one and the same time atonement, holocaust and communion.

29:10. The imposition of hands on the victim's head is a rite that is frequently found in sacrifices. This gesture does not really mean that one is passing one's own sins onto the victim or that the victim is a substitute for the offerer; it is a sign of ownership, to show that *this* is the offerer's victim. Therefore, the gesture identifies who is the offerer making the sacrifice, even though it is others, the ministers, who perform the ceremonies.

29:18. This is an anthropomorphism frequently found in the Bible—describing the offering as smelling sweet to God. Far from implying a crass materialism, as if God were going to eat the tasty offering (cf. Deut 14:1–22), it is saying that God desires things to be offered up to him: that is why they are said to please him.

29:19–20. The most characteristic feature of the consecration offering is this ritual

---

reliquum autem sanguinem fundes iuxta basim eius. ¹³Sumes et adipem totum, qui operit intestina, et reticulum iecoris ac duos renes et adipem, qui super eos est, et offeres comburens super altare; ¹⁴carnes vero vituli et corium et fimum combures foris extra castra, eo quod pro peccato sit. ¹⁵Unum quoque arietem sumes, super cuius caput ponent Aaron et filii eius manus; ¹⁶quem cum mactaveris, tolles sanguinem eius et fundes super altare per circuitum. ¹⁷Ipsum autem arietem secabis in frusta lotaque intestina eius ac pedes pones super concisas carnes et super caput illius. ¹⁸Et adolebis totum arietem

ram, and take part of its blood and put it upon the tip of the right ear of Aaron and upon the tips of the right ears of his sons, and upon the thumbs of their right hands, and upon the great toes of their right feet, and throw the rest of the blood against the altar round about. ²¹Then you shall take part of the blood that is on the altar, and of the anointing oil, and sprinkle it upon Aaron and his garments, and upon his sons and his sons' garments with him; and he and his garments shall be holy, and his sons and his sons' garments with him.

²²"You shall also take the fat of the ram, and the fat tail, and the fat that covers the entrails, and the appendage of the liver, and the two kidneys with the fat that is on them, and the right thigh (for it is a ram of ordination), ²³and one loaf of bread, and one cake of bread with oil, and one wafer, out of the basket of unleav-
Lev 7:30ff ened bread that is before the LORD; ²⁴and you shall put all these in the hands of Aaron and in the hands of his sons, and wave them for a wave offering before the LORD. ²⁵Then you shall take them from their hands, and burn them on the altar in addition to the burnt offering, as a pleasing odour before the LORD; it is an offering by fire to the LORD.

²⁶"And you shall take the breast of the ram of Aaron's ordination and wave it for a wave offering before the LORD; and it shall

with the blood. The blood is put on the altar but also on the ears, hands and feet of the priest, who ought to be as far away from the people as the altar is from profane objects. The triple anointing spells out what his office entails: the priest ought always listen to the voice of God, devote himself to the work of the temple, and walk in holiness. That is what the consecration of priests is meant to imply.

29:26–28. This ceremony consisted in swinging in front of and behind oneself

that part of the victim which (now, after the offertory) belongs to the priests and is for their upkeep. The term *tenufáh* which is used for this waving and swinging passed into ordinary language; it can mean either the sacrifice in which the priests took part or the portion of the victim which was designated as theirs.

Another part of the offering (we do not now know what it was) was ceremoniously raised up and it too was kept as a stipend for the priests. The technical term *terumáh* became synonymous in ordinary

super altare: holocaustum est Domino, odor suavissimus, incensum est Domino. ¹⁹Tolles quoque arietem alterum, super cuius caput Aaron et filii eius ponent manus; ²⁰quem cum immolaveris, sumes de sanguine ipsius et pones super extremum auriculae dextrae Aaron et filiorum eius et super pollices manus eorum ac pedis dextri; fundesque sanguinem super altare per circuitum. ²¹Cumque tuleris de sanguine, qui est super altare, et de oleo unctionis, asperges Aaron et vestes eius, filios et vestimenta eorum cum ipso. Et sanctus erit ipse et vestimenta eius et filii eius et vestimenta eorum cum ipso. ²²Tollesque adipem de ariete et caudam et arvinam, quae operit intestina, ac reticulum iecoris et duos renes atque adipem, qui super eos est, armumque dextrum, eo quod sit aries consecrationis, ²³tortamque panis unam, crustulam unam conspersam oleo, laganum unum de canistro azymorum, quod positum

be your portion. ²⁷And you shall consecrate the breast of the wave offering, and the thigh of the priests' portion, which is waved, and which is offered from the ram of ordination, since it is for Aaron and for his sons. ²⁸It shall be for Aaron and his sons as a perpetual due from the people of Israel, for it is the priests' portion to be offered by the people of Israel from their peace offerings; it is their offering to the LORD.

²⁹"The holy garments of Aaron shall be for his sons after him, to be anointed in them and ordained in them. ³⁰The son who is priest in his place shall wear them seven days, when he comes into the tent of meeting to minister in the holy place.

The sacred meal

³¹"You shall take the ram of ordination, and boil its flesh in a holy place; ³²and Aaron and his sons shall eat the flesh of the ram and the bread that is in the basket, at the door of the tent of meeting. ³³They shall eat those things with which atonement was made, to   Mt 7:6 ordain and consecrate them, but an outsider shall not eat of them, because they are holy. ³⁴And if any of the flesh for the ordination, or of the bread, remain until the morning, then you shall burn the remainder with fire; it shall not be eaten, because it is holy.

---

language with a religious offering or tribute (cf. 25:1).

29:31–37. The meal which follows the consecration was part of the whole ceremony and had a sacred character; no lay person could partake of it. Moreover, anything not eaten had to be burned. All the little details to do with the consecration offering serve to stress the transcendence and holiness of God. Everything to

do with the rite, be it the people or the things they use, should reflect the fact that it is all centred on God.

The consecration ceremonies lasted seven days (vv. 35–37), because they involved also the consecration of the altar and other items to do with worship. They were festive celebrations, expressing the joy of those who serve the Lord: "Serve the Lord with gladness! Come into his presence singing!" (Ps 100:2).

---

est in conspectu Domini; ²⁴ponesque omnia super manus Aaron et filiorum eius, ut agitent ea coram Domino. ²⁵Suscipiesque universa de manibus eorum et incendes in altari super holocausto in odorem suavissimum in conspectu Domini; quia incensum est Domino. ²⁶Sumes quoque pectusculum de ariete, quo initiatus est Aaron, elevabisque illud coram Domino; et cedet in partem tuam. ²⁷Sanctificabisque pectusculum elevatum et armum oblatum, quem de ariete separasti, ²⁸quo initiatus est Aaron et filii eius; cedentque in partem Aaron et filiorum eius iure perpetuo a filiis Israel; quia oblatio est et oblatio erit a filiis Israel de victimis eorum pacificis, oblatio eorum Domino. ²⁹Vestem autem sanctam, qua utetur Aaron, habebunt filii eius post eum, ut ungantur in ea, et impleantur in ea manus eorum. ³⁰Septem diebus utetur illa, qui pontifex pro eo fuerit constitutus de filiis eius, qui ingredietur tabernaculum conventus, ut ministret in sanctuario. ³¹Arietem autem consecrationis tolles et coques carnes eius in loco sancto. ³²Et vescetur Aaron et filii eius carnibus arietis et panibus, qui sunt in canistro, in vestibulo tabernaculi conventus. ³³Et comedent ea, quibus expiatio facta fuerit ad implendum manus

The consecration of the altar

³⁵"Thus you shall do to Aaron and to his sons, according to all that I have commanded you; through seven days shall you ordain them, ³⁶and every day you shall offer a bull as a sin offering for atonement. Also you shall offer a sin offering for the altar, when you make atonement for it, and shall anoint it, to consecrate it. ³⁷Seven days you shall make atonement for the altar, and consecrate it, and the altar shall be most holy; whatever touches the altar shall become holy.

Mt 23:19

Lev 6:2
Num 28:3–8
Ezek 46:13–15

The daily burnt offering

1 Kings 18:29
2 Kings 16:13
Heb 7:27

³⁸"Now this is what you shall offer upon the altar: two lambs a year old day by day continually. ³⁹One lamb you shall offer in the morning, and the other lamb you shall offer in the evening; ⁴⁰and with the first lamb a tenth measure of fine flour mingled with a fourth of a hin of beaten oil, and a fourth of a hin of wine for alibation. ⁴¹And the other lamb you shall offer in the evening, and shall offer with it a cereal offering and its libation, as in the morning, for a pleasing odour, an offering by fire to the LORD. ⁴²It shall be a continual burnt offering throughout your generations at the door of the tent of meeting before the LORD, where I will meet with you, to speak there to you. ⁴³There I will meet with the

Ex 25:22

29:38–46. Daily sacrifices were held in Israel from very early on, as we know from the story of Elijah (cf. 1 Kings 18:29) and from the offering made by Ahaz, king of Israel (2 Kings 16:13). But apparently it was not until after the Exile that they were conducted with all the detailed ritual described here (cf. Ezek 46:13–15; Lev 6:2–6).

In the language of worship a tenth-measure of flour is the equivalent to a tenth of an ephah of fine flour (cf. Lev 5:11; 6:13), that is, the tenth of the capacity of a receptacle that would hold 21 litres or five gallons (cf. the note on Ex 16:32–36). A hin (used for oil, wine or water) was about 3.6 litres.

Religious worship in Israel underwent many changes over the years, but despite the ever-present danger of falling into a mere external formalism it always held on to the idea that men can obtain access to God, who is present among his own people. The Christian liturgy makes

---

eorum, ad sanctificandum eos. Alienigena non vescetur ex eis, quia sancta sunt. ³⁴Quod si remanserit de carnibus consecrationis sive de panibus usque mane, combures reliquias igni; non comedentur, quia sancta sunt. ³⁵Omnia, quae praecepi tibi, facies super Aaron et filiis eius. Septem diebus consecrabis manus eorum ³⁶et vitulum pro peccato offeres per singulos dies ad expiandum. Mundabisque altare expians illud et unges illud in sanctificationem. ³⁷Septem diebus expiabis altare et sanctificabis; et erit sanctum sanctorum: omnis, qui tetigerit illud, sanctificabitur. ³⁸Hoc est quod facies in altari: agnos anniculos duos per singulos dies iugiter, ³⁹unum agnum mane et alterum vespere; ⁴⁰decimam partem similae conspersae oleo tunso, quod habeat mensuram quartam partem hin, et vinum ad libandum eiusdem mensurae in agno uno. ⁴¹Alterum vero agnum offeres ad vesperam iuxta ritum matutinae oblationis et libationis in odorem suavitatis, incensum Domino, ⁴²holocaustum perpetuum in generationes

people of Israel, and it shall be sanctified by my glory; ⁴⁴I will Ex 24:16; 40:34
consecrate the tent of meeting and the altar; Aaron also and his
sons I will consecrate, to serve me as priests. ⁴⁵And I will dwell
among the people of Israel, and will be their God. ⁴⁶And they
shall know that I am the LORD their God, who brought them forth
out of the land of Egypt that I might dwell among them; I am the
LORD their God.

The altar of incense

30 ¹"You shall make an altar to burn incense upon; of acacia
wood shall you make it. ²A cubit shall be its length, and a
cubit its breadth; it shall be square, and two cubits shall be its
height; its horns shall be of one piece with it. ³And you shall overlay it with pure gold, its top and its sides round about and its
horns; and you shall make for it a moulding of gold round about.
⁴And two golden rings shall you make for it; under its moulding
on two opposite sides of it shall you make them, and they shall be
holders for poles with which to carry it. ⁵You shall make the poles
of acacia wood, and overlay them with gold. ⁶And you shall put it
before the veil that is by the ark of the testimony, before the
mercy seat that is over the testimony, where I will meet with you.
⁷And Aaron shall burn fragrant incense on it; every morning when Lk 1:9

Ex 37:25–28; 40:26
1 Kings 6:20–22; 7:48
Num 4:11
Rev 8:3–5; 9:13

---

a reality of what was figure and symbol in the Old Testament: "Christ, indeed, always associates the Church with himself in this great work [the Liturgy] in which God is perfectly glorified and men are sanctified. The Church is his beloved Bride who calls to her Lord, and through him offers worship to the eternal Father" (Vatican II, *Sacrosanctum Concilium*, 7).

30:1–10. The altar of incense (cf. 37:25–28; 40:26) was a place in Solomon's temple in front of the Holy of Holies (cf. 1 Kings 6:20–22; 7:48). Incense was used in religious worship from very early on both in Mesopotamia and in Canaan. Being a sweet-smelling substance it is very good for conveying an atmosphere and for perfuming venues where big crowds gather for either religious or profane events; above all, it symbolizes praise making its way up to heaven.

vestras, ad ostium tabernaculi conventus coram Domino, ubi conveniam vos, ut loquar ad te. ⁴³Ibi conveniam filios Israel, et sanctificabitur locus in gloria mea. ⁴⁴Sanctificabo et tabernaculum conventus cum altari et Aaron cum filiis eius, ut sacerdotio fungantur mihi. ⁴⁵Et habitabo in medio filiorum Israel eroque eis Deus; ⁴⁶et scient quia ego Dominus Deus eorum, qui eduxi eos de terra Aegypti, ut manerem inter illos: ego Dominus Deus ipsorum. ¹Facies quoque altare ad adolendum thymiama de lignis acaciae ²habens cubitum longitudinis et alterum latitudinis, id est quadrangulum, et duos cubitos in altitudine; cornua ex ipso procedent. ³Vestiesque illud auro purissimo, tam craticulam eius quam parietes per circuitum et cornua. Faciesque ei coronam aureolam per gyrum ⁴et duos anulos aureos sub corona in duobus lateribus, ut mittantur in eos vectes, et altare portetur. ⁵Ipsos quoque vectes facies de lignis acaciae et inaurabis. ⁶Ponesque altare contra velum, quod ante arcam pendet testimonii, coram propitiatorio, quo tegitur testimonium, ubi conveniam ad te. ⁷Et adolebit incensum super eo Aaron suave fra-

he dresses the lamps he shall burn it, [8]and when Aaron sets up the lamps in the evening, he shall burn it, a perpetual incense before the LORD throughout your generations. [9]You shall offer no unholy incense thereon, nor burnt offering, nor cereal offering; and you

Heb 9:7 shall pour no libation thereon. [10]Aaron shall make atonement upon its horns once a year; with the blood of the sin offering of atonement he shall make atonement for it once in the year throughout your generations; it is most holy to the LORD.'

Ex 38: 24–31 **The half-shekel tax**

2 Sam 24
Num 1 [11]The LORD said to Moses, [12]"When you take the census of the people of Israel, then each shall give a ransom for himself to the LORD when you number them, that there be no plague among them

Mt 17:24 when you number them. [13]Each who is numbered in the census shall give this: half a shekel according to the shekel of the sanctuary (the shekel is twenty gerahs), half a shekel as an offering to the LORD. [14]Every one who is numbered in the census, from twenty years old and upward, shall give the LORD's offering. [15]The rich shall not give more, and the poor shall not give less, than the half shekel, when you give the LORD's offering to make atonement for yourselves. [16]And you shall take the atonement money from the people of Israel, and shall appoint it for the service of the tent of meeting; that it may bring the people of Israel to remembrance before the LORD, so as to make atonement for yourselves."

30:11–16. In Israel tribute had a markedly religious character to it (cf. 38:24–31). Because each and every Israelite belonged to God, the authorities could not use them for their own advantage, nor could they extort taxes from them. Taking a census could cause temptation (cf. 2 Sam 24), because those in charge ran the risk of registering as belonging to them what in fact belonged to God alone; every census involved the risk of a plague or some other punishment (v. 12). To avoid anyone having that sort of twisted intention, every adult was given the *right* to help support divine worship; poor and rich are equal before God and have identical rights: that is the idea behind what it says in v. 15.

grans mane. Quando componet lucernas, incendet illud; [8]et quando collocabit eas ad vesperum, uret thymiama sempiternum coram Domino in generationes vestras. [9]Non offeretis super eo thymiama compositionis alterius nec holocaustum nec oblationem, nec libabitis libamina. [10]Et expiabit Aaron super cornua eius semel per annum in sanguine sacrificii pro peccato; et placabit super eo in generationibus vestris: sanctum sanctorum erit Domino». [11]Locutusque est Dominus ad Moysen dicens: [12]«Quando tuleris summam filiorum Israel iuxta numerum, dabunt singuli pretium expiationis pro animabus suis Domino; et non erit plaga in eis, cum fuerint recensiti. [13]Hoc autem dabit omnis, qui transit ad censum, dimidium sicli iuxta mensuram sanctuarii—siclus viginti obolos habet—; media pars sicli offeretur Domino. [14]Qui habetur in numero a viginti annis et supra, dabit pretium; [15]dives non addet ad medium sicli, et pauper nihil minuet, quando dabitis oblationem Domino in expiationem animarum vestrarum. [16]Susceptamque expiationis pecuniam, quae collata est a filiis Israel, trades in usus tabernaculi con-

The bronze basin

Ex 38:8; 40:30
1 Kings 7:23–39

[17]The LORD said to Moses, [18]"You shall also make a laver of bronze, with its base of bronze, for washing. And you shall put it between the tent of meeting and the altar, and you shall put water in it, [19]with which Aaron and his sons shall wash their hands and their feet. [20]When they go into the tent of meeting, or when they come near the altar to minister, to burn an offering by fire to the LORD, they shall wash with water, lest they die. [21]They shall wash their hands and their feet, lest they die: it shall be a statute for ever to them, even to him and to his descendants throughout their generations."

The oil for anointing

Lev 8:10ff
Ex 37:29

[22]Moreover, the LORD said to Moses, [23]"Take the finest spices: of liquid myrrh five hundred shekels, and of sweet-smelling cinnamon half as much, that is, two hundred and fifty, and of aromatic cane two hundred and fifty, [24]and of cassia five hundred, according to the shekel of the sanctuary, and of olive oil a hin; [25]and you shall make of these a sacred anointing oil blended as by the perfumer; a holy anointing oil it shall be. [26]And you shall anoint with

---

30:17–21. The bronze basin or bath for the washings (cf. 38:8; 40:30) made it easier for the priests to do all the purifications their role involved. Unlike the other elements in the sanctuary, no great detail is laid down as regards the basin. We do not know its exact dimensions, although there is a reference to there being a huge receptacle in Solomon's temple (the "sea of bronze": cf. 1 Kings 7:23–26), upheld by twelve statues of bulls; there were other smaller containers as well (cf. 1 Kings 7:38–39).

30:22–33. The oil of unction (cf. 37:29) was a mixture of olive oil and various aromatic substances, many of them imported and very expensive. Given that oil was used both for personal embellishment (cf. Ruth 3:3; 2 Sam 12:20; Mt 6:17) and for healing wounds (cf. Is 1:6; Mk 6:13; Lk 10:34; etc.), the complicated mixture in the oil of unction is another indicator of the importance given to divine worship and of appreciation for the transcendence of God, who requires maximum moral perfection of his ministers.

---

ventus, ut sit monumentum eorum coram Domino et propitietur animabus illorum». [17]Locutusque est Dominus ad Moysen dicens: [18]«Facies et labrum aeneum cum basi aenea ad lavandum; ponesque illud inter tabernaculum conventus et altare. Et, missa aqua, [19]lavabunt in eo Aaron et filii eius manus suas ac pedes. [20]Quando ingressuri sunt tabernaculum conventus, lavabunt se aqua, ne moriantur; vel quando accessuri sunt ad altare, ut ministrent, ut adoleant victimam Domino. [21]Et lavabunt manus et pedes, ne moriantur: legitimum sempiternum erit, ipsi et semini eius per successiones». [22]Locutusque est Dominus ad Moysen [23]dicens: «Sume tibi aromata prima myrrhae electae quingentos siclos et cinnamomi boni odoris medium, id est ducentos quinquaginta siclos, calami suave olentis similiter ducentos quinquaginta, [24]casiae autem quingentos siclos, in pondere sanctuarii, olei de olivetis mensuram hin. [25]Faciesque unctionis oleum sanctum, unguentum compositum opere unguentarii; unctionis oleum sanctum erit. [26]Et unges ex eo tabernaculum conventus et arcam testamenti [27]mensamque cum vasis

it the tent of meeting and the ark of the testimony, [27]and the table and all its utensils, and the lampstand and its utensils, and the altar of incense, [28]and the altar of burnt offering with all its utensils and the laver and its base; [29]you shall consecrate them, that they may be most holy; whatever touches them will become holy. [30]And you shall anoint Aaron and his sons, and consecrate them, that they may serve me as priests. [31]And you shall say to the people of Israel, 'This shall be my holy anointing oil throughout your generations. [32]It shall not be poured upon the bodies of ordinary men, and you shall make no other like it in composition; it is holy, and it shall be holy to you. [33]Whoever compounds any like it or whoever puts any of it on an outsider shall be cut off from his people.'"

Ex 37:29 **The incense**

[34]And the LORD said to Moses, "Take sweet spices, stacte, and onycha, and galbanum, sweet spices with pure frankincense (of each shall there be an equal part), [35]and make an incense blended
Ex 25:22 as by the perfumer, seasoned with salt, pure and holy; [36]and you shall beat some of it very small, and put part of it before the testimony in the tent of meeting where I shall meet with you; it shall

---

This oil was used to anoint the main items used in divine worship and also consecrated persons, specifically, priests, prophets and particularly, the king (vv. 25:30; 1 Sam 24:7; 26:9, 11, 23; 2 Sam 1:14, 16; 19:22). That is why the title of the "Anointed" is the one which most specifically identifies the future King-Messiah and which in the New Testament applies to Jesus, our Lord: "The word 'Christ' comes from the Greek translation of the Hebrew *Messiah*, which means 'anointed'. [. . .] Jesus fulfilled the messianic hope of

Israel in his threefold office of priest, prophet and king" (*Catechism of the Catholic Church*, 436).

30:34–38. The recipe used for the incense (cf. 37:29) was quite complicated: some later rabbinical treatises describe an even more complex mixture, involving sixteen separate ingredients. All we can say is that many of the substances used for it were not native to Palestine, and that the use of incense was a further refinement in divine worship. It is therefore another indication that it is

---

suis, candelabrum et utensilia eius, altaria thymiamatis [28]et holocausti et universam supellectilem, quae ad cultum eorum pertinet, et labrum cum basi sua. [29]Sanctificabisque omnia, et erunt sancta sanctorum: qui tetigerit ea, sanctificabitur. [30]Aaron et filios eius unges sanctificabisque eos, ut sacerdotio fungantur mihi. [31]Filiis quoque Israel dices: Hoc oleum unctionis sanctum erit mihi in generationes vestras. [32]Caro hominis non ungetur ex eo, et iuxta compositionem eius non facietis aliud, quia sanctum est et sanctum erit vobis. [33]Homo quicumque tale composuerit et dederit ex eo super alienum, exterminabitur de populo suo». [34]Dixitque Dominus ad Moysen: «Sume tibi aromata, stacten et onycha, galbanum boni odoris et tus lucidissimum; aequalis ponderis erunt omnia. [35]Faciesque thymiama compositum opere unguentarii, sale conditum et purum et sanctum. [36]Cumque in tenuissimum pulverem ex parte

be for you most holy. [37]And the incense which you shall make according to its composition, you shall not make for yourselves; it shall be for you holy to the LORD. [38]Whoever makes any like it to use as perfume shall be cut off from his people."

The craftsmen for the sanctuary

Ex 35:30–35

31 [1]The LORD said to Moses, [2]"See, I have called by name Acts 6:3 Bezalel the son of Uri, son of Hur, of the tribe of Judah: [3]and I have filled him with the Spirit of God, with ability and intelligence, with knowledge and all craftsmanship, [4]to devise artistic designs, to work in gold, silver, and bronze, [5]in cutting stones for setting, and in carving wood, for work in every craft. [6]And behold, I have appointed with him Oholiab, the son of Ahisamach, of the tribe of Dan; and I have given to all able men ability, that they may make all that I have commanded you: [7]the tent of meeting, and the ark of the testimony, and the mercy seat that is thereon, and all the furnishings of the tent, [8]the table and its utensils, and the pure lampstand with all its utensils, and the altar of incense, [9]and the altar of burnt offering with all its utensils, and the laver and its base, [10]and the finely worked garments, the holy garments for Aaron the priest and the garments of his sons, for

---

not good to be miserly when allocating resources whether material or personnel where divine worship is involved.

31:1–11. To ensure that the sanctuary is built with all due perfection, in line with the instructions given, God gives his spirit of wisdom to the craftsmen involved, that is, he gives them great skill.

Wisdom, so greatly appreciated among Eastern peoples, is according to the Bible a sharing in divine wisdom: God is the only Wise One; he has created the world with great skill and dexterity. Therefore, those men are wisest who best imitate God; the wise are not those who simply have theoretical knowledge or those who have greater intellectual ability or a better philosophy, but rather those who are endowed with a special skill that enables them to do what God wants. The craftsmen who make the sanctuary are equipped with the wisdom needed to

---

contuderis, pones ex eo coram testimonio in tabernaculo conventus, in quo conveniam ad te: sanctum sanctorum erit vobis thymiama. [37]Talem compositionem non facietis in usus vestros, quia tibi sanctum erit pro Domino; [38]homo quicumque fecerit simile, ut odore illius perfruatur, peribit de populis suis». [1]Locutusque est Dominus ad Moysen dicens: [2]«Ecce vocavi ex nomine Beseleel filium Uri filii Hur de tribu Iudae [3]et implevi eum spiritu Dei, sapientia et intellegentia et scientia in omni opere [4]ad excogitandum, quidquid fabrefieri potest ex auro et argento et aere, [5]ad scindendum et includendum gemmas et ad sculpendum ligna, ad faciendum omne opus; [6]dedique ei socium Ooliab filium Achisamech de tribu Dan et in corde omnis eruditi posui sapientiam, ut faciant cuncta, quae praecepi tibi: [7]tabernaculum conventus et arcam testimonii et propitiatorium, quod super eam est, et cuncta vasa tabernaculi [8]mensamque et vasa eius, candelabrum purissimum cum vasis suis et altaria thymiamatis [9]et holocausti et omnia vasa eorum, labrum cum basi sua [10]et vestes textas et vestes sanctas Aaron sacerdoti et vestes

their service as priests, [11]and the anointing oil and the fragrant incense for the holy place. According to all that I have commanded you they shall do."

Ex 20:8–11 **The sabbath rest**

Ezek 20:12 [12]And the LORD said to Moses, [13]"Say to the people of Israel, 'You
Mk 1:24
Heb 2:11 shall keep my sabbaths, for this is a sign between me and you throughout your generations, that you may know that I, the LORD,
Num 15:32–36 sanctify you. [14]You shall keep the sabbath, because it is holy for
Mk 3:6 you; every one who profanes it shall be put to death; whoever does any work on it, that soul shall be cut off from among his people. [15]Six days shall work be done, but the seventh day is a sabbath of solemn rest, holy to the LORD; whoever does any work on the sabbath day shall be put to death. [16]Therefore the people of Israel shall keep the sabbath, observing the sabbath throughout
Gen 2:2–3; 9:9 their generations, as a perpetual covenant. [17]It is a sign for ever
Ex 20:11 between me and the people of Israel that in six days the LORD

---

build it according to God's desire. Moreover, the Wisdom books will teach that the wise are not those who have most knowledge (even if that be religious knowledge) but those who live in keeping with that knowledge; that is, the wise person is the devout person.

Divine Wisdom is the attribute which is most fully described in the Old Testament, so much so that it becomes personified (cf. Prov 8:22–31). In the New Testament, for example in the Gospel of St John (Jn 1), features of the creative Wisdom of God are attributed to the Word.

31:12–17. By including here the rules about the sabbath, the sacred text wants

to show that sabbath observance is the key act of divine worship for the people of Israel. Perhaps because the rules contained in these final chapters (30–31) are later and more detailed, this section is usually seen as the one which has most to say about the sabbath.

Thus, three reasons are given (none of them social reasons) why sabbath rest is something to do with religion—the sovereignty of God (v. 13), the Covenant (vv. 16–17) and the fact that one is a member of the people of God (vv. 14–15). Christian Sunday rest means all these three things too; it commemorates the resurrection of the Lord, in which the new creation comes about, and the new Covenant and the new people of God.

---

filiorum eius, ut fungantur officio suo in sacris, [11]oleum unctionis et thymiama aromatum in sanctuario: omnia, quae praecepi tibi, facient». [12]Et locutus est Dominus ad Moysen dicens: [13]«Loquere filiis Israel et dices ad eos: Videte ut sabbatum meum custodiatis, quia signum est inter me et vos in generationibus vestris, ut sciatis quia ego Dominus, qui sanctifico vos. [14]Custodite sabbatum, sanctum est enim vobis. Qui polluerit illud, morte morietur; qui fecerit in eo opus, peribit anima illius de medio populi sui. [15]Sex diebus facietis opus; in die septimo sabbatum est, requies sancta Domino: omnis, qui fecerit opus in hac die, morietur. [16]Custodiant filii Israel sabbatum et celebrent illud in generationibus suis: pactum est sempiternum [17]inter me et filios Israel signumque perpetuum; sex enim diebus fecit Dominus caelum et terram et in septimo ab opere cessavit et respiravit». [18]Deditque Dominus Moysi,

made heaven and earth, and on the seventh day he rested, and was refreshed.'"

The tables of the Law

[18]And he gave to Moses, when he had made an end of speaking with him upon Mount Sinai, the two tables of the testimony, tables of stone, written with the finger of God.

Acts 7:38

2 Cor 3:3

11. ISRAEL'S APOSTASY*

The golden calf

32 [1]When the people saw that Moses delayed to come down from the mountain, the people gathered themselves together to Aaron, and said to him, "Up, make us gods, who shall go before us; as for this Moses, the man who brought us up out of the land of Egypt, we do not know what has become of him." [2]And Aaron said to them, "Take off the rings of gold which are in the ears of your wives, your sons, and your daughters, and bring

Acts 7:40-41

Ex 24:18

*32:1—34:35. After the account of the rules about how the sanctuary should be built, the narrative picks up where it left off in chapter 24. This last narrative section contains the account of the grave sin of apostasy committed in the desert (chap. 32) and the account of the renewal of the Covenant after that sin.

The first answer the people give to the love of God as expressed in the events of Sinai is a very grave sin of idolatry, one which merits severe punishment. But, through Moses' intercession, God stays true to his Covenant and continues to guide the course of Israelite history. In the events recounted here, the people take their sin to heart, and understand the punishment it deserves and the extent of God's forgiveness: he is "slow to anger, and abounding in steadfast love" (Ex 34:6).

Thus, we have here again the great teachings of Exodus: there is only one God, who wants to be the only God that is worshipped; he chose the Israelites to be his people, having delivered them from all kinds of danger but especially from inner wickedness; he made a Covenant time and again; and he has shown himself to be just and merciful and a close friend of men.

32:1-6. In the ancient East the bull or bull-calf was a symbol of divinity insofar as its strength symbolized divine omnipotence. King Jeroboam ordered golden calves to be put in the temples of Dan and Bethel (cf. 1 Kings 12:28) when the kingdom of the North broke away. Given that the image of a bull was being used to represent the true God, it was not so much a sin of idolatry as a sin against

completis huiuscemodi sermonibus in monte Sinai, duas tabulas testimonii lapideas scriptas digito Dei. [1]Videns autem populus quod moram faceret descendendi de monte Moyses, congregatus ad Aaron dixit: «Surge, fac nobis deos, qui nos praecedant; Moysi enim, huic viro, qui nos eduxit de terra Aegypti, ignoramus quid acciderit». [2]Dixitque ad eos Aaron: «Tollite inaures aureas de uxorum filiorumque et filiarum vestrarum auribus et afferte ad me». [3]Fecitque omnis populus, quae iusserat, de-

1 Kings 12:28
Neh 9:18
Ps 106:19ff
Acts 7:41

them to me." ³So all the people took off the rings of gold which were in their ears, and brought them to Aaron. ⁴And he received the gold at their hand, and fashioned it with a graving tool, and made a molten calf; and they said, "These are your gods, O Israel, who brought you up out of the land of Egypt!" ⁵When Aaron saw this, he built an altar before it; and Aaron made proclamation and

Acts 7:41
1 Cor 10:7

said, "Tomorrow shall be a feast to the LORD." ⁶And they rose up early on the morrow, and offered burnt offerings and brought peace offerings; and the people sat down to eat and drink, and rose up to play.

Deut 9:7–14   **The Lord's ire**

⁷And the LORD said to Moses, "Go down; for your people, whom you brought up out of the land of Egypt, have corrupted them-

Acts 7:41   selves; ⁸they have turned aside quickly out of the way which I

---

the ban on making images of the Lord; but it is also true that that commandment was aimed at avoiding any occasion of idolatry (cf. Acts 7:40–41).

While Moses was away up the mountain (cf. 24:18), Aaron proved unable to refuse the people when they pressed him to give them a god they could see and touch—the kind of god other peoples had. The contrast between Moses and Aaron in this account is intentional: Moses is in deep conversation with the Lord to equip himself to tell the people what God wants of them (cf. the note on 24:12–18); in his absence Aaron decides to act on his own initiative without taking the will of God into account. The teaching we can glimpse here is that the people must always take account of the word of God, over and above human interests or advantages. "Faith and love will be the guides of the blind, which will lead you, by a way you do not know, to

the hidden place of God. Faith is like the feet which bring the soul to God. Love is the guide that directs it" (St John of the Cross, *Spiritual Canticle*, 1,11).

The sacred writer emphasizes that the calf was made by human hands, from silver and gold, and it was made using techniques with which the people are familiar; this means it is just like any of those idols that have a mouth but say nothing, eyes but see nothing (cf. Ps 105:19–20; 115:5ff). The mention of a "feast" (v. 5) may imply idolatrous ceremonies and orgies, in imitation of what is done in other nations. So, it is perfectly clear that this was a very serious sin, a radical change of direction from the path marked out by the Lord (v. 8). The Covenant has been broken before it starts to operate.

32:7–14. The Lord's dialogue with Moses contains the doctrinal bases of sal-

---

ferens inaures ad Aaron. ⁴Quas cum ille accepisset, formavit stilo imaginem et fecit ex eis vitulum conflatilem. Dixeruntque: «Hi sunt dii tui, Israel, qui te eduxerunt de terra Aegypti!». ⁵Quod cum vidisset Aaron, aedificavit altare coram eo et praeconis voce clamavit dicens: «Cras sollemnitas Domini est». ⁶Surgentesque mane altero die obtulerunt holocausta et hostias pacificas; et sedit populus manducare et bibere et surrexerunt ludere. ⁷Locutus est autem Dominus ad Moysen: «Vade, descende; peccavit populus tuus, quem eduxisti de terra Aegypti. ⁸Recesserunt cito de via, quam praecepi eis, feceruntque

commanded them; they have made for themselves a molten calf, and have worshiped it and sacrificed to it, and said, 'These are your gods, O Israel, who brought you up out of the land of Egypt!'" ⁹And the LORD said to Moses, "I have seen this people, and behold, it is a stiff-necked people; ¹⁰now therefore let me alone, that my wrath may burn hot against them and I may consume them; but of you I will make a great nation."

Ex 33:3; 34:9
Deut 9:13
Num 14:12

Moses' prayer for Israel

Gen 18:22–23
Deut 9:26–29
Ps 106:23

¹¹But Moses besought the LORD his God, and said, "O LORD, why does thy wrath burn hot against thy people, whom thou hast brought forth out of the land of Egypt with great power and with a mighty hand? ¹²Why should the Egyptians say, 'With evil intent did he bring them forth, to slay them in the mountains, and to consume them from the face of the earth'? Turn from thy fierce

---

vation history—Covenant, sin, mercy. Only the Lord knows just how serious this sin is: by adoring the golden calf the people have taken the wrong road and have vitiated the whole meaning of the Exodus; but most of all, they have rebelled against God and turned their backs on him, breaking the Covenant (cf. Deut 9:7–14). God no longer calls them "my people" (cf. Hos 2:8) but "your people" (Moses') (v. 7). That is, he shows him that they have acted like anyone else, guided by human leaders.

The punishment that the sin deserves is their destruction (v. 10), for this is a stiff-necked nation (cf. 33:3; 34:9; Deut 9:13). The sin deserves death, as the first sin did (Gen 3:19) and the sin which gave rise to the flood (cf. Gen 6:6–7). However, mercy always prevails over the offence.

As Abraham did in another time on behalf of Sodom (Gen 18:22–23), Moses intercedes with the Lord. But this time intercession proves successful, because Israel is the people that God has made his own; he chose it, bringing it out of Egypt in a mighty way; so, he cannot turn back now; in fact, he chose it ever since he swore his oath to Abraham (cf. Gen 15:5; 22:16–17; 35:11–12). He established the Covenant with Israel, as Moses reminds him when he refers to "thy people, whom thou has brought forth out of the land of Egypt" (v. 11). Thus, promise, election and Covenant form the foundation which guarantees that God's forgiveness will be forthcoming, even if they commit the gravest of sins.

God forgives *his* people (v. 14) not because they deserve to be forgiven, but out of pure mercy and moved by Moses' intercession. Thus God's forgiveness and the people's conversion are, both of them, a divine initiative.

---

sibi vitulum conflatilem et adoraverunt atque immolantes ei hostias dixerunt: 'Isti sunt dii tui, Israel, qui te eduxerunt de terra Aegypti!'». ⁹Rursumque ait Dominus ad Moysen: «Cerno quod populus iste durae cervicis sit; ¹⁰dimitte me, ut irascatur furor meus contra eos et deleam eos faciamque te in gentem magnam». ¹¹Moyses autem orabat Dominum Deum suum dicens: «Cur, Domine, irascitur furor tuus contra populum tuum, quem eduxisti de terra Aegypti in fortitudine magna et in manu robusta? ¹²Ne, quaeso, dicant Aegyptii: 'Callide eduxit eos, ut interficeret in montibus et deleret e terra'. Quiescat ira tua, et esto placabilis super nequitia populi tui. ¹³Recordare Abraham, Isaac et Israel servorum tuorum,

Gen 15:5; 22: wrath, and repent of this evil against thy people. [13]Remember
16–17;
35:11–12 Abraham, Isaac, and Israel, thy servants, to whom thou didst
Heb 11:12 swear by thine own self, and didst say to them, 'I will multiply
your descendants as the stars of heaven, and all this land that I
have promised I will give to your descendants, and they shall
inherit it forever.'" [14]And the LORD repented of the evil which he
thought to do to his people.

The golden calf is destroyed

Ex 24:12 [15]And Moses turned, and went down from the mountain with the
2 Cor 3:3 two tables of the testimony in his hands, tables that were written
on both sides; on the one side and on the other were they written.
[16]And the tables were the work of God, and the writing was the
writing of God, graven upon the tables. [17]When Joshua heard the
noise of the people as they shouted, he said to Moses, "There is a
noise of war in the camp." [18]But he said, "It is not the sound of
shouting for victory, or the sound of the cry of defeat, but the
Amos 8:11–12 sound of singing that I hear." [19]And as soon as he came near the
camp and saw the calf and the dancing, Moses' anger burned hot,
and he threw the tables out of his hands and broke them at the

---

32:15–24. The punishment described in
these verses is full of significance. In the
first place, Moses breaks the tables on
which God wrote the Law (vv. 16, 19),
thereby showing that sin has broken the
Covenant, and that the main effect of and
punishment for sin is not to have the
Law (cf. Amos 8:11–12), that is, what
today we would call loss of the sense of
sin.

Moses destroys the calf because of
itself it has no power. The tables were
"the work of God" (v. 16), whereas the
calf was something made by men (v. 20).
And he gives the people the residue of
the calf to drink (v. 20), in a gesture

which is reminiscent of trials by ordeal
(cf. Num 5:23–24), but the main point he
is making is that sin is personal: only
those who have sinned are to be punished. And his reproach to Aaron, which
echoes that which God made to Adam
(cf. Gen 3:11), identifies the man who is
truly to blame.

The mystery of sin affects even key
figures chosen by God, and the Bible
does not disguise this fact. Elsewhere
Moses is reminded of his own sin (cf.
Num 20:12; Deut 32:51), as is David (cf.
1 Sam 12:7–9); and in the New Testament Peter's denials are also recorded in
detail (Mt 26:69–75). It is God who

---

quibus iurasti per temetipsum dicens: 'Multiplicabo semen vestrum sicut stellas caeli; et universam
terram hanc, de qua locutus sum, dabo semini vestro, et possidebitis eam semper'». [14]Placatusque est
Dominus, ne faceret malum, quod locutus fuerat adversus populum suum. [15]Et reversus est Moyses de
monte portans duas tabulas testimonii in manu sua scriptas ex utraque parte [16]et factas opere Dei; scrip-
tura quoque Dei erat sculpta in tabulis. [17]Audiens autem Iosue tumultum populi vociferantis dixit ad
Moysen: «Ululatus pugnae auditur in castris». [18]Qui respondit: «Non est clamor vincentium / neque
clamor fugientium, / sed clamorem cantantium / ego audio». [19]Cumque appropinquasset ad castra, vidit
vitulum et choros; iratusque valde proiecit de manu tabulas et confregit eas ad radices montis.

foot of the mountain. [20]And he took the calf which they had made, Num 5:23-24
and burnt it with fire, and ground it to powder, and scattered it
upon the water, and made the people of Israel drink it. [21]And Gen 3:11
Moses said to Aaron, "What did this people do to you that you
have brought a great sin upon them?" [22]And Aaron said, "Let not
the anger of my lord burn hot; you know the people, that they are
set on evil. [23]For they said to me, 'Make us gods, who shall go Acts 7:40
before us; as for this Moses, the man who brought us up out of the
land of Egypt, we do not know what has become of him.' [24]And I
said to them, 'Let any who have gold take it off'; so they gave it
to me, and I threw it into the fire, and there came out this calf."

The zeal of the Levites
Deut 33:9

[25]And when Moses saw that the people had broken loose (for
Aaron had let them break loose, to their shame among their enemies), [26]then Moses stood in the gate of the camp, and said, "Who
is on the LORD's side? Come to me." And all the sons of Levi
gathered themselves together to him. [27]And he said to them, Deut 33:8–11
"Thus says the LORD God of Israel, 'Put every man his sword on Num 25:7–13
his side, and go to and fro from gate to gate throughout the camp,

---

shapes the history of salvation, and he does this despite our infidelities.

32:25–29. To our modern minds the part played by the Levites here seems rather shocking. This account may be designed to highlight the role which Levites would play in future times: the sons of Levi are praised for being obedient to the word of God and to the Covenant (cf. Deut 33:9); here they stay loyal to Moses and are able to distinguish the guilty from the innocent. This whole section about the punish-ment of the people's sin shows that, even when sin is forgiven, punishment still applies. The Church teaches that, in addi-tion to being an offence against God, sin "injures and weakens the sinner himself, as well as his relationships with God and neighbour. Absolution takes away sin, but it does not remedy all the disorders sin has caused. Raised up from sin, the sinner must still recover his full spiritual health by doing something more to make amends for the sin [. . .]" (*Catechism of the Catholic Church*, 1459).

---

[20]Arripiensque vitulum, quem fecerant, combussit et contrivit usque ad pulverem, quem sparsit in aquam et dedit ex eo potum filiis Israel. [21]Dixitque ad Aaron: «Quid tibi fecit hic populus, ut induceres super eum peccatum maximum?». [22]Cui ille respondit: «Ne indignetur dominus meus; tu enim nosti populum istum, quod pronus sit ad malum. [23]Dixerunt mihi: 'Fac nobis deos, qui nos praecedant; huic enim Moysi, qui nos eduxit de terra Aegypti, nescimus quid acciderit'. [24]Quibus ego dixi: Quis vestrum habet aurum? Abstulerunt et dederunt mihi, et proieci illud in ignem; egressusque est hic vitulus». [25]Vidit ergo Moyses populum quod esset effrenatus; relaxaverat enim ei Aaron frenum in ludibrium hostium eorum. [26]Et stans in porta castrorum ait: «Si quis est Domini, iungatur mihi!». Congregatique sunt ad eum omnes filii Levi. [27]Quibus ait: «Haec dicit Dominus, Deus Israel: Ponat unusquisque gladium super femur suum. Ite et redite de porta usque ad portam per medium castrorum, et occidat unusquisque fratrem et amicum et proximum suum». [28]Fecerunt filii Levi iuxta sermonem Moysi;

and slay every man his brother, and every man his companion, and every man his neighbour.'" [28]And the sons of Levi did according to the word of Moses; and there fell of the people that day about three thousand men. [29]And Moses said, "Today you have ordained yourselves[s] for the service of the LORD, each one at the cost of his son and of his brother, that he may bestow a blessing upon you this day."

Ex 17:8–13
Num 12:13–14

Moses intercedes again

[30]On the morrow Moses said to the people, "You have sinned a great sin. And now I will go up to the LORD; perhaps I can make atonement for your sin." [31]So Moses returned to the LORD and said, "Alas, this people have sinned a great sin; they have made

Is 4:3
Lk 10:20

for themselves gods of gold. [32]But now, if thou wilt forgive their

---

32:30–35. This new dialogue between Moses and God sums up the content of the whole chapter. Once again Moses plays intercessor, and the Lord shows himself to be merciful and forgiving. "From this intimacy with the faithful God, slow to anger and abounding in steadfast love, Moses drew strength and determination for his intercession (cf. Ex 34:6). He does not pray for himself but for the people whom God made his own. Moses already intercedes for them during the battle with the Amalekites (cf. Ex 17:8–13) and prays to obtain healing for Miriam (cf. Num 12:13–14). But it is chiefly after their apostasy that Moses 'stands in the breach' before God in order to save the people (Ps 106:23; cf. Ex 32:1—34:9). The arguments of his prayer—for intercession is also a mysterious battle—will inspire the boldness of the great intercessors among the Jewish

people and in the Church: God is love; he is therefore righteous and faithful; he cannot contradict himself; he must remember his marvellous deeds, since his glory is at stake, and he cannot forsake this people that bears his name" (*Catechism of the Catholic Church*, 2577).

But the people still has a penalty to pay for its offence (v. 34). Throughout the course of its history Israel continues to be aware that it deserves severe punishment for this and other sins that follow. The prophets say that Israel's debt is paid for by the exile in Babylon.

The reference to the book in which God writes the names of those whom he has chosen (in a kind of census, as it were: cf. Is 4:3; Rev 3:5, 12; 17:8), is a graphic way of showing that God has special love for those who have a mission to fulfil in the work of salvation.

---

cecideruntque de populo in die illa quasi tria milia hominum. [29]Et ait Moyses: «Implestis manus vestras hodie Domino unusquisque in filio et in fratre suo, ut detur vobis benedictio». [30]Facto autem altero die, locutus est Moyses ad populum: «Peccastis peccatum maximum; ascendam ad Dominum, si quo modo quivero eum deprecari pro scelere vestro». [31]Reversusque ad Dominum ait: «Obsecro, peccavit populus iste peccatum maximum, feceruntque sibi deos aureos; aut dimitte eis hanc noxam [32]aut, si non facis, dele me de libro tuo, quem scripsisti». [33]Cui respondit Dominus: «Qui peccaverit mihi, delebo

s. Gk Vg See Tg: Heb *ordain yourselves*

176

sin—and if not, blot me, I pray thee, out of thy book which thou Rom 9:3
Rev 3:5, 12; 17:8
hast written." ³³But the LORD said to Moses, "Whoever has sinned
against me, him will I blot out of my book. ³⁴But now go, lead the Dan 12:1
Ex 3:16; 23:20
people to the place of which I have spoken to you; behold, my
angel shall go before you. Nevertheless, in the day when I visit, I
will visit their sin upon them."

³⁵And the LORD sent a plague upon the people, because they
made the calf which Aaron made.

The order to pull out. An angel will lead the way*

Num 10:11–13

33 ¹The LORD said to Moses, "Depart, go up hence, you and
the people whom you have brought up out of the land of
Egypt, to the land of which I swore to Abraham, Isaac, and Jacob, Ex 23:20
Num 20:16
saying, 'To your descendants I will give it.' ²And I will send an Deut 7:1

---

*33:1–23. The sacred writer explains
how God is going to act in regard to his
people from now on, given that they have
sinned: his presence among them cannot
be as it formerly was (vv. 1–6), when he
worked wonders which filled them with
joy; from now on there will be more to
weep about and less celebration (v. 6);
but he will continue to speak to Moses
face to face (vv. 7–11). However, Moses
pleads for God's presence to be more
active (vv. 12–17) and he even manages
to see the glory of the Lord (vv. 18–23).

33:1–6 The order to leave Sinai is based
not so much on the exodus-covenant
adjudged to Moses, but on the oath-
promise which God made to the patriarchs. This means that the situation has
changed radically due to the episode of
the golden calf.

The Lord holds to his promise to lead
the people to the promised land, but he is
no longer going to help them directly.

The presence of the angel (v. 2), which
had been seen as a sign of protection (cf.
23:20; Num 20:16), is now interpreted as
a punishment, because it means that the
Lord has decided to keep a certain distance away and send an intermediary.
This decision makes the people very sad,
and God will change his mind only after
further intercession by Moses.

The punishment God is imposing on
his people by refusing to remain among
them is reminiscent of how Adam's sin
was punished (cf. Gen 3:24). Adam's was
the first sin man committed; this is the
first sin the people commits, after it was
constituted by the Covenant of Sinai. In
the book of Genesis God sent Adam and
Eve out of his presence; here he refuses
to stay with the Israelites. There he
ordered the angel to block their way and
forced them out of paradise; here he
again makes an angel his intermediary
and forces the Israelites to take off their
jewellery, which they probably had put

---

eum de libro meo. ³⁴Tu autem vade et duc populum istum, quo locutus sum tibi: angelus meus prae-
cedet te; ego autem in die ultionis visitabo et hoc peccatum eorum». ³⁵Percussit ergo Dominus populum pro reatu vituli, quem fecerat Aaron. ¹Locutusque est Dominus ad Moysen: «Vade, ascende de loco
isto tu et populus tuus, quem eduxisti de terra Aegypti, in terram, quam iuravi Abraham, Isaac et Iacob
dicens: Semini tuo dabo eam. ²Et mittam praecursorem tui angelum et eiciam Chananaeum et
Amorraeum et Hetthaeum et Pherezaeum et Hevaeum et Iebusaeum, ³et intres in terram fluentem lacte

Gen 3:24;
32:9
Acts 7:51

angel before you, and I will drive out the Canaanites, the Amorites, the Hittites, the Perizzites, the Hivites, and the Jebusites. ³Go up to a land flowing with milk and honey; but I will not go up among you, lest I consume you in the way, for you are a stiff-necked people."

⁴When the people heard these evil tidings, they mourned; and no man put on his ornaments. ⁵For the LORD had said to Moses, "Say to the people of Israel, 'You are a stiff-necked people; if for a single moment I should go up among you, I would consume you. So now put off your ornaments from you, that I may know what to do with you.'" ⁶Therefore the people of Israel stripped themselves of their ornaments, from Mount Horeb onward.

The tent of meeting

Heb 13:13

⁷Now Moses used to take the tent and pitch it outside the camp, far off from the camp; and he called it the tent of meeting. And every one who sought the LORD would go out to the tent of meeting, which was outside the camp. ⁸Whenever Moses went out to the tent, all the people rose up, and every man stood at his tent door, and looked after Moses, until he had gone into the tent.

---

on for the feast of the golden calf (vv. 5–6); he wants them to be detached from their valuables, to show the repentant attitude that should mark the rest of their pilgrimage through the desert.

33:7–11. The tent of meeting, sometimes called the tent of witness, and also the sanctuary, normally means the main tent in the sacred precinct (cf. chaps. 25–27). Here, however, it seems to be different from the sanctuary, because the sanctuary was located in the centre of the encampment and was a place of worship, whereas this tent is pitched away from the camp and is used for consultation.

This discrepancy may well be due to the fact that this passage belonged to an older tradition than the Priestly one. Whereas the Priestly tradition lays the stress on matters to do with worship, the earlier one would have focused more on social matters.

The sacred writer, through this account, is showing that God continues to be present but at a certain distance, and that only Moses has the privilege of speaking to him "face to face" (cf. 33:20). The people are simply the silent witnesses of the conversations which take place between God and Moses, but God still shows them special favour.

---

et melle. Non enim ascendam tecum, quia populus durae cervicis es, ne forte disperdam te in via». ⁴Audiens populus sermonem hunc pessimum luxit, et nullus ex more indutus est cultu suo. ⁵Dixitque Dominus ad Moysen: «Loquere filiis Israel: Populus durae cervicis es; uno momento, si ascendam in medio tui, delebo te. Nunc autem depone ornatum tuum, ut sciam quid faciam tibi». ⁶Deposuerunt ergo filii Israel ornatum suum a monte Horeb. ⁷Moyses autem tollens tabernaculum tetendit ei extra castra procul; vocavitque nomen eius Tabernaculum conventus. Et omnis, qui quaerebat Dominum, egrediebatur ad tabernaculum conventus extra castra. ⁸Cumque egrederetur Moyses ad tabernaculum, surgebat universa plebs, et stabat unusquisque in ostio papilionis sui; aspiciebantque tergum Moysi,

⁹When Moses entered the tent, the pillar of cloud would descend
and stand at the door of the tent, and the LORD would speak with
Moses. ¹⁰And when all the people saw the pillar of cloud standing
at the door of the tent, all the people would rise up and worship,
every man at his tent door. ¹¹Thus the LORD used to speak to
Moses face to face, as a man speaks to his friend. When Moses
turned again into the camp, his servant Joshua the son of Nun, a
young man, did not depart from the tent.

Ex 33:20
Num 12:8
Deut 34:10
Jn 15:15

God agrees to stay with his people

¹²Moses said to the LORD, "See, thou sayest to me, 'Bring up this
people'; but thou hast not let me know whom thou wilt send with
me. Yet thou hast said, 'I know you by name, and you have also
found favour in my sight.' ¹³Now therefore, I pray thee, if I have
found favour in thy sight, show me now thy ways, that I may know
thee and find favour in thy sight. Consider too that this nation is
thy people." ¹⁴And he said, "My presence will go with you, and I
will give you rest." ¹⁵And he said to him, "If thy presence will not
go with me, do not carry us up from here. ¹⁶For how shall it be
known that I have found favour in thy sight, I and thy people? Is it

Mt 11:28
Heb 4:1
Lk 1:30

33:12–17. In this touching prayer Moses
makes two requests: he asks God to show
him his ways and to continue to stay with
his people. What he is referring to is not
the physical route through the desert
(Moses and the Israelites were familiar
with that) but rather the way to conduct
themselves. Other biblical texts, especially
the Psalms, uses "way", "ways" in this
sense, as does Christian asceticism.
"'Make me to know thy ways, O Lord;
teach me thy paths' (Ps 25:4). We ask the
Lord to guide us, to show us his footprints,
so we can set out to attain the fullness of
his commandments, which is charity"

(St J. Escrivá, *Christ Is Passing By*, 1).

The Lord also agrees to the second
request—to stay with his people (vv.
15–17)—which means that he refrains
from punishing them as he previously
said he would (v. 3). So, his protective
presence will still be the distinguishing
mark of Israel: "After Israel's sin, when
the people had turned away from God to
worship the golden calf, God hears
Moses' prayer of intercession and agrees
to walk (cf. Ex 32) in the midst of an
unfaithful people, thus demonstrating his
love (cf. Ex 33:12–17)" (*Catechism of
the Catholic Church*, 210).

---

donec ingrederetur tabernaculum. ⁹Ingresso autem illo tabernaculum, descendebat columna nubis et
stabat ad ostium; loquebaturque cum Moyse, ¹⁰cernentibus universis quod columna nubis staret ad
ostium tabernaculi. Stabantque ipsi et adorabant per fores tabernaculorum suorum. ¹¹Loquebatur autem
Dominus ad Moysen facie ad faciem, sicut solet loqui homo ad amicum suum. Cumque ille reverteretur in castra, minister eius Iosue filius Nun puer non recedebat de medio tabernaculi. ¹²Dixit autem
Moyses ad Dominum: «Praecipis, ut educam populum istum, et non indicas mihi, quem missurus es
mecum; cum dixeris: 'Novi te ex nomine, et invenisti gratiam coram me'. ¹³Si ergo inveni gratiam in
conspectu tuo, ostende mihi viam tuam, ut sciam te et inveniam gratiam ante oculos tuos; respice quia
populus tuus est natio haec». ¹⁴Dixitque Dominus: «Facies mea ibit, et requiem dabo tibi». ¹⁵Et ait

not in thy going with us, so that we are distinct, I and thy people, from all other people that are upon the face of the earth?"

[17]And the LORD said to Moses, "This very thing that you have spoken I will do; for you have found favour in my sight, and I know you by name."

Ex 33:1
1 Kings 19:9–18
Jn 1:18
Rom 9:15
Gen 32:30
Ex 19:21
Deut 4:33
Judg 6:22–23
Is 6:2
Jn 1:18
1 Cor 12:12
1 Tim 6:16
1 Jn 3:2
1 Kings 19:9–13
Mt 17:1–7

Moses sees the glory of God

[18]Moses said, "I pray thee, show me thy glory." [19]And he said, "I will make all my goodness pass before you, and will proclaim before you my name 'The LORD'; and I will be gracious to whom I will be gracious, and will show mercy on whom I will show mercy. [20]But," he said, "you cannot see my face; for man shall not see me and live." [21]And the LORD said, "Behold, there is a place by me where you shall stand upon the rock; [22]and while my glory passes by I will put you in a cleft of the rock, and I will cover you with my hand until I have passed by; [23]then I will take away my hand, and you shall see my back; but my face shall not be seen."

God manifests his love to his people, by coming close to them. And he does so with every soul. "You were deeper than the most inward place of my heart and loftier than the highest" (St Augustine, *Confessions*, 3, 6–11). In the fullness of Revelation the Gospel of St John teaches that God's presence among men reaches its zenith in the Incarnation: "And the Word became flesh and dwelt among us" (Jn 1:14).

33:18–23. Moses asks for a more intimate knowledge of God—to see his glory, that is, to see him as he really is. But, because God is infinite, it is not possible for man, given his creaturely limitations, to fully comprehend God. The

Bible frequently refers to the fact that "no one can see the face of God and live" (cf. v. 20; Gen 32:30; Ex 19:21; Deut 4:33; Judg 6:22–23). To show the sublime greatness of God, Scripture says that even the Seraphim hide their face in the presence of the Lord (cf. Is 6:2).

The vision of God described so mysteriously here is a work of special favour to Moses, his special friend (cf. Num 12:7–8; Deut 34:10). But not even he is allowed to see God directly; he will see only the back of him, as if to say that man can only manage to see God in the tracks he leaves behind. This vision was a very special privilege, and it is one which will also be given to Elijah (cf. 1 Kings 19:9–13). And it is in fact these

---

Moyses: «Si non tu ipse eas, ne educas nos de loco isto; [16]in quo enim scietur me et populum tuum invenisse gratiam in conspectu tuo, nisi ambulaveris nobiscum, ut glorificemur ego et populus tuus prae omnibus populis, qui habitant super terram?». [17]Dixitque Dominus ad Moysen: «Et verbum istud, quod locutus es, faciam; invenisti enim gratiam coram me, et teipsum novi ex nomine». [18]Qui ait: «Ostende mihi gloriam tuam». [19]Respondit: «Ego ostendam omne bonum tibi et vocabo in nomine Domini coram te; et miserebor, cui voluero, et clemens ero, in quem mihi placuerit». [20]Rursumque ait: «Non poteris videre faciem meam; non enim videbit me homo et vivet». [21]Et iterum: «Ecce, inquit, est locus apud me, stabis super petram; [22]cumque transibit gloria mea, ponam te in foramine petrae et protegam dextera mea, donec transeam; [23]tollamque manum meam, et videbis posteriora mea; faciem

12. THE COVENANT IS RENEWED*   Ex 19:14

34 ¹The LORD said to Moses, "Cut two tables of stone like the first; and I will write upon the tables the words that were on the first tables, which you broke. ²Be ready in the morning, and come up in the morning to Mount Sinai, and present yourself there to me on the top of the mountain. ³No man shall come up with you, and let no man be seen throughout all the mountain; let no flocks or herds feed before that mountain." ⁴So Moses cut two tables of stone like the first; and he rose early in the morning and went up on Mount Sinai, as the LORD had commanded him, and took in his hand two tables of stone. ⁵And the LORD descended in the cloud and stood with him there, and proclaimed the name of the LORD.

---

two men who appear in the Transfiguration on Mount Tabor (cf. Mt 17:1–7), where Christ's divinity is revealed. Only Christ has seen God and has made him known (cf. Jn 1:18). The blessed in heaven will attain the fullest vision of God (cf. 1 Cor 13:12; 1 Jn 3:2).

*34:1–28. This chapter narrating the renewal of the Covenant follows the same pattern as the account of its original establishment (cf. Ex 19–24); but it is shorter, concentrating on the two main protagonists, God and Moses. Thus, it begins with the preparations for the theophany and for the encounter with the Lord (vv. 1–5); then follows the revelation of God, and Moses' prayer (vv. 6–9); and it ends with the renewal of the Covenant and the so-called Rite of the Covenant (vv. 10–28). The account hinges on the remaking of the tables of

stone after the sin of the golden calf; the tables symbolize God's offer to keep to the pact and never to go back on it.

34:1–5. The theophany is described very soberly here, but it has exactly the same elements as given in chapter 19: very careful preparation by Moses (v. 2; cf. 19:10–11); the people forbidden to approach the mountain (v. 3; cf. 19:12–13); God appearing wrapped in the cloud (v. 5; cf. 19:16–20).

Comparing the two accounts, this one says less about the transcendence of God and puts more stress on his closeness to Moses: "he stood with him there" (v. 5). God's initiative in drawing close to man is clear to see; it lies at the very basis of the Covenant.

"He proclaimed the name of the Lord" (v. 6); the context would suggest that it is Moses who proclaims the name

---

autem meam videre non poteris». ¹Dixitque Dominus ad Moysen: «Praecide tibi duas tabulas lapideas instar priorum, et scribam super eas verba, quae habuerunt tabulae, quas fregisti. ²Esto paratus mane, ut ascendas statim in montem Sinai; stabisque mihi super verticem montis. ³Nullus ascendat tecum, nec videatur quispiam per totum montem; oves quoque et boves non pascantur e contra». ⁴Excidit ergo duas tabulas lapideas, quales antea fuerant; et de nocte consurgens ascendit in montem Sinai, sicut praeceperat ei Dominus, portans secum tabulas. ⁵Cumque descendisset Dominus per nubem, stetit cum eo vocans in nomine Domini. ⁶Et transiens coram eo clamavit: «Dominus, Dominus Deus, misericors

God appears

Ex 20:5–6
Num 14:18
Deut 5:9–18
Jn 1:17
Jas 5:11
Jn 1:14

⁶The LORD passed before him, and proclaimed, "The LORD, the LORD, a God merciful and gracious, slow to anger, and abounding in steadfast love and faithfulness, ⁷keeping steadfast love for thousands, forgiving iniquity and transgression and sin, but who will by no means clear the guilty, visiting the iniquity of the fathers upon the children and the children's children, to the third and the fourth generation." ⁸And Moses made haste to bow his head toward the earth, and worshiped. ⁹And he said, "If now I have

Ex 32:11–14;
33:15–17
Ps 86:1–15;
103:8–10

of the Lord, but the Hebrew could indeed be as the RSV has it, "and he proclaimed his name, 'Lord' ". The same wording appears in v. 6 implying that it is the Lord who is "proclaiming", defining himself as he promised he would (cf. 33:19). The sacred writer may have intentionally left these words open to either interpretation; whether spoken by Moses or said directly by God, they are equal from the revelation point of view.

34:6–7. In response to Moses' pleading, the Lord makes himself manifest. The solemn repetition of the name of Yahweh (Lord) emphasizes that the Lord is introducing himself liturgically to the assembled Israelites. In the description of himself which follows (and which is repeated elsewhere, cf. 20:5–6; Num 14:18; Deut 5:9–18; etc.), two key attributes of God are underlined—justice and mercy. God cannot let sin go unpunished, nor does he; the prophets, too, will teach that sin is, first and foremost, something personal (cf. Jer 31:29; Ezek 18:2ff). But this ancient text refers only in a general way to the fact that God is just, and puts more stress on his mercy. A person who is conscious of his own sin has access to God only if he is sure that God can and

will forgive him. "The concept of 'mercy' in the Old Testament," John Paul II comments, "has a long and rich history. We have to refer back to it in order that the mercy revealed by Christ may shine forth more clearly. [. . .] [S]in too constitutes man's misery. The people of the Old Covenant experienced this misery from the time of the Exodus, when they set up the golden calf. The Lord himself triumphed over this act of breaking the covenant when he solemnly declared to Moses that he was a 'God merciful and gracious, slow to anger, and abounding in steadfast love and faithfulness' (Ex 34:6). It is in this central revelation that the chosen people, and each of its members, will find, every time that they have sinned, the strength and the motive for turning to the Lord to remind him of what he had exactly revealed about himself and to beseech his forgiveness" (*Dives in misericordia*, 4). On "God's jealousy", see the note on 20:5–6.

34:8–9. Moses once more implores the Lord on behalf of his people; he makes three requests, which sum up many earlier petitions: he begs God to stay with the people and protect them in their hazardous journeying in the desert (cf.

found favour in thy sight, O Lord, let the Lord, I pray thee, go in the midst of us, although it is a stiff-necked people; and pardon our iniquity and our sin, and take us for thy inheritance."

The Covenant*

[10]And he said, "Behold, I make a covenant. Before all your people Jn 1:17
I will do marvels, such as have not been wrought in all the earth or Rev 15:3
in any nation; and all the people among whom you are shall see the
work of the LORD; for it is a terrible thing that I will do with you.

33:15–17), to forgive the very grave sin they have committed (cf. 32:11–14), and finally to make them his own property, thereby distinguishing them from all other peoples (cf. 33:16) and restoring them to their status as "his own possession" (cf. 19:5). These three requests are ones that were constantly on the lips of the people of Israel and in the hearts of everyone who acknowledges God (cf. Ps 86:1–15; 103:8–10; etc.).

*34:10–28. This section, which is considered to belong to the Yahwistic tradition, has a very ancient origin; it is probably older than the narrative into which it is set (just as other law sections of the book are). As in the text of the moral Decalogue (cf. 20:1–21), there is a preface which recalls the wondrous things God has done and which form the basis of the precepts and rules which will now be listed. This discourse of the Lord, begins in a solemn style, describing God's decision to establish a Covenant with his people.

The historical introduction (v. 10) does not confine itself to the marvels of the Exodus but covers all the wonderful things that God is doing all the time. God's initiative is the very origin and basis of the Covenant; Israel is to be a permanent witness to his protective presence.

If Israel were to make pacts and alliances with polytheistic nations, that would be equivalent to accepting their gods and exposing themselves to the danger of idolatry (vv. 12–13) or syncretism.

The establishing of the Covenant is followed by the so-called "Ritual Decalogue" (vv. 14–28). Although v. 28 refers to there being "ten commandments", it is not easy to reduce all these rules to ten. Most scholars agree that this "code" or codification of laws (cf. the note on 20:1–17), in its original form and as later modified, was not initially part of the book of Exodus. The regulations included here have basically to do with worship and they are so couched as to suggest that they belong to a people already settled and therefore able to organize the pilgrimage feasts (unleavened bread, Pentecost, Tabernacles), even though the rules given for them here are rather embryonic.

"You shall break their pillars and cut down their Asherim" (v. 13). The pillars were commemorative stones such as obelisks (cf. the note on 23:24–25). The Asherim were wooden monuments in the form of tree-stumps decorated in some way in honour of the fertility goddess Ashera (Astarte in Greek).

---

quidem durae cervicis est, sed tu auferes iniquitates nostras atque peccata nosque possidebis».
[10]Respondit Dominus: «Ego inibo pactum coram universo populo tuo; mirabilia faciam, quae numquam visa sunt super totam terram nec in ullis gentibus, ut cernat cunctus populus, in cuius es

Ex 23:20
Deut 7:1

11"Observe what I command you this day. Behold, I will drive out before you the Amorites, the Canaanites, the Hittites, the Perizzites, the Hivites, and the Jebusites. 12Take heed to yourself, lest you make a covenant with the inhabitants of the land whither you go,

Ex 23:24–25

lest it become a snare in the midst of you. 13You shall tear down their altars, and break their pillars, and cut down their Asherim 14

The Ritual Decalogue

Ex 20:3–5
Deut 4:24

14(for you shall worship no other god, for the LORD, whose name is Jealous, is a jealous God), 15lest you make a covenant with the

Acts 15:20

inhabitants of the land, and when they play the harlot after their gods and sacrifice to their gods and one invites you, you eat of his sacrifice, 16and you take of their daughters for your sons, and their daughters play the harlot after their gods and make your sons play the harlot after their gods.

Ex 20:4

17"You shall make for yourself no molten gods.

Ex 12:2; 23:14

18"The feast of unleavened bread you shall keep. Seven days you shall eat unleavened bread, as I commanded you, at the time appointed in the month Abib; for in the month Abib you came out

---

34:14–17. Verses 14 and 17 can be taken as a new wording of the first two commandments (cf. 20:3–5), centred on a ban on idolatry and the making of images. Verses 15 and 16 are prescriptions designed to prevent idolatry: they contain marriage imagery of the sort often found in the prophets from Hosea onwards (cf. Hos 2:4–25), meant to convey the idea of exclusive fidelity to God. Every idolatrous act is seen as prostitution or adultery against the Lord because the Covenant links man to God with the strength of the marriage bond. The image of married love continues into the New Testament, which applies it to Christ's love for his Church: "Husbands, love your wives, *as Christ loved the church*" (Eph 5:25). The Second Vatican Council repeats this teaching in these simple words: "Christ loves the Church as his bride, having been established as the model of a man loving his wife as his own body" (*Lumen gentium*, 7).

34:18–20. The keeping of the feast of the unleavened bread could be the third precept of this "Ritual Decalogue", and the rule about the first-born, the fourth. Here the month of Abib is given as the time the people came out of Egypt, but, unlike 12:2, it does not say it is the first month of the year. On the law about the first-born, see what is said in the note on 13:12.

---

medio, opus Domini terribile, quod facturus sum tecum. 11Observa cuncta, quae hodie mando tibi: ego ipse eiciam ante faciem tuam Amorraeum et Chananaeum et Hetthaeum, Pherezaeum quoque et Hevaeum et Iebusaeum. 12Cave, ne umquam cum habitatoribus terrae, quam intraveris, iungas amicitias, quae tibi sint in ruinam; 13sed aras eorum destrue, confringe lapides palosque succide. 14Noli adorare deum alienum: Dominus Zelotes nomen eius, Deus est aemulator. 15Ne ineas pactum cum hominibus illarum regionum, ne, cum fornicati fuerint cum diis suis et sacrificaverint eis, vocet te quispiam, et comedas de immolatis. 16Nec uxorem de filiabus eorum accipies filiis tuis, ne, postquam ipsae fuerint fornicatae cum diis suis, fornicari faciant et filios tuos in deos suos. 17Deos conflatiles non facies tibi. 18Sollemnitatem Azymorum custodies: septem diebus vesceris azymis, sicut praecepi tibi, in tempore constituto mensis Abib mense enim verni temporis egressus es de Aegypto. 19Omne, quod

from Egypt. [19]All that opens the womb is mine, all your male[x] cattle, the firstlings of cow and sheep. [20]The firstling of an ass you shall redeem with a lamb, or if you will not redeem it you shall break its neck. All the first-born of your sons you shall redeem. And none shall appear before me empty.

[21]"Six days you shall work, but on the seventh day you shall rest; in plowing time and in harvest you shall rest. [22]And you shall observe the feast of weeks, the first fruits of wheat harvest, and the feast of ingathering at the year's end. [23]Three times in the year shall all your males appear before the LORD God, the God of Israel. [24]For I will cast out nations before you, and enlarge your borders; neither shall any man desire your land, when you go up to appear before the LORD your God three times in the year.

[25]"You shall not offer the blood of my sacrifice with leaven; neither shall the sacrifice of the feast of the passover be left until

Ex 13:1–3; 13:11

Ex 20:8

Ex 23:14–17

Ex 12:1–4; 23:18

34:21. The precept on sabbath rest, the first in this code, is oriented to an agricultural society (that is, not to the sort of circumstances that applied in the crossing of the desert: cf. the note on 20:8). No religious reasons for this rest are mentioned, whether because this is a very concise wording or because it comes from a very early source (from a time when the idea of the sabbath's being the day of the Lord had not yet come into its own). Divine revelation, even on commandments, was a gradual thing and would not reach its full development until the New Testament.

34:22–24. The annual feasts of Pentecost and Tabernacles are the subject of the sixth commandment in this code. The fact that there are three pilgrimages each year seems to imply that religious wor-

ship is already centralized in the temple of Jerusalem. For a detailed comment on the main feasts of the chosen people, see the note on 23:14–17.

34:25. The seventh and eighth precepts of this code have to do with the Passover. The Code of the Covenant (cf. 23:18) is worded similarly to this, but here the Passover is not linked to the feast of the unleavened bread, despite the fact that they were held at the same time from very early on. This passage gives grounds for thinking that they were originally two different celebrations, with different purposes and rituals. The Passover was much the older; it betokened God's special protection; and it was a true sacrifice, perhaps the only one held in the context of the home and not in the temple (cf. the note on 12:1–14).

---

aperit vulvam generis masculini, meum erit; de cuncto grege tuo tam de bobus quam de ovibus meum erit. [20]Primogenitum asini redimes ove, sin autem nec pretium pro eo dederis, franges cervicem eius. Primogenitum filiorum tuorum redimes, nec apparebis in conspectu meo vacuus. [21]Sex diebus operaberis, die septimo cessabis etiam arare et metere. [22]Sollemnitatem Hebdomadarum facies tibi in primitiis frugum messis tuae triticeae et sollemnitatem Collectae, quando, redeunte anni tempore, cuncta conduntur. [23]Tribus temporibus anni apparebit omne masculinum tuum in conspectu omnipotentis Domini Dei Israel. [24]Cum enim tulero gentes a facie tua et dilatavero terminos tuos, nullus insidiabitur

x. Gk Theodotion Vg Tg: Heb uncertain

Ex 23:19
Deut 26:1

the morning. 26The first of the first fruits of your ground you shall bring to the house of the LORD your God. You shall not boil a kid in its mother's milk."

27And the LORD said to Moses, "Write these words; in accordance with these words I have made a covenant with you and

Ex 24:10, 18;
20:1
Mt 4:2

with Israel." 28And he was there with the LORD forty days and forty nights; he neither ate bread nor drank water. And he wrote upon the tables the words of the covenant, the ten commandments.[t]

2 Cor 3:7–16
Mt 17:2
2 Cor 3:10

Moses' shining face

29When Moses came down from Mount Sinai, with the two tables of the testimony in his hand as he came down from the mountain, Moses did not know that the skin of his face shone because he had been talking with God. 30And when Aaron and all the people of Israel saw Moses, behold, the skin of his face shone, and they were afraid to come near him. 31But Moses called to them; and Aaron and all the leaders of the congregation returned to him, and Moses talked with them. 32And afterward all the people of Israel

---

34:26. These last two precepts are also to be found in other lists of laws (cf. 23:19). They bring to a close this Ritual Code or Decalogue which contains a diverse series of laws, though all of them have to do with worship. For this reason, these precepts no longer apply, since Jesus Christ has come and it is he who renders true worship to the Father.

34:27–28. The conclusion of the Covenant is described as soberly as its introduction (v. 10). On the meaning of the forty days, see the note on 24:12–18.

34:29–35. The account of the events at Sinai ends with Moses in sharp focus, his face reflecting the glory of God.

"His face shone" (vv. 29, 30, 35). The Hebrew word *qarán*, which means "to shine, to be radiant", is very similar to *qeren*, which means "horn". Hence St Jerome's translation in the Vulgate: "And his face turned with bright horns", which has had its influence on Christian tradition and art. Michelangelo, for example, gave his famous statue of Moses two bright lights, one on each side of his forehead. Anyway, the sacred author's point is that Moses was transformed due to the fact that he had been so near God. The veil covering his face emphasizes the

---

terrae tuae, ascendente te et apparente in conspectu Domini Dei tui ter in anno. 25Non immolabis super fermento sanguinem hostiae meae; neque residebit mane de victima sollemnitatis Paschae. 26Primitias frugum terrae tuae afferes in domum Domini Dei tui. Non coques haedum in lacte matris suae». 27Dixitque Dominus ad Moysen: «Scribe tibi verba haec, quibus et tecum et cum Israel pepigi foedus». 28Fuit ergo ibi cum Domino quadraginta dies et quadraginta noctes; panem non comedit et aquam non bibit et scripsit in tabulis verba foederis, decem verba. 29Cumque descenderet Moyses de monte Sinai, tenebat duas tabulas testimonii et ignorabat quod resplenderet cutis faciei suae ex consortio sermonis Domini. 30Videntes autem Aaron et filii Israel resplendere cutem faciei Moysi, timuerunt prope

t. Heb *words*

came near, and he gave them in commandment all that the LORD
had spoken with him in Mount Sinai. ³³And when Moses had fin-   2 Cor 3:16
ished speaking with them, he put a veil on his face; ³⁴but whenever Moses went in before the LORD to speak with him, he took
the veil off, until he came out; and when he came out, and told the
people of Israel what he was commanded, ³⁵the people of Israel
saw the face of Moses, that the skin of Moses' face shone; and
Moses would put the veil upon his face again, until he went in to
speak with him.

13. BUILDING THE SANCTUARY*

The sabbath rest

Ex 20:8;
31:12–17

35 ¹Moses assembled all the congregation of the people of
Israel, and said to them, "These are the things which the
LORD has commanded you to do. ²Six days shall work be done,   Num 15:32ff
but on the seventh day you shall have a holy sabbath of solemn
rest to the LORD; whoever does any work on it shall be put to death;

---

transcendence of God: not only can the
Israelites not see God; they cannot even
look at the face of Moses, his closest
intermediary.

St Paul refers to this episode in order
to show the radical superiority of the
New Covenant and the meaning of apostolic ministry, for with the coming of
Christ all has been revealed and man has
direct access to the Father (cf. 2 Cor
3:7–18).

*35:1—40:8. The last section of the
book tells how the sanctuary and all its
furnishings were made. In order to show
how faithfully the Israelites obeyed, the
sacred writer repeats even word for word
the orders given in chapters 25–27 and
30. Even his little additions serve to show

how exactly those men carried out the
Lord's instructions. It is a lesson on the
quality a Christian's obedience should
have.

35:1–3. The precept on sabbath rest
came at the end of the instructions for
building the sanctuary (31:12–17); here it
is placed first, giving it all its due importance, for the day dedicated to the Lord
should be kept even when the work being
done is done at God's own bidding.

This is the only passage in the Old
Testament to mention the ban on lighting
fires on the sabbath (though that may be
implied in 16:23). It is very much to the
point, since metals would have had to be
smelted to make much of the sanctuary
fittings.

---

accedere; ³¹vocatique ab eo reversi sunt tam Aaron quam principes synagogae. Et postquam locutus est
ad eos, ³²venerunt ad eum etiam omnes filii Israel; quibus praecepit cuncta, quae audierat a Domino in
monte Sinai. ³³Impletisque sermonibus, posuit velamen super faciem suam, ³⁴quod ingressus ad
Dominum et loquens cum eo auferebat, donec exiret; et tunc loquebatur ad filios Israel omnia, quae
sibi fuerant imperata. ³⁵Qui videbant cutem faciei Moysi resplendere, sed operiebat ille rursus faciem
suam, donec ingressus loqueretur cum eo. ¹Igitur, congregato omni coetu filiorum Israel, dixit ad eos:

Ex 16:23 ³you shall kindle no fire in all your habitations on the sabbath day."

Ex 25:1-7 **Generous contributions**

⁴Moses said to all the congregation of the people of Israel, "This is the thing which the LORD has commanded. ⁵Take from among you an offering to the LORD; whoever is of a generous heart, let him bring the LORD's offering: gold, silver, and bronze; ⁶blue and purple and scarlet stuff and fine twined linen; goats' hair, ⁷tanned rams' skins, and goatskins; acacia wood, ⁸oil for the light, spices for the anointing oil and for the fragrant incense, ⁹and onyx stones and stones for setting, for the ephod and for the breastpiece.

¹⁰"And let every able man among you come and make all that the LORD has commanded: the tabernacle, ¹¹its tent and its covering, its hooks and its frames, its bars, its pillars, and its bases; ¹²the ark with its poles, the mercy seat, and the veil of the screen; ¹³the table with its poles and all its utensils, and the bread of the Presence; ¹⁴the lampstand also for the light, with its utensils and its lamps, and the oil for the light; ¹⁵and the altar of incense, with its poles, and the anointing oil and the fragrant incense, and the screen for the door, at the door of the tabernacle; ¹⁶the altar of burnt offering, with its grating of bronze, its poles, and all its utensils, the laver and its base; ¹⁷the hangings of the court, its pillars and its bases, and the screen for the gate of the court; ¹⁸the pegs of the tabernacle and the pegs of the court, and their cords; ¹⁹the finely wrought garments for ministering in the holy place, the holy garments for Aaron the priest, and the garments of his sons, for their service as priests."

²⁰Then all the congregation of the people of Israel departed from the presence of Moses. ²¹And they came, every one whose

«Haec sunt, quae iussit Dominus fieri: ²sex diebus facietis opus, septimus dies erit vobis sanctus, sabbatum et requies Domino; qui fecerit opus in eo, occidetur. ³Non succendetis ignem in omnibus habitaculis vestris per diem sabbati». ⁴Et ait Moyses ad omnem coetum filiorum Israel: «Iste sermo, quem praecepit Dominus dicens: ⁵'Separate apud vos donaria Domino'. Omnis voluntarius et proni animi offerat ea Domino: aurum et argentum et aes, ⁶hyacinthum et purpuram coccumque et byssum, pilos caprarum ⁷et pelles arietum rubricatas et pelles delphini, ligna acaciae ⁸et oleum ad luminaria concinnanda et aromata, ut conficiatur unguentum et thymiama suavissimum, ⁹lapides onychinos et gemmas ad ornatum ephod et pectoralis. ¹⁰Quisquis vestrum sapiens est, veniat et faciat, quod Dominus imperavit, ¹¹habitaculum scilicet et tentorium eius atque operimentum, fibulas et tabulata cum vectibus, columnas et bases; ¹²arcam et vectes, propitiatorium et velum, quod ante illud oppanditur ¹³mensam cum vectibus et vasis et propositionis panibus; ¹⁴candelabrum ad luminaria sustentanda, vasa illius et lucernas et oleum ad nutrimenta luminarium; ¹⁵altare thymiamatis et vectes et oleum unctionis et thymiama ex aromatibus; velum ad ostium habitaculi; ¹⁶altare holocausti et craticulam eius aeneam cum vectibus et vasis suis, labrum et basim eius; ¹⁷cortinas atrii cum columnis et basibus, velum in foribus atrii; ¹⁸paxillos habitaculi et atrii cum funiculis suis; ¹⁹vestimenta texta, quorum usus est in ministerio sanctuarii, vestes sanctas Aaron pontificis ac vestes filiorum eius, ut sacerdotio fungantur mihi».

heart stirred him, and every one whose spirit moved him, and brought the LORD's offering to be used for the tent of meeting, and for all its service, and for the holy garments. ²²So they came, both men and women; all who were of a willing heart brought brooches and earrings and signet rings and armlets, all sorts of gold objects, every man dedicating an offering of gold to the LORD. ²³And every man with whom was found blue or purple or scarlet stuff or fine linen or goats' hair or tanned rams' skins or goatskins, brought them. ²⁴Every one who could make an offering of silver or bronze brought it as the LORD's offering; and every man with whom was found acacia wood of any use in the work, brought it. ²⁵And all women who had ability spun with their hands, and brought what they had spun in blue and purple and scarlet stuff and fine twined linen; ²⁶all the women whose hearts were moved with ability spun the goats' hair. ²⁷And the leaders brought onyx stones and stones to be set, for the ephod and for the breastpiece, ²⁸and spices and oil for the light, and for the anointing oil, and for the fragrant incense. ²⁹All the men and women, the people of Israel, whose heart moved them to bring anything for the work which the LORD had commanded by Moses to be done, brought it as their freewill offering to the LORD.

The craftsmen chosen

Ex 31:2–6

³⁰And Moses said to the people of Israel, "See, the LORD has called by name Bezalel the son of Uri, son of Hur, of the tribe of Judah; ³¹and he has filled him with the Spirit of God, with ability, Acts 6:3 with intelligence, with knowledge, and with all craftsmanship, ³²to devise artistic designs, to work in gold and silver and bronze, ³³in cutting stones for setting, and in carving wood, for work in every skilled craft. ³⁴And he has inspired him to teach, both him and

²⁰Egressus est omnis coetus filiorum Israel de conspectu Moysi, ²¹et venit, quisquis erat mentis promptissimae, et attulit sponte sua donaria Domino ad faciendum opus tabernaculi conventus et quidquid ad cultum et ad vestes sanctas necessarium erat. ²²Viri cum mulieribus, omnes voluntarii praebuerunt fibulas et inaures, anulos et dextralia; omne vas aureum in donaria Domini separatum est. ²³Si quis habebat hyacinthum et purpuram coccumque, byssum et pilos caprarum, pelles arietum rubricatas et pelles delphini, ²⁴argenti aerisque metalla, obtulerunt Domino lignaque acaciae in varios usus. ²⁵Sed et mulieres eruditae dederunt, quae neverant, hyacinthum, purpuram et coccum ac byssum ²⁶et pilos caprarum, sponte propria cuncta tribuentes. ²⁷Principes vero obtulerunt lapides onychinos et gemmas ad ephod et pectorale ²⁸aromataque et oleum ad luminaria concinnanda et ad praeparandum unguentum ac thymiama odoris suavissimi componendum. ²⁹Omnes viri et mulieres mente prompta obtulerunt donaria, ut fierent opera, quae iusserat Dominus per manum Moysi. Cuncti filii Israel voluntaria Domino dedicaverunt. ³⁰Dixitque Moyses ad filios Israel: «Ecce vocavit Dominus ex nomine Beseleel filium Uri filii Hur de tribu Iudae; ³¹implevitque eum spiritu Dei, sapientia et intellegentia et scientia ad omne opus, ³²ad excogitandum et faciendum opus in auro et argento et aere, ³³ad scindendum et includendum gemmas et ad sculpendum ligna, quidquid fabre adinveniri potest. ³⁴Dedit quoque in corde eius, ut alios doceret, ipsi et Ooliab filio Achisamech de tribu Dan. ³⁵Ambos implevit sapientia,

Ex 26:31–32 Oholiab the son of Ahisamach of the tribe of Dan. ³⁵He has filled them with ability to do every sort of work done by a craftsman or by a designer or by an embroiderer in blue and purple and scarlet stuff and fine twined linen, or by a weaver—by any sort of workman or skilled designer.

36 ¹Bezalel and Oholiab and every able man in whom the LORD has put ability and intelligence to know how to do any work in the construction of the sanctuary shall work in accordance with all that the LORD has commanded."

²And Moses called Bezalel and Oholiab and every able man in whose mind the LORD had put ability, every one whose heart stirred him up to come to do the work; ³and they received from Moses all the freewill offering which the people of Israel had brought for doing the work on the sanctuary. They still kept bringing him freewill offerings every morning, ⁴so that all the able men who were doing every sort of task on the sanctuary came, each from the task that he was doing, ⁵and said to Moses, "The people bring much more than enough for doing the work which the LORD has commanded us to do." ⁶So Moses gave command, and word was proclaimed throughout the camp, "Let neither man nor woman do anything more for the offering for the sanctuary." So the people were restrained from bringing; ⁷for the stuff they had was sufficient to do all the work, and more.

Ex 26:1–14 **Building the tabernacle**
⁸And all the able men among the workmen made the tabernacle with ten curtains; they were made of fine twined linen and blue

---

36:2–7. The Israelites were so generous that Moses had to call a halt to their offerings. In view of how well the sons of Israel acted, and mindful of all that God did for his people, the prophets and future generations looked back nostalgically on the journey in the desert as an ideal, a reference point, to encourage heartfelt conversion to God (cf., e.g., Hos 2:16–17; Jer 2:6).

ut faciant opera fabri polymitarii ac plumarii de hyacintho ac purpura coccoque et bysso et textoris, facientes omne opus ac nova quaeque reperientes». ¹Fecit ergo Beseleel et Ooliab et omnis vir sapiens, quibus dedit Dominus sapientiam et intellectum, ut scirent fabre operari, quae in usus sanctuarii necessaria sunt et quae praecepit Dominus. ²Cumque vocasset Moyses Beseleel et Ooliab et omnem eruditum virum, cui dederat Dominus sapientiam, omnes, qui sponte sua obtulerant se ad faciendum opus, ³acceperunt ab ipso universa donaria, quae attulerant filii Israel ad faciendum opus in cultum sanctuarii. Ipsi autem cotidie mane donaria ei offerebant. ⁴Unde omnes sapientes artifices venerunt singuli de opere suo pro sanctuario ⁵et dixerunt Moysi: «Plus offert populus quam necessarium est operi, quod Dominus iussit facere». ⁶Iussit ergo Moyses praeconis voce per castra clamari: «Nec vir nec mulier quidquam offerat ultra pro omni opere sanctuario». Sicque cessatum est a muneribus offerendis, ⁷eo quod oblata sufficerent et superabundarent. ⁸Feceruntque omnes corde sapientes inter artifices habita-

and purple and scarlet stuff, with cherubim skilfully worked. ⁹The length of each curtain was twenty-eight cubits, and the breadth of each curtain four cubits; all the curtains had the same measure. ¹⁰And he coupled five curtains to one another, and the other five curtains he coupled to one another. ¹¹And he made loops of blue on the edge of the outmost curtain of the first set; likewise he made them on the edge of the outmost curtain of the second set; ¹²he made fifty loops on the one curtain, and he made fifty loops on the edge of the curtain that was in the second set; the loops were opposite one another. ¹³And he made fifty clasps of gold, and coupled the curtains one to the other with clasps; so the tabernacle was one whole.

¹⁴He also made curtains of goats' hair for a tent over the tabernacle; he made eleven curtains. ¹⁵The length of each curtain was thirty cubits, and the breadth of each curtain four cubits; the eleven curtains had the same measure. ¹⁶He coupled five curtains by themselves, and six curtains by themselves. ¹⁷And he made fifty loops on the edge of the outmost curtain of the one set, and fifty loops on the edge of the other connecting curtain. ¹⁸And he made fifty clasps of bronze to couple the tent together that it might be one whole. ¹⁹And he made for the tent a covering of tanned rams' skins and goatskins.

The framework for the tabernacle

Ex 26:15–30

²⁰Then he made the upright frames for the tabernacle of acacia wood. ²¹Ten cubits was the length of a frame, and a cubit and a half the breadth of each frame. ²²Each frame had two tenons, for fitting together; he did this for all the frames of the tabernacle. ²³The frames for the tabernacle he made thus: twenty frames for the southside; ²⁴and he made forty bases of silver under the twenty

culi cortinas decem de bysso retorta et hyacintho et purpura coccoque, cum cherubim intextis arte polymita; ⁹quarum una habebat in longitudine viginti octo cubitos et in latitudine quattuor: una mensura erat omnium cortinarum. ¹⁰Coniunxitque cortinas quinque alteram alteri et alias quinque sibi invicem copulavit. ¹¹Fecit et ansas hyacinthinas in ora cortinae unius in extremitate iuncturae et in ora cortinae extremae in iunctura altera similiter. ¹²Quinquagenas ansas fecit pro utraque cortina, ut contra se invicem venirent ansae et mutuo iungerentur. ¹³Unde et quinquaginta fudit fibulas aureas, quae morderent cortinarum ansas, et fieret unum habitaculum. ¹⁴Fecit et saga undecim de pilis caprarum pro tentorio super habitaculum; ¹⁵unum sagum in longitudine habebat cubitos triginta et in latitudine cubitos quattuor: unius mensurae erant omnia saga. ¹⁶Quorum quinque iunxit seorsum et sex alia separatim. ¹⁷Fecitque ansas quinquaginta in ora sagi ultimi iuncturae unius et quinquaginta in ora sagi iuncturae alterius, ut sibi invicem iungerentur; ¹⁸et fecit fibulas aeneas quinquaginta, quibus necteretur tentorium, ut esset unum. ¹⁹Fecit et opertorium tentorio de pellibus arietum rubricatis aliudque desuper velamentum de pellibus delphini. ²⁰Fecit et tabulas habitaculi de lignis acaciae stantes. ²¹Decem cubitorum erat longitudo tabulae unius, et unum ac semis cubitum latitudo retinebat. ²²Bini pedes erant per singulas tabulas, ut altera alteri iungeretur: sic fecit in omnibus tabulis habitaculi. ²³E quibus viginti ad plagam meridianam erant contra austrum ²⁴cum quadraginta basibus argenteis. Duae bases sub

frames, two bases under one frame for its two tenons, and two bases under another frame for its two tenons. 25And for the second side of the tabernacle, on the north side, he made twenty frames 26and their forty bases of silver, two bases under one frame and two bases under another frame. 27And for the rear of the tabernacle westward he made six frames. 28And he made two frames for corners of the tabernacle in the rear. 29And they were separate beneath, but joined at the top, at the first ring; he made two of them thus, for the two corners. 30There were eight frames with their bases of silver: sixteen bases, under every frame two bases.

31And he made bars of acacia wood, five for the frames of the one side of the tabernacle, 32and five bars for the frames of the other side of the tabernacle, and five bars for the frames of the tabernacle at the rear westward. 33And he made the middle bar to pass through from end to end halfway up the frames. 34And he overlaid the frames with gold, and made their rings of gold for holders for the bars, and overlaid the bars with gold.

Ex 26:31–37 **The veil**

35And he made the veil of blue and purple and scarlet stuff and fine twined linen; with cherubim skilfully worked he made it. 36And for it he made four pillars of acacia, and overlaid them with gold; their hooks were of gold, and he cast for them four bases of silver. 37He also made a screen for the door of the tent, of blue and purple and scarlet stuff and fine twined linen, embroidered with needlework; 38and its five pillars with their hooks. He overlaid their capitals, and their fillets were of gold, but their five bases were of bronze.

Ex 25:10–20 **The ark**

37 1Bezalel made the ark of acacia wood; two cubits and a half was its length, a cubit and a half its breadth, and a

singulis tabulis ponebantur pro duabus pedibus. 25Ad plagam quoque habitaculi, quae respicit ad aquilonem, fecit viginti tabulas 26cum quadraginta basibus argenteis: duas bases per singulas tabulas. 27Contra occidentem vero, id est ad eam partem habitaculi quae mare respicit, fecit sex tabulas 28et duas alias per singulos angulos habitaculi retro; 29quae gemellae erant a deorsum usque sursum in unam compaginem. Ita fecit duas tabulas in duobus angulis, 30ut octo essent simul tabulae et haberent bases argenteas sedecim: binas scilicet bases sub singulis tabulis. 31Fecit et vectes de lignis acaciae quinque ad continendas tabulas unius lateris habitaculi 32et quinque alios ad alterius lateris coaptandas tabulas; et extra hos quinque alios vectes ad occidentalem plagam habitaculi contra mare. 33Fecit autem vectem medium, qui per medias tabulas ab una extremitate usque ad alteram perveniret. 34Ipsa autem tabulata deauravit. Et anulos eorum fecit aureos, per quos vectes induci possent; quos et ipsos laminis aureis operuit. 35Fecit et velum de hyacintho et purpura coccoque ac bysso retorta, opere polymitario, cum cherubim intextis; 36et quattuor columnas de lignis acaciae, quas cum uncis suis deauravit, fusis basibus earum argenteis. 37Fecit et velum in introitu tabernaculi ex hyacintho, purpura, cocco byssoque retorta opere plumarii; 38et columnas quinque cum uncis suis. Et operuit auro capita et anulos earum

cubit and a half its height. ²And he overlaid it with pure gold within and without, and made a moulding of gold around it. ³And he cast for it four rings of gold for its four corners, two rings on its one side and two rings on its other side. ⁴And he made poles of acacia wood, and overlaid them with gold, ⁵and put the poles into the rings on the sides of the ark, to carry the ark. ⁶And he made a mercy seat of pure gold; two cubits and a half was its length, and a cubit and a half its breadth. ⁷And he made two cherubim of hammered gold; on the two ends of the mercy seat he made them, ⁸one cherub on the one end, and one cherub on the other end; of one piece with the mercy seat he made the cherubim on its two ends. ⁹The cherubim spread out their wings above, overshadowing the mercy seat with their wings, with their faces one to another; toward the mercy seat were the faces of the cherubim.

The table for the offertory bread   Ex 25:23–29

¹⁰He also made the table of acacia wood; two cubits was its length, a cubit its breadth, and a cubit and a half its height; ¹¹and he overlaid it with pure gold, and made a moulding of gold around it. ¹²And he made around it a frame a handbreadth wide, and made a molding of gold around the frame. ¹³He cast for it four rings of gold, and fastened the rings to the four corners at its four legs. ¹⁴Close to the frame were the rings, as holders for the poles to carry the table. ¹⁵He made the poles of acacia wood to carry the table, and overlaid them with gold. ¹⁶And he made the vessels of pure gold which were to be upon the table, its plates and dishes for incense, and its bowls and flagons with which to pour libations.

basesque earum fudit aeneas. ¹Fecit autem Beseleel et arcam de lignis acaciae habentem duos semis cubitos in longitudine et cubitum ac semissem in latitudine, altitudo quoque unius cubiti fuit et dimidii; vestivitque eam auro purissimo intus ac foris. ²Et fecit illi coronam auream per gyrum, ³conflans quattuor anulos aureos in quattuor pedibus eius; duos anulos in latere uno et duos in altero. ⁴Vectes quoque fecit de lignis acaciae, quos vestivit auro; ⁵et quos misit in anulos, qui erant in lateribus arcae, ad portandum eam. ⁶Fecit et propitiatorium de auro mundissimo: duorum cubitorum et dimidii in longitudine et cubiti ac semis in latitudine. ⁷Duos etiam cherubim ex auro ductili fecit ex utraque parte propitiatorii: ⁸cherub unum ex summitate unius partis et cherub alterum ex summitate partis alterius; duos cherubim ex singulis summitatibus propitiatorii ⁹extendentes alas sursum et tegentes alis suis propitiatorium seque mutuo et illud respicientes. ¹⁰Fecit et mensam de lignis acaciae in longitudine duorum cubitorum et in latitudine unius cubiti, quae habebat in altitudine cubitum ac semissem; ¹¹circumdeditque eam auro mundissimo et fecit illi coronam auream per gyrum. ¹²Fecit ei quoque limbum aureum quattuor digitorum per circuitum et super illum coronam auream. ¹³Fudit et quattuor circulos aureos, quos posuit in quattuor angulis per singulos pedes mensae ¹⁴iuxta limbum; misitque in eos vectes, ut possit mensa portari. ¹⁵Ipsos quoque vectes fecit de lignis acaciae et circumdedit eos auro; ¹⁶et vasa ad diversos usus mensae, acetabula, phialas et cyathos et crateras ex auro puro, in quibus offerenda sunt libamina. ¹⁷Fecit et candelabrum ductile de auro mundissimo, basim et hastile eius; scyphi sphaeru-

Ex 25:31–39 **The golden lampstand**

¹⁷He also made the lampstand of pure gold. The base and the shaft of the lampstand were made of hammered work; its cups, its capitals, and its flowers were of one piece with it. ¹⁸And there were six branches going out of its sides, three branches of the lampstand out of one side of it and three branches of the lampstand out of the other side of it; ¹⁹three cups made like almonds, each with capital and flower, on one branch, and three cups made like almonds, each with capital and flower, on the other branch—so for the six branches going out of the lampstand. ²⁰And on the lampstand itself were four cups made like almonds, with their capitals and flowers, ²¹and a capital of one piece with it under each pair of the six branches going out of it. ²²Their capitals and their branches were of one piece with it; the whole of it was one piece of hammered work of pure gold. ²³And he made its seven lamps and its snuffers and its trays of pure gold. ²⁴He made it and all its utensils of a talent of pure gold.

Ex 30:1–5 **The altar of incense**

²⁵He made the altar of incense of acacia wood; its length was a cubit, and its breadth was a cubit; it was square, and two cubits was its height; its horns were of one piece with it. ²⁶He overlaid it with pure gold, its top, and its sides round about, and its horns; and he made a moulding of gold round about it, ²⁷and made two rings of gold on it under its moulding, on two opposite sides of it, as holders for the poles with which to carry it. ²⁸And he made the poles of acacia wood, and overlaid them with gold.

Ex 30:22–25; 34–35 ²⁹He made the holy anointing oil also, and the pure fragrant incense, blended as by the perfumer.

Ex 27:1–8 **The altar of holocaust**

38 ¹He made the altar of burnt offering also of acacia wood; five cubits was its length, and five cubits its breadth; it

---

laeque ac flores unum cum ipso erant: ¹⁸ sex in utroque latere, tres calami ex parte una et tres ex altera; ¹⁹tres scyphi in nucis modum in calamo uno sphaerulaeque simul et flores et tres scyphi instar nucis in calamo altero sphaerulaeque simul et flores. Aequum erat opus sex calamorum, qui procedebant de hastili candelabri. ²⁰In ipso autem hastili erant quattuor scyphi in nucis modum sphaerulaeque et flores; ²¹singulae sphaerulae sub binis calamis per loca tria, qui simul sex fiunt calami procedentes de hastili uno. ²²Sphaerulae igitur et calami unum cum ipso erant, totum ductile ex auro purissimo. ²³Fecit et lucernas septem cum emunctoriis suis et vasa, ubi emuncta condantur, de auro mundissimo. ²⁴Talentum auri purissimi appendebat candelabrum cum omnibus vasis suis. ²⁵Fecit et altare thymiamatis de lignis acaciae habens per quadrum singulos cubitos et in altitudine duos; e cuius angulis procedebant cornua. ²⁶Vestivitque illud auro purissimo cum craticula ac parietibus et cornibus. ²⁷ Fecitque ei coronam aureolam per gyrum et binos anulos aureos sub corona in duobus lateribus, ut mittantur in eos vectes, et possit altare portari. ²⁸Ipsos autem vectes fecit de lignis acaciae et operuit laminis aureis. ²⁹Composuit

was square, and three cubits was its height. ²He made horns for it on its four corners; its horns were of one piece with it, and he overlaid it with bronze. ³And he made all the utensils of the altar, the pots, the shovels, the basins, the forks, and the firepans: all its utensils he made of bronze. ⁴And he made for the altar a grating, a network of bronze, under its ledge, extending halfway down. ⁵He cast four rings on the four corners of the bronze grating as holders for the poles; ⁶he made the poles of acacia wood, and overlaid them with bronze. ⁷And he put the poles through the rings on the sides of the altar, to carry it with them; he made it hollow, with boards.

⁸And he made the laver of bronze and its base of bronze, from the mirrors of the ministering women who ministered at the door of the tent of meeting.

Ex 30:17–21
1 Sam 2:22

The court of the sanctuary

Ex 27:9–19

⁹And he made the court; for the south side the hangings of the court were of fine twined linen, a hundred cubits; ¹⁰their pillars were twenty and their bases twenty, of bronze, but the hooks of the pillars and their fillets were of silver. ¹¹And for the north side a hundred cubits, their pillars twenty, their bases twenty, of bronze, but the hooks of the pillars and their fillets were of silver. ¹²And for the west side were hangings of fifty cubits, their pillars ten, and their sockets ten; the hooks of the pillars and their fillets were of silver. ¹³And for the front to the east, fifty cubits. ¹⁴The hangings for one side of the gate were fifteen cubits, with three

---

38:8. It is not known what role these women had at the entrance to the tent of meeting (cf. 1 Sam 2:22). The Septuagint Greek says that they "fasted" and the Greek version of Onkelos says that they "prayed". This is the only Old Testament text that speaks of women taking part in temple activities.

et oleum ad sanctificationis unguentum et thymiama de aromatibus mundissimis opere pigmentarii. ¹Fecit et altare holocausti de lignis acaciae quinque cubitorum per quadrum et trium in altitudine, ²cuius cornua de angulis procedebant; operuitque illud laminis aeneis. ³Et in usus eius paravit ex aere vasa diversa: lebetes, vatilla et pateras, fuscinulas et ignium receptacula. ⁴Craticulamque eius in modum retis fecit aeneam subter marginem altaris ab imo usque ad medium eius, ⁵fusis quattuor anulis per totidem craticulae summitates, ad immittendos vectes ad portandum. ⁶Quos et ipsos fecit de lignis acaciae et operuit laminis aeneis; ⁷induxitque in circulos, qui in lateribus altaris eminebant. Ipsum autem altare non erat solidum, sed cavum ex tabulis et intus vacuum. ⁸Fecit et labrum aeneum cum basi sua de speculis mulierum, quae excubabant in ostio tabernaculi conventus. ⁹Fecit et atrium, in cuius australi plaga erant tentoria de bysso retorta cubitorum centum; ¹⁰columnae aeneae viginti cum basibus suis; unci columnarum et anuli earum argentei. ¹¹Aeque ad septentrionalem plagam tentoria, columnae basesque et unci anulique columnarum eiusdem mensurae et operis ac metalli erant. ¹²In ea vero plaga, quae ad occidentem respicit, fuerunt tentoria cubitorum quinquaginta, columnae decem cum basibus suis; et unci columnarum anulique earum argentei. ¹³Porro contra orientem quinquaginta cubitorum paravit

pillars and three bases. ¹⁵And so for the other side; on this hand and that hand by the gate of the court were hangings of fifteen cubits, with three pillars and three bases. ¹⁶All the hangings round about the court were of fine twined linen. ¹⁷And the bases for the pillars were of bronze, but the hooks of the pillars and their fillets were of silver; the overlaying of their capitals was also of silver, and all the pillars of the court were filleted with silver. ¹⁸And the screen for the gate of the court was embroidered with needlework in blue and purple and scarlet stuff and fine twined linen; it was twenty cubits long and five cubits high in its breadth, corresponding to the hangings of the court. ¹⁹And their pillars were four; their four bases were of bronze, their hooks of silver, and the overlaying of their capitals and their fillets of silver. ²⁰And all the pegs for the tabernacle and for the court round about were of bronze.

Materials used

Num 1:45–46   ²¹This is the sum of the things for the tabernacle, the tabernacle of the testimony, as they were counted at the commandment of Moses, for the work of the Levites under the direction of Ithamar Ex 35:30–35   the son of Aaron the priest. ²²Bezalel the son of Uri, son of Hur, of the tribe of Judah, made all that the LORD commanded Moses; ²³and with him was Oholiab the son of Ahisamach, of the tribe of Dan, a craftsman and designer and embroiderer in blue and purple and scarlet stuff and fine twined linen.

    ²⁴All the gold that was used for the work, in all the construction of the sanctuary, the gold from the offering, was twenty-nine

---

38:21–31. There is nothing in chapters 25–31 about an account having to be made up. This passage was probably added later because the Levites (v. 21) were not instituted until later (cf. Num 3:45–46) and Ithamar became their leader later still (cf. Num 4:33). But the passage does serve to show how generous the people were.

---

tentoria, ¹⁴e quibus quindecim cubitos columnarum trium cum basibus suis unum tenebat latus; ¹⁵et in parte alter —quia inter utraque introitum tabernaculi fecit— quindecim aeque cubitorum erant tentoria columnaeque tres et bases totidem. ¹⁶Cuncta atrii tentoria in circuitu ex bysso retorta texuerat. ¹⁷Bases columnarum fuere aeneae, unci autem earum et anuli earum argentei et capita earum vestivit argento et omnes columnas atrii cinxit anulis argenteis. ¹⁸Et in introitu eius opere plumario fecit velum ex hyacintho, purpura, cocco ac bysso retorta; quod habebat viginti cubitos in longitudine, altitudo vero quinque cubitorum erat iuxta mensuram, quam cuncta atrii tentoria habebant. ¹⁹Columnae autem in ingressu fuere quattuor cum basibus aeneis, uncis argenteis; capitaque et anulos earum vestivit argento. ²⁰Paxillos quoque habitaculi et atrii per gyrum fecit aeneos. ²¹Hic est census habitaculi, habitaculi testimonii, qui recensitus est iuxta praeceptum Moysi ministerio Levitarum per manum Ithamar filii Aaron sacerdotis. ²²Beseleel filius Uri filii Hur de tribu Iudae fecit cuncta, quae praeceperat Dominus Moysi, ²³iuncto sibi socio Ooliab filio Achisamech de tribu Dan fabro et polymitario atque plumario

talents and seven hundred and thirty shekels, by the shekel of the sanctuary. ²⁵And the silver from those of the congregation who were numbered was a hundred talents and a thousand seven hundred and seventy-five shekels, by the shekel of the sanctuary: ²⁶a beka a head (that is, half a shekel, by the shekel of the sanctuary), for every one who was numbered in the census, from twenty years old and upward, for six hundred and three thousand, five hundred and fifty men. ²⁷The hundred talents of silver were for casting the bases of the sanctuary, and the bases of the veil; a hundred bases for the hundred talents, a talent for a base. ²⁸And of the thousand seven hundred and seventy-five shekels he made hooks for the pillars, and overlaid their capitals and made fillets for them. ²⁹And the bronze that was contributed was seventy talents, and two thousand and four hundred shekels; ³⁰with it he made the bases for the door of the tent of meeting, the bronze altar and the bronze grating for it and all the utensils of the altar, ³¹the bases round about the court, and the bases of the gate of the court, all the pegs of the tabernacle, and all the pegs round about the court.

The priestly vestments

39 ¹And of the blue and purple and scarlet stuff they made finely wrought garments, for ministering in the holy place; they made the holy garments for Aaron; as the LORD had commanded Moses.

39:1. "As the Lord had commanded Moses"—a phrase which is repeated throughout this chapter (vv. 1, 5, 7, 21, 29, 31) and the following one (vv. 16, 19, 21, 23, 25, 27, 29, 32). It serves to confirm that all this work was carried out perfectly: obedience is a sign of faithfulness and, as reported here, it is an encouragement to later generations to listen to the word of God and put it into practice.

---

ex hyacintho, purpura, cocco et bysso. ²⁴Omne aurum, quod expensum est in opere sanctuarii et quod oblatum est in donariis, viginti novem talentorum fuit et septingentorum triginta siclorum ad mensuram sicli sanctuarii. ²⁵Argentum autem eorum, qui in congregatione recensiti sunt, centum talentorum fuit et mille septingentorum et septuaginta quinque siclorum ad mensuram sicli sanctuarii. ²⁶Beca, id est dimidium sicli iuxta mensuram sicli sanctuarii, dedit quisquis transit ad censum a viginti annis et supra, de sescentis tribus milibus et quingentis quinquaginta armatorum. ²⁷De talentis centum argenti conflatae sunt bases sanctuarii et veli, singulis talentis per bases singulas supputatis. ²⁸De mille autem septingentis et septuaginta quinque siclis fecit uncos columnarum et vestivit capita earum et cinxit eas argento. ²⁹Aeris quoque oblata sunt septuaginta talenta et duo milia et quadringenti sicli, ³⁰ex quibus fecit bases in introitu tabernaculi conventus et altare aeneum cum craticula sua omniaque vasa, quae ad usum eius pertinent, ³¹et bases atrii tam in circuitu quam in ingressu eius et omnes paxillos habitaculi atque atrii per gyrum. ¹De hyacintho vero et purpura, cocco ac bysso fecerunt vestes textas pro ministerio sanctuarii. Et fecerunt vestes sacras Aaron, sicut praecepit Dominus Moysi. ²Fecerunt igitur ephod de auro, hyacintho et purpura coccoque et bysso retorta ³opere polymitario tundentes bratteas

Ex 28:6–13 **The ephod**

[2]And he made the ephod of gold, blue and purple and scarlet stuff, and fine twined linen. [3]And gold leaf was hammered out and cut into threads to work into the blue and purple and the scarlet stuff, and into the fine twined linen, in skilled design. [4]They made for the ephod shoulder-pieces, joined to it at its two edges. [5]And the skilfully woven band upon it, to gird it on, was of the same materials and workmanship, of gold, blue and purple and scarlet stuff, and fine twined linen; as the LORD had commanded Moses.

[6]The onyx stones were prepared, enclosed in settings of gold filigree and engraved like the engravings of a signet, according to the names of the sons of Israel. [7]And he set them on the shoulder-pieces of the ephod, to be stones of remembrance for the sons of Israel; as the LORD had commanded Moses.

Ex 28:15–30 **The breastpiece**

[8]He made the breastpiece, in skilled work, like the work of the ephod, of gold, blue and purple and scarlet stuff, and fine twined linen. [9]It was square; the breastpiece was made double, a span its length and a span its breadth when doubled. [10]And they set in it four rows of stones. A row of sardius, topaz, and carbuncle was the first row; [11]and the second row, an emerald, a sapphire, and a diamond; [12]and the third row, a jacinth, an agate, and an amethyst; [13]and the fourth row, a beryl, an onyx, and a jasper; they were

Rev 21:12 enclosed in settings of gold filigree. [14]There were twelve stones with their names according to the names of the sons of Israel; they were like signets, each engraved with its name, for the twelve tribes. [15]And they made on the breastpiece twisted chains like cords, of pure gold; [16]and they made two settings of gold filigree and two gold rings, and put the two rings on the two edges of the breastpiece; [17]and they put the two cords of gold in the two rings

---

aureas et extenuantes in fila, ut possent torqueri cum priorum colorum subtegmine. [4]Fasciasque umerales fecerunt ei, cum quibus in utroque latere summitatum suarum copulabatur, [5]et balteum, quo constringebatur ephod, eiusdem operis et unum cum eo ex auro, et hyacintho et purpura coccoque et bysso retorta, sicut praeceperat Dominus Moysi. [6]Paraverunt et duos lapides onychinos, inclusos texturis aureis et sculptos arte gemmaria nominibus filiorum Israel; [7]posueruntque eos in fasciis umeralibus ephod, lapides memorialis filiorum Israel, sicut praeceperat Dominus Moysi. [8]Fecerunt et pectorale opere polymito iuxta opus ephod ex auro, hyacintho, purpura coccoque et bysso retorta, [9]quadrangulum duplex mensurae palmi. [10]Et posuerunt in eo gemmarum ordines quattuor: in primo versu erat sardius, topazius, smaragdus; [11]in secundo carbunculus, sapphirus et iaspis; [12]in tertio hyacinthus, achates et amethystus; [13]in quarto chrysolithus, onychinus et beryllus: inclusi textura aurea per ordines suos. [14]Ipsique lapides duodecim sculpti erant nominibus duodecim tribuum Israel, singuli per nomina singulorum. [15]Fecerunt in pectorali catenulas quasi funiculos opus tortile de auro purissimo [16]et duos margines aureos totidemque anulos aureos. Porro duos anulos posuerunt in utraque summitate pectoralis; [17]duos funiculos aureos inseruerunt anulis, qui in pectoralis angulis eminebant. [18]Duas

at the edges of the breastpiece. [18]Two ends of the two cords they had attached to the two settings of filigree; thus they attached it in front to the shoulder-pieces of the ephod. [19]Then they made two rings of gold, and put them at the two ends of the breastpiece, on its inside edge next to the ephod. [20]And they made two rings of gold, and attached them in front to the lower part of the two shoulder-pieces of the ephod, at its joining above the skilfully woven band of the ephod. [21]And they bound the breastpiece by its rings to the rings of the ephod with a lace of blue, so that it should lie upon the skilfully woven band of the ephod, and that the breastpiece should not come loose from the ephod; as the LORD had commanded Moses.

The robe

Ex 28:31–35

[22]He also made the robe of the ephod woven all of blue; [23]and the opening of the robe in it was like the opening in a garment, with a binding around the opening, that it might not be torn. [24]On the skirts of the robe they made pomegranates of blue and purple and scarlet stuff and fine twined linen. [25]They also made bells of pure gold, and put the bells between the pomegranates upon the skirts of the robe round about, between the pomegranates; [26]a bell and a pomegranate, a bell and a pomegranate round about upon the skirts of the robe for ministering; as the LORD had commanded Moses.

Other vestments

Ex 28:38–42

[27]They also made the coats, woven of fine linen, for Aaron and his sons, [28]and the turban of fine linen, and the caps of fine linen, and the linen breeches of fine twined linen, [29]and the girdle of fine twined linen and of blue and purple and scarlet stuff, embroidered with needlework; as the LORD had commanded Moses.

summitates amborum funiculorum colligaverunt duobus marginibus in fasciis umeralibus ephod in parte eius anteriore. [19]Et fecerunt duos anulos aureos et posuerunt super duas summitates pectoralis in eius margine interiore contra ephod, sicut praecepit Dominus Moysi. [20]Feceruntque duos anulos aureos, quos posuerunt in duabus fasciis umeralibus ephod deorsum in latere eius anteriore secus iuncturam eius super balteum ephod. [21]Et strinxerunt pectorale anulis eius ad anulos ephod vitta hyacinthina, ut esset super balteum ephod, ne amoveretur ab ephod, sicut praecepit Dominus Moysi. [22]Fecerunt quoque pallium ephod opere textili totum hyacinthinum [23]et capitium in medio eius supra oramque per gyrum sicut in capitio loricae [24]deorsum autem ad pedes mala punica ex hyacintho, purpura, cocco ac bysso retorta [25]et tintinnabula de auro purissimo, quae posuerunt inter malogranata in inferiore parte pallii per gyrum, [26]ut sit tintinnabulum inter singula mala punica, quibus ornatus incedebat pontifex, quando ministerio fungebatur, sicut praeceperat Dominus Moysi. [27]Fecerunt et tunicas byssinas opere textili Aaron et filiis eius [28]et tiaram et ornatum mitrarum ex bysso, feminalia quoque linea ex bysso retorta, [29]cingulum vero de bysso retorta, hyacintho, purpura ac cocco, arte plumaria, sicut praeceperat Dominus Moysi. [30]Fecerunt et laminam diadema sanctitatis de auro purissimo; scripseruntque in ea

Ex 28:36–37 **The tiara or turban**

³⁰And they made the plate of the holy crown of pure gold, and wrote upon it an inscription, like the engraving of a signet, "Holy to the LORD." ³¹And they tied to it a lace of blue, to fasten it on the turban above; as the LORD had commanded Moses.

³²Thus all the work of the tabernacle of the tent of meeting was finished; and the people of Israel had done according to all that the LORD had commanded Moses; so had they done.

The finished work is presented to Moses

³³And they brought the tabernacle to Moses, the tent and all its utensils, its hooks, its frames, its bars, its pillars, and its bases; ³⁴the covering of tanned rams' skins and goatskins, and the veil of the screen; ³⁵the ark of the testimony with its poles and the mercy seat; ³⁶the table with all its utensils, and the bread of the Presence; ³⁷the lampstand of pure gold and its lamps with the lamps set and all its utensils, and the oil for the light; ³⁸the golden altar, the anointing oil and the fragrant incense, and the screen for the door of the tent; ³⁹the bronze altar, and its grating of bronze, its poles, and all its utensils; the laver and its base; ⁴⁰the hangings of the court, its pillars, and its bases, and the screen for the gate of the court, its cords, and its pegs; and all the utensils for the service of the tabernacle, for the tent of meeting; ⁴¹the finely worked gar-

---

39:33–43. The importance of every item used in divine worship is stressed once again. One cannot fail to be impressed by the insistence on every little thing having to do with it. The Church, too, stresses how important everything laid down about the liturgy is, especially things having to do with the celebration of the Eucharist. "The Eucharist is a common possession of the whole Church as the sacrament of her unity. And thus the Church has the strict duty to specify everything which concerns participation in it and its celebration. We should therefore act according to the principles laid down [. . .]. [I]n *normal conditions* to ignore the liturgical directives can be interpreted as a lack of respect towards the Eucharist, dictated perhaps by individualism or by an absence of a critical sense concerning current opinions, or by a certain *lack of a spirit of faith*" (John Paul II, *Dominicae Cenae*, 12).

---

opere caelatoris: «Sanctum Domino»; ³¹et strinxerunt eam desuper cum tiara vitta hyacinthina, sicut praeceperat Dominus Moysi. ³²Perfectum est igitur omne opus habitaculi et tabernaculi conventus feceruntque filii Israel cuncta, quae praeceperat Dominus Moysi: sic fecerunt. ³³Et obtulerunt habitaculum et tabernaculum et universam supellectilem, fibulas, tabulas, vectes, columnas ac bases, ³⁴opertorium de pellibus arietum rubricatis et operimentum de pellibus delphini, velum, ³⁵arcam testimonii, vectes, propitiatorium, ³⁶mensam cum vasis suis et propositionis panibus, ³⁷candelabrum ex auro puro, lucernas in ordine earum et utensilia earum cum oleo candelabri, ³⁸altare aureum et unguentum et thymiama ex aromatibus et velum in introitu tabernaculi, ³⁹altare aeneum, craticulam aeneam, vectes et vasa eius omnia, labrum cum basi sua, ⁴⁰tentoria atrii et columnas cum basibus suis, velum in introitu

ments for ministering in the holy place, the holy garments for Aaron the priest, and the garments of his sons to serve as priests. ⁴²According to all that the LORD had commanded Moses, so the people of Israel had done all the work. ⁴³And Moses saw all the work, and behold, they had done it; as the LORD had commanded, so had they done it. And Moses blessed them.

The sanctuary is consecrated

40 ¹The LORD said to Moses, ²"On the first day of the first month you shall erect the tabernacle of the tent of meeting. ³And you shall put in it the ark of the testimony, and you shall screen the ark with the veil. ⁴And you shall bring in the table, and set its arrangements in order; and you shall bring in the lampstand, and set up its lamps. ⁵And you shall put the golden altar for incense before the ark of the testimony, and set up the screen for the door of the tabernacle. ⁶You shall set the altar of burnt offering before the door of the tabernacle of the tent of meeting, ⁷and place the laver between the tent of meeting and the altar, and put water in it. ⁸And you shall set up the court round about, and hang up the screen for the gate of the court. ⁹Then you shall take the anointing oil, and anoint the tabernacle and all that is in it, and consecrate it and all its furniture; and it shall become holy. ¹⁰You shall also anoint the altar of burnt offering and all its utensils, and consecrate the altar; and the altar shall be most holy. ¹¹You shall also anoint the laver and its base, and consecrate it. ¹²Then you shall bring Aaron and his sons to the door of the tent of meeting, and shall wash them with water, ¹³and put upon Aaron the holy garments, and you shall anoint him and consecrate him, that he may serve me as priest. ¹⁴You shall bring his sons also and put coats on them, ¹⁵and anoint them, as you anointed their father,

Rev 9:13

Heb 9:21

---

atrii funiculosque illius et paxillos. Nihil ex vasis defuit, quae in ministerium habitaculi in tabernaculo conventus iussa sunt fieri. ⁴¹Vestes quoque textas, quibus sacerdotes utuntur in sanctuario, et vestes sacras Aaron sacerdotis et vestes filiorum eius ⁴²obtulerunt filii Israel, sicut praeceperat Dominus Moysi. ⁴³Quae postquam Moyses cuncta vidit completa, benedixit eis. ¹Locutusque est Dominus ad Moysen dicens: ²Mense primo, die prima mensis eriges habitaculum, tabernaculum conventus, ³et pones in eo arcam testimonii, abscondes illam velo; ⁴et, illata mensa, pones super eam, quae rite praecepta sunt. Candelabrum stabit cum lucernis suis ⁵et altare aureum, in quo adoletur incensum, coram arca testimonii. Velum in introitu habitaculi pones, ⁶et ante tabernaculum conventus altare holocausti, ⁷et labrum inter altare et tabernaculum conventus et implebis illud aqua. ⁸Circumdabisque atrium tentoriis et pones velum in porta eius. ⁹Et, assumpto unctionis oleo, unges habitaculum et omnia, quae in eo sunt, et consecrabis illud cum vasis suis, et erit sanctum. ¹⁰Unges quoque altare holocausti et omnia vasa eius et consecrabis altare, et erit sanctum sanctorum. ¹¹Et unges labrum cum basi sua et consecrabis illud. ¹²Applicabisque Aaron et filios eius ad fores tabernaculi conventus et lotos aqua ¹³indues Aaron sanctis vestibus, unges et consecrabis eum, ut mihi sacerdotio fungatur; ¹⁴filios eius applicabis et vesties eos tunicis ¹⁵et unges eos, sicut unxisti patrem eorum, ut mihi sacerdotio fungantur, et unctio

that they may serve me as priests: and their anointing shall admit them to a perpetual priesthood throughout their generations."

Moses' obedience to God's commands

¹⁶Thus did Moses; according to all that the LORD commanded him, so he did. ¹⁷And in the first month in the second year, on the first day of the month, the tabernacle was erected. ¹⁸Moses erected the tabernacle; he laid its bases, and set up its frames, and put in its poles, and raised up its pillars; ¹⁹and he spread the tent over the tabernacle, and put the covering of the tent over it, as the LORD had commanded Moses. ²⁰And he took the testimony and put it into the ark, and put the poles on the ark, and set the mercy seat above on the ark; ²¹and he brought the ark into the tabernacle, and set up the veil of the screen, and screened the ark of the testi-

Mt 12:4
Mk 2:26

mony; as the LORD had commanded Moses. ²²And he put the table in the tent of meeting, on the north side of the tabernacle, outside the veil, ²³and set the bread in order on it before the LORD; as the LORD had commanded Moses. ²⁴And he put the lampstand in the tent of meeting, opposite the table on the south side of the tabernacle, ²⁵and set up the lamps before the LORD; as the LORD had commanded Moses. ²⁶And he put the golden altar in the tent of meeting before the veil, ²⁷and burnt fragrant incense upon it; as the LORD had commanded Moses. ²⁸And he put in place the screen for the door of the tabernacle. ²⁹And he set the altar of burnt offering at the door of the tabernacle of the tent of meeting, and offered upon it the burnt offering and the cereal offering; as the LORD had commanded Moses. ³⁰And he set the laver between the tent of meeting and the altar, and put water in it for washing, ³¹with which Moses and Aaron and his sons washed their hands and their feet; ³²when they went into the tent of meeting, and

eorum erit eis in sacerdotium sempiternum in generationibus eorum. ¹⁶Fecitque Moyses omnia, quae praeceperat ei Dominus: sic fecit. ¹⁷Igitur mense primo anni secundi, prima die mensis collocatum est habitaculum. ¹⁸Erexitque Moyses illud et posuit bases ac tabulas et vectes statuitque columnas ¹⁹et expandit tentorium super habitaculum, imposito desuper operimento, sicut Dominus imperaverat Moysi. ²⁰Sumpsit et posuit testimonium in arca et, subditis infra vectibus, posuit propitiatorium desuper. ²¹Cumque intulisset arcam in habitaculum, appendit ante eam velum, sicut iusserat Dominus Moysi. ²²Posuit et mensam in tabernaculo conventus ad plagam septentrionalem extra velum, ²³ordinatis coram propositionis panibus, sicut praeceperat Dominus Moysi. ²⁴Posuit et candelabrum in tabernaculo conventus e regione mensae in parte australi, ²⁵locatis per ordinem lucernis, sicut praeceperat Dominus Moysi. ²⁶Posuit et altare aureum in tabernaculo conventus coram propitiatorio ²⁷et adolevit super eo incensum aromatum, sicut iusserat Dominus Moysi. ²⁸Posuit et velum in introitu habitaculi ²⁹et altare holocausti in vestibulo habitaculi, tabernaculi conventus, offerens in eo holocaustum et sacrificium, sicut Dominus imperaverat Moysi. ³⁰Labrum quoque statuit inter tabernaculum conventus et altare implens illud aqua; ³¹laveruntque Moyses et Aaron ac filii eius manus suas et pedes, ³²cum ingrederentur tabernaculum conventus et accederent ad altare, sicut praeceperat Dominus Moysi.

when they approached the altar, they washed; as the LORD commanded Moses. ³³And he erected the court round the tabernacle and the altar, and set up the screen of the gate of the court. So Moses finished the work.

Num 9:15–33
1 Kings 8:10–11
Ezra 43:15
Ex 13:21–22; 25:8
Mk 9:7
Rev 15:5, 8
Num 9:15–23

The glory of God fills the tabernacle

³⁴Then the cloud covered* the tent of meeting, and the glory of the LORD filled the tabernacle. ³⁵And Moses was not able to enter the tent of meeting, because the cloud abode upon it, and the glory of the LORD filled the tabernacle. ³⁶Throughout all their journeys, whenever the cloud was taken up from over the tabernacle, the people of Israel would go onward; ³⁷but if the cloud was not taken up, then they did not go onward till the day that it was taken up. ³⁸For throughout all their journeys the cloud of the LORD was upon the tabernacle by day, and fire was in it by night, in the sight of all the house of Israel.

40:34–38. The book of Exodus ends by speaking once again about the Lord's presence among his people, mentioning the cloud and the glory of God (cf. Ex 13:21–22). The cloud will stay with the people throughout their journey in the desert (cf. Num 9:15ff), showing them the way to go. In Christian tradition the cloud is seen as an image of faith, which guides the Christian night and day as he makes his pilgrim way to the promised land. The Fathers also saw this cloud as a figure of Christ: "He is the pillar who, keeping himself upright and strong, cures our infirmity. By night he sheds light, by day he becomes opaque, so that those who do not see are enabled to see and those who see become blind" (St Isidore of Seville, *Quaestiones in Exodum*, 18, 1).

³³Erexit et atrium per gyrum habitaculi et altaris, ducto in introitu eius velo. Sic complevit opus. ³⁴Et operuit nubes tabernaculum conventus, et gloria Domini implevit habitaculum. ³⁵Nec poterat Moyses ingredi tabernaculum conventus, quia habitavit nubes super illud, et gloria Domini replevit habitaculum. ³⁶Si quando nubes de tabernaculo ascendebat, proficiscebantur filii Israel in omnibus stationibus suis; ³⁷si autem non ascendebat nubes, non proficiscebantur usque in diem, quo levabatur. ³⁸Nubes quippe Domini incubabat per diem habitaculo, et ignis in nocte, ante oculos universae domus Israel per cunctas mansiones suas.

Explanatory Notes

(N.B. In these notes Vulgate additions are quoted in the Douay Version.)

EXODUS

This book, made up of various traditions of different dates, deals with two events: the deliverance from Egypt and the Sinai covenant, which, closely linked together, form the basis of Old Testament faith. It is dominated by the personality of Moses.

3:14: This translation is uncertain: it is, therefore, difficult to decide whether this is a refusal to disclose the name or an explanation of the divine title Yahweh revealed immediately afterwards.

7:14: Here begins the story of the ten plagues. Again the narrative is composite and originally different traditions knew of different numbers of plagues. All, however, lead up to the climax of the death of the first-born. Some of the plagues correspond to natural phenomena that are known to occur, or to have occurred in the past, in Egypt.

12:1: The feast of the Passover, the regulations for which are given here, commemorates the deliverance from Egypt. The feast of unleavened bread would probably have been added only after the entry into Canaan. The Passover foreshadows the sacrifice of Jesus (1 Cor 5:7).

16:14: The mysterious manna may have been a substance secreted by the tamarisk or perhaps an insect that feeds on its leaves and is edible. In the New Testament it is a type of the Eucharist: cf. Jn 6:31–35, 48–51.

19:3: The covenant makes Israel the people of God and binds them to the fulfilment of the commandments; it is concluded in chapter 24.

20:1–17: The Ten Commandments, in their original form even briefer than here, are found in a different version in Deut 5:6–21.

40:34, *the cloud* and the fire, that is, the *glory*, are ways of representing at the same time the presence and the transcendence of God.

Sources Quoted in the Commentary

1. DOCUMENTS OF THE CHURCH

Vatican, Second Council of the
Sacrosanctum Concilium: Constitution on the Sacred Liturgy, 4 December 1963, AAS 56 (1964) 97–138.
Lumen gentium: Dogmatic Constitution on the Church, 21 November 1964, AAS 57 (1965) 5–71.
Dei Verbum: Dogmatic Constitution on Divine Revelation, 18 November 1965, AAS 58 (1966) 817–835.
Presbyterorum ordinis: Decree on the ministry and life of priests, 7 December 1965, AAS 58 (1966) 991–1024.
Gaudium et spes: Pastoral Constitution on the Church in the modern world, 7 December 1965, AAS 58 (1966) 1025–1120.

John Paul II
Dives in misericordia: Encyclical Letter on the mercy of God, 30 November 1980, AAS (1980) 1177–1232.
Laborem exercens: Encyclical Letter on human work, 14 September 1981, AAS 73 (1981) 577–647.
Evangelium vitae: Apostolic Letter on the value and inviolability of human life, 25 March 1995, AAS 87 (1995) 401–522.
Dominicae Cenae: Letter on the mystery and worship of the Blessed Eucharist, 24 February 1980, AAS 72 (1980) 113–148.

OTHER

Catechism of the Catholic Church, New York, 1994.
Pontifical Biblical Commission
The Interpretation of the Bible in the Church, Ottawa, 1994.

2. LITURGICAL TEXTS

Roman Missal: Missale Romanum, editio typica altera, Vatican City, 1975.

3. THE FATHERS, ECCLESIASTICAL WRITERS AND OTHER AUTHORS

Augustine, St
Confessions, PL 32, 659–868.
Enarrationes in Psalmos, PL 36–37.
Quaestiones in Heptateuchum, PL 34, 547–824.
Ambrose, St
De sacramentis, PL 15, 435–482.
Basil, St
Adversus Eunomium, PG 29, 497–774.
Bede, St
Commentaria in Pentateuchum, PL 91, 189–394.

Sources Quoted in the Commentary

Cyril of Alexandria, St
Glaphyra in Exodum libri III, PG 69, 386–538.
Glossa ordinaria
Glossa ordinaria in Exodum, PL 113, 183–296.
Isidore of Seville, St
Quaestiones in Vetus Testamentum. In Exodum, PL 83, 287–322.
Josemaría Escrivá, St
Christ Is Passing By, Dublin, St Peter's (N.S.W.) and New Rochelle, 1982.
Friends of God, London, New Rochelle and Dublin, 1988.
John of the Cross, St
Spiritual Canticle: E. Allison Peers (trs. and ed.), *Complete Works,* vol. II, London, 1947.
Origen
Homiliae in Exodum: P. Fortier and H. de Lubac (eds.), *Origène. Homélies sur l'Exode* (SC 16), Paris, 1947.
Homiliae in Jeremiam: P. Nautin (ed.), *Origène. Homélies sur Jérémie*, vol. I (SC 232), Paris, 1976.
Thomas Aquinas, St
Summa theologiae: ed. T. McDermott, London 1964.

Headings Added to the Biblical Text

EXODUS

Part One
The departure from Egypt

1. THE SONS OF ISRAEL IN EGYPT 1:1
The prosperity of the sons of Israel in Egypt 1:1
The sons of Israel are oppressed 1:8

2. THE CALL OF MOSES 2:1
The birth and early years of Moses 2:1
Moses in Midian 2:11
God appears to Moses in the burning bush 3:1
The divine name is revealed 3:11
The mission of Moses 3:16
Moses is granted miraculous powers 4:1
Aaron, the mouthpiece of Moses 4:10
Moses returns to Egypt 4:18
Moses' son is circumcised 4:24
Moses meets Aaron 4:27
Moses' first audience with the pharaoh 5.1
The Hebrews' work is made heavier 5:6
Moses intercedes with the pharaoh 5:19
A new call to Moses 6:2
The genealogy of Aaron and Moses 6:14
The announcement of the plagues 6:28

3. THE PLAGUES 7:8
Moses' miraculous rod 7:8
The first plague: the water turns to blood 7:14
The second plague: the frogs 7:25
The third plague: the gnats 8:16
The fourth plague: the flies 8:20
The fifth plague: the livestock epidemic 9:1
The sixth plague: the boils 9:8
The seventh plague: the hail 9:13

The eighth plague: the locusts 10:1
The ninth plague: the darkness 10:21
The tenth plague is announced 11:1

4. PASSOVER 12:1
The institution of the Passover 12:1
The feast of the unleavened bread 12:15
Instructions relating to the Passover 12:21
The tenth plague: death of the first-born 12:29
Provisions for the Exodus 12:33
The sons of Israel leave Egypt 12:37
Further instructions about the Passover 12:43
The law about the first-born 13:1
Instructions about the feast of the unleavened bread
    13:3
Instructions about redeeming the first-born 13:11

5. THE DEPARTURE FROM EGYPT 13:17
A roundabout way 13:17
The Lord shapes events 14:1
The Egyptians in pursuit 14:5
Crossing the Red Sea 14:15
Song of victory 15:1

6. ISRAEL IN THE DESERT 15:22
The bitter water of Marah 15:22
The manna and the quails 16:1
The water from the rock 17:1
A battle against the Amalekites 17:8
The meeting of Jethro and Moses 18:1
The appointment of judges 18:13

Part Two
The people of Israel

7. IN THE DESERT OF SINAI 19:1
The Israelites arrive in Sinai 19:1
God promises a Covenant 19:3
The theophany on Sinai 19:10
The ten commandments 20:1

8. THE BOOK OF THE COVENANT 20:22
Laws concerning worship 20:22
Laws concerning slaves 21:1
Laws concerning homicide 21:12
Laws concerning violence 21:18
Laws concerning restitution 21:33

209

Headings Added to the Biblical Text

MAPS

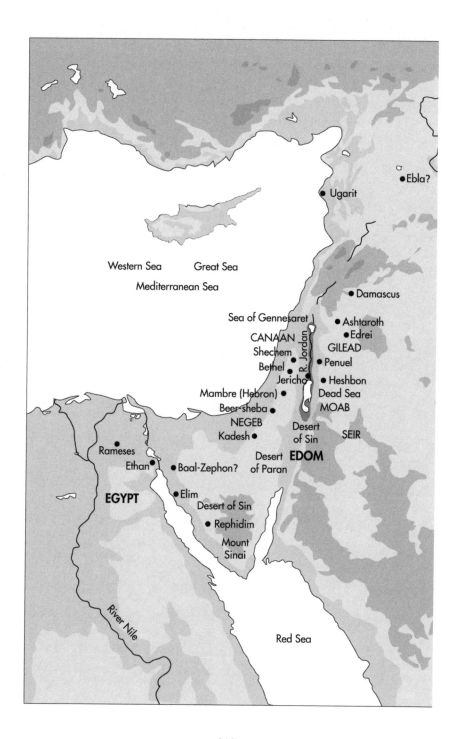

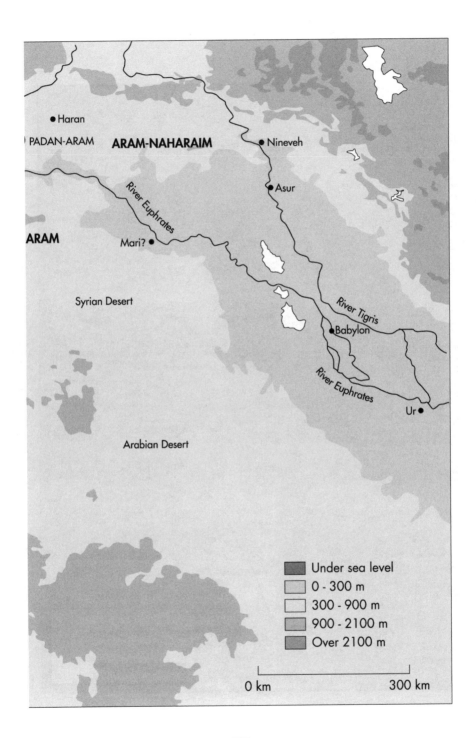

Haran

PADAN-ARAM **ARAM-NAHARAIM** Nineveh

Asur

River Euphrates

ARAM Mari?

Syrian Desert

River Tigris

Babylon

River Euphrates

Arabian Desert

Ur

	Under sea level
	0 - 300 m
	300 - 900 m
	900 - 2100 m
	Over 2100 m

0 km   300 km

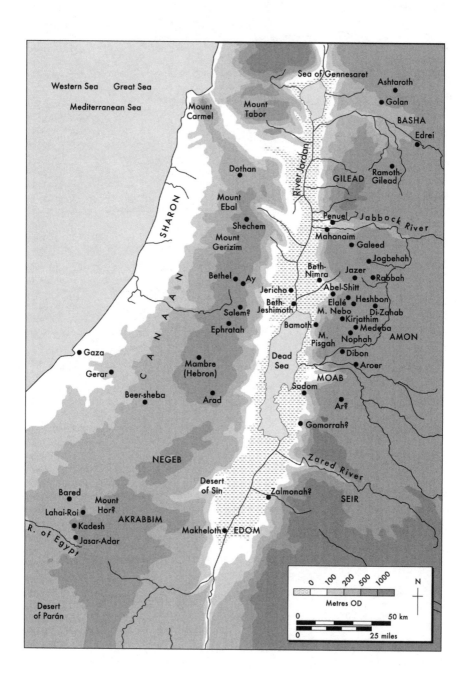